CW01064157

THE REBIRTH OF REVELATION

GERMAN AND EUROPEAN STUDIES

General Editor: Jennifer L. Jenkins

The Rebirth of Revelation

German Theology in an Age of Reason and History, 1750–1850

TUSKA BENES

UNIVERSITY OF TORONTO PRESS
Toronto Buffalo London

© University of Toronto Press 2022
Toronto Buffalo London
utorontopress.com
Printed in the U.S.A.

ISBN 978-1-4875-4307-5 (cloth)
ISBN 978-1-4875-4308-2 (EPUB)
ISBN 978-1-4875-4309-9 (PDF)

German and European Studies

Library and Archives Canada Cataloguing in Publication

Title: The rebirth of revelation : German theology in an age of reason and history, 1750–1850 /
   Tuska Benes.
Names: Benes, Tuska, 1971– author.
Series: German and European studies ; 45.
Description: Series statement: German and European studies ; 45 | Includes bibliographical
   references and index.
Identifiers: Canadiana (print) 20210242299 | Canadiana (ebook) 20210242418 |
   ISBN 9781487543075 (cloth) | ISBN 9781487543082 (EPUB) | ISBN 9781487543099
   (PDF)
Subjects: LCSH: Theology – Germany – History – 18th century. | LCSH: Theology –
   Germany – History – 19th century. | LCSH: Revelation – History of doctrines – 18th
   century. | LCSH: Revelation – History of doctrines – 19th century. | LCSH: Reason –
   History – 18th century. | LCSH: Reason – History – 19th century.
Classification: LCC BR855 .B46 2022 | DDC 274.307 – dc23

We wish to acknowledge the land on which the University of Toronto Press operates. This
land is the traditional territory of the Wendat, the Anishnaabeg, the Haudenosaunee, the
Métis, and the Mississaugas of the Credit First Nation.

The German and European Studies series is funded by the DAAD with funds from the
German Federal Foreign Office

 Deutscher Akademischer Austauschdienst
German Academic Exchange Service

University of Toronto Press acknowledges the financial support of the Government of
Canada, the Canada Council for the Arts, and the Ontario Arts Council, an agency of
the Government of Ontario, for its publishing activities.

 Canada Council Conseil des Arts
for the Arts du Canada

ONTARIO ARTS COUNCIL
CONSEIL DES ARTS DE L'ONTARIO
an Ontario government agency
un organisme du gouvernement de l'Ontario

 Funded by the Financé par le
Government gouvernement
of Canada du Canada | Canadä

To
Parvaneh,
Taraneh,
and
Ali

Contents

Illustrations

Acknowledgments

Post-tenure books are written under vastly different circumstances than dissertations. As a faculty member with the privilege of continuous employment, I have enjoyed the financial stability and institutional support that makes scholarship feasible. A summer grant from The College of William and Mary funded research on this book, as did the sabbatical leaves given me over the past decade. A number of individuals have also been extremely helpful. I would like to thank Suzanne Marchand, Lu Ann Homza, and Ron Schechter for reading portions of the manuscript. Susannah Heschel and the two anonymous external reviewers for the University of Toronto Press provided excellent feedback on the entirety of the book. I am grateful to them and to the exceptional guidance of Stephen Shapiro, my editor.

It also bears mention that I researched and wrote this book from the sidelines of my life as a mother, daughter, and faculty member. To my delight, it took shape on the bleachers of pool decks across Virginia and North Carolina and while I crammed, not able to return to my office, into tiny chairs at the Williamsburg Parent Co-operative Preschool. The final touches came as virtual school and family illness ended any expectation for prolonged periods of concentration. My father, Peter Benes, a prolific historian of early New England material culture, did not live to see this book in print. However, the work ethic he imparted and a half-century of unflinching support from my mother, Jane Montague Benes, enabled its completion. I dedicate the book to my husband and children, who have, for many years, made sacrifices, challenged and inspired me, and given me many wonderful reasons to leave my desk behind.

THE REBIRTH OF REVELATION

Introduction

In 1802, Friedrich Wilhelm Joseph Schelling made the startling claim that the German research university should aim to rebuild *Urwissen*, the universal absolute knowledge posited by God at the start of time. "All knowledge is a striving for communion with the divine essence," the ardent Romantic wrote, "for participation in the primordial knowledge of which the visible universe is the image and whose source is the fountainhead of eternal power."[1] This evocation of revelation strikes readers today as unusual, as it aligns poorly with our understanding of the modern university and followed so closely on the Enlightenment's notorious critique of revelation. "Every moment of time is a revelation of a particular aspect of God,"[2] Schelling insisted, expecting the academic disciplines to express in ideal form the divine presence in nature, history, and human consciousness. His proclamations, while surprising, indicate how enticing early nineteenth-century scholars found the theological concept and the prospect of recovering a lost original wisdom that could rectify the seeming fragmentation of the present in the years following the French Revolution.

The partially discredited idea of revelation acquired new life in the nineteenth century, as Protestants, Catholics, and Jews justified faith in an age committed to historicism, human agency, and *Wissenschaft* (or science). As Schelling's case indicates, the post-Enlightenment restoration of revelation among German intellectuals conflated knowledge and faith in intriguing new ways and reflects a surprisingly persistent entanglement of theology and the human sciences. Thomas Howard, Grant Kaplan, Suzanne Marchand, and Samuel Moyn have remarked on revelation's wide-ranging significance as a category of reflection.[3] Yet there is no decisive account of the crisis that struck revelation during the Enlightenment, its post-critical revival as a subjective, historical category in the nineteenth century, or the possibilities and challenges that the rehabilitation of revelation posed for German intellectual life more broadly.[4]

Comparing Protestant, Catholic, and Jewish reflections on revelation from 1750 to 1850, this study argues that a strategic transformation in the term's meaning secured its relevance for the modern age. Specifically, the theological reframing of revelation as an historical process grounded in human experience, rather than as the divine dispensation of doctrine, reconciled faith with reason and history, deferring their more decisive split until the later nineteenth century. Enhanced compatibility with the ideals of *Wissenschaft* ensured that concepts of revelation continued to permeate academic fields through mid-century. Granting human subjects custody over revelation likewise accorded well with repeated demands for political and social reconstruction in post-revolutionary Europe. The rebirth of revelation, however, perilously justified faith in human terms, reframing religion as a set of cultural practices and granting revelation applicability in the secular realm, for example, as a lens for envisioning the development of the self. The innovative approach German religious thinkers took to revelation nearly succumbed to the spectre of anthropocentrism, faltering as a secure foundation for doctrinal truths. After a half-century of experimentation, many theologians again gravitated to more conventional positions on revelation, weakening the appeal of faith within *Wissenschaft*.

Revelation is an important pillar of belief in the Judeo-Christian tradition, alternatively paired or competing with reason as a source of knowledge about God. The contested relationship between the two is central to the epistemology of religious belief, or the question of what justifies faith and anchors knowledge of the transcendent realm. Appeals to revelation have occasionally dismissed reason as irrelevant, unfit to evaluate divine acts, such as the miracles performed by Christ. Since antiquity, however, Jews and Christians have more often invoked reason in the form, for example, of Greek philosophical ideas, to authenticate and reinforce the content and credibility of scriptural revelations. Following precedents set by Augustine and Aquinas, Catholic theologians have consistently ascribed to reason the ability to clarify matters of faith and acquire additional truths regarding, for example, God's qualities or the immortality of the soul. Luther and Calvin more strictly limited the prerogatives of unaided reason, stressing divine incomprehensibility, such that Protestants have traditionally held more forcefully to the notion of original biblical truth. Revelation only lacks bearing on belief when faith refuses evidential grounding, or when, in the tradition of natural theology, earthly truths provide adequate justification.[5]

The respective priority of reason and revelation in the justification of belief has fluctuated over time, and, to a certain extent, this book evaluates the shifting nature of that relationship. The half-century of religious revival that followed the Enlightenment witnessed a progressive conflation of the terms and eroded the distinction between reason and revelation on new grounds. Schelling and other idealists, for example, equated the historical self-revelation of God with the actualization of absolute reason, expecting a range of academic disciplines to assemble knowledge of the divine. Other religious thinkers identified subjective inner experience as the site of revelation, extrapolating knowledge of God from critical self-reflection on the very structures of consciousness. At the same time, a parallel historicization of reason and revelation exposed both pillars of belief to the contingencies of cultural context and political expediency, thus undermining their respective prerogatives to lay absolute claim to truth. Not only were exegesis and analysis of God's worldly presence presumed to be evolving enterprises, revelatory events, such as Moses's receipt of the Torah, themselves appeared to many in the nineteenth century as strategic human actions, not vehicles for the transmission of divine wisdom.

This spiritual model fit well with the rapidly changing political landscape of post-revolutionary Europe. From 1792 to the Congress of Vienna, warfare repeatedly engulfed the continent, precipitating the dissolution in 1806 of the long-standing Holy Roman Empire, a loose conglomerate of micro-territories with varying degrees of political sovereignty. More than twenty prince-bishoprics existed in the western and southern parts of the Empire in the late eighteenth century, as well as important archbishoprics in Mainz, Cologne, Trier, and Salzburg, the corresponding dioceses of which usually extended far beyond the political jurisdiction of the principalities. However, only three Catholic states (Austria, Bavaria, and Hohenzollern-Sigmaringen) survived the process of secularization and mediatization that absorbed German-speaking ecclesiastical territories into larger principalities starting in 1802. The Napoleonic occupations consolidated large segments of Central Europe's feudal patchwork into modern bureaucratic states, instituting disputed legal reforms, including Jewish emancipation, and awakening German nationalist sentiment. Conflating reason and revelation invested greater agency in human subjects as new political movements overturned the *ancien régime*, while the emphasis on revelation's historicity suggested faith could be responsive during times of upheaval.

A certain vulnerability has always plagued revelation in its role securing religious belief. In the early modern period, the idea of revelation shifted from being an implicit conviction of faith to a proposition that required justification beyond Scripture. Among Catholics, natural philosophy first assumed the task of establishing the possibility and necessity of revelation on non-theological grounds; Protestants

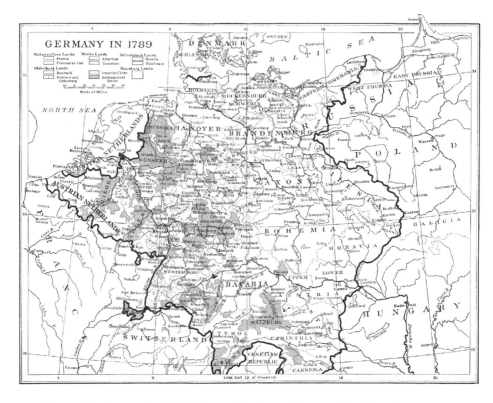

Map of the fragmented Holy Roman Empire on the eve of the French Revolution, showing the ecclesiastical principalities eliminated during mediatization (territorial restructuring) and the secularization of German states between 1802 and 1814. Map adapted from Charles Downer Hazen, *Modern European History* (New York: Holt, 1917), 18–19.

preferred historical exegesis as a platform for securing scriptural truth. By the seventeenth century, the theology of revelation had developed into a philosophical discipline that evaluated the epistemological status of revealed doctrines, especially which truths were above reason, and thus impossible to comprehend, and which of the mysteries in fact contradicted reason.[6] Systematic theories of revelation justified the possibility, necessity, and discernibility of revelation, in the process addressing the ultimate sources of human knowledge, God's attributes, and man's relationship to the divine.[7]

By the late eighteenth century, misgivings about the specifically historical nature of revelation had imperilled the intellectual standing of theology. The destabilizing effects of historicism have been noted for critical exegetical methods, the life of Jesus, and Orientalist scholarship. A debilitating form of historicism struck revelation during the early Enlightenment and, when combined with rationalist critique and the looming obsolescence of theology's methods as a discipline, spawned a defensive mission to rescue the term. Revelation in the Judeo-Christian tradition is by nature historical: an act in time through which a transcendent God discloses new knowledge or dimensions of his being to a culturally specific people. In Exodus 3:1, for example, God appears to Moses as a burning bush on Mount Horeb with instructions to deliver the Israelites from Egypt. Growing awareness of and concern for the subjective reception of such revelations, their preservation and transmission in datable texts, and the reliability of historical evidence for their existence threw the idea of revelation into disarray. Belief in miracle, prophecy, and supernatural intervention reinforced scriptural literalism, and its collapse brought into question the facticity and positivity of divine self-presentation through history.[8] Karsten Niebuhr's expedition to Arabia in the 1760s not surprisingly investigated the tidal movements of the Red Sea and the varieties of Arab manna.

At the heart of these concerns lay the problem of transcendence, or how to close the gap between the historically contingent presentation of revelation and the absolute, divine realm it purported to reference. In 1777, German writer Gotthold Ephraim Lessing observed that a "broad and ugly ditch"[9] separated revelation from the necessary truths of reason, its contingent nature only offering a shaky foundation for salvation. Commentators have distinguished three main components of Lessing's ditch, all prompted by recognition of revelation's historicity and drawing attention to the limits of human knowledge and the culturally constructed aspects of religion and faith. The temporal gap, the distance between the present and past revelatory events, raised problems of evidence, proof, testimony, and transmission. What could establish the historical facticity of God's presence on earth? The irreconcilability of reason and revelation pointed to a metaphysical gap between an historically contingent occurrence, such as St. Paul's vision on the road to Damascus, and the universal, binding religious truths revelation supposedly conveyed. The existential gap addressed the problem of religious appropriation and plausibility, or how distant, unsettling, unbelievable, or incomprehensible moments in history could be interiorized to foster faith and obedience to religious authorities.[10]

Reacting to the apparent fallibility of historical revelation, religious thinkers across the confessions, at different rates and with different degrees of radicalness, reworked its inherited meanings. In the process, revelation became a central concern of nineteenth-century German reli-gious thought, such that, by some accounts, every theological dispute since the Enlightenment has hinged on conflicting interpretations of the term.[11] The emphasis on revelation reflects, in part, its systemic legiti-mizing function. The presumed receipt of revelation from an infallible, transcendent power traditionally distinguished theology as a privi-leged science, privy to wisdom that exceeded human capabilities. The inheritance of divine revelation likewise legitimated the institutions and doctrinal expositions of the Catholic Church, as well as the author-ity of Jewish ritual law.

The nineteenth-century preoccupation with revelation also reflects the vulnerable position into which broader intellectual and cultural transformations in the German states had thrust religious thought. The declining prestige of theology as a discipline within the German uni-versity, as well as the need to prove the "scientific" credentials of the field under the new standards of modern *Wissenschaft*, forced a reckon-ing with the concept. The claim to relay and interpret revelation once sustained the privileged status of Protestant and Catholic theology at the German university.[12] However, traditional understandings of rev-elation were a liability to theology's status as a science, and they sat uneasily with the critical historical methods and philosophical rigour that legitimated other disciplines. The model of a transcendent per-sonal God dispensing fixed doctrine had also justified the preroga-tives of absolute monarchy and was ill-suited to revolutionary Europe. A political theology derived from revelation's embodiment in human experience was more compelling as Germans of all faiths and political persuasions navigated social and cultural reconstruction after 1815.

The thirty-nine states of the fragile German Confederation, torn in their loyalties between Prussia and Austria, weathered repeated con-flict between newly invigorated liberals and representatives of the old order, often buttressed by the Protestant state churches. An initial period of constitutional reform led members of the intelligentsia to believe that the German princes would institute representative government, protect civil liberties, and lift restrictions on economic life. The Wars of Libera-tion against Napoleon and the founding of nationalist student organi-zations likewise heightened expectations for German unification under parliamentary rule. But the pervasive system of political repression, censorship, and university oversight that Austrian Prince Klemens von Metternich introduced with the Carlsbad Decrees in 1819 restored monarchical authority at the expense of liberalism and nationalism. The German states also reinstated additional taxation and legal restrictions on Jewish citizens, curtailing their freedom of trade, rights of marriage and domicile, and the holding of public office. The violent Hep-Hep pogroms of 1819, which spread outwards from Bavaria, were the first in a series of anti-Jewish riots that erupted periodically in the 1830s and 1840s. Detecting the presence of revelation in this fraught landscape served to grant divine sanction to a broader range of political actors.

After examining the crisis into which revelation fell, this book documents its rebirth as a nineteenth-century concept that profoundly altered German religious studies and historical scholarship more broadly, as well as the perceived relationship between reason and faith. It argues that propositional revelation, understood as the divine dispensation of knowledge required for salvation, yielded in the early nineteenth century to two other conceptions: revelation as a subjective process of inner transformation and as the historical self-disclosure of divine being in the world. This shift disassociated revelation with the divine bestowal of doctrine, destabilizing theology's claim to absolute truth and ceding crucial aspects of religion to human, not divine origin. Such approaches were more compatible with the goals of *Wissenschaft* and political reform, but they struggled to offset the anthropocentrism otherwise inherent in human knowledge, ultimately relegating religion to an outgrowth of human needs or desires. At the same time, revelation also acquired new life as a category of historical analysis applicable to a range of human activities and as a key to understanding the dynamics of subject formation and interpersonal engagement.

The two trajectories that overtook propositional revelation as confidence in its epistemological merits waned deserve brief elaboration.[13] On the one hand, reservations about establishing the objectivity and facticity of revelation encouraged Friedrich Schleiermacher and other liberal theologians to reconceive revelation as subjective inner experience. As Martin Jay has observed, self-conscious recourse to experience was a potent weapon in the renewal of Christianity after the Enlightenment, although privileging the experiential ground of religion risked reversing the respective priority of God and man in revelation.[14] Pietists and mystics had long accepted ecstatic states and inner illumination as legitimate sources of religious knowledge, but, especially when possessed by women, these could undermine ecclesiastical institutions and the Bible. Liberal nineteenth-century theologians remained comparatively within the bounds of religious institutions, believing sacred texts formalized intuitive perceptions derived from acute states of inner awareness.

On the other hand, an ontological approach to revelation reinterpreted the term as the self-disclosure of God's being in history, an interactive process by which human and divine selfhood mutually constituted each other. From the perspective of Schelling and other idealists, revelation entailed a disclosing or self-manifestation of God through his actions in the world. The process of divine self-constitution

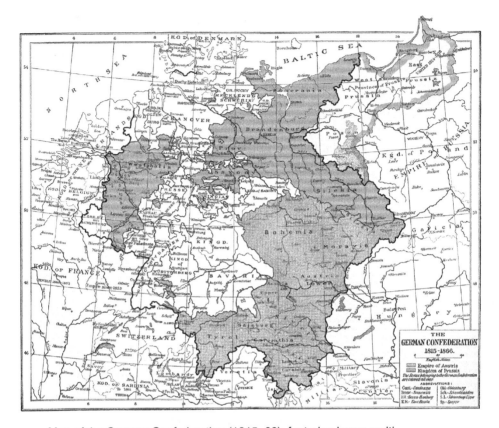

Map of the German Confederation (1815–66), featuring larger multi-confessional states. As a result of territorial restructuring, the Protestant states of Prussia and Baden incorporated large numbers of Catholics; heavily Protestant areas in Middle and Upper Franconia and the Rhenish Palatinate fell under the Catholic king of Bavaria. Map adapted from Hazen, 260–1.

depended for its fulfilment on humanity achieving awareness of God's presence in history and partaking in his realization. Knowledge of God increased with his self-disclosure, was necessarily incomplete, and attained greater perfection in response to new events. The focus on renewal legitimated the reform of liturgy, religious law, and doctrine. But it also presumed a hierarchy of religious development that favoured a presumably rational, intellectualized Protestantism.

Both models were politically nimble, capable of being mobilized to interpret and contest religious and political transformation during the

Restoration and the *Vormärz* (the years preceding the Revolutions of 1848/49). Propositional revelation invested greater authority in a transcendent, personal God and his right to dispense doctrine, religious laws, and commandments that offered salvation and governed daily life. The German princes legitimated restrictions on suffrage, civil rights, and constitutional government based on an analogous paternalism and the divine right of monarchs. The new models of revelation fostered a modern political subjectivity, not by excluding religion from public life, but by foregrounding God's presence in the historical world. The active role granted human subjects in the unfolding of revelation could justify a broad range of interventions into religious practices and institutions, as well as constraints on princely power. The historical unfolding of revelation could also, conversely, be equated with the actualization of existing state structures and reinforce a conservative alliance of throne and altar. As Mark Lilla writes, German theology "left the faint odor of revelation hanging over its celebration of modern political and cultural life, implying that it had been divinely blessed."[15]

A third, less successful response to the crisis of revelation was a reactionary reaffirmation of the historical significance of primordial revelation, seen in modified form in Schelling's proclamations. In each of the main confessions, primordial revelation traditionally referred to an oral tradition that predated Moses and provided the foundation for material later recorded in Genesis. In some contexts, *Uroffenbarung* referred to wisdom imparted to the patriarchs as a prelude to God's special covenant with Israel, but often primordial revelation was believed to have transpired during an ideal period of communion with the divine before Adam and Eve were expelled from paradise. Preserved by Noah, its wisdom filtered down to all of humankind but found surest footing among the ancient Hebrews, having become distorted or hidden from public view in pagan religions. Related to this was the idea of a universal or general revelation, derived from the natural world or human conscience and therefore accessible to all of humanity.

Through the eighteenth century, primordial revelation had offered a welcome antidote to the scandal of particularity, by which large segments of humanity were excluded from salvation by virtue of never having known revealed truths. But it could also take the form of a privilege whose transmission favoured certain peoples. Judaic primacy held that the religious wisdom of the patriarchs best preserved the earliest and most authentic deposit of God's word. But primordial revelation was also used to depict Judaism as derivative, secondary in historical importance to the sacred wisdom of older sages, such as Zoroaster. As Suzanne Marchand established for German Orientalism, the prevalence of highly speculative, diffusionary cultural histories that idealized origins as a point of purity and authenticity was grounded in the notion of God having dispensed a singular truth at the start of time. This inevitably widened the circle of peoples privy to revelation.[16]

In the nineteenth century, primordial revelation usually factored conservatively to counterbalance perceived excesses of rationalism. The lingering effects of a primeval intervention could deflect the otherwise destabilizing consequences of deriving religion from human creativity. The grounding of an otherwise subjective, radically historical experience of God in an original moment of divine disclosure narrowed Lessing's ditch. It also set a precedent for recognizing the divine origins and binding nature of tradition. Rabbis and priests derived authority from claiming custodianship of an oral tradition inherited through a chain of transmission from God. As propositional revelation yielded to subjective, experiential revelation, however, *Uroffenbarung* was reinterpreted as a primal inborn capacity for spiritual awareness implanted by God in each soul. This radically dehistoricized primordial revelation, eliminating its function as an original source in the genealogical transmission of knowledge.

The post-critical transformation of revelation from an epistemological anchor of doctrine and tradition rooted in established religious institutions to a concept that probed human consciousness, subjective inner life, and the nature of being and existence transpired differently among Protestants, Catholics, and Jews. On the whole, Protestant thinkers enjoyed the institutional privileges, state sanction, and intellectual precedents for more autonomous critical inquiry that made feasible an earlier and more radical reconceptualization of revelation. By the late eighteenth century, the centralizing bureaucratic states of Central Europe had severely weakened the ability of the Protestant and Catholic churches to govern academic theology; theologians thought of themselves as state servants whose social role was defined by the nation-state and university, not by the creedal traditions of Christianity.[17] Protestant theology, however, was particularly well suited to the ideals of *Wissenschaft* and the post-confessional state and more readily ceded its creedal and ecclesial interests. Prussia, for example, eagerly funded theological seminars dedicated to historical and philological criticism, rather than dogmatics, ethics, or pastoral concerns, and increasingly directed censorship initiatives towards political, not religious, threats.

Catholics and Jews depended more heavily on propositional revelation to sanction religious institutions, tradition, and the interpretive authority of rabbis, priests, and the papacy. The dissolution of the Jesuits in 1773 and the forced secularization of ecclesiastical lands within the Holy Roman Empire severely curtailed the Catholic Church's influence over university theology. Only six of the eighteen Catholic universities in German-speaking lands survived the revolutionary wars and the ensuing territorial reorganization of Central Europe. Only one, the university in Würzburg, remained within the territory of a formerly ecclesiastical state, effectively ending the educational traditions of *Germania sacra*.[18] After 1815, under the auspices of the *Paritätsstaat*, most Catholic clergy were trained in state theological faculties, many answering to Protestant princes, where contact with Protestant colleagues posed a particular challenge to orthodoxy.

The rehabilitation of German higher education in the early nineteenth century occurred as the Catholic Church faced its most significant crisis since the Reformation, lacking the material resources, organizational stability, and political clout to preserve its educational institutions. Rome, in fact, remained ambivalent to the weakening of German Catholic universities, many of which had been dangerous seats of Febronianism, a movement to strengthen the national episcopate.[19] Efforts in Cologne to build a Catholic equivalent to the flagship university in Berlin failed in 1815. Many Catholic faculties remained under the direction of Protestant states. Clergy were also trained in Catholic academies, lyceums, and gymnasia, as well as in Benedictine or Dominican monasteries. But only a select number of seminaries run directly by bishops could compete with university faculties in extending this training beyond the requirements of pastoral care.[20] The German College at the Pontifical Gregorian University offered Rome a counterweight to the control the German states wielded over Catholic university theology. However, it closed for twenty years in 1798. After reopening under Jesuit leadership, the moderate scholasticism of its theologians could not rival the system-building ambitions of German academic theology.[21]

Denied access to the university, Jewish religious thought developed in yeshivot, rabbinical seminaries, and, in the second half of the nineteenth century, separate institutes of higher education. University positions dedicated to Christian Hebrew studies existed, for example, as part of the *Institutum Judaicum et Muhammedicum* in Halle, founded in 1728, but ancillary and subordinate to Protestant theology. Cultural and religious training at yeshivot was, in the interpretation of Keith Pickus, "static and narrow,"[22] focused on the Torah and the Talmud and its codifiers and designed as preparation for participation in specifically Jewish society. The Haskalah, or Jewish Enlightenment, weakened the intellectual authority of the rabbinate with the creation of new institutions for the dissemination of knowledge, such as Jewish reading and literary societies.[23] Select modern Jewish schools, the enlightened *Freischulen* founded in Berlin, Breslau, and Dessau between 1778 and 1799, restructured and secularized Jewish education. Jewish attendance at German universities, especially in the field of medicine, increased accordingly, most notably after the emancipation decrees of the Napoleonic period.[24] But multiple proposals to create a chair in Jewish theology, literature, or history in the 1830s and 1840s failed; the German states refused to acknowledge the equality of Judaism, fearful it would erode assimilation and inhibit conversion.[25] The first German chair in Jewish studies did not open until 1964 at the Free University of Berlin.

Ceding the traditional privileges of revelation, Scripture, and religious law was far less attractive to religious thinkers operating in difficult institutional and social environments. The book's chapters therefore largely maintain confessional lines. Chapter 1 tracks the curtailment of propositional revelation among enlightened theologians, mostly Protestant, who reinterpreted revelation as an evolving human capacity for understanding eternal truths. The following three chapters examine how the comparative history of religion and early nineteenth-century German research on language, mythology, and natural history factored in debates over revelation and restricted the terms' epistemological significance. Chapter 5 analyses post-Kantian Protestant philosophies of revelation, charting two alternative paradigms for restoring religion under the Restoration: revelation as subjective inner feeling and revelation as a dialectical process of divine self-disclosure. The final three chapters compare how Catholic, Jewish, and Protestant theologians responded to the rehabilitation of revelation, especially to its rebirth as a subjective category of experience, while noting the implications these shifts had for religious practice and the comparative history of religion.

Liberal efforts to overhaul propositional revelation posed a serious threat to orthodoxy everywhere and never penetrated the core circle of any confession. In their extreme forms, the subjective and experiential reinterpretations of revelation positioned religion as a human creation and threatened to undo God's transcendence, the objectivity of his revelation, and the relevance of dogma, reducing religion to philosophical ethics. The escalation of human agency in the production of religious knowledge and the consequent anthropocentrizing of revelation ultimately proved untenable, as the book's final comparison of Ludwig Feuerbach and Søren Kierkegaard indicates. Feuerbach radically severed revelation from God, exposing and pursuing to its radical conclusions the anthropological origin of religion. Kierkegaard, by contrast, embraced the paradoxes of historical revelation as crucial to self-transformation as a Christian, regarding religion as an existentialist project in which revelation shaped the real, existing self. Both prospects posed significant difficulties for theology, as they respectively culminated in self-declared atheism and a virulent denunciation of the established church. The political instability and weakening

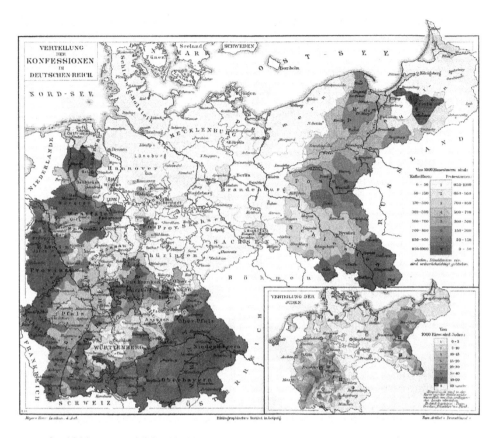

An 1886 map, published in H.J. Meyer's liberal Protestant *Konversations-Lexikon* towards the end of the *Kulturkampf*, a conflict between Chancellor Otto von Bismarck and religious authorities, depicting the distribution of Catholics and Jews (the insert) in the German Empire. The scale for Catholics ranges from 5 to 95 per cent of Christian inhabitants; the scale for Jews extends from 0.3 per cent to 6 per cent. Both confessions appear on the geographic periphery as deviations from the Protestant norm. Map from *Meyers Konversations-Lexikon*, vol. 4, 4th edition (Leipzig: Bibliographisches Institut, 1886), 816–17.[26]

of monarchical authority caused by the Revolutions of 1848/49 compounded the perceived intellectual risks of ceding control over revelation to its recipients.

Rethinking revelation in the nineteenth century nevertheless raised a host of questions, issues, and concerns of relevance beyond the specific theological dilemmas the term aimed to resolve. These encouraged a secularized reappropriation of revelation as a metaphor and conceptual framework for understanding processes and transformations in a resolutely human world. At the heart of many debates over revelation lay epistemology, reflection on the nature and limits of knowledge, on the sufficiency of reason to make ethical judgments and grasp a higher order of existence, and on its relationship to feeling, instinct, and intuition. Theologians grappled with the extent human agency factored in the production of knowledge and contemplated the prospect of losing a transcendent signifier that invested meaning, truth, and value in the world. Revelation, understood as the sudden disclosure of new knowledge, likewise raised the question of genius or how to understand innovation, inspiration, and the radical breakthrough of once unconceivable ideas.[27] As a process of historical self-disclosure, revelation persisted as a category within existentialist philosophy for capturing the constitution of the modern self and the dynamics of intersubjectivity. Finally, the capacity for revelation became a marker of cultural distinction that reinforced racialized hierarchies and inequalities, while justifying certain world historical narratives, imperial rhetoric, and missionary impulses.

By the end of the nineteenth century, a resurgence of orthodoxy visible, for example, in the resolutions of the First Vatican Council and in the "inflation"[28] of revelation in Protestant crisis theology, reversed much of the innovation that resulted from historical revelation's initial crisis. Having struggled to bridge Lessing's ditch, more theologians resorted to a naively positivist restoration of revelation's pre-critical propositional content. This defensive move shielded the authority of Scripture and ecclesiastical institutions from modern thought, but at a cost. University theology, once revered as the impervious study of supernatural forces, yielded to the field of religious studies, which approached religion non-confessionally as a social and cultural construct best grasped through methods accepted across disciplines. Faith could only make its peace with reason and history as a dominant partner that overlooked revelation's fallibilities. This silencing of a century's worth of creative negotiation therefore marks a more decisive moment in the bifurcation of reason and faith than the crisis revelation successfully weathered during the Enlightenment.

Chapter One

Historical Revelation in the Protestant Enlightenment

In 1777, the German dramatist and philosopher Gotthold Ephraim Lessing declared the "accidental truths of history can never become the proof of necessary truths of reason."[1] His statement followed upon nearly a century of rationalist critiques of revelation and varying attempts to reconcile the historical foundation of Christian revelation with its claims to universal truth and divine origins. Lessing suspected Islam was a more reasonable religion than Christianity because it did not rely as heavily on miracles and prophecies to provide historical proof of God's revelations.[2] At the same time, he cautioned against presuming that the revealed religion of Christianity was roughly equivalent to the natural religion of reason. He countered the naturalism of the notorious German deist, H.S. Reimarus, by inveighing at the height of the *Fragmentenstreit*: "Then what is a revelation that reveals nothing?"[3] Lessing tried to solve the dilemma by historicizing revelation in relation to the human capacity for reason in the *Education of the Human Race* (1780). But the difficulty of accepting revelation when its facticity depended on a shaky foundation of miracle, prophecy, and biblical literalism plagued the German theological Enlightenment, and Lessing's recourse to human agency in the production of religious knowledge posed a threat to its transcendent origins.

Tussles over the respective priority of reason and revelation were never as acrimonious in the German states as in France and commenced later than in Britain. Enlightened German religious thinkers largely defended revelation and upheld the authority of Scripture, hesitant to undermine the absolutist state and its religious institutions.[4] Nevertheless, the rationalist principles of Protestant *Aufklärer* did weaken the traditional pillars that legitimized belief in revelation. A major achievement of the theological Enlightenment was shifting the cultural significance of biblical narrative from a literal embodiment of divine truth that accurately recorded God's interventions in human history to a postconfessional historical artefact.[5] This undermined the historical record of revelation, while ceding a greater role to human actors in its reception and transmission. The greater preeminence accorded reason and philosophy in theological matters likewise legitimated natural religion as a viable alternative to revelation in acquiring knowledge of God and securing morality. Lessing mourned the resulting abyss that separated reason and revelation, as well as the tensions between faith and its historical precedents, as a "broad and ugly ditch" he struggled to cross.[6]

This chapter argues that the German theological Enlightenment brought the concept of revelation to a crisis that could only be resolved by curtailing its propositional function, shifting agency in the acquisition of religious truths to historical subjects, and embracing the contingencies that enveloped God's presence on earth. Stakes in the reframing of revelation were inordinately high. For the two and a half centuries that followed deistic challenges to the credibility of divine communication and God's self-presentation through history, revelation remained the "central technical concept"[7] in theology. The polarization of German Protestant theological camps through the nineteenth century revolved around the affirmation or denial of a positive notion of revelation and the corresponding decision of whether to accept the literal meaning and historical reliability of sacred texts.[8] The prospect of historical revelation being unintelligible or sanctioned only by ignorance or fantasy posed an existential threat to Christ's role as saviour and to God's transcendent personhood, as well as to the uniqueness, divine origins, and absolute truth of Scripture. The authority of the Lutheran and reformed churches rested on their claim to be the authentic interpreters of revelation in history and on the right to translate God's word into dogma. Challenging the sanctity of revelation also compromised ecclesiastical authority and disquieted the absolutist state.

Of particular concern here, however, is revelation's validity as an epistemological principle anchoring otherwise inaccessible knowledge about God, redemption, and the course of human history. Early German *Aufklärer* initially encouraged what Karl Aner termed a "peaceful dualism"[9] between reason and revelation. The dogmatic rationalism typical of G.W. Leibniz and Christian Wolff delineated logical criteria that confirmed the historical revelations of Scripture as genuine, deducing God's existence from a priori proofs while accepting miracles as legitimate historical evidence. Their delicate balancing act unravelled into competing camps of naturalists, who rejected revelation, and liberal reforming neologians, who drew on the idea of accommodation to preserve the revealed truth of God. Presuming God's message had been tailored to the cultural milieu of its recipients, neologians historicized Scripture while still extracting a timeless, divinely revealed core of Christianity from its contingent articulation. Historicizing revelation enhanced its compatibility with reason, in this sense, but it also severed the truth of Christianity from its transcendent origins. The progressive dismantling of propositional revelation and the erosion of its transcendent foundations culminated in a reinterpretation of revelation as mere reinforcement for an autonomous human capacity to grasp rational truths.

Protestant conceptions of revelation could only preserve their relevance, outside orthodox circles, by restricting their function in the acquisition of religious truth. The final thrust of the chapter is the open recognition by G.E. Lessing and Immanuel Kant of revelation's historicity. In the last third of the century, both philosophers of religion acquiesced to the notion of sequential, partial revelations that enhanced the human rational capacity and would eventually eliminate the need for revelation. Kant, in addition, disqualified theoretical reason as an arbiter in considerations of divine matters and restricted theology to the domain of practical wisdom, not demonstrable truth. The presumed significance of religion accordingly shifted to the inspiring of morality and ethical conduct, and the validity of religious doctrines hinged on subjective considerations of how they affected the human condition. This undermined confessional claims to exclusive truth. The immanentism inherent in a purely moral religion, as well as its necessarily anthropocentric focus, likewise jeopardized the standing of a transcendent personal God. The radical curtailment of revelation's epistemological prerogatives and acceptance of its historical embeddedness also discouraged the longing for primordial revelation. But it eased discussion of revelation into the philosophical faculties, such that subsequent theologians were compelled to engage Lessing, Kant, and other philosophers of religion.

Reason and Revelation: Spinoza, Leibniz, and Wolff

For the early German Enlightenment, the reception of the radical Dutch freethinker Baruch de Spinoza (1632–77) was far more influential than British deism, which didn't reach a German audience until the late 1720s.[10] Spinoza ignited the German critique of revelation as part of a broader political and historical assault on religion. Expelled as a young man from his synagogue and reputed an atheist, Spinoza waged a relentless campaign against divinely constituted political authority, resulting in Spinozism standing as shorthand for any radical challenge to orthodoxy and organized religion during the hundred years following his death.[11] His posthumously published *Ethics* (1677) had the deepest reverberations among German scholars who debated the extent Spinoza's identification of God and the material world constituted a denial of a transcendent, personal deity. In the *Ethics*, Spinoza proposed that there was only one substance encompassing everything, including God, hence there was no God distinct from nature. The spectre of pantheism that hung over Spinoza's metaphysics erupted most notoriously in the 1780s, in the *Pantheismusstreit* (a debate over Spinoza's conception of God and its legacy) that followed Lessing's death, but his challenge to revelation was equally severe.

In the *Tractatus theologico-politicus* (1670), Spinoza denied the divine origins of revealed religion as a means to enhance freedom of thought and expression in the civic realm. Banned four years after its publication, the book condemned religious and intellectual intolerance in the Dutch Republic and recommended a separation of political and religious authority.[12] Spinoza drove a wedge between the domains of revelation and natural knowledge to justify this position. Philosophy and theology were distinct endeavours, he argued, presiding over their own province, methods, and principles. One governed by reason, the other by revelation, neither should be subordinate to the other. "Religion and piety should not wish to have reason for a servant," he wrote, "nor should reason wish to have religion for a servant. Both should be able to rule their own realms in the greatest harmony."[13] The aim of philosophy, for Spinoza, was truth founded on universal concepts drawn from nature.

The goal of revealed religion, by contrast, was, for Spinoza, obedience. Revelation was only "indispensable,"[14] in his view, because the natural light of reason could never guarantee the moral authority of Scripture. Spinoza maintained the "usefulness and necessity"[15] of revelation only as a societal measure to secure adherence to the law and offer solace. On these grounds, he reduced Mosaic revelation to a politically expedient event. In his view, Moses presented his law as divinely ordained to ensure loyalty and compliance; his goal was to stabilize the material welfare and polity of the Hebrews. The prophetic gift was, furthermore, not specific to the Jews; other nations had also claimed to acquire their own particular laws and governance through God's external direction.

This brutally reduced the epistemological significance of revelation. According to Spinoza, revelation did not yield a clear conception of God. Without reason, the mind "discerns nothing but dreams and fantasies."[16] The prophets, he argued, were "ignorant" of both "natural and spiritual matters" because they lacked "philosophical reasoning."[17]

Charismatic figures endowed with "a more vivid power of imagination,"[18] they merely had a gift for inspiring morality in others. The first major European thinker to categorically deny miracles, Spinoza declared supernatural interventions into nature to be impossible and popular belief in them a delusion.[19] He likewise presented the divine teachings as a human fabrication, undercutting Scripture's status as inspired. As Jonathan Israel has shown, Spinoza's early advocacy of historical biblical hermeneutics proved widely disquieting.[20] In his view, God had adapted his revelations to the understanding of their recipients; they thus displayed extreme variation based on the disposition and relative eloquence and clarity of the prophets.

German considerations of the viability of revelation were decidedly more conservative. Spinoza's early interpreters, Gottfried Wilhelm Leibniz (1646–1716) and Christian Wolff (1679–1754), were unwilling to perceive a conflict between reason and faith or to declare miracles and mysteries contrary to reason. In presuming the universe consisted in a pre-established harmony, the philosophical systems of Leibniz and Wolff veered closely on the determinism that plagued their predecessor.[21] However, as representatives of the moderate Enlightenment, these rational supernaturalists distanced themselves publicly from the radicalism that tinged Spinozism. The natural theology of both Leibniz and Wolff admitted pagan precedents to Christian morality in the tradition of Christian Platonism. Yet Leibniz, in particular, was committed to upholding state authority and strengthening organized religion and maintained a marginally orthodox attitude towards the Bible and sacred history. Even if they found metaphysical speculation sufficient to establish the existence of God and his attributes, both fell far short of denying the necessity of Christian revelation.

When Leibniz encountered Spinoza's *Tractatus* in April 1671, he denounced the author's opinions and incited German scholars to refute it, despite an abiding curiosity for Dutch radical thought and his having initiated personal correspondence with the author. As councillor and librarian to the court of Brunswick-Lüneburg, the young Leibniz at least publicly aspired to a philosophical justification of revealed religion that would secure a stronger platform for political and ecclesiastical authority than fideistic principles offered.[22] His early *Discourse on Metaphysics* (1686) countered Spinoza's reputation for atheistic fatalism with a vision of the universe's predetermined harmony that preserved divine will and intelligence.[23] Leibniz built from the presumption of God as the "absolute monarch of the most perfect city," to argue he created the best of all possible worlds, one in which miracles fit into the natural order.[24]

Natural theology nearly, but never fully, sufficed for Leibniz as a means for knowing God. In the *Preface to the Novissima Sinica* (1697) Leibniz famously declared that Europeans, being morally corrupt, would benefit from Chinese docents instructing them in "the use and practice of natural religion" just as Christian missionaries in turn taught revelation.[25] Sectarian divisions, he feared, had caused Europeans to lose touch with the core truths of natural religion. In a 1709 letter to Electress Sophie, Leibniz therefore called for "Missionaries of Reason in Europe" who would "preach the natural Religion, on which Revelation is founded, and without which Revelation would always be taken poorly."[26] As Franklin Perkins has argued, however, it would be wrong to interpret Leibniz's Sinophilia as intending to promote natural theology or even deism at the expense of revelation.[27] The superior morals of the Chinese built upon the practical philosophy of Confucianism, which could not, for Leibniz, yield necessary truths without grace.[28]

The "Preliminary Dissertation" to Leibniz's *Theodicy* (1710) upheld the orthodox presumption that faith occasionally transcended the human understanding.[29] Other "motives of credibility," in his view, justified "the authority of Holy Scripture before the tribunal of reason, so that reason in consequence gives way before it."[30] Unlike the British deists, Leibniz defended miracles and mysteries as a means to preserve the distinctive historical character of Christian doctrine and avoid reducing religion to ethics. "For the true religion must needs have marks that the false religions have not," he explained, "else would Zoroaster, Brahma, Somonacodom and Mahomet be as worthy of belief as Moses and Jesus Christ."[31] Miracles, he argued, did not violate "absolutely certain and inevitable truths,"[32] only apparently contradicting contingent truths rooted in judgment and experience. It therefore sufficed to have an "analogical understanding"[33] of the mysteries. Leibniz's acquiescing to only ever achieving a partial understanding of the Christian mysteries, explains, as Avi Lifschitz has argued, why he insisted on attributing a constitutive role to signs in the cognitive process. Clear but confused ideas required symbolic mediation; only intuitive perceptions of God were clear and distinct.[34]

Like other adherents to the theological Enlightenment, Leibniz celebrated the gradual perfection of reason, which dampened nostalgia for primordial revelation. He stressed the continued relevance of ancient religious truths, whose ubiquity held the promise, in his view, of facilitating ecumenical reconciliation after the Thirty Years war and converting Jews and Muslims.[35] In a 1714 letter to his friend Nicolas Remond, Leibniz ventured that "in noticing the traces of truth among the ancients ... one extracts gold from mud, a diamond from the rough, light from the shadows; and this would in fact be perennial philosophy." While admitting that "the Orientals had beautiful and grand idea of the divinity," however, he assumed "progress in knowledge." The Greeks contributed reason and science, and the scholastics adapted what was "acceptable in pagan philosophy" to Christianity.[36] The perennial philosophy to which he subscribed did not revive the dark terrain of lost origins.

The natural theology of Christian Wolff secured for reason the further prerogative of passing judgment on matters of faith. Christian dogma, in his view, had to justify itself to reason.[37] Although Wolff preserved the divine origins and distinction of Christian revelation, Spinoza's shadow dogged him more persistently than Leibniz. His notion that the laws of nature derived from a pre-established harmony elicited accusations of a necessarian worldview.[38] The Pietist stronghold of Halle, where Wolff obtained a professorship in mathematics and the natural sciences with Leibniz's help in 1706, was shaky ground for exploring natural theology, as well, wary as Pietists were of emancipating reason from the Bible. Wolff's "Discourse on the Practical Philosophy of the Chinese," held in memory of Leibniz in 1721, presented three possible paths for achieving virtue – revelation, reason, and natural philosophy – and immediately drew accusations of Spinozism. The Chinese, in Wolff's view, had attained philosophical virtue without revelation. While admitting their "notion of the Godhead" was "confused" and Chinese ethics could never "go beyond"[39] civil justice, Wolff was banished to Marburg for seventeen years in 1723, his philosophy banned by Prussian royal decree. State officials were still willing in the 1720s to support the church's efforts to eliminate radical thought.[40]

The *Theologia Naturalis* (1734) Wolff composed protectively in Latin applied mathematical reasoning and syllogistic logic to theological knowledge, granting a broad swath of privileges to abstract reason.[41] One of four branches of metaphysics, natural theology constituted for Wolff a rational "science of God and divine things."[42] According to Wolff, God's will called "the most perfect"[43] of all possible worlds into being as a manifestation of his own wisdom. Wolff presumed that man's perfection lay in his rationality and that he could advance systematically from natural law to an understanding of God.[44] Yet the *Theologia Naturalis* also welcomed miracles, prophecies, and the mysteries of Christianity as standing "above reason."[45] Wolff's toleration of such wonders derived from the limits he placed on the rational capacity of a "finite understanding."[46] He distinguished between "necessary truths" of a mathematical sort, which permit no contradiction, and "contingent" truths, which could be otherwise, such as explanations for changes in the natural world that might, for example, seemingly preclude a virgin birth.[47]

In the metaphor of the neo-orthodox Swiss theologian Karl Barth (1886–1968), reason and revelation comprised for Wolff two overlapping spheres of equal significance.[48] Reason prevailed in the domain of mathematics and natural sciences. Some areas, including knowledge of God as the creator and ruler of the world and of the soul's immortality, could be apprehended using both capacities. But revelation, and thus theology, had exclusive rights over knowledge lying beyond human reason, such as the Christian mysteries, the Trinity, and the doctrine of grace. In Wolff's view, revealed religion exceeded the fruits of natural religion; thus he refrained from wielding reason as a weapon against Christian dogma.[49] He still expected, though, the principles of logical reason to apply within the sphere reserved to revelation.

In this spirit, the *Theologia Naturalis* detailed logical criteria for authenticating a given historical revelation as divine in origin. Revelation had occurred among all peoples through history, Wolff admitted, so as the foundation of the Christian religion, true revelation needed to be distinguished from the false. Wolff defined revelation as a "miracle in the soul" that occurs "supernaturally." God only revealed what could not be attained through reason or experience. The first qualification of true revelation was thus that it be essential knowledge that humans could not grasp "by other means."[50] Additionally, it could not contradict the truths of reason and experience or God's qualities, nor would it require humans to act contrary to the laws of nature or the soul.[51] Although revelations could contain mysteries and contradict contingent truths, they would never violate necessary truths and should conform to natural laws as much as possible.[52] Wolff proposed strict, rationalist linguistic criteria for accepting the legitimacy of verbal revelation. Besides being comprehensible, it had to use no more words than necessary, and their placement had to follow the general rules of language or speech.[53] Wolffian hermeneutics applied the demands of conceptual clarity and logic to the Bible.[54]

The controversies reverberating around Wolff eventually subsided with the excising of theology from a mechanistic approach to nature.[55] The height of his influence over theology coincided with a second Halle period after Wolff's rehabilitation under the more tolerant Frederick the Great in 1740.[56] Wolffian theologians, such as Sigmund Jakob Baumgarten in Halle and Johann Christoph Gottsched in Leipzig, applied logic to the sphere reserved for revelation. But Wolff's influence also fed an upsurge in deism and natural philosophy in the German states during the 1730s and 1740s. His interpreters often drew far more radical consequences than Wolff himself cared to admit. The Wertheim Bible, published by avowed Wolffian Johann Lorenz Schmidt in 1735, for example, was banned on the grounds that it substituted philosophy for theology. In 1741, Schmidt translated Tindal's *Christianity as Old as the Creation* (1730), expanding the reception of British deism among German audiences; Baumgarten's reviews of British deistical literature started in 1748. Not surprisingly, the "peace treaty"[57] Wolff negotiated between reason and revelation did not endure much past his death in 1754. The tension between the epistemological principles of reason and revelation remained unresolved, pitting orthodox Wolffians against more radical Protestant adaptations of his synthesis.

Reimarus and the Neologians on Pagan Salvation

The rational-supernaturalist compromise Wolff and Leibniz maintained against radical Spinozism dissolved in the second half of the century into a staunch naturalism embodied by Hermann Samuel Reimarus (1694–1767), and an attempt by the so-called neologians to rationalize the content of revelation while purging it of dogmas irreconcilable with reason.[58] The naturalist presumption that reason provided sufficient knowledge of God without revelation posed an enduring threat to organized religion, as the scandals indicate that erupted after Lessing published fragments from Reimarus's clandestine *Apologie oder Schutzschrift für die vernünftigen Verehrer Gottes* between 1774 and 1778. The more moderate neologians persisted in approaching revelation as a useful aid and supplement to natural religion. A practical, emotional, and ethical understanding of reason derived from British theology allowed them to soften the abstract logical rationalism of Wolff.[59] Their rationalization of religion made the historical shell of Christianity appear increasingly incidental to its essential message. Devaluing the historical forms of revelation opened neologians to pagan salvation but also rattled revelation's presumed access to universal, binding truth.

The natural theology Reimarus advocated in the mid-eighteenth century radically denied that historical events, such as miracles, could be the foundation for religion, as knowledge of God needed to be universal and timeless. The biblical critic and philologist transitioned in the course of his career from an orthodox Lutheran scholar to an increasingly critical reader of the Bible and eventually a Deist. For this reason, Reimarus has rightly been labelled a "hybrid figure"[60] who straddled the radical and moderate Enlightenments, often masking inward disbelief with outward orthodoxy.[61] In 1723, Pietist criticism of Wolff so disturbed Reimarus that he resigned his position in Wittenberg and settled back in his native Hamburg as a professor of Hebrew at the local gymnasium.[62] A visit to Holland and England, and the debates over the Wertheim Bible, in which Reimarus rapidly shifted his position in favour of Schmidt,[63] precipitated his descent into controversial religious territory.

Reimarus's providential deism was politically conservative, assuming that the creator had bestowed a benevolent order on a largely perfect world which fostered morality. While seeking to limit ecclesiastical authority and increase religious toleration, Reimarus believed the social and political framework was essentially as it should be.[64] Dutch radical thinking, as well as British deism, shaped his philosophical outlook, but Reimarus remained equally as hostile to Spinozism as to revealed religion.[65] As indicated in the preface to the *Vornehmsten Wahrheiten der natürlichen Religion* (1754), which is discussed more fully in Chapter 4, Reimarus cultivated his naturalist arguments in an effort to defeat French materialism and one-substance, pantheist positions.[66] He kept private the most radical aspect of his thought, a clandestine attack on revealed religion, out of fear for his position in Hamburg society and never published the subversive *Apologie* during his lifetime. This reticence distinguishes Reimarus from other members of the radical Enlightenment.[67]

In *Die vornehmsten Wahrheiten der natürlichen Religion*, Reimarus defended Christianity with the traditional arguments of physicotheology explicitly rejecting the Epicurean notion of a universe evolving naturally without God as creator. In the unpublished *Apologie*, written in the 1740s, however, Reimarus advanced the far more brazen thesis that natural theology was not merely the philosophical foundation for supernaturally revealed religion.[68] The lengthy treatise carried physicotheology to its logical conclusion that nature was sufficient to know God and Christian revelation was dispensable. The second fragment Lessing published from the *Apologie* in 1778, circumventing the censors in his capacity as librarian in Wolffenbüttel, specifically argued for the "impossibility of a revelation that all people can believe with certainty."[69] On these grounds, Reimarus denied the necessity and possibility of all historical revelation, even as found in Christianity, in favour of a universal, timeless natural religion.

Reimarus's sprawling argument built from the presumption that God would lack perfection if knowledge of the divine were not accessible to all people. God's goodness required him to desire salvation for all; his wisdom would prevent the withholding of any knowledge necessary for salvation. At the same time, Reimarus reasoned, a continual series of supernatural revelations across time and space would disrupt the perfect order of creation, producing an "absurdity."[70] The multitude of contradictory religious traditions only produced "disharmonies," in his view, resulting in "false appearances, deception and thus doubt, mistakes, uncertainty, and contradiction."[71] It was similarly unlikely that God had bestowed a special revelation on a chosen people, such as the ancient Hebrews. Their transmission of revelation would appear to rest on human authority alone and thereby undercut its divine provenance. The linguistic differences that God himself created at Babel were furthermore insurmountable, for Reimarus, confirming that Christianity could never become universal.

Belief in divine revelation threatened, for Reimarus, the eternal truths of natural theology. He was one of few *Aufklärer* willing to deny Scripture transcendent origins, being neither inspired, nor the word of God. Jesus may have taught some principles of natural religion, according to Reimarus, but most of the gospel story, including the resurrection, was, in his view, a fraud perpetuated by his disciples – an audacity that explains Reimarus's lack of followers in Germany.[72] The "only way" for God to effectively spread knowledge of the divine was, for Reimarus, "the language and book of nature, the creatures of God and the traces of divine perfections which present themselves as if in a mirror to all people ... of all places and times."[73] God must have "integrated into the natural order and the human understanding a natural propensity for such a discovery."[74] The historical revelations attributed to Christianity were a distraction from true knowledge of God which nature provided.

The *Fragmentenstreit* that followed the publication of the *Apologie* elicited a sharp defence of orthodox Lutheranism from Hamburg theologian Johann Melchior Goeze, who maintained the verbal inspiration of the Bible, the historical facticity of revelation, and the centrality of Christ to God's communication. The disregard Reimarus showed for Scripture tinged the Enlightenment commitment to moral religion with extremism. Rather than resolve the respective contributions of reason and revelation or which peoples had been privy to religious truth, the *Fragmentenstreit* exposed the tenacity of the problem and encouraged Lessing to address it himself directly.

The liberal reform movement of Enlightened Protestant theologians known as neology opted for a more moderate mediation of reason and revelation. Rising to prominence during the second half of the eighteenth century, the neologians extended the Wolffian concern for establishing the viability of revelation as a concept compatible with reason to a systematic evaluation of individual Christian dogmas. They retained the idea of revelation as a necessary principle for clarifying religious truths and easing their discovery and apprehension. But neology emptied Christian revelation of any historical content that appeared nonsensical, replacing it with reasonable truths that accorded with natural religion.[75] For Barth, who disparaged the Enlightenment for neglecting revelation, the claim this camp made to innovation clouds the more daring Wolffian step of asserting the relevance of reason in the first place; neologists, in his view, represent a "third act" that encroached on areas of the Christian faith that Wolffians let stand as transcending reason.[76] Their real contribution, in his view, lay in proclaiming morality to be the crucial principle of Christian faith and evaluating doctrines based on their practical effects on piety and virtue. Yet, the neologians did dissolve the orthodox compromise that conservative Wolffians had supported, quietly dismembering Augustinian dogma from within the established church.[77]

The rationalizing, non-dogmatic Protestantism of the neologians proved appealing to the Enlightened German states, overtaking Pietism by 1770 as the religious interpretation most favoured by Prussia. Through their positions in state offices, supporters of neology controlled university and pastoral appointments and patronage until the succession of Friedrich Wilhelm II, whose ultra-conservative minister for religion sought to restore traditional Protestantism at the cost of rationalist theology.[78] Under Frederick the Great, the absolutist Prussian state found the principles of the theological Enlightenment useful for aiding the transition from confessional politics to a reformist bureaucratic state, especially after the annexation of Catholic Silesia in 1740.[79]

Among neologians, the primary device for protecting the indispensability of revelation was accommodation theory, which preserved scriptural authority by historicizing it. By this view God had made revelation appropriate to the human condition by adapting his message to the mentality and customs of his recipients. A timeless kernel of divine truth was thus still recognizable within a specific historical event and could be extracted by understanding the cultural milieu of its audience. For leading neologian Johann Salomo Semler (1725–91), this required discarding the notion of a divinely inspired Bible and dissecting the contingent encasement of historical revelation. Semler distinguished inner spiritual truths from their historical manifestation in both Scripture and theological doctrine. In its most basic form, faith, in his view, entailed belief in "invisible things," which, even without the "historical bits" of Christianity, could reinvigorate religion better than the "dead opinions and assertions" of traditional theology.[80]

As a student of Baumgarten in Halle, Semler worked closely on his editions of British deist literature. In Latin conversations, with Baumgarten role-playing the part of deists, Semler witnessed how theology could "lose violently" yet still leave the core of Christianity intact.[81] As a pioneer in critical historical scholarship and New Testament interpretation Semler decoupled revelation from its articulation in Scripture. His "Historische Einleitung in die Dogmatische Gottes-gelersamkeit" (1759) argued that God's word was not directly present in the text of the Bible. Instead biblical truths had been communicated "in human language and through the human imagination, according to its diversity in certain regions and times."[82] This mandated a strong foundation in "worldly wisdom,"[83] namely historical, philological, and philosophical familiarity with biblical languages, customs, and history. With these tools Semler believed he could distinguish divine spirit from the historical forms of revelation, cautioning that the "majority"[84] of the Bible consisted in natural truths and was of purely historical interest.[85] Critics needed to discover the "very few tenets ... the smallest part of the Bible"[86] that cannot be known through reason, most of which pertained to redemption and God's final purpose for humanity.

The legacy of primordial revelation was incidental to Semler's defence of natural religion. In the *Versuch einer freiern theologischen Lehrart* (1777) he envisioned producing "a harmony of moral truths"[87] by collecting "from the oldest times and authors" doctrines concerning God and his relationship to humanity.[88] Especially virtuous philosophers had preserved "secret knowledge"[89] in their symbols and ceremonies, while public devotion succumbed to superstition. For Semler, however, the source of this wisdom was "of no importance."[90] He denied that earliest forms of natural religion had enjoyed the "greatest perfection";[91] knowledge of God built progressively through time. Semler's discussions of primitive Christianity also refrained from idealizing a pure faith in its infancy. As Reill has shown, Semler traced an evolving historical dialectic between inherited external forms of religion and their private moral interpretation, attributing vital causal energy to the religious spirit.[92]

The publication of Reimarus's fragments in 1774 pressured Semler to reinforce the divinity of Christ.[93] His escape from radical naturalism was weak, as Reill notes, a personal assertion of belief, rather than rational proof, that the morality embodied in Jesus transcended his historical location among the ancient Hebrews. Semler's *Beantwortung der Fragmente eines Ungenannten* (1779) defended the story of the resurrection and the transcendent spiritual power of Christ.[94] For Semler Christianity was unique in inspiring a spiritual and moral movement that perpetually transcended its historical confines and constituted a form of perfection in becoming.[95] Indeed controversy over the fragments set off a conservative turn in the final decade of Semler's life. Based on his distinction between private and public religion Semler, alone among neologians, supported the religious edict of J.C. Wöllner that bound Protestants to the doctrines of their confession. Inner morality, in his view, belonged to an invisible realm not accessible to civil society. The religious community, however, was bound by the external needs of cohesion and preserving tradition.[96]

Johann August Eberhard (1739–1809), who studied theology in Halle under Semler in the late 1750s, more emphatically denied revelation was necessary for salvation. A debate over the issue erupted in France after the publication and condemnation by the Sorbonne of Jean-François Marmontel's *Belisaire* (1767), in which the protagonist hopes to meet noble pagans, especially Socrates, in heaven. As a Wolffian, Eberhard believed that the divine purpose behind creating the best of all possible worlds was the perfection of humanity. His response to the controversy, the *Neue Apologie des Sokrates* (1772), applied Wolff's ideas about perfection to deny a range of doctrines, including original sin, grace, and eternal damnation, for being contrary to God's goodness.[97] Eberhard's defence of pagan salvation so perturbed orthodox Lutherans that they resisted his appointment as pastor in Charlottenburg until Frederick the Great intervened.[98] The cold reception Eberhard received made him welcome an appointment in philosophy in Halle in 1778, where he defended Leibnizian metaphysics against Kant's critical philosophy.[99] Despite his valuation of reason Eberhard strongly disapproved of the French Revolution and wrote in defence of absolute monarchy, citing the state's duty to regulate civil liberties in the interest of its subjects.[100]

Eberhard's dismissal of revelation as a requirement for salvation presumed the viability of rational *ur*-monotheism. He attributed a "natural origin" to early knowledge of one God. According to the deist Carl Friedrich Bahrdt, Eberhard privately confided that "Christ presented no significant doctrine that Socrates hadn't already taught."[101] Pagan peoples realized that the world "depends on and is governed by an external cause,"[102] yet had fallen into error without a capacity for abstract thought. As early humans explained the natural world through "supernatural causes," they populated nature with a diversity of spirits, thereby fragmenting their first concept God.[103] This innocent mistake did not, Eberhard concluded, warrant condemnation. In his view, the concept of eternity developed only after other abstract and transcendent ideas so that humanity "received it only late in its pure form."[104] To support his view, Eberhard briefly sketched how Zoroastrians, Hindus, Sabians, the Incas, and ancient Chinese had once believed in the true God. Their deepest history gave evidence of a monotheistic sensibility.

Augustinian tradition erred, Eberhard asserted, in not recognizing pagans were capable of moral goodness. Eternal damnation could not be part of Christian revelation because it contradicted the idea of a wise and just order. To support his argument, Eberhard unravelled Leibniz's position on the infinite continuity of sin, suggesting that his reconciliation of eternal punishment with a perfect world was an insincere accommodation to religious orthodoxy.[105] This became the occasion, despite their personal acquaintance, for Lessing to vindicate Leibniz and attack neology. He criticized Wolffians for wrongly interpreting Leibniz as a utilitarian concerned with individual wellbeing. In his view, Leibniz referred to the world as a totality, whose perfection could increase through damnation of the unreformed.[106]

Other rationalist biblical critics, including Johann David Michaelis (1717–91), retained the concept of revelation while repudiating the cult of origins. As an Hebraist and scholar of biblical languages and antiquities, Michaelis only hovered on the fringes of neology, adamant that he was not a theologian and eschewing any ties to theological faculties. Perturbed as a youth by the difficulty of reconciling the rationalist critique of revelation with the divine truth of Christianity, he abandoned plans to enter the ministry.[107] Michaelis openly declared that he never felt the presence of the Holy Spirit or the workings of supernatural grace. He trained in Wolffian philosophy with Baumgarten in Halle. In 1746 Michaelis received an appointment as professor of oriental languages at the recently founded university in Göttingen. A position within the philosophical faculty shielded him from orthodox clerics and allowed him to explore heterodox religious ideas. His fame rests on a revolutionary historical-critical approach to Scripture that embedded Hebrew within the larger Arabic language family.

A rationalist defence of revelation is found in Michaelis's *Compendium theologiae dogmaticae* (1760), a lecture series whose expanded second edition appeared in German as *Dogmatik* in 1784. Michaelis welcomed both reason and revelation as dual sources for theology in an attempt to liberate dogmatics from literal interpretations of biblical language. Biblical exegesis required the application of reason, for Michaelis, because it was the gatekeeper for evaluating the authenticity of revelation and provided a clearer conception of God's qualities than Scripture. Revelation, in turn, offered certainty when reason could only achieve mere possibility and, moreover, supplied "some grand, entirely unexpected principles" regarding higher spiritual beings.[108] In practice, the compendium was theologically more closely bound to Wolffian conservatism than Semler's work. Michaelis affirmed nearly all the traditional doctrines, including miracles, prophecy, the resurrection, the trinity, and the omnipotence and omniscience of God.[109]

Natural religion fares moderately well in the *Dogmatik*. Michaelis held it capable of teaching morality; it formed the core of most religions, preventing peoples not of the book from descending into lawless anarchy.[110] But the many insufficiencies of natural religion made revelation desirable. Through logical deductions, Michaelis reasoned that the philosophical acumen needed for natural religion was unattainable for most. It was so inefficient that considerable damage would result from the long process required for full the comprehension of moral laws. More importantly, natural religion contained no certain knowledge of the afterlife, Michaelis noted, and thus could not dissuade people as effectively from sin as revealed religion.[111] Similarly to Wolff, Michaelis provided criteria for ascertaining whether a given revelation was genuine, including miracles and fulfilled prophecies.

Likely responding to J.G. Herder's *Älteste Urkunde*, the second edition of the *Dogmatik* also considered a revelation's age when calculating its authenticity. But Michaelis explicitly dismissed the notion of primordial revelation as irrelevant for biblical scholars. A benevolent God would not have abandoned the *Vorwelt*, Michaelis conceded, but to expect revelation to be as old as the world was delusional. Even if traces survived, primordial revelation would long ceased to have counted as a "revelation for us."[112] The "first language of the primeval world" was no longer comprehensible, Michaelis insisted.[113] He accepted Mosaic authorship of the Pentateuch and declared no other surviving author exceeded the depth of his historical vision.

Rationalist biblical critics in the German states largely retained faith in the concept of revelation during the third quarter of the eighteenth century. However, the historicization of Scripture, seen as an accommodation to its recipients, meant that the direct presence of God's word no longer justified the divine origins and uniqueness of Christian revelation. Only a fine line distinguished revealed faith from natural religion, but few followed Reimarus in erasing it entirely. The desire to circumvent the scandal of particularity encouraged Enlightened theologians to value natural religion and recognize pagan salvation, but they did so on the basis of rational *ur*-monotheism, regarding the quest for primordial revelation as irrelevant and harmful to the cause of rationalism. Neologians no longer regarded the historical trappings of revelation as essential to its content, but they insisted the historical forms required precise contextualization before the timeless truths of the faith could be excavated.

G.E. Lessing on the Historicity of Revelation

The delicate balance neologians struck between reason and revelation withered under the scrutiny of Gotthold Ephraim Lessing, who, even as he decoupled the "inner truth" of Christianity from its external forms, pursued the full implications of revelation's historical embodiment. Raised traditionally in a Lutheran parsonage in Saxony, Lessing embarked on theological studies in Leipzig in 1746, only to surrender to deism and quit. As a young literary critic and journalist in Berlin Lessing pursued a subversive cultural and political agenda, nurturing a mutual dislike for the Enlightened Prussian sovereign and his militarist state.[114] His radicalism increased in the early 1760s while serving as secretary to General Tauentzien, the garrison commander in Breslau. Engrossed in Spinoza's *Ethics*, Lessing slipped away from the benign natural religion of Leibniz and Wolff and, in debates with his friend Moses Mendelsohn, gravitated towards Spinozist monism.[115] Like other deists he anchored morality in the eternal laws of nature and initially dispensed with the concept of revelation.

Lessing's unpublished "On the Origin of Revealed Religion" written around 1763 thus grappled with the value assigned revelation given the sufficiency of primitive natural religion. His answer reflects Spinoza's claim in the *Tractatus* that Scripture teaches obedience, not philosophy, as well as other arguments regarding the social utility of religion. Where Spinoza attributed religion to the deliberate deception of priests and rulers, however, Lessing saw a real human need for it. In his view, neither dogmas nor ceremonies were necessary for the true worship of God.[116] Revealed religion was a human response to the need for social cohesion. The "founder" of each faith attributed divine origins to the otherwise "conventional elements" of religion, Lessing concluded, and established himself a mediator with God. In his view, each revealed religion still contained "essential elements" of truth derived by reason, which each state modified according to its particular circumstances. The best revealed religion, in his view, "contains the fewest conventional additions to natural religion, and least hinders [its] good effects."[117]

Starting in 1771, in his new post as librarian at the Herzog-August-Bibliothek in Wolfenbüttel, Lessing began devising a strategy for salvaging a reformed concept of revelation, while still honouring deist and Spinozist criticism of the term. Deism, he now feared, ignored both the legitimate needs of the religious consciousness and the philosophical importance of Christian thought.[118] A three-front war against orthodoxy, deism, and neology accompanied Lessing's revitalization of revelation. Its chief battles were waged over the provocative *Fragmente eines Ungenannten*, which Lessing delivered in stages starting in 1774. Drawing on orthodox principles to temper Reimarus, Lessing's campaign chiefly targeted liberal reformists within neology whose pairing of reason and Christianity he found hypocritical and inconsistent.

Barth interprets Lessing as a closet neologian, sympathizing with the movement's Enlightened ambitions but disliking its methods.[119] His vitriol against the movement neology as a shallow hybrid of philosophy and theology is indeed caustic. Lessing found the rationality embraced by neologists deceptive because it obscured an underlying loyalty to revelation. "Reason submits to imprisonment," he argued in 1777, "its surrender is nothing but a recognition of its limits as secured by the reality of revelation."[120] But neologians also preserved faith as a form of revelation that revealed nothing new. "Faith is reason confirmed by miracles and signs," Lessing wrote, "and reason has become reasonable faith. The entirety of revealed religion is nothing but a renewed sanction of rational religion."[121] He took issue, for example, with Semler's continued adherence to revelation after eliminating its basis in Scripture. Semler, in his view, refused to concede the full implications of his rationalism out of deference to the church. For Lessing, the neologians were too deferential to Lutheran ecclesiastical tradition and authority and too allied with Prussian state and church institutions.[122]

In his editor's counterpropositions, Lessing conceded the legitimacy of all Reimarus's allegations. He shared his doubts about historical revelation ever grounding a universal, rational faith and condemned the false "economizing of salvation"[123] among pagans. But Lessing endeavoured to transcend these liabilities and salvage the intrinsic value of Christianity. The fragments offended theologians, he admitted, but for true Christians, the facticity of Scripture and supernatural revelation did not determine faith. Lessing justified his position by claiming "the letter is not the spirit; and the Bible is not religion." The heart of Christianity lay in its "inner truth,"[124] which justified itself, requiring "no external accreditation."[125] The inner truths of Scripture sanctified the Bible, for Lessing, not their historical manifestation in the writing of the evangelists and apostles. This subjectivism is, Toshimasa Yasukata notes, prescient of Friedrich Schleiermacher in that for Lessing the inner truth was not externally or rationally verifiable. The evidence in its favour resided in feeling, inner experience, and personal commitment, and it was recognizable only through participation in the inner truth itself.[126]

At the same time, the editor's counterpropositions repudiate a major tenet of rationalist theology by refusing to judge the truth of revealed religion based on its conformity to natural religion. Responding to Reimarus's doubting the divine origin of the Old Testament in the fourth fragment, Lessing asserted that the criteria of meeting the basic principles of natural religion were not indicative of a faith's divinity.[127] Revealed religion should, in fact, surpass natural religion. The divinity of the Mosaic books, he wrote, "must be proven in an entirely different manner than by the truths of natural religion appearing in them."[128] The human spirit had not yet progressed far enough among the Hebrews, he cautioned, to allow for a complete revelation. This response to Reimarus foreshadows Lessing's transforming the concept of revelation into a progressive, human capacity for religious awareness.

Responding to the escalating *Fragmentenstreit*, Lessing's "On the Proof of the Spirit and of Power" (1777) indicates how dramatically the radical historicization of revelation bestowed agency on human subjects in the production of religious knowledge. The public letter addressed criticism by the orthodox Hanoverian theologian J.D. Schumann that miracles and prophecies provided historical proof of Christian truth. Lessing countered that historical events could never establish a universal truth. First, a temporal gap separating the past and present made transmitting knowledge of a revelatory occurrence problematic. Lessing admitted that miracles and fulfilled prophecies directly experienced at the time of Christ would have been compelling. But living now "in the eighteenth century in which miracles no longer happen," Christians experienced doubt. "Historical knowledge," Lessing explained, only carried the strength of "human testimonies" and "reports," being an indirect medium of transmission that deprived miracles of their "immediate effect" and "force."[129] Historical truths, for Lessing, were only probable, not demonstrable. Thus, they were insufficient underpinning for the eternal verities of faith.[130]

Second, a metaphysical gap divided the merely relative certainty of an historical occurrence from absolutely binding truths. Following Leibniz, Lessing asserted that moral truths belonged to a "different class" than "accidental truths of history," being eternal and necessary. The cleft between historical revelation and reason amounted, Lessing wrote, to a "broad and ugly ditch" that he could not ford despite earnest endeavours to "make the leap." He raised "no historical objection" to the probable fact of Christ's rising from the dead, but the event did not oblige anyone to accept the incarnation.[131] Reports of miracles and prophecies were no longer powerful in his day. He presumed Christian teachings were now self-evident; even the notion of the trinity could be reconciled with reason. But recourse to historical precedents could not compel faith.

Responding to Goeze, his main opponent in the *Fragmentenstreit*, Lessing confirmed that he "wishe[d] to see religion separated from the history of religion." Goeze had argued that Christianity was rooted in the historical truth of Scripture. Lessing countered: "I refuse to deem historical knowledge of its emergence and development indispensible ...

I pronounce the objections made against the historical in religion to be relevant."[132] Scriptural tradition represented only one moment in the historical unfolding of Christianity's inner truth, in his view. The core of the faith was timeless and universal, and required no external verification.

In the *Education of the Human Race* (1780), Lessing cautioned against treating revelation as a decisive historical event through which God bestowed the absolute truth needed for salvation. The text also represents a break from Lessing's earlier model of an enduring, ahistorical primitive natural religion, as well as from Spinoza's claim that revelation merely fosters obedience without enhancing philosophical truth.[133] Revealed religions were, in his view, more than politically mandated, conventional constructs and more than a distortion of a pure, reasonable natural religion. Revelation had an important epistemological function, Lessing argued, but its contributions to religion were progressive, incomplete, and eventually superseded by human actions. Revelation, according to Lessing, was progressively assembled from partial or relative truths and dependent on the ability of particular human communities to receive them. Positive religion embodied legitimate forms of the human religious consciousness.[134] But it was originally fallible and indicated "the process by which alone human understanding in every place can develop."[135] An outspoken proponent of toleration, Lessing applied the idea of a progressive revelation rooted in reason to marginalize ecclesiastical authority.[136]

The brief text opens with several propositions concerning the relationship between reason, revelation, and history. "Revelation is education which has come, and is still coming, to the human race," Lessing declared.[137] The principles found in the initial paragraphs are elaborated in subsequent sections that traverse the historical conditions in which the Old Testament and then the New Testament supposedly emerged. Interpreters have frequently noted Lessing's contradictory assertions regarding relative priority of reason and revelation in human development. The first half published with the counterpropositions to Reimarus is more affirmative of Christian revelation, attributing to it a generating power over human reason.[138] Although indicating that revelation may be no more than a catalyst to human rationality, Lessing allows it to take the initiative and guide human reason in the age of the Old Testament.

Similar to an education that awakens existing talent, Lessing thus asserted at the start of the text, revelation provides nothing which a man could not "acquire by himself." But it allows the acquisition of knowledge to occur "more quickly and more easily." Lessing wrote: "revelation ... gives the human race nothing which human reason, left to itself, could not also arrive at; it merely gave it, and gives it, the most important of these things sooner." Revelation, in his view, must be slow and developmental because human understanding matures over time. God could not impart everything "at once," but rather had to "observe a certain order, a certain measure in his revelation."[139] By this view, history consisted in the gradual development of human consciousness, especially of religious sensibilities, and it charted the gradual expansion of rational capacities over time. For this reason, Lessing's text is often regarded as marking the inception of an idealist philosophy of history.[140] It also transformed the concept of reason typical of Enlightened theology – from being static, analytical, and individual to a collective, social form of reason that is dynamic and historical, and driven by debate and freedom of thought.[141]

The weakness and initial failure of reason explained for Lessing the need for revelation. God's original dispensation to humanity was doomed to fail, in his view, because the human rational capacity was still in its infancy. Lessing proposed that the first man was "immediately equipped with a concept of the one and only God," but that concept lost its clarity. Once "left to its own devices" human reason dismantled primitive monotheism and assigned its components to multiple entities, producing polytheism and idolatry. People would have "drifted aimlessly among those errors," Lessing concluded, if God had not provided "a better direction by means of a new impulse."[142] Revelation dominated heavily over reason in earliest history; during the childhood of the human race God "reveals purely rational truths directly."[143]

After the fall, partial revelations appropriate to the developmental level of specific recipients became God's educational strategy. No longer revealing himself universally to every individual, as Reimarus had wished, God selected special peoples to be custodians of his education, starting with ancient Hebrews. These became the future educators of the human race. Lessing explained the lack of Old Testament references to the unity of God and the soul's immortality by the fact that God was forced to "pass over in silence"[144] certain topics. The "uncouth" Hebrews had no capacity for complex doctrines. More substantial rational abilities eventually enabled the completion of revelation among them, according to Lessing. "Revelation had guided their reason," he wrote, "and now reason suddenly illuminated their revelation." The decisive moment when the Jews started to recognize and venerate God with "more practiced reason" coincided, for Lessing, with the Babylonian captivity. He believed the Jews profited from the "strength of the purer Persian doctrine," suggesting Zoroastrians had better retained some aspects of primitive monotheism.[145]

The second half of the *Education of the Human Race* shifts emphasis from revelation to reason. In later historical epochs, Lessing reckoned, reason became more highly developed and caught up with God's teachings to the point that it was able to deepen and expand revealed truths. The knowledge of the divine among the Hebrews ultimately only attained the status, for Lessing, of a "primer … for a certain age." The arrival of Christ marked a new epoch in the development of human consciousness. In his view, the onset of Christianity coincided with the moment that one segment of humanity advanced far enough in the "exercise of its reason" to be motivated towards moral action by thoughts of the afterlife.[146]

Lessing concluded that the revelations of positive religion supplied an important catalyst to the progress of reason. Christian doctrines, in his view, provided a "new guiding impulse for human reason," permitting the human race to break its dependence on revelation and employ its own powers of reason. The immortality of the soul, for example, and other teachings first expressed themselves in revealed form, but only "until human reason has learned to deduce them from its other established truths."[147] Lessing expected a similar transformation to occur from other "rational speculations on the mysteries of religion." Significantly, he declared that the "development of revealed truths into truths of reason" was "absolutely necessary" if the human race were to attain perfection.[148] Mysteries, such as the trinity, were only revealed so that they could later become truths of reason. Lessing illustrated this point with the analogy of God working as a mathematics teacher who provides the answer so students could be more certain of their calculations.

Lessing's opening intimation that revelation merely jump-starts reason without adding anything new has led some interpreters to argue that recourse to revelation was only designed to mask an argument about the natural development of human reason.[149] By this view, Lessing was an immanentist who denied transcendent revelation and confessed his Spinozism on his deathbed, provoking a second major scandal in German intellectual life. Other passages, by contrast, lend credence to a theistic or transcendentalist reading of Lessing as an apologist for Christian revelation.[150] However "dubious" the historical truth of Christianity appears, he wrote, its revelations provide an understanding of God, human nature, and their interactions "which human reason would never have arrived at on its own."[151] Yasukata proposes a convincing resolution to this tension in the idea that Lessing envisioned a perpetual dialectic between reason and revelation. Rather than being unidirectional, reason and revelation engaged in a dynamic, multilateral relationship that aimed for a higher synthesis of the type

Lessing upholds as the "eternal gospel," a third historical era exalted at the end of the text. By this account, Lessing presumed revealed truths could only help humanity develop to perfection once reason fully understood and appropriated them; revelation had to become intrinsic to the human understanding.[152]

The Kantian Critique of Revelation

The critical turn in Kant's philosophy, which began around the time of Lessing's death, shattered the uneasy reconciliation of reason and revelation within Enlightened theology and marks a watershed moment in the epistemology of belief. Perhaps due to his Pietistic Lutheran upbringing, Kant rejected the preponderancy of speculative reason in the Leibnizian-Wolffian metaphysical tradition. As Chapter 4 recounts in detail, the *Critique of Pure Reason* (1781) dismissed the three dominant rationalist proofs for God's existence, the ontological, cosmological, and physiotheological. For Kant, such speculative arguments could only be judged by their logical coherence and eloquence and were hence meaningless. The pure categories of the understanding did not apply beyond the realm of sense-experience, in his view. As the supernatural was not subject to pure reason, it was impossible, for Kant, to have theoretical knowledge of theological truths, such as God's existence or immortality. By contrast, the moral law, a self-willed sense of obligation to others, issued from the more reliable foundation of practical reason, which, Kant believed, inevitably led to the presumption of a divine lawgiver. Kant and his early interpreter, Johann Gottlieb Fichte (1762–1814), regarded revelation as a temporary measure, a stopgap that became superfluous with the eventual triumph of a rational religion based in moral law.

The first exploration of critical philosophy's implications for revelation was Fichte's *Attempt at a Critique of All Revelation* (1792), an essay that anticipated Kant's own response by more than a year. Fichte had attended the theological seminary in Jena in the early 1780s and as a heterodox Christian with Spinozist leanings was still vainly searching for a parsonage in the years following the Wöllner edit. As part of his tutoring responsibilities in rural Saxony, he happened upon Kant's critiques and in early 1790 underwent a conversion experience. In the wake of the pantheism controversy, Fichte had been willing to make determinism the foundation of a deistic system that retained God as an abstract essential first cause.[153] Kant's notion of absolute moral freedom resolved for Fichte a spiritual crisis over how to reconcile an autonomous inner will and determinism,[154] so after losing his job as a tutor in Poland, he pilgrimaged to Königsberg to study with Kant.

The *Attempt at a Critique of All Revelation* was the destitute Fichte's ploy to gain Kant's favour and solicit money for return travel to Saxony. Kant's philanthropy took the decidedly more advantages form of recommending the manuscript to his own publisher, who printed it without revision by circumventing the censor. As a marketing trick to promote sales – Kant himself had been expected to write on the topic – the first edition was published without Fichte's name. Once Kant praised the true author and corrected the first reviewers, who attributed the book to him, Fichte earned a chair in philosophy in Jena in 1794, which he lost five years later when an atheism controversy raged over his equating the moral order with the divine. Fichte planned a sequel, but work on the *Wissenschaftslehre* derailed the expansion. The critique of revelation already bears traces of Fichte's frustration with Kant's dichotomy between theoretical and practical reason and can be seen as a muted start to his idealist system.[155]

Responding to its apparent superfluity among deists, Fichte preserved a central role for revelation in the communication of religious truths and approached its conformity with reason from a post-Kantian perspective. Deists accepted that natural religion made factual assertions about the supernatural world; Fichte declared theoretical knowledge of the supernatural world to be impossible. Following Kant, he argued that religion entailed awareness that the moral law was a proclamation of God's will and the rational alignment of individual will with God's efforts to promote the highest good. Natural religion, for Fichte, built upon internal proclamations of God's will and enabled immediate consciousness of the moral law. In revealed religion, divine proclamations occurred externally through special appearances of God in the sensuous world.[156] Revelation, as Fichte defined it, was "the concept of an appearance effected in the sensuous world by the causality of God, through which he proclaims himself as moral lawgiver."[157] Prior historical events provided just as insufficient a foundation for proving revelation necessary as speculative reason; revelation had to be deduced a priori from the concepts of practical reason and moral law.

The *Attempt at a Critique of All Revelation* thus evaluated whether God would find it practically necessary to declare that the moral law was his will using supernatural appearances in the sensuous world. Fichte concluded that "whole regions of people and lands" could fall so deeply into "extreme moral corruption"[158] that only their senses could induce them to obey the moral law. For such people to advance from animality to morality, "divine authority" had to restore awareness of the moral law. God must announce himself and demand obedience, Fichte wrote, "directly through the senses."[159] Revelation thus encouraged adherence to the moral law in those not aware of the moral commandment. Rational acceptance of the content of revelation would occur after the development of inner moral feeling. Revelation established the will to obey reason, but its divine origins would lose their "utility"[160] once the revelation was rationally acknowledged.

For Fichte, as for Lessing and Kant, the historical record of revelation was irrelevant to defending the concept and its conformity with reason. Debating the facticity of miracles had, Fichte insisted, no impact on whether divine revelation was possible or necessary. False prophecies could conceivably instil the principles of rational religion as well as genuine revelations because divine origins could never be definitively determined. As an example, Fichte proposed that instead of using his prediction of a lunar eclipse to extort food from the inhabitants of Hispaniola, Christopher Columbus could have presented it as evidence that a purely rational religion he wished to impose was divinely sanctioned. The eclipse could as well have functioned as a sign of the religion's divine origin. After the inhabitants understood the natural laws behind his prediction, they would no longer regard the religion as divinely revealed but would still be rationally bound to its moral law.[161] The need for revelation diminished as rational comprehension of God's will expanded.

In his *Deduzierter Plan einer zu Berlin zu errichtenden höheren Lehranstalt* (1807), Fichte on these grounds condemned revelation as a liability to the scientific status of theology and its position in the academy. To become scientific, in Fichte's view, university theology must accept that "God's will can be known without special revelation" and that sacred texts were not unquestionable "sources of knowledge" but vehicles for religious instruction. As long as theologians opaquely laid claim to "secrets and magic, known only to themselves," Fichte wrote, they violated the standards of *Wissenschaft*.[162] To warrant inclusion in a modern philosophical academy, theology according to Fichte had to renounce revelation, divest itself of its practical ambitions, and embrace the critical methods of history and philology. Academic theologians likewise had to cease acting as "priestly brokers between God and man."[163] Fichte's vision anticipated theology's transition away from the creedal and apologetic to modern religious studies.[164]

Kant's own *Religion within the Limits of Reason Alone* (1793) addressed the historical function of revelation within existing religions, rather than its viability under the dictates of practical reason. Having himself circumvented the censors, Kant outlined procedures for evaluating revealed religions based on the extent to which they embodied rational ethical principles. He wished to demonstrate their utility in promoting a universalizable moral law while devaluing the contingent historical and cultural features of revealed religion, such as rituals, ceremonies, or prayer. The goal, in Kant's words, was "to examine in a fragmentary manner this revelation as an historical system, in light of moral concepts; and then to see whether it does not lead back to the very same pure rational system of religion."[165] The pure religion of reason functioned as an ideal type by which historical revelations could be measured.[166] Kant agreed that the historical dressing of institutional or ecclesiastical religion helped build ethical communities, but it was not relevant to the moral law. The will needed to be autonomous to act ethically. Despite Kant's insistence that the book neither disparaged Christianity nor targeted a popular audience, the Prussian regime of Friedrich Wilhelm II found fault with it. Kant claimed his intent was to expose the inability of speculative reason and natural religion to explain evil, but the book undermined ecclesiastical authority.

More sceptical than earlier rationalists, Kant detected only a partial overlap between historical revelation and the principles of practical reason. While revelation "can certainly embrace the pure religion of reason," that latter "cannot include what is historical."[167] Key segments of Kant's book are dedicated to separating and comparing "pure religious faith" and "historical faith" based in revelation.[168] Only pure faith, for Kant, was founded on the will of God; it demanded obedience to moral laws that each individual could know through his or her own reason. As an external proclamation, revelation necessarily curtailed the autonomy of the will, inhibiting a crucial component of moral behaviour. The religion of reason was, moreover, necessarily universal because the categorical imperative had to be shared and believed by everyone. It was therefore impossible to found a church on pure faith. Until now only historical faiths had been capable of uniting people in a moral commonwealth. The wider sphere of faith encompassed the many features of historical revelation that could not be derived from rational procedures.

Revealed religion was thus, in Kant's interpretation, necessarily of narrow scope. Historical faiths, by which he principally had in mind Judaism, Christianity, Islam, and Hinduism, were restricted by time and place since their foundations lay in culturally specific doctrines not fully aligned with the universal law. What Kant termed "statutory laws" set standards for ethical conduct within the historical religions. Contingent and not universally binding, such laws drew their legitimacy from supposed historical revelations and were transmitted through time as if divinely sanctioned. In place of the moral law, statutory laws substituted contingent forms of divine worship that required obedience to external authorities. Adherents of revealed religion believed themselves to be serving God, but their observances were, for Kant, "morally indifferent," as they were not self-willed. Revealed religion was prone to abuse because believers must be told that something was a divine command before recognizing it as a duty. Churches resorted, Kant wrote, to a "usurpation of higher authority to seek, under pretense of a divine commission, to lay a yoke upon the multitude by means of ecclesiastical dogmas."[169]

By this appraisal, claiming a foundation in historical revelation prevented a church from attaining universality.[170] Revelations were nothing more than statutory traditions claiming to represent a higher order, their parochial features and commandments clouding genuine expression of the moral law.[171] Kant nevertheless believed that revealed religion was indispensable as a launching pad for pure religion. Ecclesiastical faith, in his view, preceded pure religion and served as an essential "vehicle"[172] for its realization. On the one hand, historical revelation could provide the sanction of external authority to the precepts of practical reason and thereby catalyse a union of believers, offering a public forum for their moral obligations. On the other hand, revelation communicated the postulates of practical reason in popular fashion, rendering a rational idea comprehensible. Eventually, however, as it gained sovereignty, pure religious faith would dispense with revelation as an historical vehicle.

Kant's project in the service of religious Enlightenment was to delineate how historical faiths advanced and gave public form to the pure religion of reason while progressively dispensing with the statutory observances that obscured the supreme moral law. A kingdom of God would be achieved on earth, Kant declared, once the historical, revealed faiths transitioned into a universal religion of reason. Religion would be freed, he wrote, from "all empirical determining grounds and from all statutes which rest on history."[173] At this time ecclesiastical faith would no longer be needed to mediate the moral law, and the postulates of practical reason would themselves appear in the form of a genuine revelation. "The pure religion of reason," Kant concluded, "is a continually occurring divine (though not empirical) revelation for all men."[174] God's will would be accessible to all people through practical reason in the form of the moral law.

Kant held the origins of the diverse historical religions to be irrelevant for their respective ability to become universal as the pure religion of reason. In his view, "no inference regarding a religion's qualification ... to be the universal religion of mankind can be drawn merely from its origin."[175] Even before the historical emergence of faith, he speculated,

"the predisposition to the moral religion lay hidden in human reason."
Even the distorted manifestations of this moral religion in myth unin-
tentionally preserved traces of its supersensible origin.[176] For Kant,
every religion, even if revealed, harboured some original natural elements and contained principles discoverable using reason alone. In
his terms, most religions were objectively natural, but subjectively
revealed. Christianity according to Kant was both natural, in that some
components aligned with a universal religion of reason, and learned, in
that a historical tradition of revelation still secured its authority. Not yet
freely assented to by everyone, Christianity relied on the commands of
its guardians and on revelation as a means to make its moral principles
comprehensible.

For Lessing and Kant existing strategies for securing the reliability
of revelation were unconvincing. In their view, neither revelation's
presumed historical facticity nor its commensurability with reason
bestowed certainty on the propositions it conveyed. They historicized
the very knowledge dispensed by revelation, as well as the divine act
of communication, within particular historical communities. Subsequently understood as an act of the human spirit, revelation quit the
preserve of theological inquiry and became part of the general history
of consciousness.[177] The threat of historicism left theologians to grapple
with the uncertainties of having derailed revelation from its transcendent origins, however, and exposed gaps between its historical manifestation, absolute truth, and faith. For most Enlightened theologians,
primordial forms of religious awareness anticipated the natural religion that developed as the human capacity for reason increased over
time. But idealizing a primitive state would only hinder the synthesis
of reason and revelation towards which history progressed. For Lessing and Kant the history of religions documented a process by which
the rational content of revelation was progressively realized until the
human reliance on it was overcome. Revelation merely made the rational content of religion more accessible to those incapable of immediately grasping it, and for many Protestants, this included Jews and
Catholics, as well as women, children, and pagans. The theological
Enlightenment took different forms within the other two main German
confessions, as seen in Chapters 6 and 7.

Chapter Two

The Comparative History of Religion, 1770–1800

German interest in the comparative history of religion surged during the late Enlightenment after British deism reached the continent. David Hume's *Natural History of Religion* (1757) appeared in German translation in 1759,[1] and Hume's usefulness in combatting Leibnizian-Wolffian philosophy secured his reputation in Germany well before his appropriation by Kant.[2] Speculating on the origin of religion was central to the German debate over revelation and hence highly contested, with scholars divided into two broad camps sketched by Frank Manuel in his landmark study.[3] Believers in original monotheism subscribed to the orthodox assumption that true knowledge of God was revealed during creation and had passed from Adam to the descendants of Noah. By this view, aspects of primordial revelation entered pagan faiths in degenerate form, surviving as esoteric knowledge that prefigured basic Christian principles. By contrast, what Manuel terms "rationalist myths of origin" assumed that the capacity for monotheism developed gradually as humanity emerged from a state of barbarism. Idolatry and polytheism were, from this perspective, the natural first psychological responses to a threatening environment, which reason and experience eventually exposed as errors but only among peoples capable of cultivation.[4] A third position, belief in rational *ur*-monotheism, steered a compromise course, accepting revelation as a benevolent stimulus to otherwise accurate early reflection on God's presence in nature.

The cleft separating these paradigms was substantial and hinged on the credibility of primordial revelation. At stake were also fundamental assumptions about human nature and the universality of religious experience, as well as correlations between race, rational capacity, and divine truth. Histories of religion regularly challenged social and institutional hierarchies, especially in Britain where deists feared that corrupt priestcraft and state intervention had weakened purer forms of the faith.[5] In Germany comparative religious history was a venue for Protestants to adjudicate the epistemological prerogatives of reason and revelation and contest rationalist theology and its appropriation by the enlightened state. Importantly, the comparative history of religion also contributed significantly to the racialization of religion in the late eighteenth century, as it derived religious diversity from intractable qualities associated with communities of belief.

This chapter argues that the theological reframing of revelation as an historical process shaped by national communities meant that a people's presumed access to revelation functioned as a marker of race in German religious thought. Theologians had long passed judgment on human communities based on whether they enjoyed the favour of having inherited God's word and on whether they were able to acquire divine truth through natural means. In the late eighteenth century, however, the possession of revelation increasingly appeared dependent, not on God's propositional dispensations or on external environmental factors such as climate but on the intrinsic ethnic or national attributes that purportedly determined the forms assumed by the world's religions. The closer revelation was wedded to a nation's own devices and agency, the more emphatically the concept was racialized. Comparative historical narratives based on original revelation envisioned race as lineage, creating exclusive communities of descent and depicting religion as an inheritance. Rational ur-monotheism extended the prerogative of genuine religion to a broader swath of peoples. But rationalist histories also approached religion as an epiphenomenon of race in that belief systems supposedly reflected immutable physical, cultural, and psychological traits.

The starting point for the chapter is J.G. Herder's foundational response to Hume's *Natural History* that foregrounded Near Eastern and East Asian religions in the German defence of original monotheism. Herder expected comparative religious history to resurrect an otherwise obscured *prisca theologia* that reinforced the fundamental truths of Christianity and the historical reliability of Scripture. The idea of primordial revelation usually aided theologically more conservative defenders of scriptural authority. Deists, by contrast, appealed to rational ur-monotheism graced by revelation to soften the blow of equating the knowledge of God found in natural religion, ancient philosophy, and Christianity. Peter Hanns Reill's term "Enlightened theological hermeticism"[6] nicely captures the melding of rationalism, esoteric thought, and anti-dogmatic Christianity exemplified in this chapter by the Lutheran freemason Johann Andreas Starck. Because it promised to purvey elusive knowledge of spiritual truths without denying rationalism, esotericism was a "catalyst" for the theological enlightenment.[7] Starck's levelling of faiths drew staunch opposition from fellow Königsberger Johann Georg Hamann, who defended biblical literalism and the historical specificity of Christian revelation.

The theological and philosophical faculties at the Georgia Augusta University in Göttingen were the centre of more sceptical rationalist efforts to locate the origin of religion in human reflection on the environment. The chapter explores the comparative religious history of the ethnologist and racial theorist Christoph Meiners who ascribed idolatry and polytheism to the errors of unenlightened peoples. Natural religion was a farce, in his view; only the Greeks came close to attaining religious truth without revelation. Building on Meiners, the Kantian school of comparative religious history that emerged in Göttingen in the 1790s likewise credited philosophical reflection rather than divine revelation with launching humanity's gradual ascent to rational religion. Under the direction of the theologian Karl Friedrich Stäudlin, its members redirected Meiners's ethnology to locate the first inklings of Kant's moral law in pagan religions.

Even as it excised the scandal of Christian exclusivity, the comparative history of religion created cultural and ethnological hierarchies that reinforced racial thought. Proximity to religious truth continued to serve as a barometer for a nation's significance within human history, as well as for its presumed level of intellectual achievement. But embedding revelation in the historical experiences of national communities compounded the racialization of religion by making faith derivative of national qualities. Not until Schelling and Hegel redefined revelation as the self-disclosure of divine being in the 1820s did the comparative history of religion come to reflect more strongly on God's character itself, although not as a depository of propositions that clarified his attributes. As seen in Chapter 5, their conception of religious history as a dialectical unfolding of divine being unseated primordial revelation as the likely origin of religion but failed to interrupt the association of race and religion, as the teleology of God's self-revelation relegated the historical religions to subordinate roles in the ascent of Protestant Christianity.

David Hume and the Comparative History of Religion

Comparative religious history became viable in the early modern period as beliefs and practices were conceived in categories other than truth and error. Several historical shifts unseated Christian doctrine as the arbiter of religious life. Most important was an ethnological turn in European perceptions of religion that followed overseas encounters with unfamiliar rituals and beliefs and redefined religion as social practice and culture. Critical philology, newly translated religious texts, and the recovery of classical treatises provided essential sources and methods.[8] The first sustained attempt to address global religious pluralism occurred among Cambridge Platonists and the deist followers of Herbert of Cherbury in post-Reformation England. The presumed exclusivity of Christian revelation constituted in their eyes a scandalous denial of salvation to heathens, to which the idea of natural religion offered a corrective.[9] An explosion of ethnological data from missionaries, travellers, and colonial officials in the late seventeenth century enabled sustained comparison of the world's religions.[10]

Cambridge Platonists, such as Henry More and Ralph Cudworth, explained religious diversity according to the model of sacred history latent in Mosaic accounts of the beginning of the world.[11] The Old Testament exalted primitive monotheism and documented the degeneration of belief after the fall. This encouraged a "single-source" theory of religious diversity, by which all pagan cultures were rooted in age-old Jewish traditions descended through Noah from Adam. This approach recognized the Jewish patriarchs as the source of all esoteric wisdom; their reputed heirs included Zoroaster, Hermes, Orpheus, Pythagoras, and Plato, as well as Brahmins, Druids, and Sibyls.[12] Protecting the legacy of primordial revelation required embracing the idea of the double-truth doctrine.[13] By this account, paganism had two dimensions: an arcane esoteric theology and corrupt public rituals. Buried beneath popular superstitions and brutal sacrificial rites lay a learned esoteric religion which secretly preserved monotheism and other divine truths. Depending on the author's political intent, either benign philosophers had safeguarded endangered truths as mysteries or wicked priests had withheld them from the people to solidify state power.

Natural histories of religion were the first to break with paradigms of sacred history in the early eighteenth century. Rejecting primitive monotheism, these offered other mechanisms besides an initial revelation to explain the universality of religious instincts and their historical development.[14] Deists such as Pierre Bayle, incorporated religion into a general theory of human nature and interpreted the prevalence of polytheism and idolatry as a reflection of a primitive mentality. Reference to climate, psychology, human agency, and culture explained shifts in religious life, as did models of health and disease. Rationalist in tenor, natural histories of religion intended to expose the historical sources of superstition and mysticism to liberate men from the illusions of religion.[15] Overwhelmingly anticlerical, they threatened the absolute truth of dogma and the institutional authority of church.

David Hume's *Natural History of Religion* (1757) disrupted crucial assumptions that both of these traditions made about the origin of religion. For deists, the rational grounds for belief were most visible at the historical inception of religion. Presuming truth to be older than error, they thought the origin of religion testified to a universal human capacity for rationalism. Hume's radical scepticism invalidated this perspective. In his view, religion did not result from the rational contemplation of nature or from speculation on final causes. Hume likewise denied both primitive revelation and the innateness of religious sentiment.[16] Belief in an invisible, intelligent power was not "universal," he wrote, nor were conceptions of the divine "uniform."[17] Unlike sexual desire, preconceptions of a higher being were "secondary" instincts; historical accidents could prevent or pervert the development of religious principles.[18]

The *Natural History of Religion* assigned chronological primacy to polytheism. Unlike Adam in paradise, the first humans had been barbarous and needy animals, whose wants and passions left no leisure for inquiry into the causes behind events, according to Hume. The mind had to rise gradually before forming ideas of perfection. The first inklings of religion, Hume concluded, arose from "anxious fear of future events."[19] Caught in a perpetual state of apprehension and alarm, primitive people imagined "invisible, unknown powers" lurking behind objects that both articulated and alleviated their fears. This developed into polytheism and idolatry. According to Hume humanity was initially incapable of monotheism: "the stupidity of men, barbarous and uninstructed, be so great, that they may not see a sovereign author in the more obvious works of nature."[20] Monotheism evolved as nations venerated one god as their particular patron. Praise of this god escalated until he appeared as an infinite, eternal, perfect being.[21]

Hume briefly compared pagan traditions and Christianity in the *Natural History*, not to trace genealogical lines of descent but to evaluate how each stood on principles such as persecution, toleration, courage, rationality, and strength of faith. Hume's scepticism prevented a linear progressive narrative from idolatry to theism. The two principles engaged in a cyclical pattern of flux and reflux, in his view, with monotheism often generating worse results than polytheism.[22] Certain, Hume concluded, was that any form of popular religion would corrupt morality through frivolous observances and absurd opinions. Hume dismissed most religious principles as "sick men's dreams."[23] His account of the origin of religion was a provocative etiology that dismantled both the idea of primitive revelation and the grounds for believing in natural religion.

J.G. Herder's *Älteste Urkunde des Menschengeschlechts* (1774)

German work on comparative religious history responded to Hume's provocations in the mid-1770s just as Lessing released the *Fragmente* challenging the historical foundations of revelation. The two earliest commentators, Johann Gottfried Herder and Christoph Meiners, took Hume in opposite directions while both insisting their reflections constituted a natural history of religion. In the *Älteste Urkunde des Menschengeschlechts* (1774) Herder defended the historical reliability of biblical accounts of creation and scrutinized the pagan faiths of the ancient Near East for traces of primordial revelation. Following closely on a critique of J.D. Michaelis's rationalist theology, the text asserted that the truth of revelation and history could not be established abstractly.[24] Denying historical revelation to pagans, the enlightened anthropologist Christoph Meiners approached religion as an essential component of human culture and explained the early onset of idolatry as a result of rational deficiencies. The precedent set by each shaped competing schools for conceiving the origin of religion in the German states and its implications for negotiating the relationship between reason, revelation, and race.

Johann Gottfried Herder's comparative history of religion strengthened a theologically informed conception of race as lineage or ethnic descent by reconstructing the historical transmission of revelation. When narrowly defined as observable physical differences, race (*Race*) was, admittedly, an empty category ('*keine Ursache*'), for Herder.[25] He rejected the nascent natural historical division of humanity based on skin colour. Belief in cultural pluralism, monogenesis, and the unity of the human species, as well as his categorizing of difference at the level of culture, language, and spirit, has in fact earned Herder a reputation as an antiracist thinker.[26] However, speculating on cultural and spiritual differences also reinforced racial thinking in the late eighteenth century, and Herder's preference for categories such as *Volk*, nation, or tribe did not inhibit differentiation of human communities based on cultural practices or descent. "Race," Herder wrote, "has to do with a difference of origin."[27] While he denied race entailed progressive physical differentiation, the receipt and transmission of revelation did create privileged lineages of ethnic descent from a divine moment of origin.

Hume's *Natural History of Religion* deeply influenced the young Herder in the early 1760s and while he taught at the Cathedral School in Riga. His early fragment "Ueber die verschiedenen Religionen" (1766) followed Hume in attributing psychological origins to natural religion. Like Hume, Herder initially concluded that early humans were "barbaric and ignorant"; their emotional response to a threatening environment produced a polytheistic, idolatrous religion of "fear and superstition."[28] Herder, however, superimposed a pronounced national dimension on this narrative, arguing that religious "inequalities" were "a far more secure basis for deducing the spirit of a nation than the formation of the face was an indicator of temperament."[29] As people emerged from barbarism, in his view, religion developed into a "genealogy and history of ancestors, customs, and practices."[30]

The myriad national doctrines that comprised natural religion constituted, for Herder, genealogies that held the memory of a people's ancestry. Through religion, elders taught the public "what *Volk* means" and steered a community, "true to its origin, towards national preservation." Always "national and local," the particular forms of religion reflected the "thought patterns, language, and morality of a *Volk*."[31] He later affirmed that the cause of religious diversity lay in "different cultures, language, epochs, and climates."[32] Like nations, religions were, for Herder, pure, distinct, and monolithic. Faith maintained a people "without foreign assistance on the path of its own culture,"[33] and religious degeneration resulted from the absorption of "opinions from foreign peoples."[34] As the highest expression of cultural particularity, religion divided peoples into communities of descent whose bonds were inherited across generations.

Transitioning away from the liberalism of his Riga years towards a deeper religiosity and renewed interest in pietistic traditions, Herder later adapted Hume's anthropological framework and the natural history of religion to reconceive the Christian tradition of primordial revelation.[35] As a court preacher and church official in Bückeburg, capital of the small principality of Schaumburg-Lippe, a position he assumed in 1771, Herder was caught between the enlightened absolutism of his local prince and provincial Lutheran orthodoxy.[36] He opted for "mysticism" and revelation over the free-thinking philosophical path of Lessing.[37] Research on the *Älteste Urkunde* likewise reflects Herder's engagement with Hermetic texts and other esoteric literature while a freemason in Riga. The book's publisher, Hartknoch, had inducted Herder into the lodge *Zum Nordstern* in 1766.[38] Concern that the *Älteste Urkunde* hermeticized the Bible jeopardized Herder's career as a theologian. He was denied a position as General Superintendent and professor in Göttingen in 1775 because the English king, as Elector of Hannover, questioned his orthodoxy.[39] Detecting a shared kernel of original truth in multiple religions could appear to relativize Christianity and question the necessity of redemption through Christ.[40]

The comparative history of religion that Herder presented in the *Älteste Urkunde* located the origins of humanity and religion in primordial revelation and traced its historical transmission through national cultures, evaluating which human communities had served as loyal custodians of God's word. The founding moment of human culture, which seeded subsequent national traditions, was, Herder argued, a mysterious hieroglyph that God presented to the first humans. Writing from Strasbourg in 1770 Herder announced to his friend J.H. Merck the "strange discovery" of a hieroglyph that proved the antiquity of Genesis while linking it to other creation stories. The same hieroglyph he had detected in Genesis I many years ago was, Herder claimed, "so certainly the foundation of all Egyptian mythology, mystery cults, and the wisdom of Thot or Theut, etc., as my name is Herder."[41] While researching in Göttingen, Herder believed to have found it replicated in a French translation of the *Zend-Avesta*, the sacred texts of Zoroastrianism, suspected to be of great antiquity.[42] "I am interpreting and restoring a divine revelation that has been disfigured and obscured for millennia," Herder proclaimed in the *Älteste Urkunde*.[43] Genesis was a surviving fragment that was difficult to decipher,[44] but it proved the divine origins of revelation.

As an exercise in biblical exegesis, Herder's *Älteste Urkunde* favoured a doctrine of human witness, rather than divine inspiration, locating the conditions for interpreting Genesis in sensual contemplation and feeling.[45] Moses, in his view, had been a collector of ancient oral traditions. Genesis was based on older sources, perhaps even dating to the second generation of humanity.[46] Herder's approach to the Old Testament also betrays the aesthetic precepts he garnered from Robert Lowth's Oxford lectures on the sacred poetry of Hebrews. Herder assumed that God had instructed his earliest disciples through images, symbols, and suggestions, yet he was reluctant to explain Genesis in purely figurative terms. As Herder explained to his friend Hamann in 1768, refuting deist claims that the creation story was allegory required positioning the text within the ancient, highly poeticized Orient and discovering other documents that attested to a shared provenance from a common source.[47]

The stylistic abyss into which unfortunate readers of the *Älteste Urkunde* plummet was a failed attempt on Herder's part to replicate the hieroglyph's opaque symbolism and imagery, as well as the power and emotion of God's original word. In his far more lucid preparatory exercise, the "Archäologie des Morgenlandes" (1769), Herder rejected the "dry scholasticism" of dogmatic exegesis of Genesis and imagined a style that evoked "its proper poetic expression ... in its own time, its nation, and its language."[48] His goal was to illustrate the limits of reason and point to forms of truth outside of rationalism.[49] This caused some theologians to misinterpret Herder as excessively mystical or as a gushing enthusiast.[50] But even for adepts in obfuscation such as Hamann, Herder's stylistic experiment resembled the "blathering of a confused equerry,"[51] exposing an author who neither understood himself nor his material. Kant was so enraged by Herder's mystifications that he begged Hamann to translate the work "into the language of humans."[52] When Hamann defended his recently estranged friend, Kant reacted so vehemently against the perceived irrationalism of his former student that he forever turned his back on the *Sturm-und-Drang.*[53]

Part I of the *Älteste Urkunde* advances a rambling, disjointed critique of rationalist theology and Hume's attempts at natural religion. Herder condemned the "morass" in which these traditions sunk revelation. The contorted "mischief of physics and metaphysics" amounted, in his view, to "human reason disgracing ... God's simple, lucid revelation."[54] Herder's solution was to reappropriate the idea of natural religion and its historical origins "against itself with another meaning" to historically document primordial revelation. Nature was, he agreed with the philosophers of natural religion, the "first, only, most beautiful, Perfect, sufficient religion," but it did not lead to superstition and idolatry. "Natural religion in and through revelation!" he gushed. Herder welcomed the notion that creation revealed "Everywhere only the invisible, omnipresent fatherly God." "Behold!" he hammered into readers, "the pure, distilled, physical religion of nature," actually "protects invisible power and divinity against idolatry and superstition."[55]

The daily reoccurrence of morning light symbolized for Herder the first moments of creation and God's initial revelation to mankind. In the *Älteste Urkunde* a youth is beckoned onto a field where the experience of dawn enables him to "feel and act"[56] according to the first chapter of Genesis. Every morning the oldest, most magnificent revelation came alive again as an act of God in nature, Herder gushed. In the "Archäologie des Morgenlandes" he explained that light embodied "his incomprehensible being, the luster of his majesty, his permeating power, the omnipresence of his being."[57] The *Älteste Urkunde* urged readers to experience a more authentic commentary on Genesis than all learned exegesis; the magic of dawn would entice readers to approach Genesis with empathy and intuition rather than abstract reason. The Hebrews' special penchant for experiencing the presence and power of God derived from their senses and feelings, the most reliable basis of religious knowledge.[58]

The primordial hieroglyph, or the divine origin of all language and wisdom, from J.G. Herder's *Älteste Urkunde des Menschengeschlechts* (1774), vol. 1, 171.

The founding moment of human culture, which seeded subsequent national traditions, was, Herder argued, a mysterious hieroglyph God presented to the first humans. The central structure and content of Genesis as well as proof of its greatest antiquity derived from this form. The hieroglyph Herder sketched consisted in seven points arranged as an elongated hexagon with a central point or as a square with triangles issuing from the top and bottom. The design evoked symmetry and parallelism with a central vertical axis connecting heaven and earth. The seven points corresponded to the seven days of Christian creation but also to the sacred number seven prevalent in mythology. Even the human face he suspected, based on Johann Kaspar Lavater's physiognomic theories, revealed the essential structure of the hieroglyph.[59] "There in his First symbol man had," he wrote, "all his knowledge of nature, morality, religion and timekeeping ... as if written with God's finger."[60] These teachings were living images to be experienced, not abstract concepts. God's word issued in a "sensual language, the voice of signs, deeds, events, images from the heart and feelings of the people."[61] Only traces of this original knowledge had survived. However, the comparative history of religion could establish the synchronisms necessary to reconstitute it, as could, Herder noted in the *Älteste Urkunde*, research into language and the natural world.

The comparative religious history Herder sketched in the *Älteste Urkunde* deemed Sabianism – worship of the sun, moon, and stars as sources of light – to be the oldest faith. Having emerged in Chaldea and Syria, it became established across Persia, Media, Babylonia, Assyria, Arabia, and Egypt. Herder speculated that the earliest forms of pure Sabianism venerated "primordial light" (*Urlicht*) as an image of God and symbol of creation.[62] "Woven ... out of a few golden threads of the world's oldest document and of revelation!" Sabianism was, Herder marvelled, "fine, well spun, but – only a chimera,"[63] for it was also the "mother of idolatry."[64] Abraham, Zoroaster, and Moses represented, for Herder, reformers who strove to restore lost aspects of the pure religion of light. The Jewish patriarchs, he argued, returned "religion back to the simplicity of its origin."[65]

The *Älteste Urkunde* set an important precedent in German scholarship for conceiving of race as lineage and descent and for wielding primordial revelation against rationalist theology and profane natural histories of religion. It likewise identified critical fields of inquiry where remnants of early revelation could presumably be discovered. These included comparative religion and mythology, the early history of language, geography, and natural history, which could conceivably detect traces of revelation and creation in geological formations. In the wake of the *Fragmentenstreit* Herder himself tempered the fervour of the *Älteste Urkunde* with a new valuation of rationalism. As Beiser argues, renewed engagement with Lessing after his death in 1781 encouraged Herder to close the gap between reason and faith, although without progressing to Lessing's radical conclusions. Herder continued to base faith in history and biblical testimony, convinced that reason could never transcend its embodiment in history.[66] Other contemporaries, including Christoph Meiners, opted for strictly naturalist explanations for the origin of religion, which jettisoned the idea of revelation in favour of progress in human knowledge.

The Comparative Religious History of Christoph Meiners

Christoph Meiners's emphatic rejection of primordial revelation on racialist grounds offered a powerful counter-narrative to Herder and established a competing approach to comparative religious history among rationalists at the University of Göttingen. Meiners patently refused to recognize true knowledge of God in any peoples besides the ancient Jews, Greeks, or Christians. Born the son of the postmaster in Warstade in the Duchy of Bremen, the young Meiners was an autodidact able to study philosophy in Göttingen from 1767 to 1770. Due to the "shocking quantity"[67] of his productivity he earned a full professorship there in *Weltweisheit* (worldly wisdom) by the age of twenty-eight. Although an adherent of the Enlightenment and a prominent member of the Illuminati, Meiners was a conservative loyalist who defended all forms of privilege. He blamed the French Revolution on the false enlightenment embodied in Rousseau[68] and during the French occupation of Hannover reported on student organizations and his colleagues, including J.G. Eichhorn and Stäudlin.[69]

As a philosopher, the young Meiners made a name for himself defending *Populärphilosophie* and editing the anti-Kantian journal *Philosophische Bibliothek* with his friend and colleague J.G.H. Feder. His object was to apply psychology and Lockean empiricism to reform metaphysical systems inspired by Wolff. Most of Meiners's career, however, was dedicated to the comparative cultural history of humanity with an ethnological and anthropological bent. Along with A.L. von Schlözzer and J.G. Gatterer, he helped shape the Göttingen Historical School. Meiners was also a noxious racist and racial theorist. His work theorized a division of humankind into two races, the Caucasian and the Mongolian, or what Meiners also termed the "dark-colored and ugly."[70] He was an unabashed apologist for slavery and colonialism[71] and opposed Jewish emancipation.[72]

Religion represented an important subset of culture for Meiners, and its history comprised a substantial component of his comparative work. Self-identification as an "esoteric" philosopher in the early *Revision der Philosophie* (1772) likely triggered Meiners's first engagement with the topic. The pursuit of truth required, in his view, maintaining a sceptical distance from public opinions, which gravitated towards superstition and dogmatism.[73] Esoteric philosophy achieved this through "doctrines ... far removed from the existing theological system and the generally accepted opinions governing the practical life of an epoch."[74] The text, which earned Meiners the position in Göttingen,

offered a "brief sketch of esoteric philosophy"[75] in an effort to rehabilitate it. Egypt, he concluded, had suffered under a debilitating form
of esotericism, in which theology corrupted useful knowledge.[76] The
"disharmony"[77] between philosophy and theology in ancient Greece,
by contrast, allowed for respectful public criticism of religion. The rap-
prochement of faith and reason in Meiners's own day demanded, he
argued, reviving esoteric knowledge with enlightened objectives.

Hume was a ready ally in the fight against superstition and prejudice and likely confirmed Meiners's disparaging view of uncultivated
peoples. In a review of Hume's posthumous *Dialogues Concerning Natural Religion* (1779) Meiners declared himself an "admirer of his talent
and noble character." Yet he also read the text with "no little trepida-
tion" since it could endanger faith. These reservations are typical of the
negative turn in Hume's German reception that followed publication
of the *Dialogues*.[78] Meiners found it better to overestimate the dangers
of Hume's philosophy than underestimate them.[79] Yet Hume's natural
history is also readily apparent in Meiners's approach to the origin of
religion.

Meiners waged a sustained campaign against the theory of primitive monotheism, starting with his *Versuch über die Religionsgeschichte
der ältesten Völker besonders der Egyptier* (1775). This pit him directly
against Herder, although Meiners claimed only to have read the *Älteste
Urkunde* after his manuscript was in production. An addendum to the
text notes that both arrived separately "at completely contradictory
hypotheses and thoughts."[80] The *Versuch* investigated whether the
Egyptians had ever attained "a pure natural theology" that included
monotheism and correct views on creation and the soul's immortality.[81] Meiners argued against Ralph Cudworth, Thomas Hyde, and
P.E. Jablonski, who, in his view, wrongly attributed "orthodoxy" to
the Persians and Egyptians based on lineage from Noah.[82] The justification Meiners offered for his thesis was that the Egyptians were
an "original people" whose escape from barbarity transpired without
foreign assistance. Conquered peoples worshipped gods resembling
human beings, Meiners figured. But the Egyptians revered heavenly
bodies and natural objects. Their great antiquity implied, furthermore,
time to develop laws, religion, arts, and sciences to maturity without
outside influence.[83] He rejected the notion of a twofold philosophy, in
which priests guarded secret knowledge.

Within a year Meiners shifted his position on the existence of double
truth doctrines. While still denying Egyptian priests' natural theology,
he confessed in his influential essay "Ueber die Mysterien der Alten"

(1776) that failure to research "tenaciously and deeply enough" had led him to overlook in the *Versuch* the division of religion into "exoteric and esoteric."[84] The essay offered a tripartite typology of ancient mysteries based on levels of civilizational attainment. Wild peoples without communal religion, including American Indians, had shamans who conjured spirits through "sacred illusions and farcical comedies"[85] to reveal secrets of the past and future. Communal religions that worshipped humanlike gods possessed mysteries in the form of dramas that publicly enacted the history of those gods. The third type of mystery only developed once highly educated priests reflected and observed nature long enough to realize popular, public religion was wrong. Their knowledge endangered the state and the priesthood, so they concealed it in inaccessible sacred writings and oral transmissions. The cult of Demeter and Persephone at Eleusis exemplified for Meiners the most enlightened of the ancient mysteries, and he conceded to the Greeks alone accurate knowledge of God and the soul.

The model of rational enlightenment within a secret society of initiates, which Meiners saw embodied in the Eleusinian mysteries, appealed to Adam Weishaupt, the founder of the Bavarian Illuminati, highly politicized radical enlighteners. Weishaupt read Meiners's essay enthusiastically as well as a 1778 article on the teachings of Zoroaster, and both Meiners and Feder joined the order.[86] Its grades and double initiation system mimicked the structure of the Eleusinian cults. Meiners severed any thoughts of revelation from his discussion of the mysteries and regarded them as a forum for the rational transmission of knowledge.[87] This appealed to Weishaupt as he distinguished the order from the Rosicrucians and fought off the theosophical influences of his rival in the order, Adolph Freiherr Knigge.[88]

Having granted true knowledge of God to the Greeks, Meiners felt compelled to deny that privilege elsewhere. His *Historia doctrinae de vero Deo* (1780) extended the emphatic rebuttal of Egyptian natural religion to all peoples who had been capable of esoteric knowledge.[89] Indulging conspiracy theories about priests faking the antiquity of borrowed doctrines, the text combatively jettisoned the idea of primordial revelation and condemned the barbarity of those cultures lauded in Herder's *Älteste Urkunde*. True knowledge of God required substantial development of the intellectual faculties, Meiners argued, since reason must attain maturity before grasping difficult concepts. His *Historia doctrinae* set out to prove the primitive state of most peoples before contact with the Greeks.

A racialist hierarchy of cultural development enabled Meiners to hypothesize that religion was not universal. His ethnologies delineate levels of cultural development, ranging from wild (hunters), barbarian (herders), and partially enlightened (agriculturists) to the fully enlightened.[90] Overcome by the evils of war, famine, and infertility, the first two groups, Meiners argued in the *Historia doctrinae*, were "so wild that not even suspicions regarding the nature of the gods were present."[91] He therefore excluded all peoples designated barbaric from his study, including the populations of America and sub-Saharan Africa. With the exception of the Chinese, all the peoples Meiners did investigate, the Egyptians, Phoenicians, Persians, Chaldeans, and Brahmin Indians, belonged to what he later termed the third division of the Caucasian race. These "Orientals," he believed, never developed philosophy.[92] They shared cultural commonalities that had a biological foundation, especially in a high tolerance for physical pain that, for Meiners, sanctioned harsh colonial rule.[93]

The *Historia doctrinae* offers no directly racialist explanation for the failure to develop true notions of God. But, aside from some Greek source criticism, it largely levels insults against those partly Caucasian Orientals suspected of having inherited primordial revelation. Meiners denied Egyptian priests, "those lazy servants to animals,"[94] had possessed wisdom, erudition, or true knowledge of God. The Phoenicians "revered a hoard of the ugliest gods" with "inhumane brutality."[95] Herodotus confirmed, for Meiners, that Chaldean priests were "most salacious and vicious."[96] The Brahmins falsified chronologies to deny the Greek origin of their wisdom. Meiners's discussion of Chinese concepts of God was most dismissive, perhaps because he later classified the Chinese as Mongolian, not Caucasian. "Like all other barbarians," Meiners wrote, the Chinese "submitted to the most odious superstitions."[97] Confucius was no better than other fabricated prophets such as Orpheus, Zoroaster, and Hermes with whose names later writers adorned their books to "convince their compatriots that they drew from the same well of truth."[98]

Meiners's subsequent publications in the history of religion largely relinquished philosophical debates over natural religion in favour of ethnological research on religious rites, cults, practices, and objects. Rather than present findings chronologically or geographically, the *Grundriß der Geschichte aller Religionen* (1785) classified early religions "according to the natural sequence of their most important components,"[99] drawing together evidence from various cultures on common practices such as sacrifice, fasting, and burials. Meiners still rejected the idea of primitive monotheism and criticized Hume for insinuating that monotheists were "persecutory and longed to proselytize, and polytheists, by contrast, tolerant."[100] Primitive religion was, for him, the source of superstition, repression, and immorality. It progressed through the stages of fetishism, ancestor worship, and reverence for heavenly bodies until producing the idea of a national god.

In the *Allgemeine Kritische Geschichte der Religionen* (1806) Meiners finally conceded the universality of religion, perhaps responding to the religious awakening that followed the French Revolution, though disparaging its effects. Knowledge and worship of higher beings sprung, he concluded, "unstoppably from general predispositions in the organization of uncultured men."[101] Overhauling Hume's fear theory, he attributed polytheism to "the lack of a correct understanding of nature or the inability of crude men to investigate the true causes behind natural appearances."[102] With racial overtones, the text separates aspects of religion reflecting "general human nature" from the effects of nationality, climate, geography, and personality.[103] The insufficient intellectual abilities of barbaric nations, not psychological need, caused them to misattribute natural events to the intervention of invisible powers.

Meiners thoroughly racialized the origin of religion in this text. The exact number of *Ur-Religionen*, in his view, corresponded to early racial divisions, which were more significant, in his view, than potential common origins. The rapid diffusion of peoples across new environments would have altered a shared religion beyond recognition. For this reason he redefined "original religion" to designate the faith of practitioners who were markedly distinct from neighbouring peoples. The most original religions, he concluded, were found in Egypt and India, where "beautiful and light people encountered a dark and ugly race, and the latter were subjected by the former."[104] The spread of religion correlated furthermore with the expansion of dominant peoples. It was "more natural," Meiners concluded, that "crude, weak people started to worship the gods of cultivated and powerful nations, as the reverse."[105] But he also feared differences in the "abilities and external circumstances" of "truly enlightened and moral people" and "wild people in all parts of the earth" set limits to the reach of monotheism.[106] Religious truths could never overcome immutable racial differences.

A commitment to enlightened rationalism encouraged Meiners to deny primordial revelation and deprive all ancient esoteric traditions, except the Greek, of the privilege of divine wisdom. Racialized hierarchies of civilizational attainment permeate his comparative religious history to the extent that peoples incapable of enlightenment remained mired in the conceptual errors that produced original polytheism. Meiners explicitly rejected the notion that religion contributed to the progressive education of the human race. For Meiners, the defence of colonialism, slavery, and aristocratic privilege was more compelling than the promise of enlightenment. A fully rational religion did not, in his view, await at the end of history, nor would the revival of oriental truths restore a pristine theology. By contrast, the Göttingen school of Kantian theologians, who in the 1790s likewise doubted primordial monotheism on rationalist grounds, detected in history the gradual triumph of a universal religion of reason.

J.A. Starck and J.G. Hamann on Rational *Ur*-Monotheism

The question of whether esoteric wisdom derived from original revelation or rational reflection inspired considerable debate in the 1770s, especially among affiliates of Masonic societies that claimed inheritance of ancient theology. One of the main advocates of rational *ur*-monotheism, the Lutheran theologian Johann August Starck (1741–1816), chided Meiners for restricting true knowledge of God to the Eleusinian mysteries, finding more widespread evidence of a natural religion that prefigured Christianity. The priestly elites of multiple cultures had advanced to accurate knowledge of God, Starck believed. Concessions to primordial revelation made his allegiance to rational *ur*-monotheism more palpable, and Starck appealed to the notion of priestly societies having inherited scattered fragments of divine wisdom. Unlike Herder, however, Starck veered far from the scriptural tradition when interpreting the legacy of revelation. Dismissing the special role of the ancient Hebrews in its preservation, Starck reduced the content of primordial revelation to a rationalist core of religious truths accessible without knowledge of Christ. The deist overtones of his comparative religious history and Starck's rationalist veneration of mystery cults angered conservative Biblicists such as Johann Georg Hamann (1730–88). Denouncing Starck for crypto-Catholicism, Hamann defended Christianity's foundations in Scripture and historical revelation.

Born in Schwerin to a family of Mecklenburg theologians, Starck studied theology, philosophy, and oriental languages in Göttingen with Michaelis and A.F. Büsching in the early 1760s. His devotion to freemasonry began in 1761 when a mobile French military lodge accepted Starck as a member. Following Büsching to St. Petersburg to teach at a Lutheran school in 1763, Starck joined the theosophical-Rosicrucian and alchemical circles of a Russian general who traced his own order back to the Templar Knights. In 1765 Starck moved to Paris to work with Near Eastern manuscripts in the royal library. He converted to Catholicism in France, possibly to gain access to freemasonic texts at religious institutions or to symbolically free himself from the bonds of confessionalism.[107] Religious conviction seems not to have played a role, and Starck later hid the event, although it resurfaced pointedly two decades later.

As the assistant rector of a gymnasium in Wismar, Starck organized a spiritual branch of the freemasonic Templar Order in 1767, *Zu den drei Löwen*. The Grand Lodge of Germany proclaimed that medieval building fraternities had bequeathed to the order a secret science based on a Christian mystery that Jesus had confided to the apostles. The Rite of Strict Observance restricted knowledge of this wisdom to the highest degrees of initiation to protect its purity. Starck argued that the Knights Templar had been separated into military and sacerdotal members and organized his own clerical branch of the order, which claimed exclusive inheritance of the spiritual truths. Appointing himself 'chancellor of the clergy,' Starck declared he possessed secret knowledge and negotiated unsuccessfully to secure financing and organizational recognition for his order.

Returning from a trip to Russia in 1768, Starck stopped in Königsberg as a guest of Hamann's publisher and Kant's landlord, the freemason J.J. Kanter. Starck remained in the east Prussian city for nearly a decade, working his way to a full professorship in theology and a position as court chaplain. To cover his lodging expenses Starck wrote for Kanter the anonymous *Apologie des Ordens der Frey-Mäurer* (1770), which sketched his emerging views on natural religion. This text defended freemasonry against subversion and other criticisms by exalting the esoteric wisdom of ancient mystery cults. Unable to reveal the secrets of his own order, Starck justified freemasonry through analogy. At the core of ancient mystery cults, according to Starck, had been rational truths that aligned with the doctrines of Christianity. Exposing them would have endangered the state which relied on popular religion. Starck reassured readers that freemasonry guarded equally essential truths, which in no way jeopardized public religion, morality, or the state.[108]

The way Starck connected Christianity and its pagan precedents infuriated Hamann despite their shared interest in ancient languages and the history of the early church. In 1774 Hamann walked out on the public lecture Starck held defending his dissertation upon appointment to the Albertina university. Starck proposed that primitive Christianity, including the practice of baptism, incorporated rites and ceremonies from heathen mystery cults and that its core doctrines, such as monotheism and the immortality of the soul, derived from a natural religion of reason.[109] As a student of his nemesis Michaelis, Starck embodied for Hamann the distasteful religious politics of the enlightened Prussian state.[110] Yet he defiantly chose Starck as his personal confessor, perhaps to covertly strengthen his Lutheranism.[111]

Hamann's dislike of enlightened theology ensued from a series of well-known personal crises. Raised in Königsberg's old bathhouse, the son of a bather-surgeon, Hamann left the local university without a degree, his speech impediment discouraging a career in theology or academia.[112] His early professional ambitions to become a merchant collapsed dramatically during a failed mission to London in 1758 where he was undertaking secret negotiations on behalf of the trading firm of his university friend J.C. Berens. Living wildly after talks failed, Hamann discovered sexual misconduct by his British contact and sought refuge in a garret where he binge-read the Bible. The religious conversion that followed led Berens to reject Hamann's marriage proposal to his sister. Resulting quarrels with Berens distanced Hamann from the principles of the Enlightenment, and, as a badly paid minor tax official, he nurtured a lifelong resentment of Friedrich the Great's bureaucratic state.

In the *Socratic Memorabilia* (1759) Hamann had characterized the relationship between paganism and Christianity in orthodox terms as allegorical and typological. Paganism was a dream-like intuition of Christianity.[113] The text was a personal defence of creedal Christianity against the efforts of Berens and Kant to reenlist Hamann to the cause of the Enlightenment. He conceded that pagans possessed some knowledge of God, but without direct revelation their natural consciousness and rational capacities were insufficient for salvation, which depended on a personal relationship to Christ. Hamann reappropriated the figure of Socrates as a forerunner of Christ, not a proto-rationalist; in a 1772 supplement he criticized Eberhard's defence of the figure. According to Hamann, Christianity represented a prophetic fulfilment of providential developments anticipated under paganism.[114]

Hume offered Hamann an apparent ally in unseating the deist reduction of Christianity to natural religion. His scepticism, according to Hamann, exposed the futility of the Enlightenment's dogmatic rationalism and proved reason insufficient for appreciating religious truths.[115] Hamann translated the *Natural History of Religion* into German but deemed it too dangerous to print.[116] In 1781 he published an influential German version of Hume's *Dialogues*, welcoming the criticism it contained of the argument from design. Nature was one component of revelation, for Hamann, but he found it too weak to be the sole foundation of faith.[117] Hamann refused to regard revelation as the handmaiden of enlightened reason. Religious truths, in his view, could never be abstracted because revelation was always encased in contingent historical forms. The spirit was bound to the letter; divine communication was material, symbolic, and historically conditioned.[118]

The first of Hamann's mystery writings, the *Hierophantische Briefe* (1775), explicitly targeted Starck, defending the revealed mysteries of Christianity against the natural religion of enlightened theologians. In the form of seven letters, in which an early Christian apologist responds to a hierophant, an interpreter of esoteric principles, Hamann faulted Starck for reducing the Christian faith to a rational core that could be abstracted from its historical appearances. In Hamann's terms, this produced a "material nothing or a spiritual something."[119] The spiritual content of Christianity lost its historical power, reducing its otherwise meaningful pagan and Jewish precedents to a lifeless empirical foundation. He held Starck's deism to be empty and impotent, lacking the inspiration that only the Holy Spirit provided.

When responding to Herder's *Älteste Urkunde*, Hamann had already labelled Starck a "Roman-apostolic-Catholic heretic and crypto-Jesuit."[120] The *Hierophantische Briefe* caricatured Starck as "a blind caviller of the papacy."[121] His reverence for hierarchy in secret societies betrayed echoes of Catholicism, as supposedly did Starck's preference for precedents set by the early church over Scripture. Deism and popery, according to Hamann, both denied the power of the living spirit, failing to recognize its embodiment in Scripture and the historical world, and succumbed to idolatry and superstition. He indicted Starck, furthermore, for failing to honour the extent that Luther had eliminated all form of "pagan horrors"[122] from the true faith. Nestled between the spirit and the letter, the pearl of Christianity was, Hamann concluded, "a concealed life in God, truth in Christ the mediator, and a power" that could not be adequately captured in rituals, dogmas, or visible works nor reduced to ethics nor judged according to reason.[123]

Starck confirmed his conflation of natural religion, pagan mysteries, and Christian truth in the controversial *Hephästion* (1775). The work venerates natural religion, emphasizing in deist terms the prevalence of morality and divine truths among pagans. Starck presumed an act of primordial revelation. The "pure and exalted truths" preserved in pagan mystery cults were a "beneficial gift"[124] "from the hand of the creator in its first beauty."[125] Yet he emphasized the importance of enlightenment and rationality in their comprehension. A "more reasonable edifice" lay concealed, Starck surmised, behind the "foolish and dispensable" external religion of pagans.[126] The universal religious principles Starck detected in pagan faiths correspond to those identified by Herbert of Cherbury.[127] These included belief in one God, morality, knowledge of the afterlife and the soul's immortality, and an awareness of reward and punishment after death. Starck denounced Herder's *Älteste Urkunde* as "incomprehensible quartos in alchemical and cabbalistic style"[128] and declared his "unwillingness" to waste time on "futile" efforts to understand him.[129]

The second part of the *Hephästion* undercut the significance of Hebrew antiquity for the development of Christian truths, which in Starck's view were more indebted to the natural religion of pagans. Breaking with Michaelis, he denied any close relationship between the Old and New Testaments; the Jewish cult did not offer a typological preview of Christ.[130] Instead, Moses had tailored his revelations to the cultural milieu of the Hebrews, whom Starck deprecated as a "very miserable,"[131] "uncultivated,"[132] and "inconsequential people."[133] As the Hebrews worshipped a national god, their understanding of the divine was "narrow-minded,"[134] Starck concluded, lacking awareness of the trinity, as well as concepts of omniscience and omnipotence. Their sense of morality was likewise restricted to this world with no appreciation of reward and punishment in a future life. Only during the Babylonian exile did exposure to pagan knowledge of the soul's immortality render the Hebrew religion philosophical.

The *Hephästion* elicited strong rebuttals, including an *Antihephästion* by the orthodox theologian G.C. Pisanski, and severely damaged Starck's popularity in the Königsberg consistory and theological faculty.[135] Hamann again defended conservative, orthodox Lutheranism against Strack in *Konxompax: Fragmente einer apokryphischen Sibylle über apokalyptischen Mysterien* (1779). Written in the voice of a pagan prophetess, it is widely considered to be Hamann's most impenetrable composition.[136] The text took collective aim at Starck, Meiners, Lessing, and the neologist G.S. Steinhart, whom Hamann accused of downgrading religion to philosophy and placing it in service of the enlightened state. All were guilty, he pronounced, of undervaluing revelation in the acquisition of theological truths and reducing religion to a rationalist core concerning God, morality, and the afterlife. Hamann ridiculed Starck and Meiners for perceiving in ancient pagan mysteries "the sacred fire of a natural salvific religion,"[137] a contradiction in terms, while presuming Christian doctrines precluded the esoteric and mysterious. Lessing, he believed, wrongly jettisoned the historical foundations of Christianity and decoupled its spirit from the letter.

Hamann turned the tables on his opponents by reinterpreting their association of pagan mysteries, freemasonry, and rationalist theology as a form of theosophical mysticism. Enlightened philosophy, he taunted, was a new mystery religion with its own priests and devotees who idolized reason and indulged in secret, unspoken mysteries. This resulted, Hamann wrote, in an "eternal mystical, magical and logical circle of human deification and divine incarnation."[138] Religious truths could not be acquired either through rational or mystical abstraction. The incarnation and resurrection, Hamann concluded, were the only authentic mysteries, and salvation depended on inspired scriptural encounters with the flesh and blood of Christ.

Under pressure Starck quit Königsberg in 1777 for a string of other positions before settling down as a court chaplain in Gießen in 1781. As indicated in his anonymous *Freymüthige Betrachtungen über das Christenthum* (1780) Starck slowly began to distance himself from theological rationalism. He still insisted that the mysteries contained true knowledge of God but conceded that Christianity was more than a "restoration of natural religion." To reduce a revealed religion to "mere deism" denied the crucial role of Christ as redeemer and mediator; while not directly inspired, Scripture, in his view, was God's word.[139] Starck argued in 1781 that Christ was sent so the truths contained in paganism did not remain particular and restricted. Starck's own *Ueber die alten und neuen Mysterien* (1782) still sanctified the esoteric wisdom of ancient mystery cults for having preserved a rational natural religion, partly in response to Meiners's denials, but approached paganism more critically. He denied that contemplation of nature was sufficient, without revelation, to evoke the idea of one God. "What one learned about the nature of things in the mysteries," he wrote, could only be "an affirmation of revealed truth ... a means to perceive it."[140] Revelation, he now insisted, taught more than humankind could achieve on its own.

A flood of genealogical research on ancient mystery cults followed the Masonic congress convened in Wilhelmsbad in 1782 by Duke Ferdinand of Brunswick, which abolished the Rite of Strict Observance and declared freemasons were not successors to the Knights Templar. In the search for alternative origins of masonry, the question of whether esoteric mysteries originated in primordial revelation or the rational observation of nature was significant. In the *Compass der Weisen* (1779) the Rosicrucians traced the secrets back to the first revelation Adam received from God; despite the fall his knowledge was never "entirely extinguished" and flowed via Noah to Egyptian priests, such as Hermes, the Jewish patriarchs, Zoroaster, and Moses.[141] By contrast, the Illuminati, especially the Vienna lodge of Ignaz von Born, continued to embrace the idea of esoteric philosophy as a way to uphold the values of a strictly rationalist enlightenment.

Conflicts with leadership in the Strict Observance, as well as increasing religious and political conservatism, gradually distanced Starck from freemasonry during the early 1780s until his complete break in 1785. Nevertheless in 1786 the enlightened *Berlinische Monatsschrift* denounced him as a covert Jesuit. The resulting legal suit and literary scandal radicalized Starck as a reactionary. To his enemies Starck appeared to embody the danger of Catholics secretly infiltrating Protestant institutions. High-degree masonry and its gradations of wisdom were, according to his accusers, an effort to secretly instil Catholic doctrines.[142] Starck subsequently indulged all manner of conspiracy theories against the Enlightenment he once embraced. His popular *Triumph der Philosophie* (1804) lambasted French philosophers and in particular the Illuminist order founded by Adam Weishaupt, for precipitating the French Revolution and its violent destruction of throne and altar.

For Starck, the idea of an early dispensation inhibited the racialized condemnation of pagan peoples to whom Meiners denied the Enlightenment necessary to attain true knowledge of God. However, it justified deprecating the ancient Hebrews, whose isolation and unphilosophical bent supposedly prevented full appreciation of God's qualities and the soul's immortality. Unlike Herder, Starck failed to articulate a convincing genealogical relationship linking pagan mysteries to Christianity and freemasonry; the affinities he traced were largely ahistorical. Hamann's defence of historical revelation resisted the notion of timeless religious truths. Yet his understanding of paganism prefiguring Christianity also failed to engage the diffusionary model, exemplified in the *Älteste Urkunde*, by which primordial revelation extended into particular religions. This required a greater departure from Scripture than Hamann was willing to allow but did mesh well with heterodox supernaturalism.

The Göttingen School of Comparative Religious History

Protestant theologians influenced by Kantian philosophy turned to comparative religious history in the 1790s as a means to document the progressive realization of rational religion through time. Kant's *Critique of Judgment* (1790) and his *Religion within the Limits of Reason Alone* (1793) offered a model for imagining the origin of religion and explaining the apparent presence of divine wisdom in pagan religions without primordial revelation. Under the guidance of Karl Friedrich Stäudlin (1761–1826), a small group of Kantian theologians in Göttingen organized comparative religious history into a distinct field warranting specialized journals. He and his disciples, Immanuel Berger and Christian Wilhelm Flügge, are, for this reason, often regarded as marking the prehistory of religious studies as a field.[143] Their approach, following Kant, denied primordial revelation on the grounds that early humans first needed to develop the idea of God before being receptive to his word. As a project, comparative religious history in a Kantian key rapidly fizzled out. Berger and Flügge both left academic life for pastoral positions shortly after 1800. The group's relative negligence of empirical research and the rapid transformation of critical philosophy severely compromised their aspirations. Yet Kantian philosophy did offer an attractive antidote to Hume's sceptical position on natural religion.

Stäudlin is best known as an historian of scepticism and moral philosophy interested in dogmatic responses to doubt.[144] Born in Stuttgart to the son of a government advisor with antiquarian interests, he trained in exegesis, biblical criticism, and oriental languages at the Tübingen *Stift* from 1779 to 1784. Meiners encouraged him to study the history of philosophy.[145] This precipitated a crisis of faith that placed Stäudlin in a "very distressing situation."[146] After reading Hume, he abandoned Leibnizian-Wolffian theology. Stäudlin travelled extensively in England, engaging closely with his legacy before receiving an appointment in Göttingen, where he lectured with a strong Swabian accent.[147] Theologically, Stäudlin adhered to a fairly conservative rational supernaturalism, accepting a mutually reinforcing relationship between reason and revelation while deferring to Christian truths. His autobiography characterizes Christianity as "a revealed doctrine, commensurate with reason, but also transcendent, supernatural, and based in holy scriptures."[148] Reason was needed to comprehend Christianity and inhibit superstition, for Stäudlin, but it could never be a sovereign "lawgiver."[149]

Politically conservative, Stäudlin feared that radical scepticism was the "sickness of his age"[150] responsible for destroying the social fabrics of France and the United States. His *Geist und Geschichte des Skepticismus* (1794) denounced the French Revolution as caused by "dogmatic disbelief and wanton mockery ... spreading among the people."[151] Kant's critical philosophy offered an antidote that could secure faith without resorting to dogmatism or mysticism. Stäudlin found in Kant "many of my doubts lifted and much of what I only perceived darkly to be enlightened."[152] The actual extent of Stäudlin's Kantianism is debated.[153] The special role he reserved for the Christian church suggests that Stäudlin might merely have clothed his apologetics in "fashionable" Kantian terminology. His conception of church history dismissed any idea of progress from statutory to universal religion, depicting instead a constant struggle among statutory religions without an increase in moral faith.[154]

Before Kant published his treatise on religion, Stäudlin sent him his own *Ideen zur Kritik des Systems der christlichen Religion* (1791). In return, Kant considered publishing his *Streit der Fakultäten* (1798) in a journal Stäudlin founded; under pressure from the censors it appeared instead as a monograph dedicated to Stäudlin.[155] His *Ideen* gingerly applied Kant to Hume's account of the origin of religion. In the *Critique of Judgment*, which Stäudlin cited extensively, Kant had derived religion from a "pure moral requirement of existence" that produced feelings of gratitude, obedience, and humility. Practical reason led the first humans to presume "a moral, law-giving being beyond this world." The concept of God was thus, for Kant, not a result of theoretical reflection on nature or of self-interest; it was a subjective sensibility.[156] Stäudlin used this position to assert, in supposed alignment with the Mosaic books, that early humans had an underdeveloped conception of one God, as well as a moral consciousness, before revelation.

Stäudlin argued that the origin of the idea of God had to be separated from the question of original monotheism. The Mosaic books, which Hume as an historian should have followed, indicated to Stäudlin that the first concepts of God were "quite paltry and human." Moses, in his view, recounted only the inception of monotheism, not of religion in its entirety. For this reason Stäudlin rejected orthodox assumptions that the world religions resulted "from a degeneration of the first religion."[157] Following Meiners he attributed the religious ideas of the first humans to "a diversity of sources and causes" dictated by local conditions.[158] Deficits in the historical record, however, meant that Stäudlin could only explain the origin of religion speculatively. Following Kant, he declared religion to be latent in the human capacity for reason. God, according to Stäudlin, was "originally contained in the substance of reason and was already active in man, even when he was only vaguely aware of it."[159] Contemplating the beauty and wonder of nature could awaken the idea of God, but it was solidified, for Stäudlin, by an innate moral consciousness.

Kant's moral law was, for Stäudlin, fully commensurate with the doctrines of Christianity. "Several centuries ago Christ already taught," he argued, "what Kant has now proven based on the nature of the human capacity for knowledge."[160] His *Ideen* conceptualized how to evaluate both the dogmas and epistemological foundations of positive religion based on Kantian principles. However, Stäudlin also insisted that Christianity transcended critical philosophy in crucial respects. Some doctrines, such as Christ's commandment to love, couldn't be derived from the moral law nor could full knowledge of God or the afterlife be acquired using reason alone. For Stäudlin, revelation from a higher authority was necessary to reinforce the moral law.

In 1797 Stäudlin founded the *Beiträge zur Philosophie und Geschichte der Religion und Sittenlehre*, which ran for five issues. Dedicated to the "history of religions or rather of the diverse types of faith,"[161] the publication encouraged specialized studies as a prelude to a general history. Although he also wrote on Buddhism, Stäudlin's contributions were largely programmatic and established the journal's Kantian platform. His "Über den Werth der kritischen Philosophie" (1797–99), for example, defended the "harmony, the compatibility" of Christianity and critical philosophy.[162] Stäudlin endeavoured to secure a space for revelation and miracles in Kantian philosophy, arguing that supernaturalism didn't contradict the moral law. He denied that critical philosophy had a "wild revolutionary spirit"[163] that threatened the church's institutional authority.

During the atheism controversy that followed Fichte's dismissal from Jena in 1799, Stäudlin wrote a Latin vindication of him, arguing that critical philosophy did not lead to atheism.[164] However, in its wake Stäudlin was less favourably disposed to Kant and increasingly reluctant to reduce religion to morality. "Indeed I attributed too much authority to [Kant] and therefore did not bestow on Jesus and his morality the honor they deserved," Stäudlin explained, "later I realized that critical moral philosophy is one-sided and that one must either relinquish Christianity entirely or concede to it a greater regard than I have." By 1815 Stäudlin no longer believed in the necessity of an absolute moral principle and sought instead to salvage the "truth and divinity of Jesus' moral teachings even in their positive and historical aspects."[165] His position shifted towards a scepticism in which faith was the only response to the insufficiency of philosophical knowledge.[166]

Two of Stäudlin's students, Immanuel Berger and Christian Wilhelm Flügge, developed the Göttingen project of comparative religious history by fusing Kantian principles with the ethnological approach of Christoph Meiners. Born in Ruhland in the Oberlausitz, Immanuel Berger (1773–1803) held a position as a theological *Repetent* in Göttingen after completing studies there and before taking a pastoral job in the Ore mountains of Saxony in 1802. During his brief academic career he applied the insights of Lessing, Kant, and Fichte to comparative religious history. According to Berger, Lessing's critique of Christianity's historical foundations implied that philosophy was necessary to secure faith, and his *Education of the Human Race* offered a model for how to meld historical revelation and philosophy. Following Kant, Berger proposed that historical developments were a "vehicle"[167] for God to promote "a pure religion of reason among humankind."[168] Berger also agreed with Fichte that the postulates of practical reason required God, as the "moral educator of the human race," to use revelation to promote morality.[169]

Berger's "Ideen zur Philosophie der Religionsgeschichte" (1798), published in Stäudlin's *Beiträge*, discarded primordial revelation on the grounds that a prior concept of God was necessary to accept his communications. The origin of religion thus did not coincide with creation, according to Berger, but with philosophy and "reflection,"[170] activities requiring people to transcend their material instincts and physical needs. Even before the onset of rationality, however, awareness of the moral law guided underdeveloped cultures, in his view, according to a typology that advanced from sensuousness to understanding to reason. Gradually separating the highest being from its physical embodiment, sensuous religion, according to Berger, progressed from fetishism to the worship of sacred animals and assumed its highest form in Sabianism. The moral law was apparent, for Berger, in a tendency towards universalizing maxims for behaviour. In *Verstandsreligion*, creation itself was taken as evidence of God's influence in human affairs, and maxims extended to the entire world, encouraging monotheism. The final stage in Berger's typology, *Vernunftreligion*, was achieved once people realized that a highest moral being created and ruled the world and bound humankind to its law.

Berger's *Geschichte der Religionsphilosophie* (1800) applied this typology to actual historical communities, excluding revealed religions, which, in his view, were rooted in tradition and authority, not free reflection. Fetishism, in his view, offered glimpses of rational religion, presuming a higher being capable of influencing the world. But the connection between an object and its principle always appeared substantive, resulting in the "degeneration, deterioration of religious ideas."[171] Berger defended the chronological priority of monotheism with an anthropological explanation for its emergence among patriarchal nomads. Concern for herd and household had encouraged, in his view, speculation on "a highest creator and governor" who provided for humankind as a father did for a family. The religious philosophy of the ancient Hebrews was thus not, for Berger, "a work of very deep or even supernatural wisdom."[172] Berger followed Meiners in assuming religion to be an anthropological constant and correlated the developmental levels of rational religion with ethnological hierarchies.[173] He decried Sabianism as a "system of deception and deceit which created the greatest evil on earth from otherwise innocuous errors."[174] Berger likewise condemned the Egyptian astrology and animal worship as "bigotry" and "extreme fanaticism."[175]

More historically oriented was Christian Wilhelm Flügge (1773–1828), whose empirical research did more than affirm the onset of rational religion.[176] Born the son of a craftsman in Winsen an der Luhe near Luneburg, Flügge, like Berger, studied theology with Stäudlin and admired Meiners. He briefly served as a lecturer in theology and university chaplain in Göttingen, where he fused Kantianism and neology until economic pressures pushed him into pastoral service near Luneburg in 1801.[177] Flügge characterized his own period as profiting from a beneficial "autonomy of reason in moral affairs," made possible by the state tolerating the freedom necessary to apply reason to religion.[178]

The history of religion was, in Flügge's view, a branch of the general history of the human spirit, distinct from church history or the history of dogma. Its object, Flügge explained in his "Versuch über das Studium der Religionsgeschichte" (1797), was to document a gradual process of "religious enlightenment."[179] Seeing "veiled truths" in pagan traditions, rather than mere error, allowed the historian to extend a "thread" through the labyrinth of alternative religions to arrive "in the realm of reason."[180] As a Kantian, Flügge credited critical philosophy with enabling religious history to detect in false faiths "imperfect traces"[181] of the moral law. Flügge, too, rejected primordial revelation in favour of the slow, natural development of the human rational capacity. He attributed, for example, natural origins to the concept of immortality with multiple starting points and diverse causes.[182]

Local cultural particularities were more significant to Flügge than questions of origin.[183] The inception of religion remained shrouded in an "enigmatic darkness."[184] Debate on the topic, he believed, should desist from speculative "squabbling"[185] and not aspire to constructing a "family tree of religions."[186] More pressing for Flügge was effective source criticism. Religious ideas needed interpretation based on their climatic, ethnological, and regional cultural context. Flügge studied ancient Saxon, Sami, and Celtic mythology and imagined creating a geography of religions. However, he overlaid such analysis with universalizing reflection on how the laws of reason present in the human soul generated such ideas as eternity. His essay on Indian mythology, for example, found knowledge of the trinity in Hinduism and Zoroastrianism, as well as among the ancient Egyptians and Goths. He offered a Kantian explanation for these commonalities, suggesting the "idea lies in universal human reason."[187]

The Göttingen school of comparative religious history dissolved by the turn of the century. Stäudlin briefly continued his journal as the *Magazin für Religions- Moral- und Kirchengeschichte*, which examined both "philosophical and revealed religions" from the perspective of history, ethnography, and geography.[188] All remnants of Kantian philosophy had been excised from this journal, however, and the Napoleonic invasion stopped publication in 1806.[189] While discovering rational religion in pagan faiths mollified Meiners's strident racialism among Kantians in Göttingen, their ranking of human communities along a progressive trajectory still produced prejudicial hierarchies that undercut Judaism and asserted the universal validity of an intellectualized Protestantism.

Historicizing revelation in the late eighteenth century meant that the cultural contingencies shaping its reception, such as ethnicity and perceived mental acuity, factored more prominently as explanatory factors in the comparative history of religion. For this reason, the two main narratives German scholars evoked to compare the belief systems of human communities contributed to a racialization of revelation. Tracing the historical transmission of primordial revelation prioritized ethnic descent and lineage, dividing chosen peoples who preserved God's word from fallen communities who succumbed to error. Explaining the failure of certain groups to develop true knowledge of God based on physical, cultural, or social idiosyncrasies more directly racialized communities of belief, depicting religion as an extension of race. In neither case was race a biological category. But the linguistic, cultural, and spiritual qualities that defined a *Volk* and shaped its religion were equally essentialized and intractable.

Chapter Three

God's Word in Comparative Mythology, 1760–1830

The destruction of two manuscripts bookends the tumultuous years in which the Romantic mythologist Johann Arnold Kanne sought to reconstruct primordial revelation by reassembling the original tongue supposedly descended from the word of God. From an unheated Berlin tavern in the spring of 1806 Kanne heard the march of Prussian soldiers mobilizing against Napoleon. Destitute, he tossed into the oven a "small manuscript" intended for sale to a publisher, briefly warmed himself on the flames, and joined up.[1] His recently completed *Erste Urkunden der Geschichte* (1808), a response to J.G. Herder's similarly titled publication, had stalled at a Leipzig censor concerned that the text "impugned" Christianity.[2] After defeat at Jena, Kanne escaped French captivity, barefoot and clutching a letter from Jean Paul Richter, and joined the Austrian army. Initially suspecting Kanne had left for India, Jean Paul discovered him languishing half dead in a lazaretto and arranged for F.H. Jacobi to buy Kanne free.[3] By 1808, his *über*-prolific pen and Jacobi's continued assistance earned Kanne a professorship in archaeology and history at the Realinstitut in Nuremburg. After his rebirth as an awakened Christian in 1814, however, Kanne felt compelled to ignite his lengthy *Panglossium* manuscript, which had been designed to distil evidence of the *Ursprache* from historical tongues. He declared himself "cured of raptures ... in my linguistic research"[4] and started preparations for a work on Christ in the Old Testament.

The German search for an *Ursprache* capable of disclosing God's earliest revelations peaked in a brief wave of enthusiasm during the nationalist stirrings that accompanied the Napoleonic occupation, when new philological methods rendered conceivable the linguistic project envisioned in Herder's *Aelteste Urkunde des Menschengeschlechts*. Until his conversion, Kanne believed that a lost *Ursprache* harboured secret knowledge of the divine as it had appeared in unadulterated form in the moments following creation. He learned over two hundred, mostly non-European languages in hopes of resurrecting its forms.[5] This project had deep roots in the Christian tradition. The Gospel of John proclaims: "In the beginning was the Word, and the Word was with God, and the Word was God," implying that creation transpired as an act of speech and was invested with hidden symbolic meaning. The tale of Babel derived all human languages from a single divine source, suggesting national idioms retained aspects of the divine logos present in God's original word.

Kanne's fascination with the *Ursprache* responded more specifically, however, to a late eighteenth-century critique of theological rationalism and the enlightened conceptions of language that sustained it. In the 1770s, Herder and Hamann, whose comparative histories of religion featured in the last chapter, inaugurated a linguistic turn in Protestant theology that took seriously scriptural claims that God first disclosed himself as the word and that revelation transpired as an act of speech. In their hands, language study assumed significance in the search for primordial revelation, both as direct evidence of God's self-disclosure and a comparative methodological tool for identifying synchronisms and patterns of historical transmission across mythological traditions. As Kanne's crisis of conscience indicates, the search for an Asian *Ursprache* sat uneasily with scriptural authority. The prospect that yet undeciphered languages or scripts preserved God's word encroached on Judaic primacy and Hebrew's status as the language of paradise. Christian apologists often preferred to concede the human origin of language, despite its heretical implications, to refute hermeticists who believed Egyptian hieroglyphs harboured esoteric wisdom.[6]

Early nineteenth-century German scholars regarded language as both a crucial medium of revelation and a window onto national history. The dual function of language, this chapter argues, further grounded revelation in the world of human experience, eliminating the ability of God's word to serve as an unencumbered conveyer of propositions. German language theory in this regard hastened the transition away from propositional revelation. The chapter also develops the story of philology's entanglement in the "theology of origins" addressed, but expanded in other directions, in Maurice Olender's *Languages of Paradise* (1992).[7] Scholars responding to this foundational work have shown that in the nineteenth century language correlated powerfully with race, ethnicity, national culture, and the presumption of privileged access to divine truth. Historical tongues supposedly united in their forms both lingering traces of God's word and the national, cultural spirit of the communities who inherited revelation. This presumed dual entanglement of language encouraged philologists to speculate on the respective significance of 'Aryan' and 'Semitic' peoples as custodians of revelation, as well as on their racial characteristics and presumed cultural legacies. This is well-trod territory, and the ambitions of the chapter are more limited.

On the one hand, it establishes why the *Ursprache* as an idea factored so prominently in the theological defence of revelation by investigating the role of language in Hamann and Herder's critique of abstract reason and their defence of cultural particularism against enlightened universalism. Like many German scholars, the pair turned against French intellectual precedents in the tumultuous years following the Revolution. In their view, language's role as a sanctuary for surviving vestiges of divine revelation rendered it an essential and formative vehicle of human understanding. At the same time, as a repository of national uniqueness, language also revealed which cultural communities had inherited and accurately preserved the original word of God. The theological imperative of defending revelation drove their arguments for the linguistic conditionality of knowledge. But they preserved revelation at the cost of associating it more closely with the fallible contingencies of human experience.

On the other hand, the chapter highlights how significant Herder's notion of God's primal hieroglyph was for two different interpretations of the divine word in creation, one concerned with discursive language and etymology and another with signs and symbolism. Philological reconstruction of the *Ursprache* was central to the related projects of Kanne, Friedrich Schlegel, and the Orientalist poet Friedrich Rückert. Each in succession occupying the chair for Oriental Languages at the University of Erlangen, Kanne and Rückert both embarked on an empirical reconstruction of the "absolute language" that their mentor Johann Jakob Wagner envisioned in a fusion of Schelling's identity philosophy and Herder's *Aelteste Urkunde*. For Kanne, the most speculative of the Romantic mythologists, the chaotic web of imaginative etymological bonds linking early Oriental myths approximated the universality of the *Ursprache*. Rückert, by contrast, expected the translation of world literature into German to transform his mother tongue into a new and redemptive ideal language.

The pictorial dimensions of Herder's hieroglyph led the Heidelberg Romantics Joseph Görres and Friedrich Creuzer, by contrast, to bypass discursive language for symbolic forms. Neither approach to reviving original revelation enjoyed longevity. Schlegel rejected the form divine revelation assumed in Indian religious doctrines, converting to Catholicism and proclaiming the primacy of the Old

Testament and Hebrew. Kanne embraced Bible-centred Christianity at the age of forty-one, and even the liberal Rückert eventually surrendered to the cultural certainties of dogmatic Christianity and classical antiquity. Speculative Romantic mythology collapsed in the wake of the Creuzer Affair, a protracted public denunciation by liberal neo-humanists of Creuzer's claiming oriental origins for Greek culture in the *Symbolik und Mythologie der alten Völker* (1810–12). The sober comparative philology of Franz Bopp likewise deflated sweeping generalizations that derived all tongues from a language of paradise. Yet the precedent set by Romantic mythologists ensured that language persisted as a crucial avenue for investigating the origin of religion, resurfacing after mid-century with Ernst Renan and Friedrich Max Müller as an explanation for the belief structures of particular cultural communities.

The Divine Origins of Language: Hamann and Herder

In the 1770s Hamann and Herder reconceived the theological significance of language while attacking the rationalist theology of Johann David Michaelis and his enlightened cohort, refuting their instrumentalist conception of language and overturning a theologically influential belief in the arbitrariness of the sign.[8] The process bound revelation to historically conditioned languages in the name of orthodox Lutheranism and set a precedent for idealizing original language as the purest embodiment of primordial revelation. As a philologist and translator, Michaelis, whose position on revelation features in Chapter 1, had explicit expectations for the religious function of language, set in part by French theories of the sign. His *Ueber den Einfluss der Sprachen auf die Meinungen der Menschen* (1759) argued that ideas existed independently of language and that human expressions could be perfected to more accurately express divine truth.[9] The text offers numerous examples of how the truths of divine revelation could be purged of distortions arising from the historical and social context in which scripture was written by identifying how nationally specific aspects of the biblical languages had altered the message of God. Language's ability to serve as a neutral vehicle for thought was a precondition for rationalist exegesis, as well as for deriving the divine from the qualities of abstract reason. Denying words an essential connection to their referents appealed to enlightened opponents of mysticism and esotericism, but for Hamann it wrongly destroyed the mysterious, hidden meanings contained in Scripture. In his view, the divine spirit could never have been revealed in the abstract languages of philosophers.

Recognizing that culturally specific and symbolic forms of language mediated the human encounter with God was central, for Hamann, to restoring the doctrine of revelation and aligned with his understanding of God's presence in the human world. His first critical engagement with Scripture occurred in a dilapidated London boarding house in 1758 while searching for an indication that God would forgive his sins. The inward faith that emerged from the crisis celebrated God's willingness to humble himself and accommodate to the historical existence of fallen man. The condescension of a trinitarian God thus lay at the core of Hamann's theology and his approach to revelation.[10] The *Tagebuch eines Christen* (1758), which Hamann kept while resolving a depression, stressed "how God in his revelation submits to human concepts and history."[11] Revelation, in his view, entailed God's adapting with humility to the forms of human understanding and making himself accessible to man.

The word assumed priority for Hamann as a medium of revelation more significant than nature, history, and the incarnation. "God reveals himself," Hamann marvelled in his journal, "the creator of the world an author."[12] This perspective reflects the influence of Christian cabbalism, as well as Hamann's aesthetic valuation of the biblical text as poetry. But it is also rooted in a traditional Lutheran theology of the word, in which language mediates between the divine and the profane. The living, spoken, and written word was, in this view, the concrete form through which the Holy Spirit became real and present in the world.[13] According to the doctrine of inverberation, language was central to divine incarnation; God created the material world and called things into being through speaking, an act Adam replicated by naming the animals in Eden.[14] "The word of this spirit is a labor as grand as creation," Hamann concluded in 1758, "and a mystery as profound as the salvation of men."[15] Rationalist biblical exegesis wrongly silenced the deep spirituality of Scripture by neglecting figurative meaning in favour of a literal, materialist reading that bypassed the forms of language to reach pure ideas.

Hamann's emphasis on the word bestowed a linguistic character on creation and the natural world, which in turn endowed research on natural history and geology with religious urgency. As the embodiment of God's speech to man, nature for Hamann was replete with allegorical or symbolic imagery. "Every phenomenon of nature was a name," he explained, "the sign, the symbol, the promise of a fresh and secret and ineffable but all the more intimate chosen union, communication and communion of divine energies and ideas. All that man in the beginning heard, saw with his eyes, contemplated and touched with his hands, all this was a *living word*. For God was the Word."[16] For Hamann, all of history and creation presented itself in the secret language of the divine. The material world itself was a symbolic text that could be read as a poetic expression of God's grace. "All we have left in nature for our use are jumbled verses and *disjecti membra poetae*," he concluded in *Aesthetica in Nuce* (1762).[17] Hamann was an empiricist and a sensualist, assuming thought and reason emerged in the mind's response to external factors. The philosopher's duty lay in reassembling and interpreting the linguistic fragments of creation to redeem God's word.

Unlike believers in natural religion, however, Hamann preserved a strong sense of God's transcendence, recognizing in creation the sovereignty of a divine will most clearly articulated in Scripture.[18] The books of nature and history were, for Hamann, merely "cyphers, secret symbols" that required "the key ... expounded in holy scripture."[19] The Bible transformed the divine spirit into a human idiom,[20] and historical languages represented a further accommodation of God to the fallen world. In depicting man as a vessel for the divine word Hamann drew on the Lutheran phrase "*communicatio idiomatum*," used to explain consubstantiation and how Christ could have both divine and human attributes. "To speak is to translate," Hamann asserted, "from an angelic language into a human language, that is to translate thoughts into words, – things into names – images into signs."[21] This position rejected a tradition of negative theology that dismissed the categories of human language as incapable of capturing the infinite nature of God and thus undermined the possibility of revelation and of God's incarnation as man.[22]

Privately Hamann condemned Herder's *Aelteste Urkunde* as a "monstrum horrendum," but it did confirm his assertion that primordial revelation had been transmitted in both symbolic and discursive form. On the one hand, Herder depicted the divine hieroglyph as a pictorial symbol or "God's first attempt at writing with man."[23] This implied that written language preceded speech and that God's word first appealed to the eye. Writing, he figured, began as pictographs, runes, and hieroglyphs with phonetic alphabets developing later. Its first forms had been highly symbolic and laden with the same imagery that pervaded the natural world. The hieroglyph's imprint on later writing systems had bequeathed, moreover, elements of God's intelligence to all forms of knowledge, scholarship, and the arts. On the other hand, the hieroglyph had been the "original archetype and standard for all human language."[24] This implied that the earliest human idioms contained "a small circle of sounds mostly held in common"[25] from God's original revelation. Herder suspected in the *Aelteste Urkunde* that Hebrew,

Phoenician, Syrian, and Persian were descendants of a yet unspecified older language.

The generation of Jena Romantics inspired by Hamann's and Herder's work transformed a late eighteenth-century debate on the origin of language into a search for the actual *Ursprache* of humankind and speculated on its association with particular human communities.[26] Herder's frequent pairing elsewhere of language and nationhood suggested that remnants from God's word had become cloaked in national particularities as they descended through time. This discouraged a propositional understanding of revelation, which required greater transparency of language. In the first decade of the nineteenth century, a generation of emerging orientalists, the most influential being Friedrich Schlegel, applied new philological rigour to the quest for uncovering the closest descendants of the divinely inspired *Ursprache* and aspired to an etymological and poetic reconstruction of original revelation and its custodians. The resulting historicization of language contributed to revelation being depicted more as an outgrowth of the national attributes associated with communities of descent than as a transcendent gift of God.

The *Ursprache* and Biblical Revelation: Friedrich Schlegel

The progressive embodiment of revelation in historical experience and its racialization as a function of nationality are both visible in Friedrich Schlegel's efforts to restore primordial revelation through language study. Herder's *Aelteste Urkunde* led Schlegel to presume the existence of an original revelation whose traces remained in mythology, Greek philosophy, and the cabbala.[27] He reread the text while preparing *Über die Sprache und Weisheit der Indier* and praised its "beautiful sentiment" as "the only good thing" Herder ever wrote.[28] Herder nearly found, Schlegel later recalled, "in the oldest revelation the key to all philosophy, all fables, traditions and mythology."[29] After reading *Sacontala* in 1797 and conversing with Friedrich Majer, he suspected that the source of all religion could be found in India.[30] In 1802, Goethe introduced Sir William Jones's translation of the *Gitagovinda* to the Jena Romantics, who saw in it revelations that had until then only been known in their Christian forms.[31] Within weeks Schlegel left for Paris, determined to study Sanskrit, Persian, and Hebrew, which he did for two years under Alexander Hamilton and Antoine-Léonard de Chézy. Schlegel embarked on this quest deeply committed to *Naturphilosophie*, seeing affinities between its conception of the divine presence in nature and the Hindu doctrine of emanation.

Later in Cologne, Schlegel reinterpreted the history of religion based on his philological research. His *Philosophische Vorlesungen*, held from 1804 to 1806, laid out a "philosophical theory of revelation"[32] that sanctified languages descended from the *Ursprache*, while recognizing the potential benefits of Catholicism in its preservation. Primordial revelation factors prominently in the text as a constraint on autonomous reason, a likely reflection of Schlegel's encounter with French traditionalism, a counter-revolutionary revival of Catholicism that emphasized origins. He believed the movement's founder, Joseph de Maistre, correctly theorized the relation between revelation and philosophy, defending the former against abstract reason.[33] Schlegel proposed in the lectures that history began with a "double revelation." In accord with *Naturphilosophie*, he speculated that an "earth spirit" ignited human reason. But, more critical now of idealist philosophy, Schlegel also insisted, like the French traditionalists, that the "stimulating impact of the divine"[34] was necessary to jumpstart humanity's rational capacity. Although the encounter with nature evoked a longing for the infinite, a second, more exclusive positive revelation was needed before select peoples acquired reliable knowledge of God.

If Schlegel's confidence in Hellenistic syncretism once threatened to conflate reason and revelation, the manner in which he now distinguished them produced a portentous hierarchy of cultures and languages. All peoples developed reason, in his view. But receipt of positive revelation established a "decisive distinction" among nations. God bestowed revelation only on "certain people and nations, not all," Schlegel wrote.[35] Similarly, only natural languages began as an imitation of sounds or an expression of inner feeling. Those displaying great artistry and development in antiquity had "another origin … revelation." "An *Ursprache* was present," Schlegel wrote, "that arose at once and was artistic and genial to the highest degree."[36] Later in the *Vorlesungen über Universalgeschichte* (1805–6) Schlegel presented language as both a litmus test for measuring divine favour and a roadmap for tracing ethnic descent. The "cultivated" nations of Asia and Europe spoke idioms, in his view, descended from a "divine language."[37] Schlegel associated the location of revelation with the "empire of Brahma."[38] His model for the diffusion of Indian religious concepts bound the transmission of revelation to specific historical cultures, establishing an uneven scale of national claims to God's word.

Schlegel's concern for primordial revelation led him away from pantheistic natural religion to a Catholicism heavily rooted in the Old Testament that emphasized a strong, personal creator God who transcended nature and appeared as a father and king.[39] This transition accompanied a political reorientation from cosmopolitan republicanism to a conservative nationalism centred on the Holy Roman Empire. In the Cologne lectures, Schlegel still conceded that emanation doctrines reflected a concept of God that reason could not generate; all mythological traditions contained, in his view, legitimate, but misunderstood, revelation. Yet he stressed the necessity of a third revelation through Christ and the Church's divinely sanctioned role in preserving and transmitting revelation. While reason could diagnose deficiencies in mythological traditions, philosophy could not reconstruct lost aspects of revelation. "A continual revelation in the sense of the Catholic Church," Schlegel affirmed, "would be wise to accept."[40] Interpreting revelation should, he concluded, be reserved for the church and its theologians. Protestants erred in abiding solely by Scripture and dismissing the importance of symbolism in transmitting religion. Catholic symbolism provided an objective form, he concluded, for relaying revelation, which philosophy could then interpret scientifically.[41]

An apology for Schlegel's immanent conversion to Catholicism, *Über die Sprache und Weisheit der Indier* (1808), resolved any remaining tension between biblical revelation and the cultural legacy of the *Ursprache* in favour of the former. The text still regarded Sanskrit and its descendants as historically most proximate to the divine word, distinguishing profane 'mechanical' languages from the benighted family of inflected tongues. But Sanskrit's place of honour in relation to the *Ursprache* was offset by Schlegel's searing critique of how original revelation had degenerated in Indian religious doctrine. "Wild inventions and savage errors everywhere predominate," Schlegel wrote, "and an impression of anguish and sorrow, naturally resulting from the first rejection of, and estrangement from, revealed truth."[42] Superstition and idolatry encouraged nature worship, which distorted Indian knowledge of God and the soul into a materialist veneration of creation. "A system of pure reason,"[43] in his view, inevitably produced pantheism, the philosophical equivalent of deism. Without a dualist framework, all things appeared to be one with God. By conflating good and evil pantheism also destroyed moral life and curtailed free will. The world appeared as necessary and absolute, a destructive form of fatalism.[44]

A tribute to the purity with which Mosaic revelation captured God's original teachings closed *Über die Sprache und Weisheit der Indier*. Schlegel credited the *Aelteste Urkunde* with offering "splendid tips" on the exceptional position of holy Scripture among other oriental systems. Moved by Herder's *Vom Geist der ebräischen Poesie* (1782), Schlegel now insisted the Hebrews had guarded divine truth more assiduously than the Indians, Egyptians, and Persians. The purity of their transmission was due to Hebrew culture and linguistic tradition remaining in "uncompromising isolation"[45] from neighbouring peoples. Messlin notes that Schlegel's exclusion of Hebrew from languages shaped by revelation was an "isolated opinion specific to the linguistic theory of the India book."[46] In the *Geschichte der alten und neuen Literatur* (1812), Schlegel declared Hebrew to be "the proper language of revelation" despite its lesser antiquity. The prevalence in Hebrew of aspiration, a short gust of air that accompanies sounds, recalled the "higher spirit" expressed in prophetic languages, for Schlegel. Because all contemplation of the divine was symbolic and the mind dealt only in images during states of inspiration, Hebrew was also ideally equipped to bear God's word. It was particularly rich in imagery and tropes; the grammatical edifice of Sanskrit, by contrast, was better suited to abstract reasoning.[47]

Schlegel exited the field of Indology convinced that the "inaccessible, obscured origins"[48] of language prohibited unmediated access to primordial revelation. He later reflected that expecting to discover anything approximating the language of paradise was "a big mistake" that overlooked the "unfathomable distance" separating the historical record from the first humans. The value of Hebrew as a language of revelation lay in its aesthetic properties, not its historical proximity to God's original word. Scholars were not capable of acquiring "even the most remote, intuitive notion" of the divine *Ursprache*.[49] In the *Philosophie der Sprache und des Wortes* (1828–9) Schlegel instead advocated a careful mapping of the several *Ursprachen* "in a more precisely limited sense of the word" which stood as the oldest tongues within specific families.[50] Schlegel's preference for Mosaic revelation over pantheistic natural religion ultimately extinguished his longing for a divine *Ursprache* of pagan provenance.

J.A. Kanne's Elusive *Ursprache*

The prospect of reconstructing the divine *Ursprache* from its surviving remnants remained viable longer within the framework of idealist philosophy, which, under Schelling's influence, recognized language as a crucial vector for attaining the absolute and extracting the ideal from its embodiment in the real. Two language scholars inspired by Schelling's disciple Johann Jakob Wagner laboured to recover 'absolute' language as the clearest embodiment of the divine. As seen in the chapter's opening vignette, Kanne used speculative etymology to unlock linguistic affinities among mythological traditions he believed had originated in God's word. This was a conservative project, seeking to restore religion to revolutionary Europe. Republican politics were "of the devil," Kanne remarked in 1815; he expected a strong monarchy to safeguard the inner spiritual life of a people.[51] For this reason, his aspirations for recovering the *Ursprache* were more universalizing, and revelation remained more closely tied to God's original intervention. Friedrich Rückert, by contrast, embraced philology during the national awakening of Germany under French occupation as a means to recreate the absolute first language. In his view, revelation's continued presence, through language, in the historical world legitimated as God's plan the causes of political self-determination, liberal reform, and German nationalism.

Born to a Pietist family in Detmold in the small principality of Lippe, Kanne felt torn from any early age between philology and the mystical faith of his reformed Catechism teacher Jakob Ludwig Passavant. An attempt to study theology at the university in Göttingen in 1790 nudged Kanne towards irreverence and the "time of my inner darkness."[52] The shock of his first colloquium, an exploration of Genesis with the Orientalist Johann Gottfried Eichhorn, required Kanne to take five weeks medical leave. Eichhorn's critical-historical method and his assertions about the Pentateuch's aesthetic content led Kanne to doubt the historical reliability of Scripture. "I was no longer a Christian," Kanne recalled in his autobiography, "but a deist."[53] Classical philology was the logical alternative, and Kanne trained under Christian Gottlob Heyne, whose historicist concept of myth aimed to uncover the lived reality of ancient Greece.[54] Kanne's first exploration of Greek myth, the *Analecta Philologica* (1802), followed Heyne in forsaking its aesthetic content for an historical core that explained the earliest manifestations of the Greek spirit.[55]

A visit to Frankfurt in the winter of 1797, and a reunion there with Passavant, reawakened Kanne's religious sensibilities and began to alter his expectations for mythology. Passavant was a disciple of the Swiss mystic J.K. Lavater, who saw in magnetic trance conditions and physiognomy the presence of the divine in human life. Kanne joined his pastor in trying to experience God with the senses, praying under the open sky to draw down the heavens.[56] According to Dieter Schrey, this encounter with Lavaterianism directed Kanne to the presence of the divine in the world, while reinforcing his rejection of quotidian life as an impediment to higher experiences.[57] Already in the *Mythologie der Griechen* (1805), Kanne began correcting Heyne's neglect of religion by supplementing his historical approach to myth with religious paradigms.[58] Yet Heyne's indifference and likely Kanne's own incapacity for cordial relationships left him vainly aspiring to academic employment. Squandering a small inheritance, he succumbed to "a wild dashing through all sorts of disorderly misfortunes,"[59] barely surviving on the publication of satirical literature.

J.J. Wagner's adaptation of Schelling's identity philosophy offered Kanne a theoretical framework for conceiving of the divine presence in the world. The pair roomed together as students in Göttingen and forged a friendship that endured until Kanne's vitriol became unbearable in 1809. After his release from Austrian service, Kanne joined Wagner in Würzburg, where Schelling had procured for him a professorship in philosophy. Wagner had initially welcomed Schelling's ideas for overcoming Kantian dualism. Their immediate personal aversion to each other, however, quickly morphed into professional squabbling. After the publication of Schelling's *Philosophie und Religion* (1804), which derived the real from the absolute using the notion of descent, Wagner increasingly carved for himself an independent profile by polemicizing against Schelling's abstractions.

In his lectures on the *Philosophy of Art*, held in 1802–3, Schelling had positioned language at a crucial intersection between the real and the ideal, sanctifying historical tongues as vessels of God's creative powers. He proposed that human idioms originated in the "absolute idea of language," which was of divine origin. The "speaking word of God, the logos" represented in Schelling's view the "eternal and absolute act of self-affirmation … the divine act of creation."[60] In his *System der Idealphilosophie* (1804), Wagner concurred that the historical languages allowed humans to replicate God's act of creation. The "absolute in language" was, in his view, couched in national terms and articulated most clearly in religious doctrines. Wagner, moreover, imagined profound benefits arising from a "philosophical expert in language" who constructed a "natural history of language," which illuminated the changing relationship between the ideal and the real across history.[61]

Herder's notion of God's primal hieroglyph steered Wagner's speculations into a language-based project for identifying the "original schematic of cognition" in antiquity. In his *Ideen zu einer allgemeinen Mythologie der alten Welt* (1808) Wagner presumed religion to be the "germ" of the entire spiritual development of mankind and used language to trace its inception and growth. [62] Like Herder, Wagner concluded that primordial human understanding had been visual, cloaked in the language of symbolism and imagery. Writing objectified subjective impressions of the world, and its earliest form had been ideographic. Only cultures capable of "greater freedom of reflection and an energetic will" could further objectify linguistic impressions through letter writing.[63]

Language also took prominence, for Kanne, as the embodiment of original revelation. "Because the idea of the primeval world generally resides in language," Kanne explained, "and history is an idea, mythological and linguistic research will never part."[64] Within six months in 1805 he completed the sprawling *Erste Urkunden* (1808), incorporating Wagner's identity philosophy as its conceptual foundation.[65] Sanskrit, Kanne concluded, was best situated to reveal "holy history,"[66] and Indian myths harboured the earliest records of humanity. As Jean Paul noted, however, Kanne had yet to learn Sanskrit, and the actual linguistic labours of the *Erste Urkunden* actually centred on Greek and Hebrew. His work nevertheless exemplifies the "linguistification" of mythological thought that occurred around 1800.[67]

Etymology offered Kanne a tool for reducing the multiplicity of mythical traditions to shared original forms. He presumed the existence "in the original land" of "a philosophical edifice of words and language" created by the first god-man. The divine inspiration of all knowledge at the time ensured that the *Ursprache* was a "language of gods"[68] and the foundation for later historical tongues. Much of the *Erste Urkunden* is consumed with establishing lexical correspondences among languages with a liberal "generosity" that produced chaos.[69] Kanne argued that words could be related not just by sound or external referent but according to the "way ideas connect them."[70] As the earliest priestly languages devolved into common forms, their symbolism was subject to loose reinterpretation, so a shared symbol could mediate seemingly unrelated words.

After his appointment to the Realinstitut in Nuremberg in 1808 Kanne became increasingly invested in the mysticism of his old friend, Adolph Wagner (1774–1835), uncle to the future composer. Adolf Wagner had introduced Kanne to the works of Jacob Böhme while the two were students in Jena. Along with the natural historian G.H. Schubert, the pair met regularly in the theosophical library of the Nuremburg baker Matthias Burger. Kanne detected in Christian mysticism "a certain consonance with the idea of antiquity."[71] Böhme suspected that national tongues contained hidden symbolic truths derived from a divine language revealed at creation; subsequent mystics had aspired to direct communion with the divine by resurrecting the mysterious meanings of words and their embodiment in nature.[72] The miracle of the apostles speaking multiple tongues at the feast of Pentecost implied that Babel could be overcome through enthusiastic transport. The mystic Louis Claude de Saint-Martin, an important figure for Kanne, proposed in 1782, for example, that the holy spirit had enabled Christ's disciples to converse in the *Ursprache* itself; the theosophist Justinus Kerner argued that animal magnetism and sleep talking could restore the powers of the *Ursprache*.[73]

Arrival in Nuremburg likewise coincided for Kanne with a shift towards Schelling, in residence there and also intrigued by mysticism.

Schelling had sent Kanne a prepublication version of the *Freedom* essay ostensibly to see him react, but he welcomed the text as an "investigation of admirable depth."[74] "You cut it too short with Schelling," Kanne wrote to J.J. Wagner in August 1809.[75] Responding to Friedrich Schlegel's concern that pantheism was deterministic, the essay drew upon core doctrines of Jacob Böhme that postulated a cyclical self-generation of the divinity from an undifferentiated original moment containing both dark and light principles.[76] Kanne appreciated how Schelling explained the origins of evil in this text, linking it to human freedom. He broke with J.J. Wagner over his opposing claim in the *Theodicee* (1809) that sin and the fall were due to external circumstances.[77]

In the *Pantheum der aeltesten Naturphilosophie, die Religion aller Völker* (1811), Kanne applied Schelling's derivation of freedom and the fall to his own defence of "dualistic pantheism … the true philosophy."[78] Schlegel, in his view, had incorrectly charted an historical degeneration of religious doctrine from emanation to pantheism and failed to comprehend the historical and philosophical connections between pantheism and dualism.[79] Like Schelling, Kanne relied on the idea of opposing forces within the divine to carve a space for freedom and evil. Pantheism entailed, for Kanne, a perpetual contretemps between spirit and the flesh, "an idealism and realism that penetrate and animate each other reciprocally."[80] He avoided completely identifying God with nature by claiming that the material world only represented the absolute in degenerate form. Denying now that the first god-men inhabited paradise, Kanne asserted that original knowledge was compromised. Mythology in the *Pantheum* appeared to him as "a degradation – a condition of diminished spiritual life."[81] As a result, Kanne placed greater emphasis on the original, presumably monotheistic, source from which the surviving myths and languages had derived. This could only be recovered, in his view, by restoring the *Ursprache*.

While working on the *Pantheum* Kanne drafted the *Panglossium* manuscript, which in his words presented "a system of all languages … in which is proved that and how all languages emanated from one *Ursprache*."[82] Kanne had expected by distilling the "inner system of language" to better appreciate the "idea of the primeval world" as articulated in myth, religion, and the earliest philosophy.[83] Even by the standards of the time, however, his etymological acrobatics were unconvincing. According to Schelling, Kanne's "erudite combinations and analogies … are mostly bizarre, in the end prove nothing … the treasure of a beggar."[84] Kanne ultimately failed to reconstruct anything approaching the lexicon of a mother tongue. His vision of the *Ursprache* was merely the "phantasm of knowing all languages."[85]

The religious awakening that developed in German territories under Napoleon caught Kanne in 1814, after which he rejected his earlier speculation in favour of Mosaic revelation. He could no longer in good conscience use language to trace primordial revelation in mythology. For the later Kanne scholarship was a "dangerous precipice";[86] divine truth came not in the form of abstract ideas but as lived experience. In a fit of anti-intellectualism, Kanne "threw most of my papers right into the fire."[87] When he accepted a chair in Oriental Languages at the University of Erlangen in 1818 the senate worried about accepting "a scholar ... who might prefer prayer to teaching colloquia."[88] His religious turn so irked Jean Paul that he kept notebooks in the six years preceding Kanne's early death in 1823 preparing an "Anti-Kanne" that parodied his "*Über*-Christianity."[89]

Kanne was still convinced that national tongues derived from an *Ursprache* and that pagan traditions preserved elements of a "common original transmission" from the first revelation, however "dejected and maimed." In *Christus im alten Testament* (1818), he conceded that despite the "horror of magic" that had disrupted man's relationship to God: "the same word that bears witness to the advent of darkness, is also a witness to the earlier light of life."[90] However, Kanne admitted that his earlier treatises on the topic lacked the "guiding star of scriptural revelation" and therefore failed to recognize the primacy of Hebrew. All humanity may have shared the light of the first revelation, but its survival required additional intervention. "For truth to have been preserved in its purity," Kanne wrote, "nations would have had to continually receive new divine revelations."[91] Therein lay the value of Scripture. After his conversion Kanne honoured the language of the Old Testament as the "language of spirit."[92] The real value in researching pagan religions and traditions lay in the subsequent ability to recognize the unique revelations bestowed upon the Hebrews.

The Language of Revelation Nationalized: Friedrich Rückert

The nationalization of God's word, aligning revelation with peoples other than the ancient Hebrews, is more prominent with the liberal nationalist Friedrich Rückert, whose early intellectual development transpired in uneasy tension with Kanne's precedent. "Regarding my dissertation," Rückert wrote to Jean Paul in June 1811, "I beg you ... to generously forgive the unsuitably expansive linguistic wit, that you yourself felt compelled to remark upon in Kanne's work, with which, by the way, my own fragile little piece would not think of comparing itself in content or scope."[93] Born the son of a Protestant magistrate in

Lower Franconia, Rückert entered the University of Würzburg in 1805 intending to pursue a law degree, shortly after Bavaria relinquished the city during the reorganization of territory under Napoleon. He abandoned his father's career track to study classical philology and mythology with J.J. Wagner. Unlike Kanne, however, he maintained a national framework when transcending Babel, expecting German to assume the forms of a revitalized ideal language and thereby build a new kingdom on earth. Kanne himself feared the radical transformations that German unification might bring in 1815.[94]

The speculative tenor of Rückert's philology can largely be attributed to Wagner's influence, especially to his call for a philosophical natural history of language. Rückert acknowledged "my teacher Wagner"[95] in his poems from Rome, having studied Greek mythology and *Naturphilosophie* with him.[96] Specific evidence of his debts is visible in his adapting Wagner's tetrachic organizational principle to etymology.[97] However, more than Kanne, Rückert maintained a critical distance from Wagner, especially regarding his feud with Schelling. He ridiculed Wagner's desire to be among the "sovereigns ... he is no republican; he only wants to be the monarch and to tolerate no other near him." According to his son Heinrich, Rückert preferred the early Schelling as a "pioneer of the religion of humanity" and "sat at his feet as a student in Würzburg."[98]

Rückert's own defection from Greece dates to his attending Friedrich Creuzer's Heidelberg lectures in the winter semester of 1808–9.[99] According to his son, however, Rückert remained "free of all the fantastical confusion in which Creuzer and his followers lost themselves."[100] Liberal Protestants rejected Creuzer as politically dangerous and gravitating too sharply towards conservative Christian mysticism.[101] Rückert, however, shared a Neo-Platonist desire to reconcile Christianity with ancient pagan religion and philosophy. As he wrote to his former student Paul de Lagarde in 1860, the "highest goal of our oriental philology" is to prove that the "pure (deistic) kernel of Christianity was already present in the Upanishads."[102] Rückert's short epic "Bau der Welt" (1812) traces the afterlife of original revelation as it meanders through major historical cultures before taking true form among Hebrews and Christians. Rückert argued that each nation "cultivated" its own piece of the lost "art and wisdom" present in paradise.[103]

The defeat of Prussia in 1806 renewed among German Protestants the quandary of how to reconcile Christian universalism with nationalism, and Rückert more than Kanne developed the national dimensions of Wagner's association of language and religion. Rückert's programmatic *Philological-Philosophical Dissertation on the Idea of Philology* (1811) envisioned German becoming an "ideal" or "universal language" which expressed the character of the nation. Building on Wagner's expectations for absolute language, Rückert declared language was "the revelation of the divine in humanity."[104] It emerged "from the idea of absolute life"[105] in a divine act and allowed humans to perpetuate God's creation. Such speculation led the classicist Franz Passow to declare his dissertation "the product of a fool."[106] Written in elegant Latin, but barely passing its defence at the University of Jena, Rückert's dissertation proclaimed philology's lofty goal to be "knowledge of humanity through the word." This required reconstructing what he variously termed "the totality of language," "the idea of language itself," or "absolute language."[107] The philologist's task was to scrutinize the various national tongues for evidence of what each embodied of the "divine idea of humanity" and reassemble it in defiance of Babel.[108]

The benefits of philology lay for Rückert in the ability to reconstruct the original relationship between humanity and the divine. He concurred with Kanne that the unfolding of revelation lay at the core of human history and that language held the key to its interpretation. However, Rückert was not willing to elide national distinctions among mythological traditions to abstract a common idea of the divine, as Kanne had been.[109] For Rückert, the diversity of historical languages corresponded to significant distinctions in the religions of their speakers. Each nation expressed "the principal idea" of its inner life in language; this was necessarily "its relationship to the divine." Philologists, he wrote, must investigate "the myths and doctrines of individual nations and times through their languages."[110] In Rückert's view, religious differences could be traced back to linguistic variations among cultural communities. The universality of life could never be expressed through a fallen language; it was only possible in "the ideal language."[111]

Rückert's main criticism of Kanne, the only author referenced in the *Dissertation*, centred on his methods for reconstructing the totality of language. Kanne had, in his view, obscured the precise connections among languages from different times and regions and "thrust all languages back into boundless chaos." This destroyed the "original clarity of the divine idea" and condemned the human understanding to flit "in blind irreverence from one contradiction to another." Kanne failed to recognize that "fixed rays" emanated from the idea of God in quasi-mathematical figurations that resembled Wagner's tetrachic forms. Rückert proposed in its place to weave "a single system" out of the internal relationships of all words.[112] He preferred deduction over Kanne-style combinations as his etymological principle, deriving the multiplicity of languages from one fixed root, "Eh," the centre and origin of language.[113]

Rückert likewise rejected Kanne's notion that historical reconstruction could reproduce the ideal language. His method, as Wiener notes, was "totally unhistorical"[114] and broke with the presumption that the oldest extant language must be the most perfect. "The absolute life of the idea is in no language"; Rückert concluded, "the true language has not yet been created, but it must be created."[115] For this reason, Willer describes Rückert's ideal language as an *"absoluta effigies,"* characterized by its imitative and mimetic functions.[116] Kanne, for his part, dismissed Rückert's goal of "creating an ideal language out of German," accusing him of "toiling in vain; it only resides in all languages."[117] The limitations of idolizing one language, in his view, were equivalent to distilling the idea of the divine from a single religious cult.

The events of the Napoleonic occupation bound Rückert's language study to the politics of liberal nationalism. During Austria's brief war against Napoleon in 1809 Rückert rushed to the aid of Archduke Charles, turning against his native Bavaria, which had allied with the French to protect its elevation to a kingdom, but only managed to reach Dresden after Vienna surrendered.[118] Wagner himself had favoured northern languages, especially modern German, as capable of articulating "the ideal in the ideal," noting based on Kanne's early comparative study that German was an idealized extension of ancient Greek.[119] Rückert concurred that at the end of history, one *Volk* would appear that united the scattered parts of the original divine idea. Germans were "a universal people" and their mother tongue was "equally universal" because "it incorporated its own idea and all the other ideas of the remaining languages."[120] Rückert concluded, moreover, that translation was the best method for reassembling "the fragments of foreign languages" in German and thus rebuilding Babel.[121]

After a year of teaching, Rückert surrendered a lectureship in classical philology to write poetry while serving as an editor to Johann Friedrich Cotta's *Morgenblatt für gebildete Stände.* "Poetry is my only action," he mused in 1813 as volunteers flocked to the Wars of Liberation.[122] Rückert's reputation as a poet stems from a collection of thirty *Geharnischte Sonette* (1814) which reminded German speakers "Only one sole bond has endured/The language you otherwise scorn/Now you must love her as your last."[123] The Congress of Vienna silenced any lingering expectation that a German national state might emerge in 1815, and Rückert got caught in the web of the Restoration. In 1816, a request to compose poems for the Freemason Lodge in Coburg led to suspicions of his joining secret societies. The Württemberg minister of police cautioned Rückert's publisher that the poet must either leave the state or drop all political opposition. Karl-August Wangenheim, the future minister of culture under King Wilhelm I, intervened on Rückert's behalf.[124] Rückert, in turn, supported his campaign against local estates seeking to preserve their traditional privileges.

The opportunity to study non-European languages came in Vienna in 1818 on a return trip from Italy, where Rückert took tea with Christian Bunsen in Rome. For four months Rückert studied Farsi, and some Arabic and Turkish, with Joseph von Hammer while residing with Friedrich Schlegel, then imperial court secretary to Archduke Charles. His first translations appeared shortly thereafter, in 1819 an edition of Jalal al-Din Muhammad Rumi's ghazals and in 1821 the *Östliche Rosen* adapted from the ghazals of the mystic poet Hafiz. In 1827 Rückert learned Sanskrit well enough to read "Nal and Damayanti" from the *Mahabharata* within three months.[125] According to his son, Rückert only needed a six-to-eight-week period of immersion to become versed in a new language.[126] He mastered an astounding forty-four distinct tongues in his lifetime.[127] These efforts aimed to recreate the mutual understanding that existed among nations before Babel. "Resurrect from rubble creation's past," he entreated, "Solve the confusion of languages that caused construction to falter;/Raise for us the idea of the master's plan, build well!"[128] When at last the scattered fragments of humanity were rejoined "in the heart of Europe," he predicted, "A new paradise will be reclaimed."[129]

Kanne's death opened the chair for Oriental Languages in Erlangen, to which Friedrich Rückert succeeded in 1826 despite concerns about his lack of theological training.[130] He cultivated contact with Schelling here and even more so with Schubert, although with reservations.[131] Heinrich Rückert speculates that the interest his father developed in pantheism while working on the *Weisheit des Brahmanen* may have sustained their relationship despite Schelling's fading interest in *Naturphilosophie*.[132] Theologically Rückert sided in Erlangen with the historical-critical school of his close friend, the classical philologist and philosopher Joseph Kopp. Although "never completely satisfied by it," Rückert expected that "the mild rational course is destined for victory." Rückert's son Heinrich describes him as an "enlightened" Protestant who valued the "true religiosity of man" irrespective of its external forms.[133] Not surprisingly, Rückert grew increasingly disaffected by Schelling's pietism, confiding to his son: "Schelling has finally through mythology ... arrived at Christianity, which he now wields egregiously, senselessly as the newest gnostic."[134] This break occurred after their time together in Erlangen, however, as Schelling still strategized on how to bring Rückert to Munich after his own departure, and Rückert visited him there in 1836.[135]

Disaffected by the religious atmosphere of the by then heavily Pietist Erlangen, Rückert followed a call to Berlin in 1841.[136] The contract he negotiated with the Friedrich Wilhelm University only required Rückert to spend winter semesters in the Prussian capital. His self-imposed isolation reflects a deteriorating relationship to Schelling. Initially, Rückert regularly attended Schelling's Berlin lectures, "because the topic (revelation) he treated, so attracted me." Halfway through the semester, however, he stopped attending, frustrated by Schelling's speculative philosophical system.[137] Later he reported that "Schelling takes it badly that we don't often visit."[138] Rückert partly blamed the philosopher for luring away "all public interest"[139] in his own courses. By 1843 Rückert wrote to his wife Luise that he could no longer face visiting the family: "We have nothing in common but empty civility."[140] Rückert generally ignored the "outcries of the sundry religious movements" in Berlin and dismissed Schelling in a letter to his son as an "*Über*-Christian."[141]

A day before revolution struck Berlin in March 1848, Rückert retreated to his Bavarian estate and negotiated a permanent release from his teaching responsibilities. Few students had subscribed to Rückert's grand project due in part to increasing scholarly specialization among philologists. Never having engaged intellectual and social life in the Prussian capital, he "happily" exchanged his "unbearable post" for the "old beloved solitude" of the province.[142] Political resignation and Luise's death marred Rückert's last years. After Friedrich Wilhelm IV rejected German unification under a liberal constitution in 1849, the "failed German empire" forced Rückert further into the "empire of poetry."[143] "Rückert's life neared its end under great sorrow and affliction," Paul de Lagarde concluded, "he set the unreachable goals of detecting language in many languages and humanity in many peoples: for this reason he met none of them."[144]

The Symbolism of God's Word: Joseph Görres

The presumption that revelation took form as the word did not necessarily privilege philology in comparative mythological research during the Romantic period. While likewise responding to the hieroglyph Herder idealized in the *Älteste Urkunde*, Joseph Görres, a Catholic, and his colleague Friedrich Creuzer emphasized its symbolic qualities as a pictorial image, rather than its foundational status as primordial language. Görres never trained as a philologist, and Creuzer flouted the norms of the discipline; his preference for mystical symbols over textual analysis radicalized the acerbic campaign classical scholars waged against him.[145] In his *Mythengeschichte der asiatischen Welt* (1810) and immediately preceding texts Görres retained the notion that creation took form as the word of God. But the influence of Schelling's *Naturphilosophie*, and the notion that hieroglyphs were ideographic, not phonetic, meant that etymology and comparative language studies factored only tangentially as methods for reconstructing revelation. The *Ursprache*, in his view, consisted of signs and symbols whose forms referenced a lost God, but these had only a weak connection to the historical languages of human communities.

Raised in the Rhineland, Görres initially welcomed the French Revolution as a manifestation of Kantian political philosophy but retreated from Jacobian political activism after the rise of Napoleon. Disillusion with enlightened republicanism following a 1799 trip to Paris steered Görres, like many of his generation, towards religion, cultural nationalism, and the distant past. Close friendship with Clemens Brentano brought Görres under the influence of the Jena Romantics, and his interest in mythology congealed under the spell of Schelling's *Naturphilosophie* and identity philosophy.[146] A neo-Platonic conception of the world emerging from a divine *Urgrund* and descending as spirit into material existence meant that Görres bestowed greater ontological significance on the finite realm than the early Schelling, however. As an emanation of God, nature, for Görres, was not merely an imperfect stage within a dialectical process that restored the absolute, nor did the absolute, in his view, fully embody the divine.[147]

Glauben und Wissen (1805), written while Görres taught science at a Koblenz gymnasium, proposed that myth transmitted memories of creation, which he imagined as an act of divine self-consciousness. "Out of boundless, inexpressible exuberance the divinity emerges into being," he narrated, "out of an unfathomable resolution of being it proceeds in glorious splendor, itself revealing the power of its accomplishments."[148] The divine principle, in his view, existed prior to and transcended the identity of the real and ideal. Reason and speculation were therefore insufficient for comprehending the absolute.[149] Görres depicted the act of creation as a nearly unintelligible linguistic performance, whose signs and symbols myth struggled to interpret. "The infinite articulated itself in a few letters," he explained. The meaning contained in the "mysterious words" was impenetrable, Görres continued, "and difficult to decipher the dark language spoken by the gods."[150] Like Herder, he believed the early human race was confronted with "the silent hieroglyphs of life, the language of images in which nature conversed."[151] Religion originated as people learned to interpret "the broken sounds of the elements"[152] as secrets of the gods. Commentators have seen aspects of Görres's later mysticism in his fear that the "hieroglyph of creation" was an "enigma," "eternally unfathomable,"[153] approachable only through longing and desire.[154]

In his *Aphorismen über die Kunst* (1802) Görres had drawn qualitative distinctions between the language of images (*Bildersprache*) and the language of words (*Wörtersprache*), and myth fit developmentally into a stage when humanity navigated the world with symbols, rather than discursive language. Symbolic representation, according to Görres, was most appropriate for depicting appearances in external nature. Egyptian hieroglyphs were designed, he figured, to capture "myths of nature" and therefore constituted a "graphic physics of cosmology."[155] The greater flexibility provided by conceptual language, which had grammar, rhythm, and structure, by contrast, was adequate to spirit and the rhetorical arts. Görres held that the language of images originated in the "empire of the cold, silent, dead hieroglyph, the symbol," but progressed gradually into the "warm, conversant, lively representation … of visual arts,"[156] a transition that echoes the narrative of mythology becoming spiritual and taking ideal form in ancient Greece. This dating of writing systems corresponded to a genealogy that held Chinese and Egyptian to be the oldest languages and conflicted to a certain degree with later chronologies that held Sanskrit most proximate to revelation.

In 1806 a lectureship brought Görres to Heidelberg where he collaborated closely with Creuzer and favoured a national paradigm in the interpretation of myth, tracing the German cultural inheritance from its presumed origins in India, Persia, Egypt, and Greece to northern Europe.[157] All religion, he concluded in "Wachstum der Histoire" (1807) began as pantheistic *Naturreligion* grounded in the elements and heavenly bodies, which transmitted God's word symbolically. "The elements speak to man in fluent tones," Görres now noted. Humankind found itself in a dreamlike state, in a "miraculous night,"[158] but nature, he now had greater confidence, "speaks the secretive words clearly, certainly, and intelligible to all."[159] At the moment of mythology's inception, however, humankind still did not think discursively. "Man emerged in all his being and essence as a grand symbol of nature," Görres wrote in 1807, "he could only think in symbols."[160] The transition from hieroglyphic to letter writing occurred once religion entered a second phase characterized by a concern for the living forms of nature and eventually an anthropomorphic conception of the gods. This lifted humanity out of blind submission to nature and eased the transition to a religion of spirituality.

Creuzer shared Görres's conviction that the language of creation and early thought was symbolic, not discursive.[161] "Especially dominant in antiquity, the plasticity and figuration of writing and speech," he wrote in the *Symbolik und Mythologie der alten Völker* (1810), is "not to be regarded as arbitrary and metaphorical, but as a means of expression that is necessary in and for itself."[162] His presumption of original monotheism, however, put a far more positive spin on the language of symbolic forms. Creuzer refused to adapt theories about writing originating in "primitive ventures"[163] to religious symbols. Symbolization he asserted, "stamps form on our thought, a necessity that even the most abstract and sober spirit cannot escape." Image and word were not successive developments, but "wed together"[164] for Creuzer such that the earliest forms of thought and belief, whether expressed verbally or in images, were necessarily pictorial and sensualist. The first myths were no more than "articulated symbols"[165] and thus spatial rather than historical. Even before protecting esoteric wisdom became necessary, priests favoured symbols given their supposed original bond with a higher world; human forms of representation, including language, by contrast, appeared to him arbitrary.[166]

The *Ursprache* Görres detailed in the *Mythengeschichte* differed substantially from that which Kanne hoped to reconstruct. (While Görres acknowledged "universal agreement in the results" of both their works, he noted the "differences in our approaches"[167] and later confessed to the Grimm brothers that he couldn't agree with Kanne on all points.[168]) When the divine emerged from the timeless "depths of eternity,"[169] according to Görres, it did so as a materially articulated word that constituted man and creation, the "hieroglyphs of earlier revelation."[170] The language of the first humans was accordingly a *Natursprache* bound to the rigid laws of mechanics. Its elements derived from the material world and, as held true for physical compounds, basic laws of chemistry, crystallization, and aggregation, governed the thought processes possible in this language. "Atomic conglomerates arise, in which ... the sounds and forms of nature come together without higher abstraction and organic interaction,"[171] Görres explained, producing pictorial fragments that conjoined without true composition. Chinese characters and Egyptian hieroglyphs, as well as originally monosyllabic languages, were the most ancient vestiges of the original *Natursprache*, in his view. Pantheism dominated during this early period, and humankind lived together as an *Urvolk* in a theocratic state.

A shift in language followed the onset of true world history, according to Görres, inaugurating a second period of creation characterized by the "self-revelation" of "the idea of life based on a higher universal self-understanding."[172] Sanskrit and Zend marked, for Görres, the old-est languages of this period, to which he attributed, like Schlegel, the qualities of "organic construction" and "grand grammatical combina-tions." "Overcoming the inertia of atoms," he proposed, they "weave themselves together in complex passages."[173] The dispersion of mythol-ogy from the original homeland, however, did not follow the path of linguistic descent. Görres proposed that three types of myth branched out from Central Asia and organized his survey of religious cultures geographically, moving west from China and Mongolia, through India, Iran, and Asia Minor to northern Europe.[174] Like Creuzer, Görres pre-sumed that the first and purest expression of monotheism could be found in India, although he acknowledged its presence in China. The Hebrews west of the Euphrates, including Abraham, had originally worshipped Brahma, he concluded; aspects of Moses's faith resembled Indian doctrine, and like the Indians, according to Görres, the Hebrews had not been able to preserve pure monotheism, which Christianity reawakened.[175]

The presumption that original revelation transpired as a speech act set the conceptual framework for how Görres interpreted the forma-tion of myth. The hieroglyph emblazoned on creation at the start of time entered history as a symbol, in his view, not as discursive lan-guage. Philology thus had little methodological significance in Görres's model for retrieving God's word. His inability to engage Asian sources or ground his assertions in textual evidence proved a liability in the work's reception. Unlike Creuzer, Görres also failed to substantially analyse actual mythological symbols in the *Mythengeschichte*.[176] His standing in Heidelberg was precarious long before its publication, and the same liberal Protestants, including J.H. Voß, who attacked Creu-zer and his speculative, orientalizing project, prevented Görres from obtaining a permanent professorship there. He returned to Koblenz, briefly studying Persian, before retooling himself in Munich as a con-servative Catholic publicist.

Strong reactions against Creuzer's *Symbolik* rapidly plunged the sweeping comparative mythology of Görres and Kanne into disrepute. However, efforts to trace the historical legacy of the divine *Ursprache* in surviving national tongues had by then already contributed to ground-ing revelation more solidly in the world of experience. The conceptual link Romantic mythologists identified between language and the origin of religion was likewise enduring. For Friedrich Max Müller mythol-ogy was a disease of language, the grammatical peculiarities of Indo-European languages encouraging a proliferation of divine beings that produced polytheism. Ernst Renan attributed belief in one God to the effects of the supposedly immobile roots of Semitic verbs. Language's divine inheritance was less significant in this case, however, than its inner structure. Speculation on the national tongues most proximate to the divine *Ursprache* continued through mid-century, but more compelling to language scholars were by then the effects of grammatical peculiarities on the thought processes of speakers, a reflection of the direction taken by comparative-historical linguistics after Franz Bopp.

Chapter Four

Revelation in Nature from Physicotheology to G.H. Schubert

"We have an older revelation than any written one – nature," Schelling wrote concluding his *Philosophical Investigations into the Essence of Human Freedom* (1809). "If the understanding of this unwritten revelation were made manifest," he continued, "the only true system of religion and science would appear ... in the full brilliance of truth."[1] Schelling's confidence in nature as a viable site of revelation is surprising given the strong philosophical objections that had been raised since Kant's first critique against the argument from design, otherwise known as the physicotheological proof for God's existence, which built from evidence in the natural world to the idea of an intelligent creator. The book of nature had since the Renaissance offered an alternative realm for acquiring divine truth, a sphere of relative freedom shielded from the institutionalized authority that the church and universities wielded over philological practices.[2] In Spinoza's wake, however, many heterodox strategies for explaining higher purpose and intentionality in nature risked accusations of pantheism or atheism for equating God with the material world and denying a transcendent creator. The most emphatic insistence on the theological significance of natural history actually came from German opponents of revelation, deists such as the notorious Hermann Samuel Reimarus, who argued reason could extrapolate full knowledge of God from the environment. Schelling's assertion that nature bore more authentic traces of revelation than ancient languages represents a postcritical repristinization of nature, one welcomed by the natural historian Gotthilf Heinrich Schubert and other Romantic scholars but distinct from eighteenth-century physicotheology.

This chapter argues that shifting German perceptions of God's revelation in nature undermined propositional revelation in the late eighteenth century and endowed the material world with unprecedented agency in fulfilling God's plan for humanity. The doctrine of the two books, proclaiming parity between God's works and his word, ensured that debates over revelation extended into the realm of natural history, a broad swath of inquiry that addressed issues similar to those found in the biblical creation stories. The descriptive, taxonomic conventions of early modern natural history had yielded by the late eighteenth century to strongly historical lines of inquiry concerning generation, development, causation, and origin.[3] Descartes's separation of earth history and cosmic history justified limiting the applicability of biblical narrative to terrestrial events and raised the prospect of an infinite, eternal, and possibly uncreated universe.[4] But explaining teleology in the natural world without recourse to theology and an intelligent creator remained a pressing problem well into the nineteenth century.[5] Mechanical explanations for change grounded in Newtonian principles failed to adequately account for the emergence of lifeforms, for example, or the beauty of the natural world. The search for a self-sufficient principle of generation and change within nature, in turn, impugned God's transcendence.

The contours of German consideration of nature as a medium of revelation differ from the well-known Genesis-and-geology debates, which were a "British preoccupation" with only the "rare German contribution."[6] The invisibility of German scholars in the empirically driven conflict may stem from a general disregard elsewhere for the speculative tendencies of *Naturphilosophie*, a tradition of German idealist reflection on nature. The potent philological methods of German higher criticism initially put far greater pressure on the historical reliability of Genesis than the natural sciences, displacing the most heated debates over Scripture onto the philosophical faculties.[7] The anthropological turn in early nineteenth-century Protestantism also rendered science less relevant to theologians; the notion that religion should invoke feelings implied that religious claims could not be adjudicated using natural scientific knowledge.[8] For these reasons, what Frederick Gregory terms "de-natured theology" emerged earlier in Germany than in Britain, where theologians were more reluctant to accept religion and science as separate spheres.[9] Protestant German theologians largely failed to develop a strong tradition of natural theology.[10] By contrast, until their dissolution the Jesuits constituted what Marcus Hellyer terms "an order of natural philosophers" with an Aristotelian curriculum devoted to physical questions and open to experimental philosophy and Newtonian mechanics.[11] But Catholic approaches to nature posed fewer challenges to propositional revelation and therefore factor less prominently in this chapter.

The first half of the chapter charts the erosion of the physicotheological proof, which in accordance with propositional revelation emphasized a transcendent God whose qualities could be reliably known through nature. Intelligent design presumed observers could arrive at a first cause and deduce God's attributes and being from the works of creation. Yet Kant's critical turn, *Naturphilosophie*, and critical-historical exegesis eroded the epistemological certainty with which natural historians derived religious truths from the material world. Waning confidence in the viability of revelation in nature opened a natural historical equivalent to Lessing ditch's, compounding the crisis revelation faced in the late Enlightenment by weakening nature's connections to the transcendent realm. A postcritical repristinization of nature as a site of revelation followed, however, from competing presumptions that the material world symbolically embodied God's word and facilitated God's self-revelation through history. Early nineteenth-century German scholars rehabilitated the idea of revelation in nature by judiciously granting greater self-sufficiency to vitalist forces within the natural world itself, reinforcing the assumption, also visible in the study of language, for example, that revelation was deeply rooted in the historical world of experience.

The second half of the chapter documents through Schubert's engagement with the creation story a postcritical restoration of revelation's viability in nature that sought to compensate for the epistemological liabilities of the physicotheological proof. Before his conversion in late 1811 to conservative, Christ-centred biblical Christianity, Schubert interpreted God's revelation in nature as a material embodiment of God's living word. His view of nature represents a significant form in which revelation returned to the material world, secondary only to the later Schelling's claim that natural history reflected the historical self-disclosure of God's being. By the 1820s Schubert had restyled much of his speculation on the forces animating nature to accommodate Lutheran orthodoxy. This turn is not surprising given Schubert's embrace of conservative, patriarchal politics during the revolutionary years and Napoleonic occupation. Under the Restoration he found denying a personal God unsustainable, especially after the militantly nationalist theology student Karl Sand murdered the conservative playwright August von Kotzebue in 1819, precipitating the repressive Carlsbad Decrees.

Natural Theology and the Collapse of Intelligent Design

The long shadow Baruch Spinoza cast over the German Enlightenment, sketched in Chapter 1, resulted in a more persistent adherence to intelligent design in the German states than in France where vitalist materialism and in England where Newtonian mechanics more readily edged revelation out of nature. Whether Spinoza's equation of *deus sive natura* or his claim in the posthumous *Ethics* (1677) that "whatever is, is in God," there being but one necessarily existing infinite substance (nature), actually amounted to pantheism or atheism has been debated. Apologists have proposed that Spinoza did not identify God with all of nature but with 'naturing nature' (*natura naturans*) or absolute subject – the infinite, invisible, active dimensions of nature. By this account, substance – nature seen as a conditioned object or *natura naturata* – is the visible effect of God's powers, distinct and causally dependent on God as a free cause. Another view holds that Spinoza radically naturalized God to the extent of denial, equating him with the material world and denying his personhood, transcendence, and free will to curb the superstitions that resulted from traditional belief.[12] Regardless, because it evoked a transcendent creator, the argument from design lessened the danger of attributing self-sufficiency to the laws of nature and held a crucial line on naturalism and freethinking.

By the early eighteenth century Spinoza's positioning of the divine in the material world had drawn almost universal condemnation, if not for outright atheism then for degrading God and Christian doctrines such as the separation of body and soul. Christian Wolff, who features in Chapter 1, decried the fatalism and determinism inherent in the positing of a single, all-encompassing substance or spirit. Without free will, there could be no moral responsibility; if nature blindly followed geometrically necessary laws, creation lost the capacity for goodness and lacked a higher purpose or meaning.[13] Until his revival in the 1780s, Spinoza remained the preserve of iconoclasts and the radically heterodox, and German theologians and philosophers welcomed the physicotheological proof. Its ready reconciliation of reason and revelation, at least until Kant's critical turn, appealed to the moderate Enlightenment. Natural historians likewise welcomed the argument from design as a means to align Newtonian accounts of transformation in the natural world with the stewardship of a personal creator.

Despite his many intellectual debts to Spinoza, G.W. Leibniz, for example, gradually ceased evoking Spinoza's understanding of substance when criticizing Cartesian dualism, cognizant that his own doctrine of pre-established harmony risked accusations of determinism.[14] As evidenced by his speculative history of the earth, *Protogaea* (1749), Leibniz believed the principle of sufficient reason required the physical world to be explained mechanistically through the application of general laws. Yet he also insisted on final causality and developed a variant of the physicotheological proof. "It is in reflecting upon the works," Leibniz wrote in 1686, "that we are able to discover the one who wrought."[15]

The cosmological is one of three proofs for God that Leibniz presented in the *Monadology* (1720). The text argues that monads, or simple substances, owe their existence to a supernatural origin. Leibniz likewise held that the perfect agreement found among all single substances in the universe betrayed a common cause and synchronism in God. Leibniz concluded that "created things owe their perfection to the influence of God," but the necessary presence of original imperfection meant that creatures were also "distinguished from God."[16] Some commentators have detected overtones of pantheism in the possibility that Leibniz maintained the ontological dependence of creatures on God. But God's serving as the principle behind things did not necessarily imply that he formed part of them.[17]

Natural theology gained heightened visibility among both Protestants and Catholics during the Enlightenment when the book of nature offered reformers a welcome corrective and supplement to scripture. Christian Wolff affirmed that as the "science of what was possible through God,"[18] natural theology, grounded in reason, was a necessary prelude and complement to revelation, providing evidence of God's existence and his attributes. Reflection on creation and the material world was the third pillar of natural theology, for Wolff, in addition to the ontology of divine existence and the psychology of the soul. In his *Vernünfftige Gedancken von den Absichten der natürlichen Dinge* (1723) he argued that God designed nature to be a "mirror of his perfections" so that humanity recognized him as a free being of supreme wisdom, benevolence, and power. Honed by reason and experience, "earth-description" was, Wolff argued, a "ladder on which we can ascend to God" and thereby arrive at the final cause behind nature's causal-mechanical laws.[19]

Significantly, the physicotheological proof depended on a tenuous teleological progression from empirical observation of contingent existence to metaphysical certainties. Wolff introduced the term teleology into philosophy to describe the science of ascending from the laws of physics to a final cause.[20] As a form of "experimental theology,"[21] Wolff wrote in 1728, "teleology" showed "how God is known from natural things."[22] The Halle philosopher Alexander Baumgarten, a disciple of Wolff and Leibniz, similarly treated "the science of divine ends in creatures" as "teleology." His *Metaphysica* (1739) classified cosmology and natural theology as subsets of metaphysics, raising for Kant the question of how a science of knowledge could reliably build on experience.[23] The viability of ascending to a transcendent realm based on revelation in nature soon proved as uncertain as the knowledge derived from historical revelation in the world of human experience.

The physicotheological proof featured prominently in the natural historical writings of the pre-critical Kant. Like Leibniz, Kant in his *Universal Natural History and Theory of the Heavens* (1755) offered a mechanistic explanation for the origin of the universe, proposing compelling theories of the Milky Way and the formation of nebulae. Universal forces of attraction and repulsion satisfactorily accounted, in his view, for the emergence of celestial bodies and their motion. Kant refused to acknowledge the immediate hand of a supreme being in his cosmology, denying that God, for example, directly set the planets in motion. Rather, in his view, gravity condensed gaseous clouds of primordial matter into masses, which, given the uneven density of substances across the universe, orbited around the heavier centres. The independent ability of nature to raise itself to perfection was, in his view, the strongest testament to a wise author. "There is a God precisely," he wrote, "because nature can proceed even in chaos in no other way than regularly and orderly."[24]

In *The One Possible Basis for a Demonstration of the Existence of God* (1763), a text which foreshadows the first critique, Kant reaffirmed the utility of a modified cosmological proof despite expressing preference for the certainty of logic over the a posteriori method of "ascending to knowledge of God through means of natural science."[25] Inverting Descartes's ontological argument, the first section of the text argues that the concept of a perfect being was not sufficient to establish his actual existence. For Kant, God was more effectively conceived as the absolutely necessary being whose existence provided the very ground for the possibility of anything actual, including conceptual thought.[26] The longer second section applies this observation to refine the process by which experience and the senses built from empirical things to knowledge of a wise creator. Although "incapable of mathematical precision and certainty," the cosmological proof, in his view, had the "preference of general utility,"[27] inspiring morality and elevated sentiments in humanity.

The weakness of standard cosmological proofs, Kant cautioned, was the inability to establish an absolutely necessary cause behind creation, to penetrate beyond an existing harmonious order to a moment of origin. God could convincingly be regarded as "the master craftsman but not the creator of the world," he wrote, "one who has ordered and formed matter to be sure, but has not produced and created it."[28] Empirical evidence of nature's perfection was in itself insufficient to ascend to a time before existence. Harmonious adaptation could have resulted from the "mechanical necessity of universal laws,"[29] Kant cautioned, and reflect "absolutely natural cosmic events."[30] Only the addition of the ontological proof could establish that the very possibility of matter's existence depended on an ultimate ground. The harmonious unity that marked the contingent arrangement of things in the world represented the realization or actualization of a set of possibilities, according to Kant, that could only originate in a primordial necessary being. He concluded *The One Possible Basis* with a tribute to the "important knowledge of God and his properties such as Reimarus provides in his book on natural religion."[31] This reference to a deist later vilified for excessive naturalism, however, recalls the threat natural religion could also pose to revelation.

The physicotheological proof had the potential to undermine the necessity of special revelations after creation, an uncertainty compounded by the introduction of French vital materialism to the German states and the accompanying suspicion that autonomous forces, not God's intentions, lay behind the apparent purposiveness of nature. In the years around mid-century French naturalists, including Pierre Louis de Maupertuis and the Comte de Buffon, severely curtailed the applicability of the machine paradigm to the life sciences. Buffon's *Histoire naturelle* (1749–1804) imposed a genealogical-causal imperative on what had been classificatory practices, while extricating natural history from physicotheology.[32] His concern for the dynamic transformation of living forms and his insistence on their material continuity opened speculation on whether nature possessed its own internal principles of self-organization. The editor of Buffon's German translation, the physiologist Albrecht von Haller, insisted on intelligent design, divine providence, and the necessity of a directive force outside of nature.[33] Through the influence of Maupertuis at the Prussian Academy of Sciences, however, French vital materialism slowly eroded the sufficiency of mechanistic explanatory schemes in the German states where, in addition to Spinozism and Epicureanism, the prospect of invisible forces steering the transformation of nature also evoked the equally unsettling spectre of hermeticism, neo-Platonism, and the occult.[34]

Unwilling to rely on a divine creator, German scientists sought alternative explanations for biological generation, emergence, and reproduction, as well as for geological change and cosmological history.[35] Georg Ernst Stahl at the Halle medical faculty theorized that an external force animated organisms; matter, in his view, was inert until set in motion, a supposition compatible with Pietist notions of divine spirit penetrating the material world. But the concept of a soul was not convincing for all lifeforms.[36] Chemical or physical reductionists sought to explain physiological processes, including the inception of life, with reference to galvanism, magnetism, or the effects of oxygen. *Lebenskraft* theorists proposed various irreducible forces within nature capable of steering development, including desire, instinct, *Bildungstrieb*, or in the case of the influential Scottish physician John Brown, 'exciting powers.' All effectively dispensed with theological explanations for teleological transformation.

The threat vitalism posed to natural religion explains the strong reaction Reimarus, whose most radical claims appear in Chapter 1, had to the proliferation of materialism.[37] His *Abhandlungen von den vornehmsten Wahrheiten der natürlichen Religion* (1755) sharply distinguished natural religion from French materialism, which, in his view, resigned the world either to self-sufficient necessity or random generation. The "blind motive power of nature"[38] was incapable, Reimarus insisted, of spontaneously generating life out of matter. Chance was equally unlikely to have created an ordered, harmonious universe, as a random association of letters could have produced Vergil's *Aeneid*. The physical world resembled, for Reimarus, "a grand machine"[39] subject to mechanical laws that originated with an autonomous, intelligent being. He faulted what he termed "our newer pantheists" for presuming that "even matter ... could live, perceive, and think"[40] and for conflating God with the world. One of the most advanced animal theorists of his time, Reimarus later developed a theory of innate physiological drives to reinforce his claim in this text that animal behaviour was too well adapted to habitat not to derive from an intelligent creator.[41]

Kant's first critique more severely compromised the argument from design, however, by disrupting how it reconciled reason and revelation. Aiming to rein in the dogmatic metaphysics of Wolff and Baumgarten, *The Critique of Pure Reason* (1781) denied theoretical reason any capacity to acquire knowledge of God. Transcendental theology "stretches its wings in vain," Kant asserted, in "attempting to soar above the world of sense by the mere power of speculation."[42] He discredited the three main rationalist proofs for the existence of God as illusions that failed at making the "tremendous leap" between experience and pure thought. Kant repeated his earlier objections to the ontological proof: it confused a logical with a real predicate when deriving the existence of an *ens realissimum*. But the supposition that God existed as the necessary ground of all possibility was no longer convincing to him as the idea of an absolutely necessary being was itself a concept of pure reason and existence could not be derived from it. The cosmological proof – distinct, for Kant, from the physicotheological in building upon indeterminate existence – unjustifiably evoked the principle of causality to transcend the sensible world. "To advance to absolute totality by the empirical road is utterly impossible," Kant concluded. The "wide abyss" separating the "solid ground of nature and experience"[43] and pure reason was unsurmountable. Only by remaining within the limits of sensibility could practical reason establish the necessary existence of God, he proposed, building from moral laws to the condition of their possibility.

The physicotheological proof survived Kant's critical turn only in severely weakened form, narrowly resuscitated in the *Critique of Judgment* (1790) in the context of his declaring nature "purposive for our cognitive faculty."[44] The purposiveness of nature was a transcendent principle of judgment, Kant conceded, meaning that while nature's purposiveness was not assertable as an objective fact, it was a regulative, a priori principle for making experience intelligible. The mind, in his view, inherently relied on teleology when interpreting organisms and nature as a totality. On these grounds, Kant granted the idea of intelligent design a heuristic role in scientific inquiry, deviating from Hume who, while inspiring Kant's critique of physicotheology, ascribed belief in a divine author to the product of imagination.[45] The ends of nature, in Kant's view, could not be thought without the idea of intentional causality, even if a higher being was not objectively verifiable. The idea of another Newton who clarified "even the genesis of but a blade of grass from natural laws that no design had ordered" was "absurd," in his view.[46] But practical reason could generate no knowledge of the "original source"[47] of organisms. On the question of whether a divine being designed the world, Kant wrote, "we can pass no objective judgement whatever, whether it be affirmative or negative,"[48] even if teleological reflection made it impossible to imagine any other source for natural ends than an intelligent author.

For these reasons, Kant concluded the physicotheological proof "falls short"[49] as a basis for theology. By encouraging reflection on the idea of a supreme being, however, it did make credible a moral teleology grounded in practical reason. Kant still ascribed a final end to creation in the *Critique of Judgement* and regarded nature as the product of design, but from the perspective of the moral law.[50] It, rather than the ontological proof, completed the "defective representation"[51] of the original grounds of nature in its physical ends. "The physicoteleological argument cannot in fact do anything more than direct reason in its judging of the source of nature," Kant wrote, "and draw our attention to a cause … which through the character of our cognitive faculty we must conceive as intelligent – and in this way make us more susceptible to the influence of the moral proof."[52] As the author of the world, God set a final end for creation that conformed to the moral law. The beauty observed in nature likewise led to the idea of God as the pleasure it inspired emulated moral feelings of gratitude.[53]

By the 1790s the collapse of the physicotheological proof undercut the epistemological rewards reaped by regarding nature as a site of revelation, such that outside of orthodox circles natural history appeared incapable of providing reliable knowledge of God or his attributes. Contemplating nature could, according to Kant, reinforce belief in the moral law. But the argument from morality relied on contemplating *human* nature and realizing that one's inner sense of duty was a divine command. When placed within the bounds of practical reason, revelation awakened feelings of moral obligation in communities not yet capable of rational religion. The very possibility of its existence derived from the failure of nature on its own to inspire adherence to the moral law. Even if the idea of purposive nature was a principle of reflective judgment, Kant confined to the realm of regulative, not constitutive reason, any attempt to stipulate a final cause or intelligent creator outside the bounds of the moral argument.

Naturphilosophie without Revelation

Naturphilosophie eliminated the last vestiges of intelligent design in Kant, inaugurating what Schelling dubbed a "Spinozism of physics"[54] intended to bridge the divide between experience and pure thought, all while rejecting the limited role granted revelation under the auspices of practical reason. In so doing, it fully unravelled the propositional value of revelation in nature. Schelling had declared himself a Spinozist in 1795 while breaking with theological orthodoxy at the Tübingen *Stift*, along with G.W.F. Hegel and Friedrich Hölderlin. While agreeing with Kant that the origin of matter could not be explained mechanistically, he refused in the *Ideas for a Philosophy of Nature* (1797) to locate the grounds for purposive nature in a transcendent God. All previous systems, he feared, wrongly "take refuge in the creative power of a divinity, from which the actual things together with their ideas proceeded and sprang forth."[55] Allowing purposiveness to enter nature from an external source destroyed, in Schelling's view, the very organic quality of nature that Kant's reflective principle of judgment sought to understand. "This purposiveness is something which could not be imparted to [the things of nature] at all from without," he wrote, "they are purposive originally through themselves."[56] *Naturphilosophie* did not conceive of nature as a site of revelation until after 1800 when Schelling no longer viewed revelation in epistemological terms.

Injecting J.G. Fichte's idealist conception of subjectivity into Spinoza, Schelling conceived of nature as a living organism fundamentally aligned with the rational capacities of the mind.[57] In the textbook designed for his course on *Naturphilosophie* in Jena, he thus depicted nature as pure, autonomous productivity, animated by an interplay of opposing forces. As unconditioned being, the "highest constructing activity,"[58] nature was not the product of a higher being, nor was its free development subject to mechanical laws. "Nature suffices for itself," Schelling wrote, and must "be explained from the active and motive principles which lie in it."[59] The "unconscious productivity" of nature created, in his view, regular forms and actions that embodied the absolute and made it visible.[60] Magnetism, electricity, and chemical processes were, for Schelling, examples of the "powers"[61] permeating nature. The forces shared regular and analogous structures enabling nature to be apprehended as an "organic whole."[62] Different aspects of the universe, from the heavens to the earth and its minerals, plants, and animals to the cultural history of its inhabitants, expressed a unified underlying plan.

Similarly to Kant, Schelling believed that the human mind immediately recognized purposiveness in nature. Kant, however, failed in Schelling's view to explain how an awareness of its teleological development came to shape human cognition. The possibility of such knowledge lay, for Schelling, in the essential and reciprocal connection that existed between the knower and the object of thought. Specifically, nature, in his view, expressed and realized the laws of the mind; its living activity consisted in an absolute act of cognition. "Nature should be Mind made visible, Mind the invisible Nature,"[63] Schelling wrote, "eternal nature" was "just Mind born into objectivity."[64] This confidence in unmediated, pre-reflective experience reflects, Bruce Matthews argues, a Pietist epistemology rooted in the immanent presence of the divine as it was revealed in nature.[65] The identity Schelling drew between mind and nature derived from absolute reason at this point, however, not from a transcendent God's revelation.

Following the French Revolution, Schelling had rejected the traditional authority of biblical revelation and its implications for political authority. In "Ueber Offenbarung und Volksunterricht" (1798) he thus argued that the Kantian retention of revelation to reinforce the moral law was unjustified. Published in Fichte's *Philosophisches Journal* shortly after Schelling joined him in Jena as an unpaid lecturer, the essay endorsed co-editor F.I. Niethammer's indictment of revelation's resurgence as a postulate of practical reason.[66] Kantians, in Schelling's view, preserved as "contraband smuggled in by the back door"[67] the very same concept of revelation declared illusory by the critique of pure reason. Their retention of the term solidified its "reality" as if revelation were a "natural object."[68] "Once proven that the conditions for the construction of a concept are false or impossible, it must vanish from the system of concepts," Schelling declared, "the term revelation can no longer assert its scientific dignity."[69]

The internal driving force steering the teleological development of nature consisted instead, for Schelling, in a world soul that infused the material world with spirit but remained independent of divine intention or design. His essay *Von der Weltseele* (1798) deduced from visible natural forces, such as light or magnetism, the qualities of a "common principle" that propelled nature forward as the "first cause" of life and change over time.[70] The *Weltseele* belonged to the eternal realm of the "immeasurable, absolute," according to Schelling.[71] Omnipresent, yet irreducible to the particular, it organized the world as a system. Although the "original forces"[72] animating the natural world had once been "One and the same,"[73] Schelling proposed that they adhered to a dialectical "world-law,"[74] each existing by virtue of its conflict with an opposite and together providing the "creative drive"[75] behind polarities, such as the earth's magnetic fields, electricity, and temperature.

When Heinrich Heine declared pantheism to be the "clandestine religion of Germany"[76] in 1834, his suspicions centred on the dubious figure of the *Naturphilosoph*. Less than a decade earlier the French biologist Georges Cuvier condemned *Naturphilosophie* as "a new form of the metaphysical system of pantheism."[77] The self-sustaining, inner dynamism German scholars perceived in the natural world incorrectly bestowed, in his view, an autonomous existence on nature and dismissed the importance of God as its rightful creator and governor.[78] Accusations of pantheism were endemic to German intellectual life in the half-century following the *Pantheismusstreit*. The label was at best an over-determined "slogan"[79] with vague theological ramifications, but *Naturphilosophie* did raise specific doctrinal concerns. Resorting to notions of emanation to explain generation and development contradicted Christianity by insinuating the evolving forms of being could be identical with the perfect God of Christianity.[80] Reconciling the ideal and material realms also undermined the basis for the Christian dogmas of the soul.[81] For the later Schelling, however, the most powerful charge against the identification of God with nature was the potential constriction of human freedom that followed from assuming that the necessary laws regulating nature expressed God's will.[82] The prospect that *Naturphilosophie* curtailed the possibilities for freedom and failed to explain evil in the world required reconfiguring God's relationship to creation as a process of self-unfolding or potentiation, a project undertaken in the *Freedom* essay.

Schelling's rejection of revelation's scientific credibility ceased once he reconceived it as the unfolding of divine being in the *System of Transcendental Idealism* (1800), a shift detailed in Chapter 5. In the second edition of *Von der Weltseele* (1806), in an introduction not included in the original, the term revelation creeps into the vocabulary of *Naturphilosophie* as a means to describe the realization of God's presence in the material world. This change is only explicable through his having redefined revelation as the self-disclosure of God's being. Reason he still affirmed as the principle of absolute identity, marking an original and necessary unity between the finite and infinite. But the absolute's coming into being in the world now stemmed from an "infinite desire to reveal itself ... a willing-of-the-self."[83] Visible nature, or matter, was the "mark" of this desire for actualization and, significantly, contained the "true history" of "God's being." The most exalted goal of science was, Schelling now concluded, "to verify the living presence of a God in the totality of things and in the particular." "Come hither to physics," he wrote, "apprehend the Eternal!" In an important distinction, Schelling declared that "nature is not simply the product of an incomprehensible creation, but rather creation itself; not the appearance or revelation of the Eternal, but precisely the Eternal itself."[84] The physical world was from this perspective not a machine whose harmonious order pointed to an intelligent transcendent creator; rather, nature embodied and gave form to the historically unfolding self-revelation of God.

Nature Divested of Sacred Tradition

By the late eighteenth century, natural history's utility in verifying Scripture stood on as shaky ground as the physicotheological proof, and related efforts to deduce scientific truth from sacred texts often forfeited their status as revelation. Nature's presumed connection to the revelation found in Scripture also faltered, in other words, as confidence diminished in its ability to extend a ladder to God. Critical-historical exegesis severely undermined the efficacy of *physica sacra* in securing the Bible's authority. In his lengthy introduction to J.G. Eichhorn's *Urgeschichte* (1790) Johann Philipp Gabler thus dismissed recent efforts to secure the truth of Genesis by proposing it depicted not creation but transformations in an already existing earth. Gabler agreed with Eichhorn that Genesis merely represented a "poetic portrait of the world's creation," and it was "futile labor ... to reconcile the truth of nature with the poetic fantasy of the primitive world."[85] In his view, the value of the creation story lay in the "simple idea"[86] that a single God brought the world into existence. Its claims represented, for him, the primitive speculation of an "ancient sage" mired in "childish Oriental concepts of the primitive world" but trying vainly to comprehend the origins of nature, humanity, and evil.[87] Such paltry accounts of nature neither held relevance for scientific research nor reliably confirmed God's word.

David Hume's conjecture that religion emerged in response to the natural world raised the prospect to which Gabler alludes that pre-Christian religions were not distortions of primordial revelation but primitive science. On these grounds, the controversial French mythologist Charles Dupuis welcomed the natural scientific content of pagan traditions but explicitly disassociated them with revelation, arguing that when correctly interpreted myths, and even Christianity itself, only contained encrypted knowledge of natural phenomena mixed with sexual symbolism. "The gods were Nature herself,"[88] Dupuis announced in the *Origine de tous les cultes* (1795), published in the third year of the revolutionary calendar and which as the Secretary of the National Convention, a parliament of the French Revolution, Dupuis modelled on ancient Egypt. The first humans were Sabianists, according to Dupuis, who worshipped the heavens, sun, moon, stars, as well as the elements, eventually speculating on the existence of an invisible cause that animated nature. This "universe-god"[89] was then imagined in dualist terms as competing forces of masculine and feminine, light and dark, and good and evil.[90]

According to Dupuis, mythical accounts of gods and heroes served as allegories of the natural world. Recognizing that peoples' attention was more easily drawn to "the marvelous than the true,"[91] natural scientists couched their knowledge in "the wondrous character of an enigma."[92] Mythology was nothing more, for Dupuis, than "poetical and allegorical astronomy";[93] "the personified beings of physics and astronomy became men and heroes."[94] For this reason an "astronomical key"[95] was required to effectively interpret religion. This claim privileged mathematically trained scholars over philologists and historians in control of the ancient past.[96]

As seen in his interpretation of the zodiac, Dupuis's account of ancient science retained the narrative scheme of primordial revelation without evoking divine intervention. In his view, the zodiac was an astronomical and agricultural calendar whose figurative images referred to seasonal events; the crab, cancer, for example, indicated a reversal in the sun's motion.[97] Dupuis proposed that the placement of the zodiac figures indicated the state of the sky at the moment the zodiac was created, making it possible to reconstruct astronomically where and when it emerged. In the "Mémoire sur l'origine des constellations, et sur l'explication de la fable par le moyen de l'astronomie" (1781) Dupuis concluded that the zodiac originated in the region where Egypt borders on Ethiopia. This was the "original dwelling"[98] of astronomical knowledge, the "common source" from which all other peoples derived their wisdom.[99] Dupuis's findings encouraged Napoleon's 1798 expedition to Egypt and further research on the Zodiac of Dendera, whose pilfered stones arrived in Paris in 1821.

Conservatives and religious reactionaries strongly opposed the *Origine de tous les cultes*, and Dupuis's public standing grew uncertain after Napoleon's 1801 concordat with the Church. He had studied astronomy with the atheist Joseph de Lalande and reckoned that precession, the millennial motion of the solstices and equinoxes among the constellations, could be retro-projected to the moment captured in the zodiac. After obtaining a precession globe to test his theory, Dupuis calculated that the summer solstice had occurred in Capricorn when the zodiac was created. Hence it had originated between 13,000 and 15,000 years ago, depending on whether the solstice occurred at the beginning or end of Capricorn.[100] This was more than nine millennia earlier than the presumed biblical date of creation. Dupuis went so far as to argue that Christianity was one of many local variants of a universal solar religion; Christ, in his view, had been a sun god. The price for extracting natural historical truths from religious traditions was, for Dupuis, sacrificing their status as revelation.

One response to the bifurcation of sacred tradition and natural history in the late eighteenth century, and a second means to restore nature's status as revelation, built upon the mystical presumption that the material world symbolically embodied God's word, a controversial position dear to Hamann, Herder, and Görres, as well as to G.H. Schubert. This view took literally the dictum that God's word assumed material form during creation, drawing upon a vitalist conception of language to preserve the divine origin of otherwise autonomous forces in nature. Kabbalists had since late antiquity intimated that letters and speech had the power to create the world. According to the *Sefer Yetzirah* (*Book of Creation*), individual letters of the Hebrew alphabet were the building blocks of the universe and corresponded to the elements and principles of life. By combining and arranging letters in speech, God had created the universe; the natural world represented the unfolding of the twenty-two letters of the divine *Ursprache*. Through the mediation of Renaissance neo-Platonists, this understanding of language entered Christian doctrines of inverberation, the attempt to interpret God's presence in the world through the concept of articulated word.

When German mythologist Friedrich Creuzer emulated Dupuis's fusion of philology and astronomy in the equally unsettling *Symbolik und Mythologie der alten Völker*,[101] a text introduced in the last chapter, for example, he granted nature cults genuine religious significance by presuming the material world symbolically embodied God's word. In his view, the origin of religion lay in a primitive period when early human beings, incapable of conceptual thought, fixated on physical objects and images. Creuzer ascribed to primordial humanity an inescapable universal drive to regard nature as a symbolic realm that revealed knowledge of the divine, as well as ethical principles for human behaviour. "Among all peoples," he wrote, "an early presentiment arises ... regarding the significance of individual natural phenomena, that they give signs and ... speak to man."[102] The propensity to detect human concerns in nature arose, on the one hand, from "the secret of all life, the eternal and unseen union of the soul with nature."[103] Creuzer credited "original thinkers of our nation," likely referring to Schelling and *Naturphilosophie*, for recognizing the copula between them.[104]

On the other hand, Creuzer gave credence to the genuine existence of a "symbolic language of nature." The esoteric symbols with which a primitive priestly class expressed its knowledge did not entail a "random designation devised by humans," he speculated, but maintained an "original and divine" connection with the "foundational powers" of nature.[105] Priests developed moral directives and shaped religious practices in response to "a word from the book of nature, a character from her unchanging pictorial script."[106] This inevitably resulted in a "pantheism of the fantasy."[107] But Creuzer insisted that the "symbolic language of nature" also "imposes an eternal truth"[108] and constituted authentic revelation. Symbols encapsulated, Creuzer explained, both the "appearance of the divine and the corruption of its earthly image," unifying the necessary and the momentary and signalling the "impenetrability of its origin."[109] He notably characterized the early acquisition of religious knowledge as "more a revelation ... than antecedent thought."[110] With imposing brevity, symbols foisted direct awareness of the divine on unreflective humankind.

Being of divine origin, the symbolic language of nature successfully conveyed knowledge of a highest being, according to Creuzer, who revealed himself as the creator of the world and early assumed the form of the Christian trinity. Unlike Dupuis, he believed India to have been the seat of an ancient monotheism.[111] Creuzer held that all mythology originated in an esoteric cosmology derived by Brahmanic priests based on their observations of the heavens. This caste expressed its wisdom by means of religious symbols, which gradually assumed narrative form as mythology as priests conveyed their knowledge to lay people.[112]

Locating God's presence in the natural world was a precarious endeavour in the fraught theological landscape of the early nineteenth century. For nature to constitute a legitimate site of revelation after Kant, it could not testify to the intelligent design of a transcendent creator, blithely confirm sacred tradition, or be endowed with self-sufficient purposiveness. In the 1820s the principal avenue for restoring revelation to nature was the idealist dialectical tradition inaugurated by Schelling and Hegel, in which the material world enabled the self-revelation of God's very being. As will be seen in Chapter 5, this redeployment of revelation into the natural world depended on shifting the term from an epistemological concept to an ontological one. But another avenue for returning a transcendent God to nature, briefly condoned by a rather fringe group of German Romantics, including Creuzer and Schubert, lay in perceiving the world as a symbolic embodiment of the divine word.

G.H. Schubert in the Spinoza Renaissance

Schubert's approach to restoring revelation to nature attributed nominally autonomous forces in the material world to the lingering effects of God's creative word. This approach overcame the dualism inherent in the physicotheological proof but struggled to reconcile reason and revelation and to preserve God's transcendence. In the 1790s J.G. Herder and Schelling, partook in what Herder termed an "honorable restitution of Spinoza"[113] inspired by attacks on the philosopher during the *Pantheismusstreit*. Rehabilitating Spinoza's work, however, required curbing his reputation for determinism and atheism. Although prepared to grant limited self-sufficiency to nature, Schubert thus insisted it was also the preserve of revelation, taking *Naturphilosophie* in a conservative direction. Recourse to the divine word offered Schubert a strategy for offsetting the threat of materialism. Yet the rapid disappearance of a transcendent creator in his natural histories rendered the approach only partially successful. "Above the shimmer of nature, he often forgot the countenance of God," one eulogist commented in 1860.[114] Schubert's recourse to mysticism, the occult, and Kabbalist thought likewise limited the appeal of conceiving revelation in nature as embodied word, drawing approbation from both rationalists and orthodox theologians.

Born in 1780 in the Ore Mountains of Saxony, Schubert attributed his reverence for nature and his geological interests to the allures of the local landscape. From a young age Schubert was enveloped in the conservative piety of a provincial Lutheran minister. His father rejected the "spirit of revolt against law and order, both divine and human"[115] when the French Revolution reached Saxony. Elector Friedrich Augustus III resisted joining the Prussian-Austrian coalition against France's revolutionary government, fearing for Saxony's territorial integrity. But Schubert's father insisted that defilement of religion and hatred of God caused the "poisonous odor" and political instability emanating from France.[116] Exposure to Spinoza while attending gymnasium in Weimar, however, and induction into Herder's household as a close friend of his son Emil, dislodged these certainties. "With deism ... I was already ... acquainted and not without a certain approval," Schubert recollected, "it didn't satisfy me anymore; far more appealing, warm and captivating, were the divine teachings of certain Oriental poets."[117] On his almost daily visits, Schubert lingered in his conversations with Herder "at Egypt's pyramids, at the ruins of Babylon and Persepolis."[118] Confronted through them with the problem of the soul, Schubert questioned with "prolonged doubt" its survival after death.[119]

Herder's *Ideen zur Philosophie der Geschichte der Menschheit* (1784–91), which "inwardly so delighted"[120] Schubert, offered an initial blueprint for conceiving spirit's presence in the material world. The active presence of God in creation and his internal operation within finite substances were central themes of Herder's theology.[121] During the Spinoza controversy, Herder had insisted that "organic forces" existed as a "middle concept between spirit and substance" and between "soul and body."[122] The *Ideen* proclaimed the existence of autonomous forces (*Kräfte*) in nature whose questionable connection to a personal God drew suspicions of pantheism.[123] Herder argued for the soul's immortality in the *Ideen* by declaring divine forces distinct from their embodied forms. This restored Schubert's confidence in the soul, and he aspired in subsequent years to comprehend through their material effects the mysterious powers that Herder insisted had been wrongly maligned as "*qualitates occultas*" despite their divine origins.[124]

By 1792 Herder had begun to associate the religious and philosophical doctrines of ancient India with vitalistic pantheism.[125] His interpretation of Indian beliefs foregrounded themes of regeneration and immortality, which fed into a longstanding debate in Weimar over the transmigration of souls.[126] To Herder's express approbation, the final report Schubert composed at the Weimar gymnasium in 1798 linked the eternity of the soul to the presence of an *Urkraft* in nature. This force appeared so enduring and indestructible to Schubert that, by his own recollection, he "touched upon thoughts of some kind of reincarnation."[127] In 1801 Schubert wrote to Emil Herder that he did not recognize "the division of soul and body ... everything is living force, the air and us, everything of God and from God."[128] This contradicted the theological assumption that a life-bestowing God provided the body as a vessel for a personal soul to enter at birth and that an individual's soul survived intact after death, finding redemption in a return to God. Schubert failed to recognize the individual soul as a discrete entity bounded in any sense from the living soul of the universe.[129]

A half-hearted attempt to pursue his father's career as a theologian ended for Schubert after a brief stint at the University of Leipzig. He switched to medicine in early 1801 to hear Schelling at the University of Jena, an emerging centre for *Naturphilosophie*. Its speculative methods impacted Schubert's practical training as a physician, as did the galvanic experiments of the physicist Johann Wilhelm Ritter, also in Jena. Ritter's research on muscle response to electricity offered Schubert a practical model for conceiving the interconnectedness of life and matter. Animal magnetism appealed to the adherents of *Naturphilosophie* by supplying apparent empirical evidence of the elusive world soul.[130] For Schubert, Ritter raised the prospect that electricity or another invisible force mediated between the material and spiritual realms and could generate life in inert matter.[131] During his brief two years as a practicing doctor in Altenburg, Schubert experimented with applying galvanism to cure diseases of the nervous system, especially in deaf mutes.[132]

By 1805 Schubert had abandoned the practice of medicine, embarking on a quest to grasp "nature, the entirety of visible creation ... as a divinely perfected totality."[133] The Mining Academy in Freiberg under the direction of Abraham Gottlob Werner was the first stop in this pursuit. Werner's dynamic lectures and his circle of talented devotees inspired the German Romantic fascination with mining, mineralogy, and the science Werner termed geognosy – the systematic study of the solid earth as an integrated body. Werner earned a reputation as a Neptunist based on his theory that a hot, turbulent primeval ocean laden with soluble silica and suspended minerals once covered the highest mountains. The gradual subsiding of a primordial ocean refuted the notion of a single act of creation and cataclysmic understandings of the flood.[134] Werner's religious convictions approximated deism, and his refusal to attend drafty church services in Freiberg earned him a reputation for atheism.[135] Yet Schubert interpreted Werner's project as seeking to connect "the primordial history of the earth and its solid lands to the inner realms, the primordial spiritual history of its inhabitant, man."[136]

As a site for independent scholarship after leaving Freiberg, Schubert chose Dresden, home to a splendid library and to some Jena friends who had joined the local circle of young Romantics. In the company of the landscape painter Caspar David Friedrich, whose works Schubert used to illustrate his perspective on nature, he witnessed Napoleon's occupation of the city in July 1807 and the transfer of the Grand Duchy of Warsaw to the Saxon King Friedrich August I. The writer Heinrich von Kleist and the political economist Adam Müller joined the scene shortly thereafter. In the absence of a university, members of this dynamic circle held public lecture series to which Dresden's nobility, artists, writers, and *Bildungsbürgertum* eagerly subscribed. As part of this, in spring 1807, Schubert agreed to offer alternating lectures with Müller in the Palais Carlowitz.

As a theorist of the state Adam Müller exemplifies the conservative political tendencies of Romanticism, and Schubert's collaboration with him reflects a shared opposition to the revolutionary ideas that brought Napoleon to Dresden. Schubert planned to address the "life of nature" while Müller spoke on the "life of states."[137] Müller's lectures, the basis of his well-known *Elemente der Staatskunst* (1809), contrasted Montesquieu's static, abstract notion of the state with the idea of a living, organic state akin to a family. Müller, who had recently converted to Catholicism, looked towards the Christian political culture of the medieval Germanic monarchies as an antidote to the failures of modern statecraft. "The secret of governance can be found in obedience," he concluded in the last lecture, "all the exaltation the soul desires, in voluntary submission; all freedom, in surrender to the fatherland and Christ."[138] Excerpts from their lectures first appeared in *Phöbus*, the journal Müller edited with Kleist. Schubert then published the entirety of his own as the *Ansichten von der Nachtseite der Naturwissenschaft* (1808), but only after circumventing the local censor who sensed danger in *Naturphilosophie*.[139]

Schubert's desire to uncover spiritual truths in mysterious, morose, and clandestine places, responded to the difficult conditions of the defeated German states.[140] The topic he selected for his public debut also reflects a new interest in the popular, quasi-occult field of animal magnetism. Galvani's experiments on how muscles responded to the application of electricity had become mainstream in German scientific and medical circles by 1800. Theories of magnetism, mesmerism, and somnambulism were also evoked to explain religious mysteries, such as prophecies, visions, and the healings performed by Christ.[141] Schubert's Dresden lectures endeavoured to resuscitate areas of scientific knowledge wrongly relegated to the realm of "miraculous faith"[142] by reconstructing a lost history of human engagement with nature. In the process, he used the concept of magnetism to better understand the forces that united the universe and produced higher modes of being.

Schubert's lectures ascribed to mythology privileged knowledge of God's revelation in nature. Deeply impressed by Schlegel's *Über die Sprache und Weisheit der Indier* (1808), he claimed when he met the author that Schlegel understood his own ambitions "almost better than I myself."[143] A five-week visit by Carl von Raumer, a geologist who had studied India, further established the "deeply insightful wisdom concerning nature found among the oldest peoples."[144] Schubert assumed in the *Nachtseite* that ancient mystery cults preserved vestiges of a "deep, lost wisdom about nature"[145] that prevailed when people still lived in "holy harmony"[146] with it. Themselves a "subordinate organ of nature,"[147] pagan interpreters had intuitively grasped the symbolic forms that disclosed higher wisdom. In Schubert's view, scientific observations contained in the *Bhagavad Gita* or in the temples of Isis harkened back to "nature's direct revelation to man."[148]

Crucial to recovering this wisdom was, according to Schubert, resurrecting the "darkened phenomena" of nature. In his view, a "life soul" acted as the "invisible band" uniting the universe. Its effects were only visible, however, in animal magnetism and related forces, such as gravity. Transitions in the states of matter were likewise crucial, in Schubert's view, to grasping how nature "articulat[ed] ever more purely and exaltedly ... the higher divine ideal."[149] Religion, he conceded, opened up a "higher spiritual realm."[150] But Schubert also believed that premonitions and clairvoyance resulting from altered states of consciousness and near-death experiences represented a reaching-out towards higher sensibilities. Mesmeric trances and somnambulism sharpened ordinary human sensitivities and produced a clarity of thought that, Schubert hoped, revealed a higher order on earth.

The lectures were a resounding success and propelled Schubert into Dresden's high society.[151] Nevertheless, in his memoirs, he rejected the "misconceptions" of the *Nachtseite*, specifically citing his mistaken disregard of the Christian God's role in revelation. "I had forgotten," he explained, "that the light which illuminates the visible world ... must come from elsewhere, from above."[152] Later editions of the text qualify his claims about pagan knowledge of nature. Orthodox theologians feared that Schubert's understanding of magnetic forces undermined the importance of God in miracles. August Tholuck, who features in Chapter 8, for example, referenced animal magnetism to defend miracles against rationalists in the 1830s. But he rejected the higher insights Schubert expected from occult phenomena, preferring the way Hegelians interpreted magnetism as "a lower form, below the spiritual level."[153]

Schubert's descent into mysticism accelerated after Schelling procured for him a position as rector and instructor at the Nuremberg Realinstitut in January 1809. A visit from the Catholic theologian Franz von Baader acquainted Schubert with the writings of the French mystic Claude Louis de Saint-Martin, who had revived neo-Platonic, Kabbalist, and early Christian speculation about creation.[154] The importance of language in *Die Symbolik des Traumes* (1814), Schubert's third attempt to locate the divine presence in nature, likewise reflects the influence of his new colleague J.A. Kanne (see Chapter 2), whose conception of the *Ursprache* as revelation reinforced Schubert's notion of God's word in creation. Christian Kabbalists also offered Schubert a precedent for viewing nature through a linguistic lens, having transferred methods for deciphering language and writing onto the observation of nature. As the language of God, Hebrew letters, according to Kabbalist tradition, possessed creative energies and quasi-magical powers.[155]

Schubert's intervention in the *Symbolik* was to recognize dreams and trances as providing access to a forgotten, symbolic language of divine origin still manifest in the natural world. He connected the "materially revealed word"[156] found in the "language of nature-images"[157] (*Naturbildersprache*) with the symbolic "language of dream-images"[158] (*Traumbildersprache*) known to somnambulists, mystics, and poets. The text contributed to the idea of a psychic unconscious in the early nineteenth century and foreshadows Freud's views. Schubert linked the psyche to a lost primordial epoch imbued with divine truths but buried in secrecy and unintelligible to rational reconstruction. In his view, the suppressed unconscious, fleetingly visible in dreams and trances, opened new pathways to the divine creator.[159]

The role Schubert attributed to God's word in creation explains why he expected to detect revelation in moments when a mystical "language of hieroglyphs" briefly replaced "our ordinary language of words."[160] Revelation, in his view, had occurred in a language of symbolic imagery that more closely resembled the "dark imagery of dreams, than wakeful prose."[161] Schubert envisioned the natural world as an "embodied dream world, a prophetic language in living hieroglyphic forms."[162] Due to human sin, the rational language of conscious thought was "no longer a creative and constructive word, rather an impotent, powerless one."[163] This reversed the circumstances of creation, and Schubert argued for a restoration of the language of dreams. Echoes of the original, divine language could still be heard, for Schubert, when people entered dreamlike states or related conditions of "poetic and mythic inspiration."[164] Parapsychological states, in his view, such as magnetic sleep, somnambulism, fainting, trances, catalepsy, or insanity, briefly restored the original, mystical relationship between human beings, nature, and the divine.

After his religious awakening, Schubert rejected the "extremely unseemly" connection the *Symbolik* drew between dreamlife, "an appearance of lower order and questionable provenance" and the spirit that spoke to humanity through the "works of His creations and revelation."[165] Although writing the text during the initial phase of his spiritual rebirth, Schubert had yet to draw the intellectual conclusions that later resulted from it. Schubert confessed to his friend Köthe at the time of its publication that he wrote the *Symbolik* "constantly engaged in prayer and reading the divine word" and realized that it contained "here and there grave misconceptions."[166] Starting with the second edition of the *Symbolik* (1837), Schubert steered the text closer towards biblical Christianity. Later editions bound the soul to "self-conscious spirit,"[167] implying the unconscious was a realm of darkness, not revelation. In the *Geschichte der Seele* (1830) Schubert placed dreams in a more negative light as the realm of sick and misdirected souls.[168]

Schubert's histories had veered into dangerous territory by the time coalition forces repelled Napoleon, asserting nature as a higher authority than Scripture, one that offered alternative conceptions of creation, revelation, and the divine presence on earth. His conservative mix of mysticism, Kabbalism, and *Naturphilosophie* severely undercut traditional Protestant doctrines. Tholuck feared, for example, that somnambulism failed to offer a convincing model for moments of divine inspiration, such as the prophecies, visions, and speaking in tongues recorded in the Old and New Testaments. He conceded that consciousness often receded during such visions and that prophets exhibited certain qualities found in clairvoyants. However, biblical figures always revealed future events of religious significance, not the particular concerns of individuals, and did so while retaining memory of the episode.[169] Even for mystically inclined theologians of the religious awakening Schubert's conception of revelation in nature exceeded the limits of acceptable religious experimentation.

Physica Sacra: The *Urwelt*, Creation, and Scripture

Conversion to revivalist Christianity shifted Schubert's perspective on God's presence in nature and bound his *Urwelt* research more closely to biblical narrative. The religious awakening that swept the German states during the occupation and Wars of Liberation reached Schubert just as his wife Henriette fell terminally ill. Schubert's childhood love for Christ rekindled, both he and Kanne joined the town's revivalists.[170]

In December 1811 Schubert wrote to his friend, the Catholic portrait-
ist Gerhard von Kügelgen, that he had been reborn in "God's love,"
yet cautiously requested secrecy from his friend: "What I announced
to you in this letter, tell no one. Not that I am ashamed of the gospel of
Christ; it would just lose significance if shared by you." Two months
later Henriette was dead, and Schubert reported having felt "more
vitally than ever in my heart … that Christ is the Lord."[171] The Bavarian state shuttered the Realinstitut in 1816, and Schubert embarked on
several years of soul-searching and spiritual dislocation, albeit rapidly
remarried to Henriette's sister.

The politics of religious revival compounded the isolation Schubert
experienced in his new post as tutor to the children of Grand Duke
Friedrich Ludwig von Mecklenburg. At the court in Ludwigslust
Schubert quickly acquired "the black mark of a mystic and Pietist,"[172] a
suspicious profile in a region dominated by theological rationalism. His
defence of Claus Harms's 95 Theses discrediting reason as apostasy in
1817 placed him on thin ice even before the highly politicized murder
of the August von Kotzebue two years later. His assailant, Karl Sand,
had ties to both the religious awakening and the radical student fraternity Teutonia. In this climate Schubert appeared to Prince Adolf as a
"wicked, clandestine revolutionary and democrat."[173] As the reaction
set in, Lorenz Oken, another *Naturphilosoph* trained by Schelling, had
been forced to surrender his position in Jena for radical democratic politics and for participating in the Wartburg Fest and the liberal-nation-
alist student movement. Schubert himself had met the nationalist E.M.
Arndt in Mecklenburg, yet insisted he followed the "large honorable
part" of the nationalist movement drawn, like Harms, to a "positive
faith in Christianity."[174] Pantheism and the denial of a personal God
ventured too closely for Schubert during the tumultuous years of the
early Restoration on the political radicalism he sought to disavow.
He, in fact, blamed the audacity of Sand's crime on pantheism of his
reputed accomplice Karl Follen, who by believing in "no other God but
the shapeless force of nature (*Naturkraft*)" had contributed to the "deification of man" that justified murder.[175]

A professorship in natural history delivered Schubert from "my
Egyptian land"[176] to Erlangen in 1819, a town acquired by the Kingdom of Bavaria in 1810. The state's new flagship Protestant university
welcomed other colleagues from the Realinstitut, and he rejoined several revivalists from Nuremburg. A "constant gnawing pain"[177] over the
dominance of rationalist theology initially plagued Schubert here, but
by 1830 speculative Christian mysticism has so engulfed Erlangen that
the young Hegelian Ludwig Feuerbach left in disgust.[178] Schelling's

arrival in Erlangen transformed the new *Heimat* into an "Indian paradise" for Schubert.[179] The intimacy that developed between them derived partly from their mutual repudiation of pantheism and defence of divine personhood.

Schubert's intellectual refashioning reached a "turning point"[180] in Switzerland during an 1820 visit with the awakened pastor and physicist David Spließ. Their conversations in the hamlet of Buch confirmed Schubert in the "mission of my life ... a *physica sacra*."[181] Spließ had traversed a similar path in the effort to reconcile spirituality and natural science: from "rationalism, deism and pantheism, down to atheism: to materialist nihilism."[182] However, he now convinced Schubert to pursue "knowledge of nature in conjunction with knowledge of its creator" so that the book of nature matched Scripture.[183] *Physica sacra* entailed, for Schubert, "writing natural science for scholars of God's word." His goal starting in 1818 was to allow God to speak through the "Bible and nature, both with one voice."[184] This required repudiating *Naturphilosophie*. He condemned the "errors of materialist contemplation" that clouded his previous work and embraced instead "a different book than the visible works, the book of revelation."[185]

During the 1820s Schubert indulged in a new genre of highly speculative natural histories that, building upon a new fascination with the earth sciences, leaped from the formation of the heavens to the moral life of human beings.[186] *Die Urwelt und die Fixsterne* (1822) and its expansion in the *Allgemeine Naturgeschichte* (1826) aimed to restore the idea of a transcendent personal creator God by sketching his plans for the universe. Their account of the divine presence in nature admittedly reveals continuity with Schubert's earlier interest in invisible forces. The universality of gravity and its status as a "creative power"[187] attracted Schubert to astronomy, as did the spiritual significance of light. However, Spinoza's shadow had receded. "Thus stands infinitely more exalted, far above the soul of nature," Schubert insisted, "a comprehensive, all-prevailing, all-substantiating, self-cognizant spirit."[188]

At this time, German scholarship on the *Urwelt* still overwhelmingly placed material remains in conversation with mythological sources and staked a position on the reliability of Genesis. In *Die Urwelt und das Alterthum* (1821–2), Heinrich Link, for example, noted that "monuments of nature" were the best evidence for the earth's earliest millennia. Because the prehistoric age immediately abutted antiquity, however, the earliest human records contained important scientific knowledge.[189] Link, who knew Sanskrit and Arabic, expected the physical remains of natural history to corroborate ancient cosmogonies, the Mosaic tale of creation being merely the purest and most reliable of the many "off-spring" of a "primordial religion."[190]

Efforts to discount the natural scientific content of the creation story often cited overlap with ancient Oriental mythologies as proof of its historical irrelevance. In *Die Urwelt* (1818) J.G.J. Ballenstedt, for example, argued that Genesis replicated the "tales and myths of some ancient peoples."[191] In his view, the Old Testament was a compilation of Indian and Persian legends whose only significance was "moral … they were not supposed to teach us any new theories about creation, any secrets about nature, any history, any geography, etc."[192] He proposed that the Hebrew myths of creation and the flood did not refer to the "first emergence and primordial beginnings"[193] of the earth and its inhabitants but to "the last general transformation of our earth" that produced a climate, environment, and new life forms.[194]

Schubert himself qualifies as a restitutionist, convinced that an extended phase of natural history, in which the earth was "waste and void,"[195] preceded the six days in which God created light, humankind, and the conditions of today's world. In Hengstenberg's *Evangelische Kirchen-Zeitung*, Schubert described a moment of "standstill and inhibition" between the two eras of creation as a "slumber, which after a brief descent into unconsciousness is followed by a more powerful awakening."[196] Restitutionism supported orthodox Lutheran doctrine better than day-to-epoch conversions. Hengstenberg himself defended the notion of a second creation capable of preserving the short biblical chronology of human history.[197] Schubert cited mythology to place creation at the moment of the earth's closest proximity to the sun, which he dated based on the astronomical coincidence, six thousand years before his time, of this event occurring at the autumnal equinox. He likewise presented evidence of rapid transformations in the natural world, such as those caused by electricity, to suggest that creation could have transpired within the Bible's brief timeframe.

Higher biblical criticism had by the 1820s already justified localizing the tale of the flood, curtailing its supposed universality and limiting its geographic scope. The notion of a geological deluge survived among European geologists, though largely disassociated from biblical references, recast by the 1840s as an ice age that explained the movement of erratic boulders and deposits of course gravels.[198] Schubert persisted, nevertheless, in tying Werner's Neptunist theory of water shaping the earth's surface to the tale of Noah and the Flood, rejecting as late as 1851 the idea of glacial displacements.[199] A "general, not partial flood" had shaped the world's current environment around four thousand years ago, burying all traces of the *Vorwelt*. Schubert defended the idea of general flood with reference to mythological traditions from India to Mexico, declaring the Hebrew rendition the purest.[200] Striking astronomical events always coincided, he concluded, with the most significant moments in human history, such as the birth of Christ, and when correctly interpreted, natural scientific references in ancient mythology would reveal synchronisms that affirmed biblical chronology.[201]

The pursuit of *physica sacra* led Schubert to tour the holy land in 1836 with his wife, two student assistants, and a landscape painter. In his request to Bavarian King Ludwig I for leave and financial support, he stated his intent "to write a *physica sacra*: a natural historical description of the holy land and, namely, of the oldest book of holy scripture."[202] Schubert's goal was to defend biblical truth through empirical confirmation of its natural scientific references, as sacred geographers did. The trip took Schubert from Egypt along Moses's likely route through the Sinai Peninsula and on to Bethlehem and Jerusalem. The *Evangelische Kirchen-Zeitung* published excerpts of his travel journal starting in 1837, and a three-volume book appeared after his return. The expedition also procured a massive collection of flora and fauna, including a lion, a leopard, and Munich's first giraffe. Its lasting scientific value lay in the measurement of elevations; Schubert's party discovered one week after a British expedition that the Dead Sea lay lower than the Mediterranean.[203] For Schubert, however, this incarnation of *physica sacra* suggests how narrowly his understanding of the divine presence in nature had been circumscribed, reduced to noting the reflection of Mosaic truth in the local environment of the Holy Land.

By the 1840s German enthusiasm for speculative *Naturphilosophie* had largely fizzled out, rendered scientifically irrelevant under a new regime of positivism, naturalism, and empirical observation. Materialism still ran the risk of provoking atheism. After Schubert and Lorenz Oken both assumed posts at the university in Munich, Schubert maligned his nemesis by linking him to the physiologist Jacob Moleschott, whose materialist denial of God nearly got him fired from the university of Heidelberg in 1854. Moleschott and the zoologist Karl Vogt, nephew to Charles Follen and a delegate to the Frankfurt parliament both, according to Schubert, "articulated in full the … core of Oken's *Naturphilosophie*."[204] The older Schubert still felt compelled to argue in 1851 that the production of the world was due to "a force not of nature, but of the Creator."[205] He received an honorary doctorate in theology in 1853 for the contributions his natural history made to biblical exegesis.[206] However, by this time, the most acrimonious debates over Christian personhood and the political theology of the Restoration had run their course. Defence of the creation story assumed a new set of cultural priorities and soon had to respond more directly to British empiricism and to Darwinian theories of evolution. In this context Schubert's speculative historical trajectories were at best a liability to the cause of revelation.

Chapter Five

The Philosophy of Revelation:
Schleiermacher, Hegel, and Schelling

In his history of nineteenth-century religious thought, Karl Barth praised G.W.F. Hegel for having "splendidly rehabilitated" the biblical concept of revelation. According to Barth, Hegel silenced the "murderous attempts" of such "disturbers of the peace" as Kant and Lessing, who imposed "wretched limits" on the concept. Uncomfortable with the liberal tradition of nineteenth-century theology, especially after World War I, Barth revered Hegel for bringing to a "highly satisfactory conclusion" the "great conflict" between reason and revelation that plagued the Enlightenment.[1] Indeed a central concern of the early Hegel was to bridge the rift between Christian revelation and post-Kantian philosophical theology.[2] Eschewing the idea of natural theology, Barth himself cultivated a theology of revelation centred on Christ, the resurrection, and Scripture as an authoritative source. His understanding of the Trinity as the movement of God's self-revelation through history is indebted to Hegel, even if Barth severed the apparent ontological continuity Hegel presumed between God and humankind and doubted his own ability to achieve rational knowledge of God.[3]

The decades following Kant's death in 1804 witnessed a postcritical revival of revelation as a philosophical concept, a watershed moment for the early twentieth-century theological recovery of German idealism.[4] Although Enlightened critique weakened the epistemological function of revelation, the term found new life among German idealists in the early nineteenth century. Writing in the *Critical Journal of Philosophy*, which he edited with Schelling in Jena, Hegel observed in July 1802 that the philosophical struggle against miracles was "no longer ... worth the bother." However, he feared the victory of Enlightened reason over faith was self-destructive. "The new-born peace that hovers triumphantly over the corpse of reason and faith," Hegel declared, "has as little of reason in it as it has of authentic faith."[5] The divine had been relegated to a subjective, supersensible realm inaccessible to cognition, in his view, while reason had been reduced to mere *Verstand* (or intellect), not daring to reach for the heavens. The *Phenomenology of Spirit* (1807) started the process, for Hegel, of rehabilitating revelation and the historical and positive content of Christianity by documenting their compatibility with a higher form of reason. This speculative endeavour culminated in the lectures on the philosophy of religion, which Hegel delivered four times in Berlin during the 1820s.

The philosophy of religion emerged as an area of inquiry distinct from theology in response to critical philosophy and the perceived failures of natural religion after 1800.[6] Its roots lie in the tradition of *theologia naturalis*, which grounded religious principles in reason and observation, often at the expense of revealed theology, and detached knowledge of God from its historical basis in Scripture. The main branches of philosophical theology had reached an impasse by the late Enlightenment. David Hume effectively stymied physiotheologcial proofs of God's existence; Kant deflated the speculative metaphysical tradition that had sustained ontological proofs of the divine. By the mid-1790s Kant's alternative grounding of religion on the precepts of practical religion had itself begun to falter. The idea of God as a moral lawgiver had been "received poorly,"[7] Hegel noted in 1802. Kant's initial (mis)appropriation by the forces of orthodoxy had unleashed an indignant reaction among rationalists.[8] The fusion of critical philosophy and historical revelation likewise proved unsatisfying to supernaturalists.

The upheavals facing Protestant theology at this time lent a sense of urgency to the philosophy of religion.[9] A more convincing self-grounding principle was needed to justify religion, Hegel argued, now that scriptural testimony, supernatural revelation, and inferences from nature to God stood on shaky foundations. While accepting radical Enlightened critique, the field restored the intellectual respectability of traditional theological themes.[10] Two distinct trajectories for conceiving of God and defending knowledge and historical experience of the divine characterized the philosophy of religion after 1800.[11] One tack, favoured by Friedrich Heinrich Jacobi (1743–1819) and the reformed theologian Friedrich Schleiermacher (1768–1834), entailed surrendering knowledge of God to the illusive realm of feeling, subjective reflection, and aesthetics. The other, visible in Hegel and Schelling, established a viable platform for a speculative philosophy of religion that heeded Kant's cautions yet disregarded the doubts and self-restraint of Enlightened critics.

This chapter argues that the project of revitalizing positive Christianity after Kant transformed the concept of revelation in the religious philosophy of Schleiermacher, Hegel, and Schelling. As young theology students coming of age during the French Revolution, these thinkers accepted the Enlightened critique of revelation, as well as Kant's dual indictment of natural and metaphysical theology. However, they wished to salvage religion for the new age into which the Napoleonic occupations and the struggle for political reform brought the German states. Refusing to capitulate to Lessing's ditch, they heralded the historical character of revelation as its essential attribute, one that enabled a better understanding of how God was present in the post-revolutionary world. Revelation's function in the early nineteenth century was not to dispense stable objective truths vulnerable to the historical nature of their disclosure but to cultivate subjective states of being that enabled awareness of partial truths whose significance only became apparent within larger trajectories. Despite bitter conflicts over how historical subjects apprehended God, Schleiermacher, Hegel, and Schelling partook in a shared project of conceiving human engagement with the divine as a mutually self-determining process. Accepting the historicity of revelation entailed making God dependent for his full self-actualization on the historical world and shifting agency for the acquisition of religious truths onto humankind.

The radical process of redefinition that made revelation respectable outside orthodox circles began with Friedrich Schleiermacher's *On Religion: Speeches to its Cultured Despisers* (1799). This text undercut the once dominant propositional understanding of revelation by which God engaged in special actions to disclose definite truths that informed select people on how to attain salvation. Revelation traditionally took the form of instructions, be they supernaturally disclosed in Scripture, transmitted through tradition and the teachings of an authoritative church, or attained universally through rational reflection.[12] Schleiermacher's emphasis on feeling and religious experience transposed revelation into a universal characteristic of the human encounter with the divine. Revelation was a subjective process of inner transformation, an experiential category that made no claim to special epistemological privileges. Subjective consciousness of God was, for Schleiermacher, nevertheless an adequate basis for dogmatic theology; it could also inspire religious communion, which arose, in his view, through voluntary adherence to the unique revelation of a founder.

The religious philosophies of Hegel and Schelling expressly rejected Schleiermacher's exclusive focus on feeling and subjective reflection as an evasive, unwarranted retreat from philosophical certainty. Yet they likewise broke with the conception of revelation as received wisdom, emphasizing instead the self-revelation of God through history.

In their view, revelation was an as yet incomplete dialectical process of divine self-disclosure and self-constitution. As such, the term was a bedrock of their ontological thought. Hegel and Schelling both deemed God's being to be essentially revelatory; God acquired historical presence through the act of revelation. His realization in the human world depended, moreover, on progressive human consciousness of the divine across time. For this reason, revelation did retain certain epistemological benefits in the idealist reconceptualization, although not as a privileged source of supernatural wisdom. God's self-revelation was a precondition for human understanding and a guarantee for the presumed historical inevitability of attaining absolute truth in post-Kantian speculative philosophy.

The rehabilitation of revelation was part of a broader nationally minded project of reconstituting the foundations of German cultural and religious life after Napoleon occupied most of the German states in 1806. The idea of God's self-revelation lent credence to expectations among a revolutionary generation of intellectuals that the divine was becoming historically manifest in the institutions of German cultural and intellectual life, and at least for Hegel in the reformed states of the Restoration. Schleiermacher had faith that a shared experience of inner revelation would unite the subjective wills of individuals within the self-governing communities of the church and nation.[13] Hegel confidently designated the Prussian state and its Lutheran church as the realm in which absolute spirit attained self-conscious subjectivity. More troubled by the recalcitrance of existence, Schelling explored the unconscious dark ground that made revelation necessary and, in his view, protected the freedom of God and humankind.

Salvaging historical revelation and the content of positive Christianity dealt a severe blow to the paradigm of primordial revelation. Despite their relative loyalty to historical Christianity, neither Schleiermacher nor Hegel nor Schelling subscribed to the ancient theology narrative that inspired Herder's *Älteste Urkunde*. The effervescent remains of a lost primordial revelation were too weak a foundation for building a Christian community in the precarious climate of the Restoration. The idea that history was building to a more perfect revelation of God, one appropriate for the current age, better reinforced the promise of immanent transformation. The origin of religion was beset, for Schleiermacher, Hegel, and Schelling with a lack of self-consciousness and considerable rational and emotional deficits. Each valued the contributions the mythological traditions of Eastern peoples made to the historical process of revelation or the preconditions making it possible but conceived of revelation as a totalizing historical project, irreducible to a single moment of origin.

Schleiermacher: Revelation as Subjective Experience

In contrast to Hegel, Schleiermacher's reputation as a philosopher of religion is tarnished among strict advocates of scriptural revelation by a perceived excess of subjectivity. Barth condemned him in 1927 for "disarming" the Christian concept of revelation and reducing it to "inner emotion."[14] Schleiermacher perpetrated a "great mistake," in his view, when he conflated the "reality of religion with the subjective possibility of revelation."[15] For Barth, Schleiermacher wrongly assumed that the divine resided within the human soul and revealed itself internally. This fatefully substituted human consciousness of God for the real object of theology. Schleiermacher's conception of religion lacked an external object, according to Barth. Any treatment of subjective religious experience required, in his words, a "second component," a "counterpart."[16] With no means to postulate the objective existence of God, Schleiermacher could neither attribute an origin or a cause to revelation nor reliably attain knowledge of the divine.

The term revelation admittedly sat uncomfortably with Schleiermacher. He rejected its inherited meanings, mired as they were in Enlightenment-era debates over its relative epistemological merits.[17] Still his reconceptualization of religion as subjective human experience required a mechanism for connecting with God that both prevented religion from being reduced to a human projection and shielded it from rationalist abstraction. Retaining the term revelation enabled Schleiermacher to depict the effects on subjective consciousness of God's presence in the finite world. It likewise provided a welcome liberal model for the process of communal integration during the turbulent years following the revolutionary upheavals in France. Schleiermacher's approach to revelation was broadly subversive, as were his politics, in that it rejected the transcendent authority of a sanctioned lawgiver to dispense truth and establish religious communion. The desire to share in a particularly powerful revelation brought individuals together in ethical communities, according to Schleiermacher, with which they must freely identify.

Schleiermacher was born the son of an army chaplain in Breslau in lower Silesia to a family of Reformed clergymen. His concern for the immediacy and uniqueness of individual experiences of faith is generally attributed to his upbringing and early education among the

Moravian Brethren, a pietistic sect that emphasized the emotional side of religion and devotion to Jesus. The Moravian theological seminar Schleiermacher attended in Barby eschewed rationalism and abstract philosophy. Dissatisfied with these limited intellectual horizons, however, Schleiermacher secretly read modern philosophy before petitioning his father in 1787 for a transfer to nearby Halle, a centre of Enlightened theology. Here Schleiermacher found a mentor in J.A. Eberhard, a representative of Leibnizian-Wolffian philosophy, and partook in his campaign against critical philosophy, welcoming Kant's critique of metaphysics but not the moral proof of God's existence. After passing his theological exams in 1790, Schleiermacher served as tutor to the household of Count Dohna of Schlobitten but left over conflicting views of the French Revolution. Schleiermacher's first church appointment came in 1794 in Landsberg an der Warthe, where he immersed himself in Spinoza's non-theistic concept of the divine.

A move to Berlin in 1796 as Reformed chaplain at the Charité Hospital drew Schleiermacher into the dynamic romantic circle that frequented the salon of Henriette Herz. Sharing a house with Friedrich Schlegel, he met Schelling and Fichte, recently dismissed from Jena for atheism; composed a feminist piece for the *Athenaeum* project; advocated full civil rights for Jews; and stood by his friend's risqué depictions of sexual liaison in *Lucinde* (1800). This literary and philosophical milieu challenged Schleiermacher to defend his religious convictions; many of his friends were accustomed to regarding religion as a "disease of the mind."[18] Directed at these radicals, *On Religion: Speeches to its Cultured Despisers* acquiesced to Enlightenment criticism of revealed theology, ecclesiastical institutions, and the conventional faith of the bourgeoisie. Yet Schleiermacher contrived to capture the living experience of faith in a "higher realism"[19] that would appeal to his young cohort while avoiding Fichte's speculative idealism. In 1802 he himself quit Berlin for a self-imposed exile in Pomerania, his love for a married woman having become unbearable.

The *Speeches* wiped the Enlightened theological slate clean, rejecting natural religion, speculative metaphysics, and the emphasis moral systems placed on praxis. Religion, Schleiermacher insisted, was grounded in "immediate experiences of the existence and action of the universe."[20] An instinctive awareness, an inborn religious capacity, predisposed humankind, in his view, to contemplate its relationship to the infinite. His "neo-Spinozist realism"[21] virtually excluded consideration of a transcendent creator; Schleiermacher regarded nature as a physical-spiritual process in the tradition of Schelling's *Naturphilosophie*.[22] Intuition and feeling were, moreover, the chief mechanisms for an individual to apprehend the actions of the universe, at least in the first edition of the *Speeches*. Intuition, in Schleiermacher's view, enabled a finite event to be perceived as a manifestation of a larger whole. Religious truth thus derived not from abstract or formal reasoning but from an existential encounter with concrete particularity.[23] Scientific and philosophic thought nevertheless remained, for Schleiermacher, a critical framework for interpreting religious experience.[24] He attacked proponents of neo-pietistic conservatism for their emphasis on blind emotional faith and their submission to traditional orthodoxy and biblical literalism.[25]

The term 'revelation,' in Schleiermacher's early work, captured the subjective experience occasioned by an individual encounter with God. It provided no knowledge of God but justified faith. "Every original and new intuition of the universe,"[26] Schleiermacher wrote, was a revelation. No longer a privileged communication, revelation arose in the interior of each religious person. It was the impression the universe made upon the person contemplating it, the working of the infinite within the self. The resulting feelings of awe, Schleiermacher noted, assumed infinite variety depending on the manner an individual intuited the universe. Revelation also constituted the self-manifestation of the infinite in the finite, a primal act of spirit. The eternal activity of the universe could at every moment reveal the infinite to humankind within the realm of the finite. Schleiermacher noted, though, that it occurred "only in small and fleeting but frequent appearances."[27]

Revelation likewise designated, for Schleiermacher, the communication of an original religious intuition, provided it evoked a new sentiment in the recipient. He attributed a strong social component to religion in the *Speeches*, evoking an alternative idea of community to the ecclesiastical institutions many of his circle despised. People had a natural desire to communicate their intuitions and feelings, in his view, so awareness of God's presence could foster communal integration. "Every new doctrine, revelation, or view that awakens the sense of the universe in a respect in which it had not previously been stirred," Schleiermacher wrote, "also wins some minds for religion."[28] A religious communion arose around the original intuition of a master, he concluded, with each member of the community proclaiming the new revelation awakened by him.

This liberal understanding of revelation justified Schleiermacher's high valuation of historical religions and rendered unnecessary any derivation of religious truth from an original divine dispensation. Religious pluralism, in his view, was "necessary and unavoidable."[29] Although itself infinite and immeasurable, religion needed a principle of individualization to exist. All expressions of divine intuition were historically conditioned, in his view, such that religion assumed "an unending multitude of thoroughly determinate forms." All communions, for Schleiermacher, harboured a "glowing outpouring of the inner fire" beneath their "dead slag" of sectarianism and empty customs.[30] The founding moment of each was an "immediate influence of the deity,"[31] a revelation which members freely chose to make the "center" of the whole religion.[32]

The *Speeches* initially failed to elicit broad support beyond Schleiermacher's enthusiastic circle of Romantic admirers. Orthodox clergymen found them unintelligible; rationalists dismissed his defence of positive religions in their historical embodiment.[33] Schelling insisted that nature deserved greater prominence in the evocation of religious sentiment; its secrets were more penetrable than Schleiermacher allowed.[34] Based on the reputation of the *Speeches*, however, Schleiermacher was called in 1804 to professorship at the Lutheran theological faculty in Halle as part of a Prussian effort to reconcile the Protestant denominations. His reception was cold. Schleiermacher's association with *Naturphilosophie* drew charges of pantheism.[35] His former mentor, Eberhard, denounced him for atheism. The *Speeches* neglected to uphold a personal God in Eberhard's view, and the prospect of eternal union with the infinite violated the doctrine of personal immortality.[36]

After the Napoleonic invasion forced the closure of the university, Schleiermacher defiantly remained in Halle, leaving only once the city was incorporated into the Kingdom of Westphalia under Jérôme Bonaparte. A new position as Reformed preacher at the Trinity Church in Berlin enabled Schleiermacher to assume a prominent role in the patriotic opposition to the French and in the Prussian reform movement. Schleiermacher aligned himself with Baron H.F.K. vom Stein, whose reforms embraced the ideals of self-government and national mobilization, and campaigned for a representative political assembly under a constitutional monarch. This commitment had a theological foundation commensurate with his ideas on revelation. Similar to a confessional community, the state in Schleiermacher's view should be a voluntary association of freely choosing persons desiring to share their individual intuitions in mutual interaction.[37] His influential sermons indicted aristocratic privileges and social inequalities, while agitating for popular resistance.[38] As editor of a political newspaper he was investigated for treason and threatened with banishment after criticizing the 1813 Prussian armistice with the French.[39]

German national renewal depended, for Schleiermacher, on securing prominence for theology at the new research university planned for Berlin. By then Minister for the Interior, Count Dohna appointed Schleiermacher Director of the Berlin Academic Deputation under Wilhelm von Humboldt. He became the first dean of the theological faculty when the university was founded in 1810, serving as rector in 1815–16. As a member of the Historical School, which included Leopold von Ranke and Jacob Grimm, he historicized the academic discipline of theology while carving a niche for the philosophy of religion. The historical method, in Schleiermacher's hands, exceeded its eighteenth-century function as a tool of disenchantment that questioned the divine inspiration of Scripture and challenged Mosaic authorship. Theology in Schleiermacher's conception built on the comprehensive historical experience of the Christian faith, a prospect that drew accusations of relativizing the values of Christianity.[40] Berlin quickly became the stronghold of Schleiermacher's theological influence. Unlike E.W. Hengstenberg among conservatives, however, he never garnered a coherent liberal following; the majority of his students applied his system to moderately conservative positions within mediating theology.[41] This is perhaps due to Schleiermacher's liberal nationalist convictions drawing repeated scrutiny.[42]

A concept of revelation largely consistent with his earlier work underpins Schleiermacher's later struggles to defend positive Christianity and historical revelation against the speculative abstraction of the philosophical school.[43] Only begrudgingly did he vote to offer Hegel the chair in philosophy vacated upon Fichte's death, sensing in his speculative philosophical system a threat to historical-critical and philological inquiry.[44] Schleiermacher's monumental *Christian Faith* (1821–2) asserted that dogmatic theology could systematize religious experience without heavy reliance on scripture, creed, or rational argument. Schleiermacher built upon the assumption that piety, not knowledge or moral action, was the basis of religious communion. All religious sentiment hinged for him on an inescapable feeling of absolute dependence, which characterized the human relationship to God. An "original revelation" of God to humankind ensured that God-consciousness was inseparable from self-consciousness. "Along with the absolute dependence which characterizes not only man but all temporal existence," Schleiermacher wrote, "there is given to man also the immediate self-consciousness of it, which becomes a consciousness of God."[45] Piety, for Schleiermacher, required no prior knowledge of God. The idea of God was an expression of the feeling of absolute dependence and not its cause.

Similarly to Hegel and Schelling, Schleiermacher equated the historical evolution of human religious consciousness with enhanced states of revelation that culminated in Protestant Christianity. His philosophy of religion delineated three grades of self-consciousness, or methods for expressing the finite's dependence on the infinite, as a basis for comparing positive religions. An "animal confusion of consciousness" burdened piety while human nature was still in an "undeveloped state."[46] Fetishism, for example, crudely directed feelings of dependence on objects apprehended by the senses. This consciousness characterized the deep past but also the "rudest human races."[47] The growth of a "sensible self-consciousness,"[48] an awareness of the self in its particular relationship to nature and other human beings, expanded human self-understanding and the feeling of absolute dependence. Finally, in monotheistic religions piety was distinguished by a higher form of self-consciousness in which the finite world appears absolutely dependent on a supreme being.

Revelation in the *Christian Faith* again designated the founding moment of a religious community, a concrete historical occurrence when the divine worked upon the human consciousness. In Schleiermacher's words, revelation constituted an "inward generation of a new and peculiar idea of God in a moment of inspiration." Revelation conditioned the specific religious emotions that defined a communion; it did not supply "pure and eternal truth" in the form of doctrine. The term thus had applicability beyond Christianity to oracles; for example, revelation could arise "in a realm of complete barbarity and degradation"[49] and produce imperfect religions. Schleiermacher insisted that each religious community had a distinctive beginning, contradicting Herder's diffusionary model. Religious emotions were, in his view, specific such that "the presence of an absolutely identical element in two different ways of faith can be only in appearance."[50] There was no universal natural religion, and no primordial revelation that produced synchronisms.

Revelation found its epitome and archetype in Christ, the "supreme divine revelation," in the *Christian Faith*.[51] Its ultimate meaning was faith in redemption through Christ. Fracturing the Enlightened dichotomy between reason and revelation, Schleiermacher argued that the appearance of the redeemer was neither an "absolutely supernatural nor an absolutely supra-rational thing."[52] The coming of Christ presumed divine causality; the source of his teaching was the "absolutely original revelation of God in Him."[53] Yet it was also a natural fact prepared for by past history. Because Christian doctrines were experiential, an expression of self-consciousness, they lay beyond the determination of reason. However, revelation through Christ did not entirely transcend reason because redemption was conditioned through communication.

Dogmas were subject to the same laws of conception and synthesis as all forms of speech; reason was needed to clarify and abstract from religious experience.

Schleiermacher radically altered the meaning of revelation in liberal Protestant theology as he established a powerful and enduring platform for religion in the wake of Enlightened criticism. Revelation, in his view, was an inner transformation of the subjective consciousness that had experiential origins in the human encounter with the divine and produced a genuine, living faith. This perspective welcomed the rational clarification of religious emotion in the form of doctrine but without subjecting faith to either metaphysical speculation or the dictates of supernaturally revealed truths. Schleiermacher invalidated the notion that primordial revelation dispensed knowledge about God, which relied on a propositional understanding of revelation. The person of Jesus Christ was, in his view, the ultimate source of revelation and faith. Schleiermacher's concern for religious feelings and the individual's subjective consciousness divested Scripture and its content of their status as revelation.[54] His interventions encouraged an anthropomorphization of religion as an emanation of historical subjects that proved unsettling to later critics.

The Self-Revelation of God in Hegel

Schleiermacher's attempt to rehabilitate religion as subjective experience and feeling wrongly relinquished objective knowledge of the divine, for Hegel. His ambition following the denouement of Kantian efforts to ground God in practical reason was to secure a solid cognitive foundation for the philosophy of religion that honoured recent critiques of speculative theology and natural religion. This project recovered revelation as a central philosophical concept dedicated to the historical unfolding of being. No longer the antithesis of reason, revelation had, for Hegel, primarily ontological significance. It lay at the heart of three interconnected processes, which his religious philosophy explored: God's coming into being and attaining self-consciousness as spirit; humankind's achieving full knowledge of the self and of God; and the logical development of rational thought. Hegel's approach to revelation justified the reformed policies of the Prussian state and its church during the Restoration. His idea of divine self-revelation through history also placed the realization of God on earth in the custodianship of Protestant philosophers. He claimed for speculative philosophy the prerogative to interpret crucial Christian doctrines, the content of which was, in his view, essentially rational.

Born the son of a revenue officer in the state of Württemberg, Hegel studied Protestant theology at the renowned Tübingen Stift from 1788 to 1793. His frustration with traditional theology was mitigated in part by his sharing living quarters with Schelling and the poet Friedrich Hölderlin. The French Revolution imbued the trio with eschatological hopes of being able to reconcile the divine and secular in a cultural act of liberation that realized the Kingdom of God on earth. Hegel specifically idealized the public dimensions of ancient Greek folk religion as a model for aligning individual conscience with the communal will and making religion an ethically transformative force within the nation.[55] After assuming a position as tutor in Bern, Switzerland, in 1793, sustained engagement with Kant immersed Hegel in the Enlightened critique of dogmatic, institutional Christianity. A small inheritance enabled him to join Schelling in Jena in 1801 as an unpaid lecturer. Hegel remained until Napoleon defeated Prussian troops outside the city, reportedly finishing *The Phenomenology of Spirit* (1807) as canon thundered in the distance.

In the *Kritisches Journal der Philosophie*, Hegel indicted both Enlightened critics and defenders of subjective religious experience for prematurely surrendering the capacity to know God. His "Faith and Knowledge" (1802) dismissed the disparate work of Kant, Fichte, and Jacobi under the label of "reflective philosophy of subjectivity." According to Hegel, the three philosophers wrongly relegated the absolute to the realm of the inconceivable, leaving behind an "infinite void of knowledge."[56] The theology of an unknown God was an affront to Christianity's valuation of revelation, Hegel concluded; God wished to be known.[57] Schleiermacher gradually replaced Jacobi as the bête noire of religious subjectivism, for Hegel. Although initially encouraged by the *Speeches*, which indicated to Hegel that his age longed for religious philosophy,[58] he denounced their supposed admixture of mystical intuition and diluted Christianity in the *Phenomenology*. The theology of feeling perpetuated what Hegel termed "unhappy consciousness," or the misperception that individual existence had been severed from the absolute. For Hegel, religion could not rest solely on historical experience; it required a transcendent truth.[59]

Responding to the first volume of the *Christian Faith* in 1822, Hegel intensified his indictment of the "unsatisfactory peace"[60] negotiated between faith and knowledge, one defined as the "lack of a known truth, an objective content, a doctrine of faith."[61] Schleiermacher exemplified, for Hegel, the "universal prejudice of our culture,"[62] namely acceptance of the "contingent and capricious" nature of subjective feeling. If religion was indeed based solely on the feeling of dependence,

Hegel remarked, "a dog would then be the best Christian."[63] This caricature represents a self-interested, polemical misreading.[64] Schleiermacher's conception of feeling entailed more than physical sensation or emotion.[65] Schleiermacher was likewise not an anti-rationalist. Reason enabled the feeling of dependence to be translated into technical theological discourse.[66] Hegel in turn was admittedly concerned with the religious experience of human subjects; his God was not exclusively an object of thought.[67] Both Hegel and Schleiermacher presumed the ultimate ontological identity of the self and absolute, man and God, but differed on how to apprehend it.[68]

Revelation was arguably the most significant concept in Hegel's philosophy of religion and had both ontological and epistemological implications.[69] On the one hand, revelation referred to the personal self-disclosure of a revelatory God.[70] The *Phenomenology of the Spirit* presents God or absolute spirit as the ultimate subject of becoming. God's being disclosed itself, for Hegel, not as abstract substance or pure immediacy but as spirit.[71] Its essential quality was to be revelatory self-consciousness. Affirming divine personhood, Hegel argued that God was a subject who was ontologically and metaphysically bound to posit himself as substance.[72] This vision melded two ontotheological traditions – Spinoza's philosophy of substance and Schelling's identity philosophy.[73] On the other hand, the self-revelation of God also represented the self-actualization of absolute idea. The term had epistemological significance since all of reality could be understood as the necessary revelation of an underlying original concept. The self-revelation of God constituted, for Hegel, the forms assumed by knowledge and human self-consciousness as they progressed through history. Spirit's coming to full self-consciousness both enabled and depended upon humankind attaining gradual knowledge of the absolute.

The logical forms assumed by human knowledge thus correlated, for Hegel, with the stages of God's self-revelation. Revelation was, for Hegel, the very activity that constituted human consciousness and enabled knowledge.[74] In Hegel's view, absolute being first existed in pure thought as a self-generating concept devoid of selfhood. Truth was attained through immediate intuition and remained abstract and universal. In a second stage, spirit posited itself as an object of representation in the historical world. Eternal being gained objective existence by becoming particular, but spirit experienced the act of individuation as a form of self-alienation or "unconscious night."[75] The human sciences participated in God's self-revelation by making the determinate life of spirit explicit and self-aware. Finally, spirit achieved self-consciousness by recognizing itself in its otherness. Absolute spirit's taking form as infinite subjectivity in turn allowed human consciousness to reconcile the particular and universal in a higher unity.

This framework structured how Hegel presented the history of religion. The *Phenomenology* outlines four moments in the evolution of how human consciousness conceived of absolute being, starting with a religion of light. In revelatory (*offenbare*) religion, the third stage of development, spirit assumed its true shape and grasped the concept of itself. Hegel argued that Christianity was the consummate form of revelatory religion; revelatoriness became the "very essence and substance" of the divine.[76] The Christian God was, according to Hegel, intrinsically self-disclosing and self-manifesting. The "divine being is *revealed*," he wrote, and becomes self-conscious of itself.[77] A speculative redescription of the Trinity was, however, the final hurdle in human consciousness advancing towards absolute knowing. Religion contained true content, for Hegel, but in an inadequate form. The constitutive movements in positive Christianity had to be translated into conceptual categories before its truth could be fully comprehended. "God is attainable in pure speculative knowledge alone," Hegel insisted, "and *is* only in that knowledge, and is only that knowledge itself."[78] The immediate form of spirit in revelatory religion needed to advance to the categories of thought to complete itself.

Religion thus constituted a preliminary stage of knowledge, for Hegel, a status he clarified in the *Encyclopedia of the Philosophical Sciences* (1817), drafted as a lecture compendium after he assumed a professorship in philosophy in Heidelberg. The text is split into three sections treating logic, the philosophy of nature, and the philosophy of spirit. The last division organized its component fields into subjective spirit (anthropology and psychology), objective spirit (law and morality), and absolute spirit, under which fell art, revealed religion, and philosophy. Hegel proposed that art, religion, and philosophy each addressed the same content – God and idea – but in a different representational medium. Art engaged absolute spirit through concrete intuition and the forms of determinate existence. It offered a prelude, advancing through religion, to the liberated and absolute forms of speculative philosophy. Religion improved on the sensuous and immediate beauty of art but was hampered by pictorial thinking and storytelling discourse, which only conceptual thought could rectify.

The *Encyclopedia* characterized Christianity as a "revealed" (*geoffenbarte*), rather than revelatory, religion, referring both to its being dispensed in an historical, empirical manner by God and to its recognizing a self-revealing God. Hegel's exaltation of the Trinity as the central symbol of the living, revelatory God was heterodox at the time given its relative marginalization in Protestant thought.[79] For Schleiermacher the trinity was merely a secondary articulation of faith since it abstracted from religious experience.[80] For Hegel the structure of the Trinity disclosed the truth of a self-revealing God and symbolized how spirit became manifest in the historical world. Revelation commenced with the self-revelation of God to himself in the realm of logic, pure thought, and possibility. God existed first as idea and the precondition for creation. In a second step, the divine manifested itself in the historical world, realizing its abstract idea in nature and human consciousness. Ultimately, God came to full self-realization in the form of self-conscious spirit or absolute being reconciled with its apparent other. Christ embodied, for Hegel, the perfect reconciliation of reason and the historical world. Yet Hegel's notion of God's continual self-revelation through history notably dissolved the presumed embodiment of revelation in the historical Jesus within the broader process of attaining absolute knowledge of the revelatory God.[81]

In 1818 Hegel acceded to the prestigious Berlin chair in philosophy vacated four years earlier upon Fichte's death. Baron vom Stein, Prussia's reform-minded minister of culture, secured Hegel's appointment and served as patron to his students, including Philipp Marheineke and Wilhelm Vatke, reportedly to offset the powerbase of Schleiermacher and the Historical School. Hegel's assurance that the rational structures of the modern state provided the best framework for actualizing ethical life appealed to the liberal reform faction of Karl August von Hardenberg, which like Hegel feared both the forces of popular nationalism and traditionalism.[82] The Hegelian approach to theology generally sanctioned the existing political and social order, as well as the status of the Protestant church as a state institution.[83] By the 1820s Hegel suspected that reason and the absolute had been actualized, however precariously, in the historical institutions of the reformed Prussian state. He favoured centralized bureaucratic control of the institutions and liturgy of the Protestant state church.[84]

Conflicts between Hegel and Schleiermacher escalated over differing visions of how the church, state, and other institutions fostered ethical life and German cultural integration, especially after the German Confederation passed the Carlsbad Decrees restricting civil liberties and political activism in 1819. Hegel had a more conservative view of how state authority should relate to religious life, expecting the church to provide spiritual direction for the nation.[85] Direct encounters between the two were rare, as each dominated a distinct discipline and a separate intellectual milieu. Yet Hegel's decision to lecture on the philosophy of religion in 1821 aimed to offset the impeding publication of

Schleiermacher's *Christian Faith*. Hegel offered the popular course three more times with significant alterations before his unexpected death during the cholera outbreak of 1831.[86] The following analysis centres on the 1824 edition, which responded most directly to Schleiermacher and vastly expanded Hegel's treatment of world religions. During this period a new generation of Hegel's disciples increasingly devoted their attention to the relationship between faith and knowledge, and the cultural role of Hegelian philosophy gradually shifted away from debates over the role of the state and *Volk* in reconstruction.[87]

The lectures on the philosophy of religion claimed the same object as *theologia naturalis*, knowledge of God based on reason alone. However, Hegel presumed that God was not "inwardly empty and dead" but a "living God"[88] to be grasped as spirit that "endows itself with revelation and objectivity."[89] The philosophy of religion therefore had to capture manifestations of the divine as it appeared in nature, history, and human consciousness. The opening lectures outlined a three-part dialectical process through which humanity gained knowledge of absolute spirit. The necessary structure of God's self-revelation shaped, for Hegel, the history of religion or how humanity conceptualized God. Spirit first existed as a universal abstract concept of the divine or as logical form and pure thought. In a second moment, spirit engaged in the activity of self-production and became an object for itself. A primal moment of division established God's nature as revelatory, for Hegel, and set the conditions under which God was to be known. Religion began, Hegel argued, when God became an object of human consciousness and took form as finite spirit within the determinate religions.

The lectures distinguished four means to attain knowledge of God that culminated in Hegel's speculative philosophy; each represented a distinct way that consciousness of absolute truth manifested itself. Immediate knowledge of the divine produced an inner certainty of God or faith. This awareness dispensed with the need for empirical evidence; belief arose based simply on God's being present in consciousness. Responding to Schleiermacher in 1824, Hegel indicted feeling "the animal, sensuous form" of divine consciousness as the "very worst way in which such a content can be posited."[90] As a form of knowledge, feeling suffered from being momentary, ephemeral, and contingent.[91] By contrast, representation, the third stage of knowing, depicted the objective content and certainty of God through symbolic imagery or history, thereby allowing God to emerge as objective being. Consciousness of God finally took the form of thought once empirical observations were deemed an insufficient basis for knowledge. As a final reconciliation of the abstract concept of God and its determination in the historical world, Hegel placed a religion's cultus, the practical relationship it cultivated with God.

The history of determinate religions that Hegel presented in the lectures traced the development of human religious consciousness, which Hegel aligned with the evolving historical forms of absolute spirit. Their collective trajectory proved that God was revelatory. Each iteration of the lectures offers a different arrangement of determinate religions, although all maintain an ascending hierarchy of racial types based on proximity to Europe. Religion was, for Hegel, the most important subjective criterion for differentiating races. [92] The early lectures took proof of God as the dominant organizing principle;[93] following the July Revolution, the history of religions charted, for Hegel, the progression of consciousness to freedom.[94] Never strictly historical, the surveys resemble a typology or geography of religions.[95] At each stage, the determinate religions follow the dialectical movement outlined in the opening lectures from concept, through its concrete representations, to the cultus. Consciousness of the absolute also progresses systematically across the determinate religions from prereflective immediacy, through spiritual individuation, and ending with Christianity in which absolute spirit is realized. As a result, most of the world religions are treated as "fossilized forms"[96] left behind by the advance of spirit towards consummate religion.

Due to the increased availability of empirical sources, as well as to his work on world history and the history of philosophy, Hegel vastly expanded his treatment of Asian religions in 1824. The three categories into which this iteration divides world religions were, for Hegel, "a necessary classification that follows objectively from the nature of spirit." His account of the origin of religion explicitly refuted the idea of a lost primordial dispensation. The first religion was "the most imperfect," a fusion of nature and spirit. "The spiritual," Hegel wrote, is "still joined with the natural in their first undisturbed, untroubled unity."[97] Most Asian, African, and the Near Eastern religions fell under the rubric of immediate religion or nature religion in 1824. He deemed the religion of magic, not Sabianism, to be the "oldest, rawest, crudest form of religion,"[98] the lowest rung of spiritual consciousness found among Eskimos, Africans, Mongols, and early Chinese, all peoples at the bottom of Hegel's racial hierarchy.[99] Because consciousness remained one with nature, as if in a "sleepwalking state,"[100] this form of religion suffered from unfreedom. He associated non-European religions, which supposedly lacked faith in a monotheistic trinity, with the failure of non-Caucasian races to recognize legal rights and establish political states.[101]

In the religions of spiritual individuality, which followed nature religion, spirit became conscious of its distinction from nature by reflecting into itself and thus more capable of subjectivity. People began to perceive God not only as substance but as a subject engaged in some free activity. Given his goal in the lectures to depict necessary and rational stages progressing towards Christianity, Hegel offered a more favourable portrayal of Judaism, as a religion of spiritual individuality than previously.[102] Hegel argued that spirit first achieved subjective unity, which the Greeks lacked, in the Jewish God. God appeared as an absolute subject after the flood in the form of a punishing force distinct from nature. But, according to Hegel, the idea of God's inward self-determination was not yet complete when, in Judaism, he appeared as absolute power, wisdom, and purpose. Jewish religious wisdom stalled in abstract universality without positing the divine as self-manifesting.

The trait qualifying Christianity as the consummate religion was, according to Hegel, revelatoriness (*Offenbarkeit*). Christianity facilitated the actualization of absolute spirit by allowing finite spirit to recognize itself as revelatory. God's destiny as spirit was to be for an other, to reveal himself. "This revealing or self-manifesting," Hegel concluded, "belongs to the essence of spirit itself." Christianity was a revelatory religion because the Trinity depicted God as self-manifesting. By Hegel's definition, revelation consisted in God's "act of determining or positing distinctions" but also the ability "at the same time to take them back into himself, and thereby to be present to himself." Revelation did not disclose essential truths about God; it had no content beyond itself. Rather, it was an activity that constituted God's very being. God engaged in an "eternal act of self-revelation"[103] and was defined by that act.

The rehabilitation of revelation as the self-revelation of spirit is far removed from the orthodox defence of historical revelation in scripture. However, especially responding in 1827 to August Tholuck's accusations of pantheism, Hegel welcomed as proto-rational the historical revelation of God in positive Christianity. He emphasized the identity in content between philosophy and faith, affirming the apologetic stance of his conservative followers.[104] The revelatoriness of God needed to be disclosed in external, sensuous, and historical forms, such as doctrines or practices, Hegel affirmed.[105] These, in turn, harboured reason and truth. Similarly to Lessing, however, Hegel feared that the rational truth of Christianity could not be established based on historical proofs alone, such as miracles or prophecies, or its positive features. These were only the "beginning of verification," its sensible and unspiritual forms. The only authentic verification of divine truth,

Hegel concluded, was the "witness of spirit."[106] This was testified to in the Bible, known through theology, but only fully comprehended in philosophy.

Revelation was crucial to Hegel's reconstruction of the foundations for achieving rational knowledge of God in post-Kantian German philosophy. He detached revelation from its previous epistemological framework in which revelation signified the supernatural dispensation of otherwise inaccessible truths. For Hegel revelation had primarily ontological significance. Revelatoriness defined God's being; it was likewise the process by which God entered the historical world, came to full manifestation, and attained self-consciousness as spirit. At the same time, Hegel's system reaped the epistemological benefits of a self-revealing God. A revelatory God had to make the truth of his being apparent; human consciousness, according to Hegel, enabled spirit to achieve self-recognition. Historical necessity thus fated finite consciousness to eventually attain knowledge of the absolute. Revealed religion was merely a preliminary kind of knowledge, however. According to Hegel, the Christian doctrine of the Trinity needed speculative philosophy to translate positive, historical revelation into conceptual language, even if its content was equivalent.

Hegel vastly expanded the significance of revelation within theology by making it an ontological as well as an epistemological term.[107] The intense divisions among Hegel's disciples suggest, however, the fragility of his reconstruction.[108] Through the 1820s, a conservative, apologetic interpretation of Hegel's reconciliation of faith and reason dominated speculative theology. Karl Daub and Marheineke, both once loyal to Schelling's identity philosophy, insisted that Hegelian philosophy validated the positive dogmas of biblical revelation and confirmed Protestant orthodoxy.[109] Younger Hegelians coming to maturity at the end of the decade, including D.F. Strauss and Ludwig Feuerbach, wrested Hegelian philosophy away from Christian apologetics.[110] For Feuerbach, who attended Hegel's lectures in 1824, religion was the outgrowth of a specifically human condition; God was a human product, a projection of the human essence, and thus an illusion. Neither Hegel's philosophy of religion nor Schleiermacher's subjectivist approach ultimately protected Christianity from the psychology of religion.[111]

The Dark Ground of Revelation in F.W.J. Schelling

Hegel's rival, F.W.J. Schelling, similarly revitalized the idea of revelation as the historical self-disclosure of God's being but attributed more significance to the experiential ground of God's self-revelation.

The logical necessity by which Hegel subsumed reality to the concept destroyed, for Schelling, the status of revelation as a free act of God. A favourite of existential theologian Paul Tillich (1886–1965), Schelling insisted that conditions preceding even the emergence of God's being made revelation both necessary and free. "The act of choice is also a part of the complete revelation of God, which is realized in history as totality," Tillich wrote admiringly of Schelling in 1912. Tillich revered Schelling as the "initiator and patron of the existentialist protest," willing to place actual existence in tension with essence and to theorize a demonic ground in which God was nevertheless present.[112] Schelling's insistence on the ontological significance of revelation preceded Hegel's and remained consistent through his late lectures on the philosophy of revelation. Disaffected by Hegel's logical determinism, however, Schelling increasingly rooted God's freedom and human autonomy in the dark ground of unconscious forces latently present in the divine. For Schelling actuality and historical contingency had priority over conceptual possibility, and comprehending God's self-revelation required a positive philosophy of existence.

Born in Leonberg, Württemberg, Schelling was the privileged son of a successful Orientalist and chaplain. Despite stiff competition and his markedly young age, Schelling dazzled the faculty of the Tübingen Stift, where he trained to be a clergyman from 1790 to 1795. Along with Hegel and Hölderlin he joined the student club dedicated to the French Revolution and embraced the theological Enlightenment as an ally in the struggle against political despotism. The conservative application of critical philosophy at the Stift hardened Schelling against traditional notions of historical revelation. The superintendent G.C. Storr, a supernaturalist, used Kant to defend orthodox Lutheran dogmas. Fichte's *Wissenschaftslehre* (1794–5) convinced Schelling that revelation could not be a postulate of practical reason.[113]

Schelling's early *Naturphilosophie*, which equated the absolute with the material world, coincided, as seen in Chapter 4, with a refusal to recognize revelation as a valid scientific principle. The start of Schelling's revaluation of revelation is, nevertheless, already visible in "Ueber Offenbarung und Volksunterricht" (1798), published after Schelling joined Fichte as an unpaid lecturer in Jena. He considered in this essay the possibility of a "rational use of revelation" depicting how the ideal intersected the real. Absolute reason, he noted, was the "primordial synthesis" from which everything particularly evolves, becoming manifest in the external world. The history of religion, Schelling speculated, could constitute "a progressive revelation or a symbolic portrayal of … ideas" derived from the absolute.[114]

The new meaning Schelling subsequently attributed to revelation within absolute idealism bestowed upon it an ontological significance that anticipated Hegel, still at this time a house tutor in Frankfurt. The *System of Transcendental Idealism* (1800) reinforced Schelling's earlier suspicion that revelation might hold validity as the process by which the absolute became manifest in history. The coming into being of the self-conscious subject, as well as the manifestation of the ideal in the real, now constituted, in his view, a type of revelation. "History as a whole is a progressive, gradually self-disclosing revelation of the absolute," Schelling wrote, "[God] continually *reveals* Himself."[115] The work presented a history of self-consciousness that culminated in the transcendental subject. Schelling's task was to understand how self-consciousness developed from a point where it did not exist without succumbing to a materialist position that reduced it to a mechanical function of nature or assuming, like Fichte, that self-consciousness is wholly self-grounding.[116]

Schelling theorized the existence of a primordial unconscious that progressively encountered and overcome its limitations. This process resembled the self-disclosure of an internalized God or, in the words of Emil Fackenheim, the breaking through of a God within.[117] History, Schelling concluded, was the "never wholly completed revelation of that absolute which, for the sake of consciousness … separates itself into conscious and unconscious, the free and the intuitant; but which itself … is eternal identity." Three progressive stages in the self-limitation of the absolute's infinite activity produced the individual, conscious self and allowed the absolute to become an object. Schelling distinguished three corresponding "periods of revelation" through which God came into existence.[118] The final section of the text proposed that art, not philosophy, was the "the one everlasting revelation"[119] that most fully articulated the absolute.

After 1800 and the death from typhus, in which he felt implicated, of Auguste Böhmer, the daughter of his lover Caroline Schlegel, Schelling became increasingly preoccupied with the idea of a self-revealing God.[120] His *Vorlesungen über die Methode des akademischen Studiums*, held in Jena in the summer of 1802 as Schelling developed his philosophy of identity, mark the start of a gradual return to Christianity, completed by 1815.[121] This return reintroduced the content of Christian revelation into the term's philosophical application. In a reversal of his plans for establishing a new Greek mythology, he announced in 1802 the "rebirth of esoteric Christianity."[122] Theology, he argued, was the "direct science of the absolute and divine being" that "objectively represents the absolute point of indifference" when the ideal and the real were united. Philosophy, however, was necessary to comprehend the highest ideas regarding the divine, especially the significance of "history as the revelation of God."[123] Schelling still feared that strict adherence to the word hampered the understanding.[124] Speculative reason was needed to extract the inner truth of Christian revelation from its historical foundation.

A new emphasis on the corruptions of a fallen world accompanied Schelling's turn away from identity philosophy and encouraged a concept of revelation that bridged the divide Enlightened thinkers feared between divine truth and its historically contingent presentation. The Jena Romantics had dissolved amidst the scandal of Schelling's intimacies with and eventual betrothal to the divorced Caroline Schlegel. Facing a cool reception at the new Catholic university in Würzburg, to which he moved in 1803, Schelling reconceived the finite world as a falling away from the infinite. His *Philosophy and Religion* (1804) responded, specifically, to C.A. Eschenmayer's allegation that identity philosophy failed to explain how a perfect world of ideas could have generated a corrupt reality. The phenomenal world represented a leap or removal from the absolute, Schelling proposed, not a positive emanation. "Only history as a whole is a revelation of God," Schelling recalled, "and then only a progressively evolving revelation."[125] Under the conditions of a fallen world the state, for example, was not a viable foundation for ethical community. Instead of a revitalized public religion, Schelling longed in 1804 for a restoration of the alliance between philosophy and religion found in Greek mystery cults. Religion, in his view, had a compensatory function that transcended the external ordering of freedom.[126]

The Peace of Preßburg, following the Battle of Austerlitz, deprived Bavaria of Würzburg, which became the seat of a Grand Duchy under Ferdinand III, the former Grand Duke of Tuscany. Schelling was transferred to Munich in 1806 with an appointment at the newly established Bavarian Academy of Sciences where F.H. Jacobi, who had denounced Lessing's pantheism twenty years earlier, served as president. The ceremonial address Schelling held to honour King Maximilian I unleashed the third major controversy over God's personhood and revelation since the publication of Reimarus's fragments.[127] The last public exposition of Schelling's philosophy of art, "Über das Verhältnis der bildenden Künste zu der Natur," raised the spectre of Spinoza by depicting nature as "the sacred, eternally creative primordial force in the world, which generates all things from itself."[128] Rather than stand in opposition to the soul, nature was, Schelling claimed, a "tool" for its revelation.[129] Jacobi's rebuttal insisted on a transcendent personal God who appeared to humankind as instinct, inner drive, or an internalized echo in the soul. Revelation occurred, Jacobi wrote, "without intuition, without concepts, inscrutably and ineffably,"[130] present in inner, subjective consciousness as an object of faith, not knowledge.

Concerns about reason's limitations, as well as Hegel's jarring condemnation of absolute identity in the preface to the *Phenomenology*, which he sent to Schelling as a manuscript asking for a foreword, encouraged Schelling to investigate the experiential grounds of God's being. To assert that all is one in an indeterminate absolute was the height of naiveté, for Hegel, equivalent to depicting a night in which all cows are black. If everything belonged to God as identity, then all differences were mere appearances. Schelling had helped his former roommate obtain a private lectureship in Jena, but in 1807 their by then tenuous relationship disintegrated into open antagonism. Schelling, for his part, sought a greater sphere for divine and human freedom than he thought possible in Hegel's deriving the revelation of spirit from the dialectical logic of the concept. Hegel, in his view, could not explain how the absolute could freely choose to come out of itself. If God were a logical abstraction, then everything would proceed from him with necessity, curtailing divine freedom.

Written just before Caroline's own death from dysentery, Schelling's *Philosophical Investigations into the Essence of Human Freedom* (1809) responded to the perceived inability of German idealism to account for human freedom. The text carved out a new space for choice in revelation's unfolding against what Schelling termed the dark ground of God or non-being. The resulting "bipolar God"[131] incorporated within itself two opposing primal principles, and the process of his becoming had to navigate all that contradicted the divine. As such, the freedom essay marks a decisive shift in Schelling's work to a philosophy of existence that accounted for aspects of real experience deemed to be non-rational and autonomous, despite their origin in God. It provided the groundwork for the positive philosophy of revelation that Schelling delivered as lectures during his second Munich period. The resulting concept of revelation navigated precariously between the absolute perspective of history and the empirical self-presentation of God, bridging Lessing's ditch with a full embrace of revelation's historicity. Revelation likewise came to designate the formation of the self, a fraught process caught between the vicissitudes of history and consciousness.

To eliminate determinism in the emergence of God as a moral being Schelling defended the concrete experience of freedom, including the possibility of evil, in the face of absolute reason. This required establishing both the "freedom of God in the self-revelation"[132] and human autonomy. According to Schelling, God could only reveal himself through "free beings acting on their own, for whose Being there is no ground other than God."[133] Schelling characterized God in 1809 as a living unity of forces. His personality was shaped by the interactions between a self-determining being and an independent ground of reality within God that was inseparable but different. There were, he wrote, "two equally eternal beginnings of self-revelation."[134] A primordial, dark, or irrational principle thus conditioned, but did not determine, revelation; Schelling referred to this force as pure craving, desire, self-will, and chaos. He cautioned that "anarchy still lies in the ground, as if it could break through once again,"[135] even though self-revelation appeared to bestow rule, order, and form on the world. Schelling's conception of the dark ground of being not surprisingly appealed in the twentieth century to psychoanalytic and poststructuralist theories of an unconscious, presymbolic realm.

A primordial negating force, the independent ground of existence, thus ensured, in Schelling's view, the possibility of revelation. "Precisely that which negates all revelation must be made the ground of revelation,"[136] Schelling declared in the *Weltalter*, an unfinished work begun in 1810, revised during his Erlangen years, and only delivered as lectures in 1827. A rough draft of sorts for the later lectures on the philosophy of mythology and revelation, the *Weltalter* confirmed Schelling's turn to positive philosophy, the attempt to interpret the particular aspects of existence as a manifestation of an essential order. Refuting the idea of primordial revelation, Schelling posited here a prehistory in which God existed only as potencies of being and non-being or as the pure capacity to be. Revelation only commenced, he concluded, with the actual assumption of being; God could not be conceived as eternally actual in the sense of always having been externally revealed.

The Bavarian king, Ludwig I, recalled Schelling from Erlangen, where he had imbibed revivalist Christianity with G.H. Schubert, when he moved the university to Munich. Schelling's triumphant return to his *Wahlheimat* in the summer of 1827 inaugurated nearly a decade of provincial philosophical glory. Schelling enjoyed close ties to king and court and tutored the crown prince; he dominated the Academy of Sciences with few serious rivals and basked in the anticipation surrounding future publications. His influence over students was such that in December 1830 Schelling successfully drew them off the streets after weeks of revolutionary protests.[137] Only J.J. Görres could challenge his position. Despite a shared dislike of Hegelian religious philosophy, Schelling was largely silent on Görres's ideas about the evolution of a putative *Urreligion* due to his speculative, unscholarly method and outspoken ultramontanism.[138] Görres, in turn, rallied fellow conservatives to steer Ludwig I away from liberal accommodation and towards revivalist Catholicism at Schelling's considerable expense.[139]

Starting in 1831 Schelling regularly held lectures on the philosophy of revelation to packed lectures halls. A student preserved a copy of the inaugural manuscript; later in Berlin Schelling added a new introduction and expanded on themes present in the *Urfassung*. Franz von Baader held a parallel series that addressed revelation in Munich but in the tradition of a theosophy that honoured traditional Christian dogmatics.[140] The two once shared an enthusiasm for Böhme and mysticism, the likely source of Schelling's conviction that God only came to consciousness with the creation of the world.[141] But their relationship collapsed in 1824. Catholic protests against Schelling's philosophy of revelation eventually threatened his freedom of teaching.[142] When the ultramontane government of Karl von Abel replaced the liberal minister of the interior, L.K.E. Prince of Oettingen-Wallerstein, in 1837 new regulations forbade Protestant professors from lecturing on religion unless affiliated with the church.[143] Schelling defied the proscription, but the victory of political Catholicism made his position in Munich tenuous.

Schelling's philosophy of religion entwined the history of God's self-revelation with that of the human religious consciousness, framing it against Hegel as a positive, historical philosophy of existence. At its core lay a theogony, a history of God's becoming from a deeply prehistorical state of pure possibility and non-being to his full revelation in the historical world as Christ; Christianity was, for Schelling, a "fact ... that must be explained in purely historical terms."[144] The philosophy of revelation's final goal was to transform revealed truths, such as the Trinity and resurrection, into independent truths. He attributed a meaningful role to human subjects as partners in revelation. God's freedom in Schelling's view was bound to the contingent, historical reality of creation and human development.[145] The laborious transition in human consciousness from relative monotheism to its absolute form and eventually to a free philosophical religion restored to God the balance and unity lost at creation. While similar in its ambitions to the religious philosophy of Hegel, Schelling's project was more conservative. His failure to task the state with generating ethical community or the church with for moralizing politics was "radically apolitical,"[146] in the words of John Toews. The notion that religion transcended the political sphere undercut liberal and democratic reform and legitimized the repressive states of the Restoration.

Schelling's lectures divested revelation of any epistemological significance. As a freely created science, philosophy rendered revelation comprehensible, in his view, but without being subject to its dictates. "Revelation is proposed as an object and not as a source or authority,"[147] he affirmed. It belonged to the "realities of experience" for Schelling, like nature, art, or human consciousness.[148] Schelling agreed with non-cognitive theorists such as Jacobi and Schleiermacher that religion was rooted in an immediate intuitive act or awe. But, in his view, reason had to elevate religious hypotheses based on feeling to conceptual certainty.[149] A moment of ecstasy, Schelling argued, enabled reason to bridge the abyss between noncognitive truth and conceptual thought. "There is an ecstasy, through which a subject is placed outside his being, estranged from himself," Schelling explained, and then a second moment in which "what is estranged is given back to itself."[150] Positive philosophy sought an encounter with the dark ground of the irrational but without collapsing into subjectivism. In a moment of insight, the mind encountered what lay beyond reason and recognized its limits; this critical self-examination captured the transrational grounds of existence before returning freely to the conceptual order.[151]

The conditions Schelling set for the historical onset of revelation eliminated the prospect of a primordial dispensation. The first religion was a religion of the primordial consciousness or *Urbewußtsein*, according to Schelling, not the product of a conscious mind. "The beginning of knowledge cannot be derived from revelation," Schelling insisted. "Primordial man did not find himself in a condition that required revelation; he was ... bound to divine consciousness."[152] Schelling explicitly broke with the tradition that regarded mythology as a distortion of an original, revealed truth. "The usual bemoaning of the decline of a pure knowledge and its splintering into successive polytheism is," Schelling wrote, "as little appropriate to the religious standpoint as to the philosophical one and to the true history."[153] Humankind's initial communion with the creator was, he argued, absolutely prehistoric, a timeless moment in eternity. Separation from the divine was a precondition for revelation; it needed to be directed to an historically constituted consciousness. This perspective offered a "more joyful view"[154] than the presumption of a lost primordial revelation, according to Schelling, which failed to justify the destruction of originally pure knowledge and misjudged the extent to which underdeveloped religious consciousness stifled freedom, repressed human development, and hindered the attainment of higher knowledge.

A rather obtuse theory of the potencies, the hallmark of Schelling's negative philosophy, explained how pure existence was moulded into spiritual being. As Edward Allen Beach has deftly outlined, it had two temporal components: a premundane phase of pure possibility prior to the actualization of the potencies, and their subsequent historical activity in the realm of human culture. Creation resulted from God deciding to place the potencies in tension and invert their proper relationship. A struggle in finite human consciousness was to restore the potencies to the unity lost with the onset of time. Real existence began, for Schelling, in chaos and conflict as the first potency resisted systematic ordering and rationalization. The ensuing dynamic of historical existence was determined by the potencies' jostling to find equilibrium. The same process enabled God's coming into being within the human consciousness. According to Schelling, the evolution of mythology documented shifts in the relationships among the potencies, which in inverted form corresponded with three primary deities common to pagan religions.

Mythology had a crucial theogonic role as necessary preparation for the full self-revelation of God in Christianity. It presided over a "regeneration of religious consciousness"[155] within the lower, natural realm. Different facets of the theogonic process were also distributed across peoples so that each *Volk* represented one moment in the collective history of God's self-revelation. Natural consciousness of God attained its highest level in the Eleusinian mysteries, according to Schelling.[156] He refuted previous claims that the mysteries harboured abstract monotheism. Instead Schelling proposed that the rites of Demeter were a dramatized recapitulation of "the history of religious consciousness,"[157] through which initiates realized that all causal gods were manifestations of the same forces.

Revelation corrected and completed the insufficiencies of myth, according to Schelling, liberating humanity from the natural realm. God freely willed to restore human consciousness. This was the "sole cause of revelation"[158] and accordingly defied rational comprehension. Although not directly willed by God, paganism was an indirect precedent, a relative truth, which Christianity fully revealed. Schelling argued for the "preexistence of Christ" before the incarnation as the inverted second potency. Osiris, Shiva, and Dionysus were pagan renditions of the same divine principle that achieved fulfilment in God's Son.[159] The coming of Christ completed the self-revelation of God and marked the "end of revelation,"[160] after which no further unveiling of the relationship between the divine and human worlds was necessary. Christianity, however, subsequently progressed through three historical stages, according to Schelling, defined as the ages of the apostles Peter (Catholicism), Paul (Protestantism), and John (their coming synthesis).

Already in 1831 Schelling presented a prophetic vision of Germany presiding over the final Johannine era of true faith: post-confessional, philosophical Christianity liberated from the external forms of revealed religion. German *Wissenschaft* elevated the Protestant church to the level of "general consciousness," he declared, and allowed it to "celebrate its true triumph, its place of rest."[161] Among Germans the historical facts of Christianity would finally be appropriated as inner, spiritual truths. Schelling, as Toews argues, assumed Germany to be the universal historical culture of his day.[162] He declared the immanent victory of a philosophical religion, rooted in existence but enhanced by reason, at the heart of Catholic Bavaria – a virtually untenable position in light of the ultramontane revival.

The aura of a prophet enveloped Schelling as, at the age of sixty-five, he delivered an inaugural lecture on the philosophy of revelation in Berlin on 15 November 1841. Schelling had been lured to Friedrich Wilhelm IV's Prussia by Christian Bunsen's plea to eradicate the "dragon's seed of Hegelian pantheism."[163] His appointment to Hegel's still unfilled chair in philosophy signalled support for a conservative restoration of Christianity.[164] Schelling's opening lecture in the revelation course has famously been described as the last great university event. The initial audience included distinguished state officials, and a breathtaking assembly of prominent intellectuals filed through later sessions. For nearly all, Schelling proved a massive disappointment. Within a few years his audience dropped from over four hundred to forty.[165] By 1846 Schelling had cancelled all university lecture courses. Friedrich Engels, among the vocal Hegelian resistance, relentlessly mocked the aged Schelling as wine turned to vinegar and a shipwreck of his former glory. Schelling's faith in revelation was childish and antiquated, in his view, a vain attempt "to smuggle into the free science of thought faith in authority, a mysticism of feeling, and gnostic fantasies."[166] Indeed Schelling failed to engage the critique Ludwig Feuerbach and others had since made of revelation.

The post-critical revival of revelation in the 1820s and 1830s circumvented Lessing's ditch by making a virtue out of a liability, even though embracing revelation's historicity risked anthropomorphizing religion. Realigning the term with subjective experience and the formation of the self made it meaningful in the context of post-revolutionary Europe's rapid political transformation. But it made vastly unappealing the idea of reconstructing a lost primordial revelation. Schleiermacher declared revelation to be a subjective state of consciousness, an inner moment of transformation residing in the soul. As religion consisted primarily in feeling, revelation need not disclose propositional truths about God. Hegel and Schelling endowed revelation with ontological significance as an historical process of self-constitution that made the actualization of the divine dependent on human self-consciousness. Revelation retained an epistemological dimension. Humankind attained knowledge of the absolute as an essential component of God's self-revelation, but that truth was not dispensed as objective doctrine nor viable at the start of time. For Hegel, the self-manifestation of spirit built progressively from the lowest echelon of religious awareness, which was marred by a lack of self-consciousness and blind subjection to nature. Schelling only found revelation conceivable against the prior backdrop of experience, which was subject to unconscious, irrational forces.

Chapter Six

The Epistemology of Grace: Revelation in Catholic Theology, 1770–1850

In 1840 the Swabian theologian Franz Anton Staudenmaier, the foremost Catholic critic of G.W.F. Hegel, vigorously defended "the primal act of revelation"[1] as key to stemming the tides of rationalism and subjectivity in religion. Staudenmaier accepted Lessing's notion that God was the educator of the human race and approached revelation historically. But his *Encyklopädie der theologischen Wissenschaften* (1840) refused to limit the scope of divine guidance, as he feared Lessing had, to a mere expedient, a catalyst that hastened the otherwise self-sufficient and autonomous development of human reason. Staudenmaier insisted on "the original unity of idea and revelation," believing God's direct intervention essential to humanity's intellectual and spiritual achievement. Arguing against Friedrich Schleiermacher, Staudenmaier likewise denied that inner feeling was a sufficient foundation for religion. An external act of awakening was necessary, in his view, to arouse "the living consciousness of God in man."[2] Creation endowed humankind with potential and possibility, but primordial revelation was the spark that ignited thought, sensibility, and sacred history.

The concept of *Uroffenbarung* regularly counteracted the threat of anthropomorphism as Catholic reformers dismantled propositional revelation, this chapter argues, albeit later and with more restraint than Protestants. As a member of the Catholic Tübingen School, Staudenmaier embraced the ontological implications of idealist concepts of revelation, drawing on Schelling's positive philosophy to tame the logical abstractions of Hegelianism. In his view, revelation was the historical "self-manifestation ... of God,"[3] although Staudenmaier insisted upon the unchanging, eternal nature of the divine, which he refused to make dependent on actualization in the human world. More than a pedagogical vehicle, primordial revelation set the "foundations of our existence,"[4] according to Staudenmaier. Yet, like many Catholic theologians,

Staudenmaier also upheld primordial revelation as the precondition for a limited form of rationalism dependent on God's grace. He broke with Protestant philosophers of revelation in this regard.[5]

Through the early modern period, faith and divine authority had sufficed to secure the veracity of Catholic revelation. God's word had required little justification beyond belief in revelation itself, leaving Catholicism particularly vulnerable to enlightened critique.[6] Catholic theories of revelation found articulation in a canonical genre of treatises entitled "De religione" and "De revelatione," which together comprised the first section of the four-part apologetic discourse, "De analysi fidei," designed to prove the necessary truth and universality of Christianity.[7] The first treatise defined revelation, established its possibility and necessity, and laid out criteria for recognizing a true revelation. The second ruminated on the actual historical existence of revelation, establishing the credibility of the sources documenting revelation and proving the factuality of revelations relayed in the Old and New Testaments. These treatises recognized natural reason as instrumental in proving the existence of God, but placed strict limits on its purview, retaining the unconditional supremacy of God's grace in dispensing revealed truths.[8]

Under the sway of scholasticism, the Catholic response to the Enlightened critique of revelation began comparatively late, spreading from France to central Europe by the mid-eighteenth century.[9] The conflict between faith and knowledge was likewise less radical than among Protestants.[10] Orthodox defenders of revelation severely narrowed the scope of the term, reducing revelation to a set of supernaturally dispensed, objectified principles that had to be accepted on Church authority. They offered positivist and absolutist interpretations of revelation that demanded "unquestioning submission" to Church doctrine and rooted religious truth in an "incomprehensible decree of God's will as *potentia absoluta*."[11] This, ironically, divested revelation of its earlier associations with reason and natural religion. Ultramontane enclaves, such as the seminaries in Strasbourg and Mainz, persisted in the narrow vein of scholasticism. Bruno Liebermann's *Institutiones theologiae* (1818–22), for example, still defended revelation against deist objections in the manner of eighteenth-century French Jesuits.[12]

Between the papal suppression of the Jesuits in 1773 and the ascent of neo-scholasticism in the mid-nineteenth century, however, reform-minded Catholics participated in the broader German reevaluation and rehabilitation of revelation. The three main frameworks for restoring positive Christian revelation within Catholicism – traditionalism, semi-rationalism, and idealism – challenged papal authority, however, and the Church's traditional balance between nature and grace.[13] They thrived in the intellectual spaces opened by Gallicanism and Febronianism, movements that favoured the national episcopates over Rome and were shielded by the theological faculties in the German states. None of the three reformist tactics for salvaging revelation was able to satisfactorily reconcile reason and faith without drawing condemnation from Catholic orthodoxy. From the perspective of Rome, they culminated in either an unacceptable fideistic dismissal of reason's contributions to knowledge of God or left an unbridgeable cleft between individual, philosophical reason and the Church's authoritative communication of tradition.[14]

A reaction to the eclipse of belief during the French Revolution, traditionalism resorted to fideism to revive Catholic theology and thrived in France between 1815 and the fall of the Second Empire. Primordial revelation was the central legitimizing concept of the movement, which held unaided reason incapable of attaining religious or moral truths. For traditionalists, all religious knowledge and the human capacity to comprehend it derived from an original act of grace. The movement's founders, Joseph de Maistre and Louis de Bonald, as well as their successor, Félicité de Lamenais and his circle, rejected an anthropological approach to religion, affirming instead a theocentric view of humanity that stressed the necessity of God's direct intervention in human affairs.[15] The very possibility of acquiring knowledge lay, for them, in an original revelation and the transmission of its metaphysical and moral truths.[16]

French traditionalism found little purchase across the Rhine, however, being distinct from the German Catholic fideism exemplified by Johann Michael Sailer's *Erlebnistheologie*, which drawing on Friedrich Heinrich Jacobi and pietism, emphasized the inner, living, subjective experience of revelation.[17] A semi-rationalist approach to restoring revelation was more compelling in the German states given the legacy of Leibnizian-Wolffian philosophy and the need to engage the Kantian critique of reason. Semi-rationalism insisted that to be scientific theology must apply reason to demonstrate and explain the possibility, necessity, and factuality of revelation. This tripartite framework structures the apologetic treatises of Enlightened theologians Benedikt Stattler and Beda Mayr but also inspired the influential Catholic Kantian Georg Hermes. Members of the Tübingen School and idealist theologians such as the Austrian Anton Günther, by contrast, adapted Hegel's and Schelling's philosophies of revelation to Catholic apologetics in the 1830s. In the process, they reconceived revelation as an experiential category that captured both subjective religious consciousness and the unfolding of self-conscious existence.

The persistence of the idea of primordial revelation after this critical turn, however, indicates a reluctance among nineteenth-century Catholic thinkers to ground revelation too heavily in the human world of experience. After the Council of Trent proclaimed Scripture alone dogmatically and exegetically insufficient, the concept had featured in Catholicism as the anchor of living tradition.[18] Counter-Reformation theology drew upon primordial revelation to justify Christianity's superiority over natural religion; it also secured doctrinal truth beyond the bounds of Scripture by establishing an independent origin for Christian teachings.[19] Primordial revelation factored only weakly in scholasticism and in many forms of semi-rationalism. Yet as revelation lost its propositional value, reformist Catholics increasingly grounded religious sensibility and human cognition in an original divine act of grace. Primordial revelation offset the danger posed by natural religion, autonomous reason, and human agency.

Early nineteenth-century recourse to primordial revelation in Catholic theology should not, however, be seen as a mere continuation of early modern syncretism. A handful of early nineteenth-century Catholic historians of religion, including Friedrich Leopold Graf zu Stolberg and Karl Windischmann, identified doctrinal continuities across ancient Eastern religions in the style of Jesuit syncretists. And certainly the appeal of primordial revelation made Catholicism attractive to Romantic mythologists and converts, such as Friedrich Schlegel. Yet late eighteenth-century Catholic historians of religion, such as Franz Michael Vierthaler, had by that time already disavowed the ancient wisdom narrative, opting to follow Christoph Meiners in rejecting even rational *ur*-monotheism. When primordial revelation resurfaced in the work of idealist Catholic philosophies of revelation, it no longer supported a propositional model of revelation typical of syncretism but acquired ontological significance as the start of God's historical self-disclosure. In contrast to Protestant idealists, Catholic understandings of God's self-revelation through history, however, refused to make the self-constitution of the divine dependent on human agency and idealized the moment of origin as epistemologically significant and complete in itself.

Enlightened Catholicism and the Semi-Rationalist Defence of Revelation

The Catholic Enlightenment was a broad movement for the reform and renewal of religious practices, scholarship, and education. Delayed by a generation when compared with its Protestant counterpart, it peaked with the suppression of the Jesuits in 1773 and emphasized moral improvement and socially utilitarian theology. During the late eighteenth century Catholic sermons began to stress moral uplift, had a deeper biblical grounding, and made use of the German language. Practical reforms improved pastoral care and the liturgy.[20] The new catechisms that replaced those of the Counter-Reformation Jesuit Peter Canisius eschewed rote memorization for deduction and active comprehension, evoking reason and natural religion as allies in defending revelation. More literate, sedate forms of piety disciplined superstitions and idolatrous veneration of saints, as well as the Gothic pilgrimage culture of rural Catholics. Better administration of church properties also eased the tensions that arose between the Catholic territorial princes, local bishops, and monastic institutions over jurisdictional boundaries and the control of wealth.[21]

The Catholic Church, however, tended to resist Enlightened ideas more forcefully than the Protestant churches, maintaining that reason could be a tool but not a judge in religious matters. Only a small minority of Catholic intellectuals were rationalist theologians, such as the moral philosopher and Illuminist Jakob Danzer (1743–96).[22] Rational philosophy ran the risk of severing religion from its institutions by deriving salvation directly from God, separating religion from the Bible, and questioning the necessity of tradition.[23] Only a few radicals, including the Bamberg Franciscan Eulogius Schneider, fervent supporter of the French Revolution, guillotined in Paris in 1794, or Martin Gerberg, abbot of St. Blasien, placed themselves directly in the crosshairs of the Church.[24] Instead, the Catholic Enlightenment was largely an apologetic endeavour characterized by mediating theology. Most reform theologians believed the church could bridge knowledge and faith by making the supernatural content of doctrine objective and certain and by providing direct access to Christ's redemptive work in history.

Eighteenth-century Jesuits had assigned complementary but distinct domains to reason and revelation in the acquisition of religious truth. Reason was believed capable of comprehending factual Christian reality as manifest in nature, history, and the human world; faith detected in those realms the presence of the supernatural and divine. Within these bounds, scholasticism welcomed philosophical rationalism and granted limited license to natural religion and autonomous reason.[25] The old traditions of scholasticism offered ineffective resistance to deist and other radical assaults on religion, however, and rapidly became obsolete, especially as the Jesuit presence in the universities waned. The old monastic orders, especially the Benedictines and Augustinians, took a leading role in eroding baroque scholasticism and the Jesuit monopoly on higher education, having for centuries cultivated their own libraries and scholarly traditions. As Ulrich Lehner has shown, the Benedictine monasteries formed the heart of the Catholic Enlightenment, experimenting with new communication structures and building networks for the production and transfer of knowledge.[26]

A limited historicist turn hastened the eclipse of scholasticism as Catholic thinkers embraced biblical criticism, approached religion anthropologically, and explored the history of the Church and canon law. J.K. Barthel, an influential jurist in Würzburg, for example, historicized papal authority as a way to affirm episcopalism and the autonomy of territorial bishops, rejecting late scholastic approaches to canon law.[27] But the universal orientation of Catholicism made critical-historical philology's emphasis on the sustaining role of the vernacular in building national culture unappealing.[28] Historicism disrupted the Catholic emphasis on a continuous tradition of revelation that secured the identity of truth over time.[29] For much of the nineteenth century, orthodox Catholic theologians responded to historical criticism by debating the nuances of what it meant for God to have authored Scripture and reinforcing a theology of inspiration.[30] This hampered the acceptance of a document hypothesis and discouraged the full historicization of revelation as an act conditioned by human experience.

New developments in mathematics, Newtonian science, and psychology likewise helped break the chokehold of scholasticism, as did an infusion of Lockean epistemology. The German Catholic reception of Wolffian philosophy was, however, most crucial to scholasticism's demise. Jesuits had used rationalist arguments to defend the necessity of revelation, and many of their manuals laid out theological issues in a manner similar to Wolff's systematized philosophy, making his work readily accessible.[31] Some Protestant theologians even criticized Wolff's attempted synthesis of revelation and reason, especially his attention to natural theology, as distinctly Catholic.[32] In the absence of equivalent educational frameworks, Catholic responses to Leibniz, Wolff, and Kant were, Ulrich Lehner cautions, "rarely as original as those of Protestant thinkers."[33] However, Wolff did spark the first semi-rationalist apologies for revelation within Enlightened Catholic circles.

The most prominent of the Catholic Wolffians, Benedikt Stattler, developed a logical demonstration of revelation, understood in propositional terms, based on Wolff's criteria of sufficient reason, but believed it incapable of discerning or judging the content of revelation. Sattler entered the Society of Jesus in 1745, but as J.M. Sailer, his most prominent student and biographer, declared, "He knew remarkably well how to sharpen the coulter of reason to uproot and reseed the fields of scholastic philosophy and theology."[34] Born in Kötzing, Bavaria, in 1728, Stattler attended the Benedictine school at the abbey in Nieder-altaich before studying philosophy and mathematics in Ingolstadt. Based on his success in applying Wolff to Catholic theology he received a chair in dogmatic theology there in 1770 and earned membership in the Munich Academy of Sciences. Stattler retained his position after the suppression of the Jesuits, only to resign in 1781 after the Benedictines gained control over Bavarian higher education. He then briefly served as a priest in the Kemnath parish of the Upper Palatinate, before moving to Munich as an ecclesiastical adviser and member of Elector Karl Theodor's censorship committee.

Stattler adapted Wolff's method of definition and logical demonstration to prove the possibility, necessity, and reality of revelation, though not the truth of its content. Catholic theology, in his view, could only effectively resist deism, atheism, and materialism by acquiring the conceptual clarity and coherence of a *Wissenschaft*, at least in those areas of theology where the criteria of sufficient reason applied. The tripartite scheme of Stattler's *Demonstratio Evangelica* (1770) aimed to silence deist charges regarding the superfluity of revelation, its incompatibility with reason, and the insufficiency of proofs for its existence. Stattler expanded this and the *Deomonstratio Catholica* (1775), which argued for the Church's custodianship of revelation, for a broader audience in the nearly 900-page *Allgemeine katholisch-christliche theoretische Religionslehre* (1791). The text used rationalist philosophy to argue for the primacy of revelation, denying that "it had ever been morally possible to recognize without positive divine revelation any of the absolutely necessary or general doctrines of natural religion."[35]

The necessity of revelation derived, for Stattler, from the fact that empirical observation, inner experience, and human initiative were inadequate for attaining religious truth. He argued that it was "morally impossible" to achieve full religious knowledge based on reason alone, not "absolutely impossible."[36] Eventually, Stattler figured, some people would attain the intellectual maturity needed for adequate natural religion. Christ represented an "excess of God's beneficial goodness," and salvation was possible without his teachings.[37] But revelation was a "morally necessary expedient"[38] given the damage humanity would suffer during an otherwise protracted road to truth. Moreover, those unresponsive to philosophical demonstrations, including women, peasants, artisans, soldiers, and even the cultivated peoples of antiquity, required revelation as a form of instruction that would erase doubt regarding God's will.

Stattler worked with a propositional model of revelation as a divine dispensation of previously unknown content. Revelation constituted, in his view, "communication of certain knowledge of a truth, which does not occur through natural powers or ways of knowing, but through an action of God himself."[39] Stattler also set strict boundaries to the applicability of reason to theology and thereby to its status as a science. Reason, in his view, could generate no knowledge of the content of revelation, merely its intrinsic possibility and necessity. Only faith could accept what God proclaimed, including dogma and the mysteries of Christianity. Unlike the neologians, Stattler did not apply the criteria of moral and practical utility to Church doctrine.[40] Faith in God's grace was the sole basis for accepting the Trinity, for example, or teachings about the afterlife. On these grounds Stattler rejected Moses Mendelssohn's claim in *Jerusalem, or on Religious Power and Judaism* (1783) that reason could distil the speculative truths of religion.

Although reason could demonstrate the necessity of the Church's role in mediating Christian truth, Sattler also insisted it yield to the Church as the custodian and interpreter of God's word.[41] To this extent Stattler was "an enlightened conservative" who used modern thought to defend traditional values and uphold Catholic privileges, while disparaging German supporters of the French Revolution.[42] In his own *Wahres Jerusalem* (1787) he accused Mendelssohn of falsely grounding religion in an individual's experience of God and stressing the voluntary nature of religious associations. Catholic princes, for Stattler, had a duty to publicly enforce religion and Church authority.[43] Mendelssohn's plea for toleration and for limiting the prince's purview over religion was unacceptable, in his view, as atheists or naturalists forfeited any claim to equal civil rights.

As a member of the Bavarian Censorship Collegium from 1790 to 1794, Stattler himself aggressively suppressed critical philosophy, fearing Kant's moral system required neither a transcendent, personal God nor revelation. Without seriously engaging his Catholic reception, Sattler anachronistically defended metaphysics as a crucial pillar of theology and refused to read the second and third critiques because Kant ignored his rebuttal of the first.[44] He forbid the booksellers of Munich from distributing any of Kant's writings, and even withheld for a year the publication license for one of Sailer's books for being overly Kantian. By 1796, however, many of Stattler's own works had been indicted and several placed on the *Index Librorum Prohibitorum*. Although not denying infallibility, Stattler was strongly Febronian, insisting that bishops derived their authority directly from Christ. While his scheme of defending the possibility, necessity, and reality of revelation endured, Sattler lacked the tools to address Lessing's ditch or the incipient historicization of revelation. Unlike Wolff he sanctified the precedent of Christian tradition and presumed the dogmas of the Catholic Church perfectly replicated the teachings of Jesus.[45]

Beda Mayr, the first Catholic theologian to engage Reimarus and Lessing, made the historical turn Sattler declined, retaining primordial revelation as a shield against the dangers of autonomous reason. Born in a small town near Augsburg to successful farmers, Mayr was educated at the abbey in Scheyern before studying philosophy in Munich and mathematics in Freiburg. In 1761 Mayr entered the Benedictine abbey of the Holy Cross in Donauwörth. After his ordination Mayr spent most of his life as a monk, teaching mathematics, physics, philosophy, and rhetoric in that abbey, which thrived as a centre of the Catholic Enlightenment. The abbey's leadership protected Mayr even after a scandal erupted when an ecumenical essay of his urging reunification of the Christian confessions was published without his consent in 1777 and landed on the *Index*. He built a massive library in Scheyern, containing works in theology, history, law, the natural sciences, philosophy, and philology, which was forcibly ceded to the local prince after secularization. The state seizure and destruction of ecclesiastical property in 1803 put an abrupt end to the Catholic Enlightenment and posed a tremendous setback for higher learning and education in the Catholic territories.[46]

Mayr held historical *Wissenschaft* to be a crucial methodological tool for theology, drawing extensively on Protestant biblical criticism in his interpretation of Scripture. He was willing to accept Eichhorn's document hypothesis, though never questioned Mosaic authorship or the reliability of scriptural witnesses to revelation. Yet Mayr struggled to effectively respond to the gulf Lessing detected between historical revelation and the universal truths of reason.[47] For Mayr revelation dispensed eternal wisdom that transcended its historical recipients, even if its articulation accommodated the intellectual capacities of a given age. Lessing, according to Mayr, wrongly presumed human reason capable of independently uncovering the truths of revelation. He severely curtailed the prerogatives of natural religion even beyond that presumed by previous Catholic theologians, re-aligning Lessing's narrative of humanity's religious education to accord with a narrow Catholic apologetics.

According to Mayr, revelation was morally necessary, and reason was insufficient in pursuit of religious truths. His three-volume *Vertheidigung der natürlichen, christlichen und katholischen Religion nach den*

Bedürfnissen unsrer Zeiten (1787–9) refuted Reimarus's assertion in the second fragment that a revelation intelligible to all people was impossible and hence natural religion sufficed to know God. Mayr countered that natural religion was viable for only a fraction of the human race and thus unable to secure felicity.[48] In his view, God created man to be happy, but people could only achieve this state by following divine laws and fulfilling God's final purposes. For Mayr, unaided reason couldn't distil God's qualities, grasp the origins of evil, or discover the immortality of the soul. Even the most cultivated peoples of antiquity lacked, in his view, basic religious knowledge: "no people without revelation knew the most important truths of natural religion."[49] Pythagoras, Plato, and Greek mystery cults only possessed bits of wisdom that were "extremely deformed and … still unproven."[50]

Mayr's refutation of the natural history of religion hinged, as it did for Herder, on the existence of a primitive revelation that first made possible humankind's engagement with creation. Rational reflection on the simplest religious truths would have been entirely in vain if "God had not wanted to elevate the mental capacity of man through a continuous miracle."[51] God had granted to primitive men only the "most obvious, easily comprehensible, and necessary religious truths,"[52] such as monotheism and knowledge of God as creator and ruler of the world, presuming subsequent improvement in the capacity for religion. He welcomed the notion of progressive revelation, or humanity gradually developing the capacity for religion. For Mayr, however, primordial revelation was not grounds for granting the privilege of religious truth to the ancient religions of the Orient. While retaining *Uroffenbarung* as a weapon against natural religion, he broke squarely with earlier eighteenth-century Catholic syncretists. Mayr possessed substantial knowledge of Eastern religions based on the work of A.H. Anquetil-Duperron and Joseph de Guignes. The second volume of the *Vertheidigung* tests and then refutes whether Indian, Persian, and Chinese religions and Islam made legitimate claims to revelation based on rationalist criteria of authenticity. The Catholic Church, whose teachings had to be accepted on faith, was the only legitimate custodian of revelation, in his view.[53]

Enlightened Catholic theology granted both historical and epistemological priority to revelation in the acquisition of religious truth, erecting a barrier against rampant rationalism and Lessing's historicization of religious knowledge. Without divine intervention, Catholic theologians insisted, humanity would have lacked the capacity to develop natural religion. Any authentic wisdom possessed by pagans must, given the inability of unaided reason to discover the content of revelation, also have stemmed from an original dispensation. Stattler's arguments for the necessity, possibility, and factuality of revelation built upon logical deductions, definitions, and syllogisms but shielded the content of revelation from rational critique. Mayr retooled Lessing's conception of the education of the human race such that reason was incapable of supplanting revelation in the acquisition of knowledge. Both appealed to primordial revelation as an escape hatch that rendered inconceivable natural religion's ever progressing to divine truth. The propositional content they derived from primordial revelation was, however, remarkably scant. Limiting the scope of primordial revelation to an epistemological facility and basic knowledge of God inhibited the syncretist idealization of ancient pagan faiths, more typical of eighteenth-century Jesuit missionaries.

The Moral Necessity of Revelation for Georg Hermes

As semi-rationalism entered the nineteenth century it continued to forestall the historicization of revelation within Catholicism. Kantians such as Georg Hermes, who defended revelation with practical reason, rejected the trajectory Kant sketched from statutory to rational religion, given its perils for the Church's claim to embody unwritten tradition and preserve Christ's revelations. Despite their selective adoption of critical philosophy, Hermes and his followers subscribed to an ahistorical model of propositional revelation, which used rational criteria to derive the legitimacy of God's revelatory actions but without recognizing the progressive development of doctrine or critiquing the content of revelation. Critical philosophy allowed reform-minded Jews, like Saul Ascher, to curtail the purview of religious law. Hermes used Kant to circumvent Lessing's ditch and the historicization of Scripture, claiming instead a veneer of timeless universality for Catholicism.

Catholic theological faculties initially welcomed Kantian philosophy more eagerly than Protestants, as it provided ammunition against scholasticism and speculative metaphysics.[54] For some the *Critique of Pure Reason* simply made room for faith; others capitalized on the break it offered with Wolffian rationalism. Kant's anthropological approach to religion also appealed to Catholics for providing a seemingly stable foundation for morality at a time when Protestant biblical criticism was eroding the scriptural foundations of revelation.[55] Despite its varied threats to orthodoxy, not until 1827 was Kant's first *Critique* placed on the *Index*. Kant implied that natural reason, without revelation, provided sufficient knowledge of religious truths. Deriving moral law from practical reason also appeared to rest faith in God in an autonomous human faculty. This unacceptably subordinated theology to philosophy, while reducing Christian dogmas to moral prescriptions.[56]

Through the mid-1830s, a tendentious interpretation of critical philosophy allowed Hermes and his school to justify faith in revelation and the revealed character of Catholicism within the bounds of practical reason. By drawing on Kant, Hermes distanced himself from Stattler's deductive rationalism. As Thomas Fliethmann rightly cautions, however, the defence Hermes made of revelation was in many respects "precritical." He perpetuated the logical structure Stattler established for first proving the necessity, possibility, and reality of revelation.[57] Hermes likewise retained far greater confidence than Kant in the ability of speculative or pure reason to grasp a higher reality. In his view, theoretical reason could establish the existence of God but provided no certainty, only a degree of probability, about matters concerning historical revelation, miracles, or God's relationship to humankind.[58]

Born in 1775 in Dreyerwald and the son of a Westphalian farmer, Hermes trained in philosophy at the university in Münster from 1792 to 1794 with Ferdinand Überwasser, who favoured empirical psychology over metaphysics and acquainted Hermes with Kant and Fichte. Exposure to philosophy thrust Hermes into what he later termed the "labyrinth of doubt."[59] He defected to theology, seeking rational proof for the act of faith, as well as for the existence of God and the truth of Christian dogma. "I withdrew into myself for a second time," Hermes explained, "with the resolve from now on to philosophize myself; but to accept nothing as real or true or as unreal or untrue as long as I could still doubt, and to that end to exclude everywhere fantasy and feeling."[60] Revelation, he figured, could not be defended adequately on its own authority nor on the basis of inner conviction.

Hermes's efforts to revive Catholic theology in the Rhineland after Prussia acquired the territory in 1815 following years of French occupation and secularization, rejected the theology of feeling as wrongly allowing subjectivity to encroach on faith. Hermes likewise steered clear of historicism. He did not imagine a living tradition of revelation developing progressively nor question whether universal truths could be derived from the contingent historical facts of revelation. Rather, Hermes asserted that "rational faith (*vernünftuge Glaube*) is the highest goal of all philosophy"[61] and applied Kantian philosophy to earn the pedigree of *Wissenschaft* for theology. His first position was as a professor of dogmatic theology at the gymnasium, then in 1807 at the university in Münster. In 1820 he accepted a call to the new university in Bonn, where a Catholic theological faculty had been established, partly on the urging of Hermes himself who served as a confidential advisor to the Prussian ministry.

Hermes's defence of revelation began with a methodological presumption of doubt. His *Philosophische Einleitung in die christkatholische Theologie* (1819) proposed "to doubt everywhere for as long as possible, and to make a definitive decision only where I could justify the decision through the absolute compulsion of reason."[62] Theoretical reason could not, according to Hermes, prove the existence of divine revelation a priori. He therefore did not hold it to the higher standards of "*Fürwahrhalten*" by which speculative reason found certain judgments to be intrinsically true. The expectation was "a complete demonstration of obligation, or the moral necessity to accept this revelation as arising supernaturally from God."[63] Hermes retained a propositional model of revelation, understood as an act through which God bestows previously unknown wisdom to humanity.[64] It could be indirect – "a concept produced on human terms by man"[65] – but required authentication from God. According to Hermes, God's ability to directly produce representations in the human mind, as well as his ability to convince humankind of their truth and of the truth of his own natural convictions, established the possibility of revelation. Its necessity derived from the inability of the vast majority of humanity to otherwise acquire religious knowledge.

Practical reason, or what Hermes termed "obligatory reason,"[66] established a moral duty to accept the truth of revelation regardless of the doubts lingering from speculative reason. He advocated "a morally necessary acceptance as true of knowledge that could be doubted theoretically."[67] The act of *Fürwahrannehmen* consisted in a voluntary assent to truth not based on logical necessity or complete knowledge but on a moral duty to preserve human dignity. A discerning philosopher was not obliged by practical reason to accept supernatural revelation because his own awareness provided adequate knowledge of moral duties. But theoretical reason did at the cost of inner contradiction compel him to accept a revelation, which the practical reason of the non-philosophers deemed true.[68] By contrast, Fichte limited revelation to evoking the will to obey the moral law among peoples who had lost knowledge of the commandment and God's will.

The categorical imperative Hermes derived from practical reason and its derivative commandments required human beings to accept external assistance, including revelation. His central moral principle was "seek to represent purely and preserve human dignity in yourself and in others." From that followed that one must apply "all necessary means" to preserve human dignity. Hermes specifically mandated that people "employ all insights and experience, generally all knowledge, your own and from others, to discover the necessary means."[69] This included the experiences previous historical periods had of revelation in the form in which they were transmitted to subsequent generations. In his *Positive Einleitung* (1829) Hermes declared the truth of Christ's teachings as recorded in oral tradition and the New Testament, and as transmitted by the Church, to be necessary to fulfil humanity's moral duties. In the posthumous *Christkatholische Dogmatik* (1834) Hermes proposed that pagan religions had not entirely forsaken a limited form of practical reason; the fall had produced not an "absolute" but a "relative" lack of knowledge about man's moral obligations. Although "unproven," their doctrines served as an effective "substitute" for the moral law inspired by God.[70]

Despite his reliance on practical reason, Hermes never sought to confine Christian truth to the limits of reason alone. In his view, Scripture, tradition, and the magisterium were legitimate sources of theology. The content of revelation, including the doctrines of original sin and God's forgiveness, transcended reason, and Christians had to accept the element of mystery in faith.[71] Catholicism remained a positive religion, for Hermes, historically conditioned through God's revelation in Christ. Despite testing the conditions on which revealed truth was to be accepted, Hermes never went beyond a positivist approach to revelation.[72]

Hermesians came to dominate the Catholic theological faculties in Bonn, Münster, and Breslau and the seminaries in Cologne and Trier during the 1820s, eventually establishing their own *Zeitschrift für Philosophie und katholische Theologie* (1832–52). They found a patron in Ferdinand August von Spiegel, Archbishop of Cologne from 1824 to 1835. Opposition to Hermes was, however, severe. His first critics included Catholics committed to primordial revelation, including K.J. Windischmann, Stolberg, and Alexander von Sieger, whose *Urphilosophie* (1831) pit the epistemological principles of French traditionalism against Hermes. In 1835, four years after his death, Pope Gregory XVI placed Hermes's main works on the *Index* for adopting 'positive doubt' as a foundation for theology and challenging Church doctrine on revelation and grace. Many declared his doubt to be substantial, not methodological.[73]

Hermesians initially convinced the Prussian government to blunt the effects of the papal denunciation, and when the new archbishop of Cologne, Clemens August von Droste zu Vischering, took action against them, state intervention embroiled the affair in the *Kölner Wirren* that politicized German Catholicism. Hoping to funnel theology students into episcopal seminaries, the archbishop ordered students in Cologne and Bonn not to attend Hermesian lectures, which he had already demanded be in Latin, withheld the imprimatur of their journal, and issued eighteen theses against Hermes, to which newly ordained clergy in his diocese had to swear allegiance. Friedrich Wilhelm III subsequently ordered the archbishops' arrest, livid at the Church's infringement on Prussian educational institutions. In 1842, however, shortly after symbolically celebrating the resumption of construction on the medieval Cologne cathedral, Friedrich Wilhelm IV removed all Hermesians from Prussian theological faculties as part of his efforts to reconcile with the Church, and his school collapsed.[74]

Comparative Religious History in Enlightened Catholic Theology

Syncretism had largely abated as a missionary strategy by the early eighteenth century, but the ancient wisdom narrative persisted as a model for the history of religion. As late as the 1770s, the legacy of Jesuit syncretism still infused the work of the orthodox theologians Joseph Ringermüller and Conrad Aloys Prechtl, for example. But subsequent Catholic histories of religion broke with the ancient wisdom narrative to reinforce the necessity of continual revelation and invalidate the prospect of unaided reason attaining religious truth. Ascribing doctrinal content to primordial revelation was a liability for apologists, as deists and Spinozists often conjured an original dispensation to make natural religion more palatable. In the 1780s the campaign against rational *ur*-monotheism drove Catholic historians of religion, such as Johann Gottlieb Lindemann and Franz Michael Vierthaler, towards Christoph Meiners, who believed religious wisdom built gradually from fetishism and idolatry. These apologists retooled Meiners to argue for the necessity of revelation in humanity's escaping animalistic origins. Of his Catholic followers, only the radical Kantian Philipp Christian Reinhard deemed revelation irrelevant.[75]

The notion that pagan religions contained prefigurations of Christian doctrine still imbued Catholic histories of religion in the 1770s. The Jesuit Joseph Ringmüller (1737–83), for example, recognized in his two-volume *Allgemeine Religions- und Staatsgeschichte* (1772) the existence of a primordial revelation that contained an annunciation of Christ's coming and other Christian doctrines. Ringmüller obtained a professorship in rhetoric and eloquence at the Catholic university in Würzburg in 1762, where the Jesuit syncretist Anathasius Kircher once taught and the Society still controlled the theological and philosophical faculties.

His universal history cautioned that any echoes of truth in natural religion had their inception in an original dispensation. Monotheism and knowledge of a future incarnation had been universal, according to Ringmüller. The Chinese had acquired from Noah's descendants "pure and dignified concepts"[76] of a highest being and creator, Tiān; the Persian magii possessed important truths about the resurrection of the dead and judgment in the afterlife.[77] In contemplating pagan salvation, Ringmüller did not seek to resolve the scandal of particularity but to expose the danger of "free thinking" and proclaim "the necessity and existence"[78] of divine revelation.

The orthodox assault on rationalism likewise permeates Conrad Aloys Prechtl's *Religionsgeschichten der ganzen Welt und aller Zeiten* (1773), a tribute to the tenacity of revelation in the face of error and superstition. After studying law, Prechtl built a career as secretary and court advisor to the electors of the Palatinate before assuming the chancellorship of the Benedictine abbey of St. Emmeram in Regensburg. One reviewer maligned Prechtl as "zealously orthodox, lowering his head into the iron yoke of papal and Church authority,"[79] and indeed the *protestatio authoris* that closed his third volume preemptively retracted any assertions that displeased the Church. Prechtl condemned "exaggerated desire for knowledge"[80] as the original sin and affirmed that faith required submitting to incomprehensible matters. His survey of pre-Christian faiths aimed to prove that humanity "was not capable of ascending on its own powers to supernatural things."[81] The source of what purported to be natural religion was, for Prechtl, actually Noah's seven commandments, which transmitted antediluvian knowledge of God, his qualities, judgment, and the soul's immortality.

The spectre of rational *ur*-monotheism and the potential sufficiency of reason in the acquisition of religious truths loomed larger in the 1780s and 1790s in the wake of Lessing's reflections on the education of the human race and Kant's critique of revelation. In this environment Catholic theologians found in Christoph Meiners an unlikely ally for defending the importance of revelation in the history of religion. Meiners himself harboured considerable reservations about Catholicism. In his *Allgemeine kritische Geschichte der Religion* he proposed that baroque Catholic devotion to relics and icons resembled African fetishism. Popular customs and the rites of Catholic priests were rooted, Meiners claimed, in the same type of superstition, magic, and sorcery as fetish worship.[82] Elsewhere he condemned zealots who believed revelation transcended reason and argued that "cultivated reason, healthy philosophy, or true enlightenment" had fuelled the Reformation, purifying religion of irrational elements.[83] In two travel reports published in the

Göttingisches Historisches Magzin in 1788 and 1789, Meiners even concluded that southern Germans bore more Slavic blood than residents of the enlightened, Protestant north and that this explained their superstitious nature, racializing in the process southern German Catholicism.[84]

Catholic reformers nevertheless found in Meiners's histories a platform for negotiating a significant but limited sphere for reason in religious development while still countenancing revelation. Meiners himself paid lip service to the compatibility of reason and revelation, while vigorously defending enlightenment as an impediment to superstition.[85] His earliest Catholic interpreters include Johann Gottlieb Lindemann (1757–1829), a priest in Isenbüttel, Lower Saxony, and the author of an influential, seven-volume *Geschichte der Meinungen älterer und neuerer Völker* (1784–95). Like Meiners, Lindemann attributed the diversity of religious opinions across the globe to local customs, political systems, and climactic conditions and, in large part, sketched a narrative of progressive enlightenment through the application of reason. "Reason and religion advance in step," Lindemann claimed, "they are two sisters who never forsake each other, and where there is great enlightenment ... knowledge of religion has also attained great heights."[86] However, he denounced those opponents of religion who in his day asserted that cultural refinement gradually produced an abstract idea of monotheism. "The history of reason and of nations alone proves," he wrote, "that humanity on its own did not arrive at the concept of a single highest being."[87]

Across the decade in which Lindemann published his *Geschichte*, he gradually abandoned primordial revelation as an explanation for the significant commonalities he found in the beliefs of ancient peoples who had religion. In 1784 he insisted on the existence of a "universal world religion" encompassing a small number of doctrines or "*ur*-truths" that survived the Flood in myriad form across the globe.[88] By 1792 Lindemann refused to see all religion as the remains of a primeval world and explicitly rejected what he termed the neo-Platonic derivation of mystical, allegorical religious imagery from one source. "To me, this type of explanation seems totally unnatural," he wrote, "for it attributes knowledge of the most hidden causes in nature to wild and unknowing nations and presumes to find deeply metaphysical spiritual ideas in the flaccid daily customs of dumb, unrefined people."[89] On these grounds, Lindemann opposed Meiners's proposition that ancient Greek mystery cults had taught monotheism. Natural religion led humanity to certain truths of reason, in his view, but without further revelation the human understanding suffered in "weakness, uncertainty, and confusion."[90]

Other Catholic adherents of Meiners dismissed primordial revelation entirely in favour of histories that located the origin of religion in fetishism. When Charles de Brosses controversially proposed fetishism as the earliest religious state in his secretly published *Du culte des dieux fétiches* (1760), he retained the notion of primal monotheism and its universal disintegration in a defensive nod to orthodoxy. De Brosse believed that figures on ancient Egyptian mummies, papyri, and obelisks could not be interpreted allegorically or symbolically; their supernatural powers had derived directly from the material qualities of the object. Religion, from this perspective, originated in unreason, a position that prevented the French Academy, which refused de Brosse entry, from accepting the term fetishism until 1835.[91] Translated into German in 1785, his book captured the attention of Meiners, and through him the enlightened Salzburg pedagogical reformer Franz Michael Vierthaler (1758–1827), who, however, dismissed *Uroffenbarung*.

Vierthaler composed his massive *Philosophische Geschichte der Menschen und Völker* (1787–1819) in part to expose the effects of natural religion without the benefit of revelation. Born the son of a stonemason in upper Austria, Vierthaler earned an education as a choirboy in the cloister of Michelbeuren, singing in the chapel of the local archbishop. When his voice broke, he transferred to the Jesuit gymnasium in Burghausen and then studied logic and classical rhetoric at the university in Salzburg. He eventually obtained a professorship in pedagogy there. Enlightened pedagogy held that reason and experience could be evoked to prepare pupils for the positive doctrines of revealed religion. Vierthaler thus advocated use of the Socratic method to guide youngsters to the principles of natural religion and general morality. In his view, however, knowledge of positive Christian doctrines could not be drawn logically from experience or reason. "Reason," he declared, "never elevates itself to belief in an eternal being."[92] Revelation accordingly retained a significant position in the new Catholic pedagogy of the late eighteenth century.

Vierthaler broke with diffusionary narratives that linked redeemable aspects of pagan religions to an original dispensation and organized his history of religion around geography and political history. "I do not believe in an *Urvolk*," Vierthaler wrote, "or in a nation that invented all knowledge and instructed all cultivated peoples."[93] He excluded China from his work given its idealization by Jesuit missionaries.[94] Mythologists, in his view, wrongly presumed culture migrated across nations, and Vierthaler proposed instead a model of autonomous intellectual development in which similarities could be explained through shared psychological predispositions. In his view, religion was an "odd mixture of madness and truth."[95] Incapable of monotheism, the first people were "primitive fetishists" who worshipped stones, shells, posts, and lions' tails; ancient mystery cults originated from the "disgraceful source"[96] of shamanism, not esoteric religion.[97] Rejecting as a "chimera"[98] the notion of a paradisiacal state of nature allowed Vierthaler to advocate for a strong state and institutional control of religion.

By the 1780s primordial revelation had lost its utility as a bulwark against natural religion in Enlightened Catholic histories of religion. Breaking with the tradition of Jesuit syncretism, Catholic apologists defended the necessity of revelation by foregrounding the disastrous results of unaided reason in the development of pagan faiths. Despite his overtly Protestant regard for the progressive rationalization of religion Meiners provided welcome fodder for an unappealing characterization of non-Christian faiths. After secularization and once the threat of natural religion subsided, primordial revelation resurfaced nearly intact among Catholic theologians, but its revival by the likes of Stolberg and Friedrich Brenner represents a strategic return to the ancient wisdom narrative, not a direct line of continuity.

Syncretism in Post-Kantian Catholic Histories of Religion

In the early nineteenth century, Catholic scholars reclaimed a diffusionary model for the history of religion that restored primordial revelation as an anchor for doctrine and for the human faculties. During the religious revival that followed the Napoleonic invasions, Friedrich Leopold von Stolberg traced the religions of the ancient Near East back to Noah, defending Judaic primacy and the literal truth of the Mosaic books. This was a conservative move that blithely sidestepped critical exegesis. Interpreting primordial revelation as a subjective process of inner transformation was a more timely justification for deriving all religion from an original dispensation. Kajetan Weiller and Friedrich Brenner built on Jacobi's fideistic understanding of revelation to reframe the Catholic history of religion in traditionalist and anthropological terms. For them, as for the Protestant revivalist August Tholuck, primordial revelation offset the liabilities of grounding religion in subjective experience by providing an external, transcendent source for religious sensibility. Loyalty to positive Christian doctrine as an inheritance of oral tradition shielded Catholic histories of religion, an established apologetic genre, from the criticisms that befell Friedrich Creuzer. Karl Windischmann, nevertheless, felt compelled to counter the liabilities of both experiential theology and comparative mythology by foregrounding the philosophical content of ancient theology.

The influential first book of Friedrich Leopold von Stolberg's fifteen-volume *Geschichte der Religion Jesu Christi* (1806–18) fuelled the resurgence of syncretism in early nineteenth-century Catholic histories of religion, as did new anthropological arguments for the necessity of original revelation. The renowned poet's conversion to Catholicism in the home of Princess Amalia von Gallitzen in Münster on 1 July 1800 marked a significant transition within German Catholicism away from Enlightened semi-rationalism and precipitated the conversion of other prominent figures. Raised amongst Pietist Moravians, Stolberg had experimented with orthodox Lutheranism before embracing a narrow, monarchical Catholicism seeped in Roman orthodoxy and the baroque scholasticism of the Jesuits.[99] A trip to Italy in 1791 and Gallitzen's revivalist circle solidified his resolve, as did a political realignment following the French Revolution towards Adam Müller. A prolonged public outcry followed the conversion, stoked by liberal humanist disgruntlement.[100] Stolberg defended his decision with an historical apology for Catholicism couched in the guise of universal religious history.

Stolberg's son Cajus had studied with Creuzer in Heidelberg and reported back on his preparations for the *Symbolik*, piquing the father's interest in comparative religious history.[101] As Stolberg wrote to his son in 1819, the *Geschichte* "traces the mythologies of oriental and occidental peoples ... back to ancient traditions, whose essence and core can only be found in holy scripture."[102] Unlike Creuzer, Stolberg remained fiercely loyal to positive religion. His recovery of mythological and other historical sources reinforced the truth of the biblical record, such that Stolberg's friend Jacobi, fellow member of Gallitzen's *sacra familia*, feared he enslaved his conscience to the Church and clergy.[103] The Cologne archbishop Droste zu Vischering had encouraged Stolberg to document the record of God's revelation to humanity. The goal of the *Geschichte* thus mirrors that of Herder's *Älteste Urkunde* as Stolberg's recovery of primordial religion also curtailed Enlightened rationalism in favour of a literal interpretation of the Old Testament.[104]

Biblical literalism and the principle of prefiguration dominate Stolberg's account of pre-Christian faiths. Citing Jesuit precedent, he defended Mosaic chronology against geology and the historical records of the Babylonians, Egyptians, Chinese, and Indians. The history of science, especially astronomy, in his view, confirmed the divine inspiration of the Old Testament. Stolberg also uncovered mythological evidence of the Flood and the dispersion of peoples after Babel. Most important to Stolberg, however, were the "many and evident traces"[105] among pagan peoples of Christianity's two greatest secrets: the coming of Christ and the Trinity. Along with monotheism, these truths made up the content of primordial revelation. Even the ancient Jews, he insisted, had known the Trinity, the immortality of the soul, and the idea of a messiah. Stolberg attributed the degeneration of original truth to the lack of further revelations among pagans and to the absence of institutions, such as the Catholic Church, to maintain tradition.

A fideistic reinvention of revelation as a process of inward transformation, inspired by Jacobi, likewise encouraged Catholic apologists to sanctify primordial revelation as the origin of religious sensibilities. In the 1780s, Sailer had drawn Jacobi's emphasis on feeling and the experience of faith into the Catholic theological critique of Kant. His followers subsequently deflected the threat unmediated inner revelation posed to the Church by embracing a traditionalism that credited external divine intervention with awakening humanity's sensibility for the divine. This upheld primordial revelation as a crucial moment in the constitution of contingent being while preserving its epistemological significance as the foundation of all knowledge. It likewise justified the Church's claim to custodianship of oral tradition. In the context of the early nineteenth century, the presumed anthropological necessity of revelation in the development of human existence proved more resistant to rationalist critique than Stolberg's by then outdated propositional model of revelation.

In this vein, the Catholic theologian Kajetan Weiller undertook an anthropological defence of revelation in his *Ideen zur Geschichte der Entwickelung des religiösen Glaubens* (1808–14), a text written after he broke with critical philosophy. Born in 1762 to a Bavarian bag maker, Weiller joined the Benediktbeuren Abbey as a novice in 1778, then studied theology and philology at the Munich Lyceum. After his ordination, he briefly held a benefice in Dichtl, before returning to the Lyceum in 1799 to teach practical philosophy and pedagogy, eventually serving as rector. Deeply committed to the Catholic Enlightenment in these years, Weiller advocated a rationalist, Kantian approach to religion to the consternation of the local nuncio. In 1802 a speech he delivered to conclude the school year resulted in a public scandal when Weiller purportedly separated morality from revelation and denied the latter.[106] After Schelling moved to Munich in 1806, Weiller organized the resistance to *Naturphilosophie* and identity philosophy. As a school reformer, he temporarily prevented Schelling from being taught at Bavarian gymnasia.[107] After the dismissal of liberal minister Maximilian Joseph von Montgelas, when the tides turned in favour of Schelling and orthodoxy, Weiller lost his professorship.

A close friendship starting in 1801 with Jacobi restored Weiller's faith in revelation. In a eulogy held in the Bavarian Academy of Sciences in

1819, Weiller credited Jacobi with being the first to regard feelings as "exquisite revelations" and as an "an inborn revelatory force,"[108] a direct source of supernatural knowledge. "He showed," Weiller recalled, "that the original revelation proceeds ... from feeling, and thus that the last positive surety rests on that."[109] Weiller admired how Jacobi reconciled faith and philosophy by recognizing their common foundation in sentiment, thus ending a mutual process of self-destruction that threatened to unravel Christianity. Like Jacobi, he presumed the idea of God resided eternally within the human soul and that religion first revealed itself as feeling. Delight at reading the first volume of Weiller's *Ideen* in turn enticed Jacobi to resume the project that launched the *Theismusstreit* with Schelling, and he dedicated *Von den göttlichen Dingen und ihrer Offenbarung* (1811) to his friend.[110] Weiller had challenged the epistemological foundations of absolute idealism and attributed inner revelation to a transcendent personal God, which helped Jacobi assail Schelling.

In the *Ideen*, Weiller no longer regarded religion as an extension of Kantian moral law. Rather, he credited primordial revelation with implanting a feeling for the sacred in the human soul and enabling reason to grasp the divine. According to Weiller, Lessing wrongly presumed revelation to be a mere catalyst for what humanity could attain more laboriously on its own. An "external impulse from an already awakened reason,"[111] in the form of God's word, was needed to draw humanity out of an animal state of nature. Weiller interpreted original revelation as an historical and psychological event, an inner transformation sparked by a supernatural miracle. It awakened the senses to religion and roused in the human mind inklings of divine wisdom. Like Jacobi, Weiller regarded feeling as an organ of truth and presumed religious knowledge built from sentiment to concept. This approach to revelation justified original monotheism. "Where is a land inhabited by man," he asked, "where this light and life has not penetrated?"[112] The original faith, in his view, had been a religion of the heart, feelings, and desires, which structured various mythological traditions.

An argument for the anthropological necessity of revelation likewise drew Friedrich Brenner, regent at the archbishop's seminary in Bamberg, Bavaria, to a position resembling Weiller's modified traditionalism.[113] Born into modest circumstances as a hatter's son, Brenner trained in theology and the philosophy of Kant and Schelling at the University of Bamberg until secularization downgraded the institution to a lyceum. After ordination, he completed a doctorate in Landshut under Sailer, who emphasized an inner, living Christianity, before returning as a professor of dogma to his hometown. Influenced by Weiller's *Ideen*,[114] as well as by Schleiermacher's *Speeches*,[115] Brenner conceived of revelation as a process of inner transformation but preserved the authority of a transcendent personal God and the possibility of objectively knowing the divine. His histories of religion were more aggressively apologetic than Weiller, designed to justify Catholic dogma and the institutions of the Church. As one of "few conservative stragglers,"[116] Brenner retained Judaic primacy, restricting over the course of his career the extent he conceded revelation to pagan peoples.

The Catholic apology Brenner formulated in *Versuch einer historisch-philosophischen Darstellung der Offenbarung* (1810) built upon a subjectivist, fideistic revival of revelation. In his view, humanity required an inner awakening by a transcendent, external God to escape an animal state. The natural world merely confirmed inner sentiment as a "refraction of the eternal *ur*-light … that shines within the soul of man."[117] The core of religion was not, for Brenner, inner feeling or morality, which risked eclipsing transcendence and God's personhood, but the relationship between humankind and the divine. He thus believed the historical unfolding of revelation centred around the idea of God's kingdom. Brenner's *Versuch* traced the progressive unfolding of this idea in the patriarchal, Mosaic, and prophetic periods of ancient Israel. His *Freye Darstellung der Theologie in der Idee des Himmelreichs* (1815) investigated how the religious systems of subsequent peoples grasped it. "All nations rejoice in God's revelation," he granted, "and are to a certain extent in possession of his kingdom."[118] However, through symbolism and unaided reason, poetry and philosophy rapidly distorted this early religious sensibility necessitating the correctives of later particular revelation.

The disrepute into which the Creuzer Affair drew comparative mythology called into question the syncretism typical of revivalist Catholic histories of religion. In the *Antisymbolik* (1824) J.H. Voss had painted Creuzer as a crypto-Catholic, guilty of mysticism, papism, and undue reverence for priests and mysteries. Although such rhetoric was less threatening to Catholics, Carl Joseph Windischmann (1775–1839) and others attempted to safeguard Catholic histories of religion from the liabilities of Romantic mythology. Born in Mainz, Windischmann studied medicine and philosophy during the French Revolutionary Wars, which uprooted him to Aschaffenburg, where he briefly served as court physician to prince-elector and archbishop Friedrich Karl Joseph von Erthal. In 1803, in the absence of a medical school, Windischmann attained a professorship there in world history and the history of philosophical systems. He famously mentored the young Franz Bopp, whose comparative linguistics soberly reinterpreted Windischmann's lectures on the history of philosophy. Windischmann's biographer dates his concern for the religions of the East to 1810 and his personal friendships with Schelling, Görres, and Friedrich Schlegel, whose works Windischmann posthumously edited. Windischmann reviewed the *Mythengeschichte* in 1810 and planned to collaborate with Görres on a neo-Platonist interpretation of Egypt.[119]

An acquaintance with Stolberg, whose sons briefly lived with Windischmann, and with Cologne archbishop Droste zu Vischering, redirected Windischmann from mystical pantheism to positive Christian revelation. His return to the Church as a practicing Catholic in 1813 demanded a more sober approach to comparative religious history. As Windischmann wrote to Bopp in February 1815: "Creuzer's and Görres's books ... I can only present to you as offering inspiration and multiple viewpoints, – but shield yourself from deception and confusion – it is not antiquity, primal feeling in these books, but images and phantasies. I entreat you to study my work as a way to tame the latter."[120] Windischmann's own history wed together reason and revelation in a traditionalist derivation of divine truth from God's first incarnation as the word. He believed that God's creative word, "this animated, invigorating, interpretive, affirming, reprimanding, punishing, comforting, exalting word (λόγος),"[121] was the basis of human rationality. Philosophy could illuminate the "path of revelation in the region of spirit"[122] due to this connection.

Windischmann's *Philosophie im Fortgang der Weltgeschichte* (1827–34) sought to restore proto-Christian doctrines to China, India, and Persia, arguing that the "soul's untiring struggle and battle for its true substance, for its spirit and freedom"[123] characterized intellectual life before Greek antiquity. Belief that "paternal power and authority" was a "manifestation of the heavens and its undivided will"[124] sustained, for example, the power of the Chinese emperor, according to Windischmann. Hegel, who likewise claimed the emperor was regarded as the son of heaven, accused Windischmann of plagiarizing his lectures on the philosophy of history.[125] Windischmann retorted that the Chinese perceived the world as reflecting the highest will of a single creator God. Relying on his colleagues in Bonn, Windischmann likewise concluded that barren highlands north of the Indus and Ganges had been home to Aryan tribes who preserved an antediluvian religion of light and peace.[126] But Windischmann also highlighted what the physician termed the "pathological side"[127] of corruption that unaided reason inflicted on an original dispensation.

The return to syncretism in early nineteenth-century Catholic histories of religion reinforced the epistemological significance of primordial revelation, while curbing the prerogatives of unaided reason in the purported education of the human race. In the precedent set by Stolberg, Catholic apologists claimed Church doctrine descended through Noah from an oral tradition that only the institutions of the Church could preserve with integrity. Proto-Christian principles, such as the soul's immortality and redemption, supposedly infiltrated ancient pagan religions, but lacking further revelation they succumbed to human error. A commitment to positive religion set the apologetic histories of Stolberg, Weiller, Brenner, and Windischmann sufficiently apart from speculative comparative mythology, and recourse to Judaic primacy and prefiguration helped dignify their otherwise sweeping diffusionary narratives. Catholic scholars offset the threat reason posed to revelation by deriving humankind's rational powers from an original act of grace and even attributed the awakening of a subjective feeling for the divine to an external intervention. As will be seen, they likewise shied away from a full-fledged ontological reinterpretation of revelation, in part to protect the Church's authority as the custodian of oral tradition.

Catholic Philosophies of Revelation: J.S. Drey and Anton Günther

As among Protestants, idealist Catholic philosophies of revelation took a subjective and experiential turn that is most visible in the Tübingen School of Johann Sebastian Drey and the Vienna School of Anton Günther. More intent on preserving God's personhood and transcendence, however, they resisted the Protestant precedent of downgrading primordial revelation and making full actualization of God dependent on humanity. Günther's interpretation of revelation as the self-disclosure of being drew on Cartesian epistemology to buttress a dualistic, anthropological approach to religion. For Günther, who in certain respects anticipates Kierkegaard, self-consciousness provided a reliable foundation for knowledge of relative and absolute being. Drey likewise believed that human existence could be derived from God's original consciousness and understood revelation as the self-disclosure of being. Despite their postcritical defence of Catholic theology, however, each maintained a prominent epistemological role for primordial revelation to offset the consequent partial grounding of religion in human consciousness. Revelation guaranteed, in their view, the scientific standing of philosophy and took precedence over reason, but its impact was limited to an initial act of grace deep in the past.

Hegel's unitary concept of God's self-revelation helped Catholics dismantle a problematic dualism that had crept into the scholastic, instructional model of revelation between knowledge and faith, nature and grace, and reason and history.[128] However, Schelling was arguably more decisive than Hegel for the Catholic theological encounter with idealist philosophy and the subjective experience of religion.[129] Hegel's monism elicited charges of pantheism, and he appeared both to subordinate faith to knowledge and substitute logical necessity and abstract concept for the freedom of a personal God. Hegel likewise viewed Catholicism with a "depreciative attitude,"[130] as an inadequate actualization of the concept of religion. In his view, Catholicism failed to negate the external, sensuous world for the spiritual; the papacy's territorial claims violated the principles of the modern state, including religious freedom; and the clergy's power over the laity exhibited a slavish deference to authority.[131]

The Catholic preference for Schelling is visible, for example, in Jakob Sengler's *Ueber das Wesen und die Bedeutung der speculativen Philosophie und Theologie* (1834–7). After studying theology in Tübingen and hearing Schelling's lectures in Munich, Sengler joined the philosophical faculty in Marburg while two dioceses boycotted Protestant control of university theology. Sengler campaigned against Hegel's philosophy as rationalism radicalized, a system that reduced God's being to abstract logic and sacrificed divine freedom and personhood for the absolute necessity of reason as a concept.[132] Schelling's philosophy of revelation restored, in his view, God as the free subject of revelation and emphasized the concrete historical character of his self-actualization. "The great events of God's revelation are truly the object of his newest philosophy," Sengler wrote admiringly of Schelling: "above all he seeks to develop creation as a free act to dispel pantheism and deism."[133]

Building upon Schelling, Sengler's mentors in Tübingen orchestrated the Catholic reinterpretation of revelation as God's historical self-disclosure, crediting an original act of grace with priming the human consciousness to facilitate revelation in nature and history. Eager to engage post-Kantian philosophy, the Tübingen School presided over a significant period of Catholic theological revival prior to the First Vatican Council. Located in the *Wilhelmsstift*, Tübingen's Catholic seminary, named after the Lutheran king of Württemberg, the school had its own journal, *Die theologische Quartalschrift*. Johann Sebastian Drey (1777–1853), one of the founding members, remained on the faculty until 1846 and cultivated many of his later colleagues, who included Johann Adam Möhler, Johannes Kuhn, Johann Baptist Hirscher, and Staudenmeier. These reformers developed an historically oriented Catholic theology that drew on both the philosophy and the history of religion to locate Christianity within a broad historical context, significantly shaping subsequent Catholic approaches to religious diversity.[134]

Born to poor shepherds in Ellwangen, Swabia, Drey depended for his education on the generosity of a parish priest. He completed his seminary training in Augsburg in 1799; studied Kant, Schleiermacher, and Schelling after being ordained as a priest; and briefly taught at the Rottweil lyceum under the Confederation of the Rhine. After the founding of a seminary in Ellwangen to accommodate Württenberg's new Catholic population in 1812, Drey was called as a lecturer in dogmatics and apologetics. In 1817 Wilhelm I moved the institution to Tübingen as the university's first Catholic theology faculty. Drey welcomed the open confessional setting but endured tense relations with Rome. In 1815 the papacy condemned his interpretation of confession, and a reputation for unorthodoxy cost him the bishopric of Rottenburg in the 1820s.[135]

An effective Catholic apologetics, according to Drey, had to articulate a post-Enlightenment theology of revelation that could establish the divine origin of positive Christian revelation based on scientific principles. Responding to Lessing, Drey considered in the 1820s how God engaged human consciousness and the material world to promote salvation. Revelation is "for all humanity what education is for the individual," he concluded in the "Aphorismen über den Ursprung unserer Erkenntnisse von Gott" (1826) – a progressive transformation of subjectivity and the development of humankind's rational abilities.[136] As "eternal, absolute reason – God,"[137] in his view, ignited the human capacity for reflection, a precondition for further revelations.[138] But, for Drey, revelation did not consist in timeless propositions about God. The Church was a living, historical community, and his reformist ambitions depended on approaching Catholicism as evolving over time.[139] Drey affirmed the truth of Christianity by documenting the history of human religious consciousness, including the crucial role of the Catholic Church in its development.

Drey's affirmation of positive, direct divine intervention in history occurred within the challenging context of an idealist, subject-centred approach to religion.[140] In his *Kurze Einleitung in das Studium der Theologie* (1819), Drey defined religion as subjective feeling or the consciousness of a connection with and dependence on God. Following Schleiermacher, he concluded that religion resulted from an original revelation of God within the soul that endowed humanity with an awareness of an invisible world and higher powers. But, for Drey, religion was also an objective truth because inner feelings reflected an external reality revealed by God. People perceived the universe as a pure revelation of God's being until the fall, and this knowledge was slowly being recaptured through history.[141]

Drey's justification of Catholic theology as a science, the *Apologetik als wissenschaftliche Nachweisung der Göttlichkeit des Christenthums* (1838–47) based on lectures held at the *Wilhelmsstift*, upheld primordial revelation as both an epistemological and an ontological necessity. Schelling found irksome that Drey's courses in Tübingen criticized his own lectures on the philosophy of revelation,[142] differing perhaps in whether revelation provided a stable foundation for knowledge. Drey's first volume approached revelation as an idea, not as an event or concrete doctrine. All knowledge of God, Drey asserted, was rooted in a primordial, necessary, external revelation. Subjective awareness of God was, in his view, a precondition for human existence such that even the first people had a radical, ontological dependence on God.[143] The second surveyed the historical course of revelation to Christ; the third covered Christian revelation in the Catholic Church.

Drey's theory of revelation balanced the objective determination of God in the world with subjective human consciousness. He believed that "congruence of the external and internal" comprised "the complete truth and reality of religious knowledge."[144] An initial inner revelation implanted the idea of God in humanity, which was itself a calling into being of human existence. Drey spoke of the "radical determination of man through the original consciousness of God."[145] At the same time, revelation through external appearances that objectively reflected the existence of the divine was a necessary correlate to subjective religious awareness. Human consciousness developed fully and achieved clarity through objective revelation. Primordial revelation thus ignited, for Drey, human consciousness, primed the faculty of reason, and supplied the first conception of God and his relationship to humanity and the world.

As for Schelling, history was a continual self-manifesting of God's creative activity, for Drey. God exerted a never-ending influence on human consciousness with the goal of guiding and awakening religious knowledge and enabling the development of religious communities. Drey ascribed four purposes to revelation that reflect his mediating role within Catholic theology. On the one hand, revelation filled the traditional role of "instruction,"[146] supplying the content of Christian doctrine. On the other hand, revelation also had the purpose of "awakening life"[147] and took the form of an "inner, direct [force]" with supernatural origins in the spirit.[148] He listed both external and subjective criteria for recognizing a genuine revelation that included "eliciting conviction and touching the living spirit," in addition to the personal qualities of the recipient and its clarity and consistency. Revelation likewise served to create a positive religious community and make redemption possible after the fall.

Mythological accounts of the origins of humanity corroborated the existence of primordial revelation, for Drey, but he relied exclusively on Scripture to reconstruct its historical unfolding. Unlike Schelling, who appreciated paganism as a stage in revelation, Drey deemed it a "disruption" or "negation" of revelation.[149] His student F.A. Staudenmaier, by contrast, regarded pagan faiths as necessary facets of religion and presentiments of the redeemer known to Christians. In his view, memories of primordial revelation survived in the form of an "inner spiritual longing"[150] to rediscover "in a covert and secret manner"[151] the personhood of God. Staudenmaier retained a partially instructional model of revelation and detected fragments of dogmatic truth in pagan religions. This reflects the insistence among Catholics, in contrast to Hegel and Schelling, that a fully complete personal God was present at the inception of time. Staudenmaier clarified that "God reveals ... his being and knowledge, not himself, for he is to himself eternally revealed."[152] The epistemological function of revelation thus extended, for him, from the human capacity for reason to the content of religious truth. The ontological turn in Catholic concepts of revelation was weaker than among Protestant philosophers and still retained elements of propositional revelation, perhaps contributing to its failure to withstand a resurgence of ultramontanism at mid-century.

Anton Günther's path to Schelling was more circuitous. Born in 1783 in Lindenau in northern Bohemia to a blacksmith's family, Günther trained with the Augustinians before entering the Charles-Ferdinand University of Prague. Unconvinced by the necessity of supernatural revelation, he pursued a law degree. Exposure to the history of philosophy marked, however, "a turning point in my life,"[153] Günther later noted, because Kant, Fichte, and Herder destabilized in his mind the relationship between reason and revelation. A move to Vienna in 1810 to tutor the Bretzenheim-Regetz family drew Günther into the Catholic revivalist circle of Klemens Maria Hofbauer whose loyalists included Stolberg, Friedrich Schlegel, and Adam Müller. While visiting a country estate, a priest convinced Günther to return to historical revelation in Christ. "The light finally dawned on me," Günther recalled, "that only an act, not knowledge, had redeemed the world ... I recognized the insufficiency of natural religion and revelation through human reason."[154] By 1821 Günther had been ordained a priest. He briefly joined the Jesuits in Galicia but broke off his novitiate to pursue "the grave, loud, lamenting call, the need of our time":[155] reconciling faith with speculative philosophy. Of initial concern to Günther was, specifically, how reason, manifest in pagan nature cults and Judaism, related to Christian revelation.

A close friendship with the physician Johann Heinrich Pabst of the Vienna medical school steered Günther's queries through Schelling's *Naturphilosophie*. Dissatisfied with Schlegel's supposition that a confusion of symbol and object precipitated paganism, Günther credited Schelling with recognizing an authentic spiritual dimension in nature. In the jointly authored *Januskópfe der Philosophie* (1833), he and Pabst credited Schelling, "a love-drunk defender of her rights,"[156] with depicting nature not as "mere materiality" but "as something alive ... as spirit ... analogous to thought, a kind of consciousness."[157] The assumption that nature could achieve a limited form of consciousness offered in their view an important corrective to Descartes's mechanical physics and explained pagan error. Schelling's freedom essay also helped them restore the dualism that eluded Spinoza by presenting the material world as a falling away from God. While acknowledging the "absolute identity of all being," they concluded, Schelling realized that achieving self-consciousness required differentiation. God and world, nature and spirit were, for him, "as identical as they were different" and "must be conceived in their identity as God, and in their difference and particularity as world."[158]

Alerted to Hegel's alleged pantheism while a novitiate, Günther campaigned aggressively against philosophical monism and determinism while selectively adopting Hegel's conception of revelation as the dialectical self-disclosure of being. As he and Pabst explained in the *Januskópfe*, Hegel rightly identified being with self-consciousness but had "already suffered a shipwreck in the harbor" when he imagined "thought as the immanent self-revelation of spirit." Hegel, Günther asserted, tainted spirit by failing to maintain an absolute distinction between key contradictory principles. He also denied God's freedom and personality by writing a natural history of his actualization. Hegel "didn't conceive spirit's being as personality," Pabst continued, "but as individuality or particularity ... as mere appearance and the revelation of universal being."[159] Schelling, by contrast, upheld God's personhood by distinguishing God from the dark ground of revelation, a position Günther held to be closer to the Christian creation story. Dualism was the antidote, Günther concluded, to an entrenched tradition of monist pantheism.

Fortifying Catholic theology against pantheism required, for Günther, securing faith with philosophy. Only *Wissenschaft*, in his view, provided the "objective foundation for subjective faith"[160] that prevented the facts of historical revelation from being reduced to a product of the human spirit; fideism and traditionalism wrongly eclipsed the powers of reason. His first major publication, the *Vorschule zur speculativen Theologie des positiven Christenthums* (1827–8), attempted an "ideal reconstruction of Christianity as a world-historical fact"[161] in the form of a philosophy of revelation grounded in the doctrines of creation and the Trinity. Written as an epistolary exchange between the priest Peregrinus Niger and his nephew Thomas Wendling, the text reinterprets revelation as the development of being using primordial revelation as an epistemological anchor that justified philosophical speculation and inhibited an anthropomorphization of religion.

Central to Günther's project was a Cartesian anthropology of religion designed to safeguard dualism, divine personhood, and the philosophical credibility of revelation. He believed Descartes rightly identified self-consciousness as the "only true and secure"[162] foundation for speculation. "Involuntary (natural, instinctive) knowledge of being"[163] was, for Günther, key to all forms of knowledge. Individuals, in his view, immediately recognized "life ... as the self-revelation of being,"[164] grasping existence as inherently revelatory. Self-consciousness provided, on the one hand, knowledge of the Trinity, which, following Hegel, Günther presumed to be the structure by which absolute and relative being unfolded. Three "coefficients"[165] or "moments of self-consciousness"[166] represented stages, in his view, in the self-realization of being. Itself empty and unconditioned prior to the onset of self-revelation, indeterminate being, for Günther, consisted in pure potential. Driven to realize itself, being became determinate through objectification before attaining self-consciousness as subject. Günther assumed absolute and relative being shared an "essential form"[167] such that the development of human consciousness mirrored both the initial process by which God attained self-consciousness and the subsequent acts through which the Father became the Son and Holy Spirit.

On the other hand, in an adaptation of Descartes's ontological proof for God's existence, Günther likewise asserted that self-awareness was the foundation of a relationship to God. Knowledge of the self required demarcating boundaries, and cognizance of one's limitations and finitude necessarily produced an awareness of dependence on a higher being. "Originally and inseparably connected with the thought of being," Günther wrote, "is knowledge that this being is conditioned ... not through itself, but through an Other."[168] As self-consciousness could not be doubted, nor could the existence of a higher ground of being. "As certain as my knowledge of myself," Günther proclaimed, "is my knowledge of God. If the idea of the self is real, so must also the idea of unconditioned being come into reality in the word of God."[169]

Günther's grounding of religion in a human faculty did not, however, condemn it to the fallibilities of a cultural construct. Unlike Feuerbach, who traced the ultimate source of revelation to humankind, Günther did not interpret self-consciousness as the cause of the God idea.[170]

An anti-Hegelian overhaul of the Christian creation story, emphasizing dualism and dynamic reciprocity between irreconcilable entities, allowed Günther to disrupt the Spinozist conflation of God and the world. Belief in emanation unnecessarily dogged dialectical thought, for Günther. The first volume of the *Vorschule* imposed an "absolute dualism"[171] on the doctrine of creation, insisting that God was in fact not dependent on the historical world for his full self-realization. An initial revelation *ad intra* ensured that "God was revelatory to himself before creation."[172] Günther insisted that the world was "external and next to God,"[173] the product of a subsequent revelation *ad extra*, in which God freely posited an existence distinct from himself. Creation was "not the necessary vehicle and condition of his self-consciousness," Günther explained, "God did not first find and comprehend himself through the founding of the world."[174] Instead, creation emerged from God's self-consciousness only as a thought after the process of self-constitution was complete. An excess of love, not necessity, brought the world into existence for beings external to God.

Rather than allow for the dialectical sublation of opposites in a higher synthesis, Günther maintained what has been termed a contrapunctual dualism in the fundamental categories of existence and reflection: God and the world, nature and spirit, concept and idea, and understanding and reason. Despite being distinct from God, nature, for Günther, was animated by a world soul and evolved towards consciousness. Governed by necessity, however, it could never achieve the free self-consciousness of which spirit was capable. Knowledge of nature was always directed outwards to the world of appearances and limited by conceptual thought. The human capacity for understanding (*Verstand*) produced the most exalted knowledge of nature found in paganism, according to Günther, but even in its highest form *Verstand* was incapable of reaching God.

Free and independent, spirit, by contrast, was fully engaged in the ontological process of self-revelation and awakened to self-consciousness. The human faculty of reason (*Vernunft*) generated knowledge of spirit in the form of absolutely certain ideas. Charged with transforming the object of faith into philosophy, *Vernunft* possessed an intuitive grasp of ontological truths, including the unconditioned ground of being and the causes behind appearances. These contradictory categories intersected dynamically in humankind, which Günther characterized as a "living union of opposites"[175] and an "organic synthesis of spirit and nature."[176] Created in God's image and traversing the same dialectical process of self-constitution, human beings were also, in his view, animals subject to nature. Their knowledge was not absolute, and even an individual's first idea of selfhood depended on revelation.

In some respects, Günther interpreted revelation quite conservatively as an objective historical fact, a unique act that could not, as Hegel held, be subsumed within a larger conceptual structure. At the same time, his confidence in the historical facticity of revelation derived from the assumption that the events comprising it also represented the ontological self-realization of the idea of God, a process which could be derived with certainty from the structure of consciousness. The *Vorschule* scrutinized specifically what Günther termed the "promised land of two revelations":[177] universal primordial revelation through creation and revelation through the second Adam or Christ. As the precondition for all human thought, the first revelation guaranteed that the content of Christianity could be known. Building from awareness of the self, it provided knowledge of the ontological grounds of absolute and relative being: the existence of a trinitarian creator, humanity embodying his image, and the irreconcilability of nature and spirit. Despite their dependence on primordial revelation, these truths were, for Günther, the domain of philosophy and reason. The second revelation, knowledge of redemption through Christ, fell to theology and faith but existed in perfect accord with primary revelation.[178]

Despite living in relative isolation in Vienna, Günther assembled a broad following of devotees, including former Hermesians, united by an anti-Hegelian commitment to neo-dualism. Günther's theological school was the largest in German-speaking Europe with centres in Bonn and Breslau, as well as Vienna. Günther himself rejected calls to succeed to university chairs vacated by Hermes, Drey, and Schelling, enjoying instead the protection of influential cardinals, including Melchior von Diepenbrock.[179] The Revolutions of 1848–9 brought a reversal of his fortunes, however. The journal Günther edited, *Lydia*, had lashed out at materialism and communism, and he was forced out of Vienna and deprived of his position as state censor. By 1852 his works were under investigation, idealism was on the wane, and Günther's opposition to Hegel had become less relevant. On the initiative of Cologne archbishop Johannes von Geissel, Günther was condemned for deviating from Catholic doctrines of the Trinity, creation, and the distinction of knowledge and faith.[180] A conservative turn in Catholic theology had by then begun to erode the centrality of self-consciousness in idealist conceptions of revelation.

The Neo-Scholasticism of Joseph Kleutgen

The outbreak of revolution in 1848 severely rattled the Catholic Church, forcing the once liberal Pius IX to flee Rome, a prominent minister assassinated and the Papal States under the short-lived, radical republic of Giuseppe Mazzini. The reaction that followed pit the papacy against liberalism, nationalism, and anticlericalism, justifying an "unscrupulously brutal"[181] restoration of Church discipline. Pius IX replaced Febronian bishops in the German states with an episcopate more loyal to Rome and wrested government control over theological education from the state bureaucracies.[182] In 1851 Mainz bishop Wilhelm Emmanuel von Ketteler, for example, withdrew Catholic theology students from the university in Gießen and reopened the diocesan seminary in Mainz under Jesuit leadership. The Church secured an alternative locus of power in the resurgence of popular piety and in new political movements, some of which Ketteler helped organize, including precursors to the Catholic Center Party.

The Jesuit resumption of control over Catholic theological education undermined speculative idealism, traditionalism, and ontologism on the grounds that these movements failed to synthesize modern philosophy with positive Christian revelation. In their place, a revival of Aristotelian philosophy, medieval metaphysics, and the work of Thomas Aquinas made neo-scholasticism the dominant philosophical stance of German Catholic theology. The return of scholastic thought occurred first in diocesan seminaries independent of the state theological faculties and was aided by the papal condemnation of prominent historical-idealist theologians between 1855 and 1866, including Anton Günther.

The theologian most closely associated with the rise of neo-scholasticism in the German states is Joseph Kleutgen, who helped prepare the dogmatic constitution *Dei Filius* adopted by the First Vatican Council in 1869 as well as the Thomistic encyclical *Aeterni Patris* for Leo XIII. Born to a pious Catholic family in Dortmund in 1811, Kleutgen nearly lost his childhood faith after reading Herder, Lessing, and Schiller. He initially registered as a student of philology in Munich hoping to study Plato and joined the *Burschenschaft* 'Germania' during the Revolution of 1830. When Ludwig I expelled all foreign students in the fraternity, Kleutgen, a Prussian, returned home. Two years later, his faith rekindled, Kleutgen embarked on theological studies in Münster and then at the seminary in Paderborn. He joined the Jesuits as a novitiate in Brig, Switzerland, in 1834, becoming a naturalized Swiss citizen. Kleutgen taught philosophy in Freibourg and Brig before being called in 1843 to the Jesuit-directed German College in Rome as a professor of sacred eloquence. He served as the secretary of the Jesuits from 1858 to 1862.

In 1848 Kleutgen followed the severely compromised Collegium Germanicum into exile, blaming the revolutionary upheavals on the ethos of the Reformation and Hegelian philosophy. Scholasticism offered, in his view, the sole means to safeguard the authority of the Church and tradition. "In the darkness of the present a tender star arose," he reflected in 1855, "and since we experienced this event, I no longer doubt an imminent, peaceful transformation of things."[183] As consulter to the Congregation of the Index, he was in a position to enact this change, preparing, for example, the report upon which Günther's condemnation was based. So useful was Kleutgen's assault on modern philosophy that Pius IX rescued him from the scandal ensuing from the attempted poisoning of Princess Katharina von Hohenzollern in the convent of Sant'Ambrogio in Rome, which erupted during Kleutgen's tenure as special confessor to the nuns. The Inquisition found Kleutgen guilty of promoting false sainthood and of sexual relations with a nun and recommended he be confined to a Jesuit house for three years, forbidden to hear confessions.[184] He left Rome for the secluded shrine of Our Lady in Galloro where he wrote his main works. Pius IX, however, recalled Kleutgen to Rome in preparation for the First Vatican Council.

Kleutgen's multivolume *Die Theologie der Vorzeit, vertheidigt* (1853–60) condemned German Catholic theology for having abandoned scholasticism and for misconceiving the relationship between the natural and supernatural order. Engaging critically with Hermes and Günther, he resurrected the traditions of scholasticism as a unifying, stable foundation for dogmatic, practical, and speculative theology. This work and Kleutgen's *Die Philosophie der Vorzeit, vertheidigt* (1860–3) presented scholasticism as an antidote to the failures of post-Cartesian philosophy and found eager reception among a broad swath of theologians stranded between rationalism and fideism and disturbed by liberal attacks on papal authority. Cartesian doubt had been the basis of both post-Kantian theology and traditionalism, Kleutgen argued, and he rejected as a presumptuous exclusion of grace any system of knowledge, such as Günther's, based on a subject's own self-reflection.[185] Like the Reformation and the recent revolution, it fostered "an audacious revolt against authority, ruthless tearing down of tradition, miscalculated self-confidence and the aspiration to build anew on one's own."[186] A stable system of knowledge could only be constructed, Kleutgen claimed, on the way St. Thomas understood the act of philosophical self-reflection. God's necessary knowledge of his own eternal essence offered a reliable platform for metaphysical abstraction.[187]

To resolve the relationship between faith and reason Kleutgen elevated theology above philosophy and endeavoured to correct "misconceived notions about science and revelation"[188] held by his predecessors. Theology, he argued, was the "science of faith" (*Wissenschaft des Glaubens*) whose foundations lay in divine revelation and grace, rather than in reason and experience. The supernatural act of faith, motivated by a revealing God and his infallible word, alone made theology possible. Revealed truths were not subject to philosophical proof; the believing mind had to assent freely to their authority. The philosophy of revelation was thus a vain endeavour because reason without the light of grace could never transcend natural religion. Kleutgen exalted "reason illuminated by faith"[189] as the principle that raised theology above other disciplines. Philosophy and history were useful aids in extracting doctrinal content from revelation, defending it from error, and establishing the positive fact of Christian revelation. But they could never be sources themselves of religious truth, and therefore apologetics could only vindicate faith and defend the credibility of an otherwise supernatural science.

Kleutgen resurrected a propositional concept of revelation rooted in divinely inspired Scripture and tradition. The unwritten word of God, proclaimed by the apostles and safeguarded by the Church, supplemented the doctrines found in Scripture and justified papal infallibility. Kleutgen denied the existence of subjective inner revelation, which encouraged false prophets and undermined Church authority. Similarly, he rejected the idea of God's progressive self-revelation through time. He agreed that religious knowledge improved but denied humanity any ability to autonomously complete or perfect revelation. The teachings of the Church merely refined how the content of revelation was determined and presented; its doctrines were God-given and accepted on the basis of faith and divine authority. On these grounds, Kleutgen rejected the rationalist position that humanity had developed from primitive barbarity. The first humans enjoyed a state of "religious morality"[190] made possible through primordial revelation.

The German Catholic restoration of revelation ended with a silencing of those innovative early nineteenth-century theologians who successfully aligned the concept with developments in modern philosophy. After the revolutionary upheavals of 1848–9, Kleutgen's more conservative propositional understanding of revelation better upheld the authority of the Church and provided greater doctrinal stability. Given the massive disruptions Catholic institutions withstood at the start of the century, the extent to which Catholic thinkers experimented with revelation is noteworthy. By the 1830s, Catholic interpretations of revelation had expanded to include subjective inner transformation and the historical self-revelation of divine being. However, revelation retained a more pronounced epistemological dimension within Catholicism, continuing to provide varying degrees of reliable access to religious knowledge. Primordial revelation likewise preserved an important function within Catholic theology as a transcendent anchor for the human capacity to grasp religious truths and for the Church's claim to have inherited custody of oral tradition. The slide towards depicting religion as a human construct was, in other words, successfully inhibited, even if finding a satisfactory balance between reason and revelation proved elusive.

Copper engraving by Johann Georg Puschner of Shavuot services in a synagogue in Fürth in the Franconian Imperial Circle, commemorating the revelation of the Torah on Mount Sinai, in Paul Christian Kirchner, *Jüdisches Ceremoniel* (Nuremberg: P.C. Monath, 1734); Jüdisches Museum Berlin, Inv.-Nr. GDR 78/6/0, Photo: Jens Ziehe, acquired through the Gesellschaft für ein Jüdisches Meseum in Berlin e.V.

Chapter Seven

Revelation in Jewish Religious Thought from Mendelssohn to Geiger

On 7 June 1840 in a synagogue recently dedicated in Dresden, the Conservative rabbi Zacharias Frankel staged an unusual celebration of Shavuot, the Jewish festival of revelation honouring the day God gave the Torah to the Israelites on Mount Sinai. In the Ashkenazi tradition, religious services on Shavuot customarily included special liturgical insertions praising the Ten Commandments, the bestowing of the law, and God's appearance to Moses, as well as Torah readings related to revelation and the spring wheat harvest.[1] Frankel omitted many of the liturgical poems, or piyutim, though not the singing of the *Akdamut*, an eleventh-century poem in Aramaic. A choir of men and boys, positioned in the second gallery, responded to the chants of the cantor, at one point singing a German hymn with the Christians in attendance. As the choir sang, Frankel and his assistants took the Torah scrolls from the ark and processed across the dais. Later from the pulpit Frankel interpreted the religious significance of the festival through the verse "You shall be to Me a kingdom of priests and a holy nation." As the chosen people of revelation, Jews had the obligation, he recalled, of passing down the wisdom given to Moses until the knowledge it provided of God reached all of humanity.[2]

Liturgical reform and intellectual upheaval transformed how Jewish Germans celebrated Shavuot in the early nineteenth century. Eager to uphold the divine origins of oral law, statues and prescriptions not recorded in the Torah, the neo-Orthodox rabbi Samson Raphael Hirsch, for example, saw the *Offenbarungsfest* as an occasion for reinforcing the authority of the Talmud, the central text of Rabbinic Judaism. The Torah, he noted, made no reference to its own festival, indicating that it relied on oral tradition for the completion of revelation. The "oral part of the Divine Revelation," he argued on the occasion of Shavuot, was the "key and indispensable complement to the Written Law."[3] By contrast,

Leopold Zunz, the liberal proponent of the *Wissenschaft des Judentums* and later author of a major historical study of Jewish liturgy, believed Shavuot was an occasion for reflection on personal virtue and morality.[4] "May we become more aware of ourselves," he urged on Shavuot in Berlin in 1822 just before resigning his post at the reform Beer temple, and "contemplate what we must do to fulfill God's commandment within."[5] Other prominent reformers, such as Samuel Hirsch, delivered similarly edifying sermons for the festival reflecting on the personal relationship between an individual and God.[6]

The diversity of these approaches reflects the extent emerging denominational divisions shaped the post-Enlightenment reconstruction of revelation within German Judaism. The cultural resonance of Shavuot likewise suggests why the crisis that struck revelation in the late eighteenth century more radically challenged Jewish religious beliefs, ritual practices, and civic identities than those of Protestants or Catholics. The critique of revelation confronted German Jews before they had achieved political and social equality, resulting in a "much more profound crisis of self-doubt," as Michael A. Meyer observes, that combined religious concerns with issues of identity and belonging.[7] The importance of revelation within Judaism extended beyond its epistemological role as a font of knowledge about God, morality, and the human condition and beyond securing biblical truth. Jews risked their presumed historical distinction – having received revelation as the chosen people of God, overturned paganism, and given ethical monotheism to humanity. Reducing God's revelation to Moses on Mt. Sinai to the product of human religious consciousness threatened to demote Judaism to the particular expression of one nation's local faith.

Revelation also anchored Jewish religious law, as the "origin and reservoir"[8] of the mitzvoth (or precepts) recorded in the Torah, as well as, by some accounts, the commandments found in the Mishnah, Talmud, and rabbinic codes. Orthodox Jews believed oral law had been revealed to Moses on Mt. Sinai and preserved intact until written down after the destruction of the second temple. A medieval tradition of Jewish historical writing created genealogies tracing the transmission of oral law back to revelation.[9] Without revelation, customs and rituals lost the sanction of divine authority and opened themselves to revision or rejection. Unlike in Catholicism, the scope of the traditions sanctioned by revelation extended beyond dogma and the institutions of religion to the total life of Jewish communities.[10] As the perceived obligations of Jews to religious law bore directly on the possibilities for emancipation, debating the extent and nature of revelation also spoke to the position of Jews within civic society.

This chapter analyses how Jewish German scholars reworked the concept of revelation in the wake of Enlightened critique, selectively adapting Protestant initiatives in rationalist theology, critical philosophy, and idealist thought. Two traditions of conceiving revelation, dating to the medieval period, are visible in Jewish responses to the crisis of revelation. The first drew on Spanish philosopher Yehuda Halevi's theory of revelation as a single collectively experienced historical act on Mt. Sinai, the second, based on Moses Maimonides, assumed a continual, universal revelation in which each age discovered components of an eternal truth. Scholarly rediscovery of Maimonides's *Guide for the Perplexed* progressed slowly through the mid-nineteenth century, due in part to apprehensions about his equating revelation with ennoblement of the human intellect.[11] By contrast, Halevi's philosophy of religion combined a rationalistic attitude towards nature and empirical human existence, attractive to Jewish reformers, with a romantic, mystical attitude towards spiritual reality. He suggested to nineteenth-century interpreters that the prophets, and by extension the Jewish people, possessed a superhuman spiritual capacity particularly suited to revelation.[12]

Even liberal Jews who welcomed halachic reforms preserved for longer than Protestants and Catholics the divine origins, propositional content, and epistemological function of revelation despite Scripture losing its status as inspiration. Only in the 1840s did Jewish scholars welcome the notion of a progressive revelation, in which knowledge of God evolved with the human race, or reframe revelation as subjective inner illumination. Liberal religious thinkers then gravitated towards Maimonides's position that sensual experiences of an historical event did not suffice as the intellectual foundations of revelation.[13] By mid-century the most radical reformers, including Abraham Geiger, were willing to acknowledge that the human spirit produced religious knowledge and that revelation was a form of human consciousness, albeit one particularly well developed in the history of the Jewish people.

The tenacity of precritical concepts of revelation within Judaism represents a strategic response to the specific demands facing Jewish religious thinkers in the early nineteenth century. On the one hand, insisting on the historical reality of a supernatural revelation bestowed to Moses and the patriarchs maintained the uniqueness of Judaism and its distinction from Christianity, especially as reformers unravelled ceremonial law, modernized religious services, and argued for the universality of Jewish religious concepts. In the effort to redefine Judaism as a doctrine or faith, similar to the Christian confessions, not as rigid adherence to the law, the notion of propositional revelation also helped secure a core set of beliefs. Denying the divine origins of oral and written law was itself radical enough without wholeheartedly severing the spirit of Judaism from revelation.

On the other hand, many ways liberal Protestant theologians responded to the crisis of revelation were unappealing to Jews because their salvaging of the concept often denigrated Judaism as an antiquated, Oriental faith ill suited to a modern religious sensibility. Protestant efforts to bridge Lessing's ditch, to assert the eternal truth of Christianity despite its reliance on historical revelation, often characterized Judaism as an obsolete stage in the evolution of a universal and rational faith. Idealist philosophies of religion likewise dismissed Judaism as a deficient form of religious consciousness through which the divine had to progress before reaching full realization. As Susannah Heschel notes, anti-Jewish stereotypes helped critical biblical scholars resolve the tension between historical analysis and the doctrine of revelation.[14] The exegetical principle of accommodation maintained that eternal truths of revelation had been historicized in Scripture to fit the cultural level and mentality of their recipients.[15]

Given these pressures, nineteenth-century Jewish responses to the critique of revelation can usefully be interpreted as a 'revolt of the colonized' that resisted the intellectual hegemony of Christianity by engaging in counterdiscursive practices. Jews, for example, created hybrids or composite narratives that salvaged a positive image of the Jewish past while adopting some principles and conclusions from biblical criticism.[16] Maintaining the historical veracity of God's revelation to the Jews inverted the self-understanding of Protestants and Catholics and unsettled accepted truths about the respective historical significance of pagan philosophy, Judaism, Christianity, and Islam.[17] David Myers has drawn attention to the persistence of Jewish anti-historicism in the nineteenth century,[18] and one response to the challenge of revelation was to bypass Lessing's ditch entirely by extracting God's eternal truths from history. Foregrounding the positive evidence of experience, especially collective national witness of the revelation to Moses, also helped offset the dangers of historicism. Neo-orthodox scholars, such as Samson Hirsch, as well as some reformers, placed certain aspects of revelation outside of time.

Claiming the mantle of primordial revelation had limited appeal for Jewish scholars, however. For one, the scandal of particularity, often solved in Christianity with reference to an early universal revelation, was not as glaring within Judaism because the Seven Noahide Laws referenced in the Talmud conceded a degree of religious knowledge to gentiles and provided a historical basis for a universal ethics. The Noahide

Laws implied that morality based on revelation was accessible without Scripture and commensurate with rational religion.[19] They helped Moses Mendelssohn, for example, equate Judaism with the natural religion of reason. The idea of primordial revelation also often undermined the importance of the ancient Hebrews in the history of religion by weakening the distinction between Judaism and paganism and celebrating Indian or Persian traditions as older, more authentic, and closer to God. Liberal Jews likewise resisted the notion of an original religious wisdom being transmitted orally until the time of Moses because it set a precedent for recognizing oral law as revealed, not a product of postbiblical developments. At the same time, the idea of religious wisdom predating Moses also allowed reformers to challenge the binding character of written law and could paradoxically serve to unseat tradition.

Revelation and the Law: Moses Mendelssohn

Religious Enlighteners across the German confessions shared the challenge of justifying revealed religion and the authority of Scripture and tradition against reason and critical-historical exegesis.[20] The Jewish Enlightenment, or Haskalah, also applied science and philosophy to renew religious traditions and sources. The maskilim, a relatively small cohort of Jewish scholars centred in Prussia, began in the late eighteenth century to supplement canonical training in the Torah and Talmud with the European culture of the Enlightenment. However, reconciling texts rooted in revelation and prophetic inspiration with outside intellectual currents, often in other scholarly languages, posed additional hurdles for Jews. Jewish scholars grappled with unique issues such as the relationship between the halacha and the laws of the state and the degree of religion's involvement in daily life. These sharply divided modernizers and the rabbinic elite, long entrusted with authority over religion, generating troubling new intellectual fault-lines.[21] Serious political consideration of emancipation also began with efforts to restructure the absolutist state and entangled religious reform with debates over the status of Jews in civic society.[22]

Despite close personal relationships among the maskilim and Christian *Aufklärer*, confessional chauvinism often prejudiced the self-justification of Enlightened forms of religion and made the transfer of critical methods perilous for Jews, as for Catholics. Deism, for example, could readily be reconciled with Judaism, especially as it denied the Trinity and original sin and insisted on free will. Many deists identified the Seven Noahide Laws or the Ten Commandments with natural religion.[23] But Enlightened Protestants were inclined to depict Judaism as the antithesis of natural religion, as a particular, national faith whose blind adherence to the law was unethical and intolerant.[24] Establishing Christianity as a purely spiritual religion often entailed transcending its historical origins and purging its Jewish elements.[25] As Jonathan Hess argued, the normative visions of universalism that proliferated under the Enlightenment created new, strikingly modern forms of antisemitism that jeopardized the place of Jews in German society.[26]

As middle-class German Jews acculturated in the late eighteenth century and acquired secular training, retaining revelation legitimized and gave divine sanction to traditional observances and practices. It likewise offset a sudden devaluation of Talmud study in Jewish education. The chief architect of the early Jewish Enlightenment, the poet Naphatali Herz Wessely, thus preserved the epistemological value of revelation as the uncontested source of all religious knowledge. His *Words of Peace and Truth* (1782) relegated reason and revelation to separate spheres, insisting that immersion in the universal "teaching of man" was imperative for Jews to effectively engage broader society and fully comprehend the Bible. But the "teaching of God," in his view, had been directly revealed to Moses and preserved in oral and written law.[27] Without divine assistance, Wessely concluded, Jews would lack knowledge of doctrines necessary to fulfill spiritual obligations.[28]

Moses Mendelssohn, one of the few Jewish disciples of Leibniz and Wolff, equated, by contrast, the doctrinal content of Judaism with natural religion but still defended the divine origins of the law, setting an uneasy precedent for assessing the significance of revelation in Judaism. Born in 1729 in Dessau to a poor Torah scribe, Mendelssohn studied the Bible, the Talmud, Jewish philosophy, and Hebrew under the rabbi David Fränkel, whom he followed to the Prussian capital in 1743 at the height of Wolff's influence. Working in the firm of a silk manufacturer, Mendelssohn published extensively on metaphysics, aesthetics, and natural theology before contributing, as an observant Jew, to the Haskalah's revival of biblical exegesis through a German translation of the Pentateuch in Hebrew letters. His defence of revealed religion in *Jerusalem, or on Religious Power and Judaism* (1783) responded to the controversies unleashed by Lessing's publication of Reimarus's *Fragments*. It also answered the theologian J.K Lavater's public challenge to convert to Christianity and reflected on C.W. Dohm's 1781 plea, encouraged by Mendelssohn, for the civic improvement and political equality of Prussian Jews, reframing the role of Jewish revelation in the context of limiting state power over religion.

A lifelong friend of Lessing, Mendelssohn had defended him against allegations of Spinozism that followed his death in 1781. But Lessing's notion of a progressive revelation in which divine guidance shepherded reason until it attained full cognizance of God and morality did little to justify the importance of revelation in Judaism. In the *Education of the Human Race* (1780) Lessing argued that Judaism represented the childhood of humanity, an early and temporary stage in the process of historical revelation. In his view, the early Israelites had been uncivilized and primitive, possessed only a rudimentary concept of God, and lacked a doctrine of immortality. He likewise regarded postbiblical literature as a corruption of Mosaic law, denying Judaism the capacity for progress.

Mendelssohn had read the entirety of Reimarus's manuscript after Lessing showed it to him in Wolfenbüttel and felt compelled to respond to the fourth fragment's contention that the Old Testament was not written to reveal a religion.[29] His argument that Judaism combined revealed legislation with the natural truths of reason recast the relationship, raised by Spinoza, between the Hebrew Bible and natural reason. Spinoza had favoured a purely political interpretation of the Mosaic books. In his view, the Pentateuch outlined a system of religious government that established the Jewish polity but contained no metaphysical truths. Mendelssohn concluded that the Mosaic books contained revealed legislation but no doctrines, opting against the use of progressive historicism to bridge Lessing's ditch. Not having been revealed, the eternal truths of Judaism stood above history, for Mendelssohn, and could not be supplanted, refined, or modified.

This position followed Wolff in distinguishing eternal rational truths from those found in Scripture. Mendelssohn defended the Sinaitic revelation as an attestable historical event that had been collectively witnessed by the entire Hebrew nation: "a matter of history on which I can rely with certainty."[30] The Mosaic books were an accurate record of God's words, for Mendelssohn, and their divine content to be interpreted literally. He remained remarkably inattentive to historical-critical scholarship and its challenges to Mosaic authorship. However, for Mendelssohn, the eternal truths of reason were distinct from the revealed truths of history.[31] "One has taken supernatural legislation for a supernatural revelation of religious propositions and doctrines necessary for man's salvation," he criticized.[32] According to Mendelssohn, revelation had no epistemological validity; it targeted the will, not the understanding.[33]

The eternal truths of Judaism thus did not derive from God's revelation to Moses, nor were they historically particular. "Judaism boasts of no exclusive revelation of eternal truths that are indispensable to salvation, of no revealed religion," Mendelssohn asserted.[34] Human powers alone were sufficient to demonstrate and verify religious wisdom.

He proclaimed Judaism the only universal religion of reason because it didn't distort natural religion with irrational dogma. Christianity, according to Mendelssohn, was exclusivistic in demanding adherence to revealed mysteries, such as the Trinity.[35] Yet, as Allan Arkush argues, Mendelssohn at times undermined his own denial of revealed religious doctrines, suggesting that Israelite knowledge of God before the revelation was insufficient because it lacked a proper understanding of divine mercy and did not prevent the descent into idolatry.[36] In a similar vein, Mendelssohn also admitted the possibility of primordial religious knowledge, suggesting its inheritance distinguished the historical role of the Jewish people.

As the Sinaitic revelation only dispensed historical truths, Mendelssohn concluded that the Torah contained primarily prescriptions, laws, ordinances, and rules of life, not doctrine. The commandments had a pedagogical value, for Mendelssohn, as practical precepts for keeping alive and pure religious truths, which could be learned elsewhere without revelation. The covenant with God required strict obedience to ritual as an "unalterable duty and obligation,"[37] at least until a new revelation altered the commandments given on Mt. Sinai. For Mendelssohn, ceremonies, practices, and actions were a more reliable way to convey knowledge than signs, images, or scripts, which were vulnerable to distortion and unintelligible to many. The law reminded Jews of the eternal truths of reason and encouraged reflection upon them. The Torah thus destined the Jews to be a priestly nation that preserved and proclaimed authentic ideas of God.

Declaring Jewish ritual law to be the inviolable purview of revelation severely undermined Dohm's stipulation that regeneration be a precondition for civic equality. Mendelssohn advocated emancipation based on natural rights theory, imagining what David Sorkin calls a "fragile dualism" between a secular state and voluntary religious associations.[38] The state, according to Mendelsohn, should neither make religious conformity a precondition for equality, nor should it intervene in matters of conscience. He characterized Judaism as a "church" or confession, on par with Protestantism and Catholicism. The political laws that guaranteed ancient Hebrews an independent national life were no longer valid, in his view, and he dismissed the notion of restoring a Jewish commonwealth. This separation of church and state, as Hess argues, was subversive in that it juxtaposed Christianity's own self-deceptive claims to universality with a recognition of its actual coercive nature and aspirations for global political power.[39]

The redefinition of Judaism in the late eighteenth century as a faith or confession weakened its association with a particular national *Volk* or ethnicity. As the absolutist state transferred the control synagogues held over religious practice to the heads of households, rabbis lost their status as officials capable of enforcing Jewish law and functioned more as spiritual leaders and theologians.[40] In this context, Mendelssohn's insistence on the revealed character of Mosaic law and its inviolability struck many liberal Jews as oppressive, while Conservatives resented his questioning the doctrinal content of the revelations found in the Torah and rabbinic literature. By the mid-1780s reformers began subjecting ceremonial law to rational investigation and modernizing synagogue services, mandating decorum and propriety from attendees and rendering prayers and the liturgy in the vernacular. Mendelssohn's defence of historical revelation, by contrast, supported strict religious observance. He admitted no historical development in Judaism and yielded to reformers only in his acceding to a 1772 ducal edict in Mecklenburg-Schwerin that internment of the dead be delayed for three days in defiance of Jewish custom.[41]

Kant and Pre-Mosaic Revelation: Saul Ascher

Immanuel Kant's critical turn cast doubt on Mendelssohn's claim that Judaism reconciled rational religion and historically revealed legislation. Kant and Mendelssohn held each other in high esteem, having met once in person, and carried on an extensive correspondence in the decades before the latter's death. Kant read and admired Mendelssohn's *Jerusalem*, though wrongly construed the text as an effort to transcend the historical foundations of Judaism for a universal rational religion.[42] Kant's own interpretation of Judaism, articulated most clearly in *Religion within the Limits of Reason Alone* (1793), disputed its ability to make such a transition. In his view, Judaism was a juridical-political system bereft of universal ethical content. Moral law, for Kant, had to be both universal and self-imposed, not the result of submission to an external authority. Judaism exemplified the limitations of statutory religion, in his view, encouraging blind, irrational obedience with no basis for evolving to a purely spiritual or rational faith.[43]

Jewish reformers interpreted Kantian philosophy as a platform for critiquing ceremonial law, external acts, and outward observances with the notion that purified Judaism was a rationally viable religion.[44] One response to Kant was to emphasize universal and ethical aspects of Judaism and interpret laws and ceremonies as pedagogical or motivational means to achieve a moral end. This required an historicist understanding of religion. Judaism could shed its external legal elements while keeping its ethical content intact.[45] However, critical philosophy also launched new, secular forms of moral and political Jew hatred.[46] Depicting Judaism as unfit for morality made emancipation contingent on Jews abandoning ritual law for a more rational religion.[47] Jews also came to represent the impurity of reason and the imperfections of the material world, the body, and the profane, while Christians claimed the supposed prerogatives of autonomous reason, the supreme qualification for participating in the body politic.[48]

The techniques Protestant scholars evoked to salvage revealed religion in a Kantian key thus compounded the vulnerabilities of Judaism's perceived adherence to external statutes. However, in the same year Fichte published his *Attempt at a Critique of All Revelation* the young Jewish journalist Saul Ascher reworked Kant's challenges to the benefit of a rationalized Judaism in *Leviathan oder ueber Religion in Rücksicht des Judenthums* (1792). Ascher later denounced Fichte's nationalism and distaste for the French Revolution as antisemitic, but he was the first of many to reconcile Judaism with Kantian principles.[49] Unlike Fichte, his approach was too subversive to precipitate a case of mistaken authorship. Ascher strategically reframed the strongly antisemitic accounts of rational religion's historical development typical of Kant, in part by rejecting Mendelssohn's characterization of Judaism as revealed legislation.

As encountered in Judaism, revelation was compatible with a religion that embodied Kant's idea of moral autonomy, Ascher argued, because it strengthened an existing faith and provided a mere catalyst to the understanding. For Ascher, Judaism was a faith defined by its doctrines, not a religion of the law; as such its social function was equal to that of other confessions under the Prussian state. He drew upon the idea of pre-Mosaic revelation to curtail the significance of halachic rituals and rabbinic authority. The essence of Judaism had, he admitted, been laid down in the earliest stage of its historical development, suffering corruption after its constitution through Mosaic law. But no unbroken line of continuity linked this early revelation and oral tradition. Like other reform-minded Jewish scholars, Ascher was reluctant to idolize primordial revelation as an authoritative source of religious truth. In his view, Judaism, once restored to its original state, would surpass Christianity as a means to safeguard the autonomy of the will necessary to promote genuine morality in the Kantian sense. On these grounds he proposed a "reformation" of Judaism that restored its essential function as a regulative religion that governed the understanding.

Born in 1767 to a well-established and acculturated Berlin family, Ascher belonged to the second generation of maskilim. Although not educated in a yeshiva, he studied Hebrew and the Talmud alongside secular training in the humanities, later earning his living as a book-seller. As a political publicist, briefly arrested for his coverage of a financial scandal, Ascher earned a reputation as an Enlightened advo-cate of the French Revolution and Napoleon. Jerome Bonaparte granted Jews full equality under the law in the Kingdom of Westphalia in the same year Fichte delivered his *Addresses to the German Nation* (1808). The consistory of rabbis Napoleon established under Israel Jacobson modernized synagogue services by introducing German language ser-mons and Jewish confirmation ceremonies. The reversal of emancipa-tion edicts after Napoleon's defeat made Ascher a vocal opponent of German nationalism. His *Germanomanie* (1815) accused E.M. Arendt and F.L. Jahn of mysticism and antisemitism and challenged Fried-rich Rühs's nationalist opposition to Jewish equality. Members of the *Burschenschaften* burned the work as un-German at the Wartburgfest of 1817.

Ascher criticized Mendelssohn for not approaching Judaism as a set of doctrines, making the religion appear unworthy of philosophical inquiry. Judaism, in his view, was distinct from Mosaic law, and Men-delssohn wrongly "restricted the whole purpose of revelation in Juda-ism to the Mosaic constitution."[50] To broaden this view, *Leviathan* opens with an anthropological analysis of religion as a universal condition necessary for social life. Its purpose, for Ascher, was to enhance the felic-ity of communities and to teach social responsibility. All religions, in his view, presupposed an exalted being, theorized the human relationship to the divine, and cultivated that relationship. They differed according to the accepted source of religious knowledge: nature, revelation, or reason. According to Ascher, revealed religion rightly recognized that faith could not be subordinated to reason, but he held revelation could only occur once a people sensed a gap in their knowledge.

Historicizing Judaism allowed Ascher to restore moral autonomy to Jews by depicting them not as blind adherents to an eternal law, but as agents who embraced the commandments as a strategic response to specific historical conditions. His history of Judaism follows a frame-work of progression from regulative to constitutive religion, a Kantian distinction between religions having the capacity to constitute knowl-edge or govern thought and behaviour. Early Judaism merely consisted, for Ascher, in "concordant beliefs"[51] that formed the kernel of faith but lacked external manifestation. Religious truths came together as a set of doctrines but did not have the force of law. "The Eternal selected Judaism as the means," Ascher wrote, "to teach a number of men to think in unison."[52] According to him, the special revelation to the Jews began with Abraham and the patriarchs. During this period, Jews lived together in a theocracy, a society based on a divinely revealed moral purpose. The period of revelation ended with the onset of a political hierarchy instituted under Mosaic law. At that point Judaism became a constitutive religion, administered by priests according to a set of fixed symbols and rituals.

Ascher argued that Kant mistook the later constitutive form of Judaism for its true essence. In his view, the Sinaitic revelation was a temporary measure to create a polity, ensure discipline, and preserve the doctrines of Judaism. But the means had been mistaken for the ends. The commandments, Ascher wrote, "therefore do not constitute the true essence of Judaism, but are mere predicates of belief, means to preserve revelation in Judaism as a constitutive religion."[53] Religious law was merely an "exalted social constitution"[54] and would no longer have full force once Judaism could be reestablished as "pure faith in God and his prophets."[55] Ascher was the first to apply the term 'orthodoxy' to Judaism as a position opposed to his own historicist approach.[56] In his view, the Talmudists recognized that the Torah could be adapted to new circumstances, but their particular application had ossified, causing the law to degenerate into "a symbol without spirit or life."[57]

Judaism's essential articles of faith required purification, according to Ascher, and he delineated fourteen doctrines that reconstituted early Judaism and guaranteed "true autonomy of will."[58] Judaism was better suited to cultivate autonomous moral development, Ascher argued, because it supplied rules for the understanding without regulating the will. Christianity was unfit to embody the ideal universal religion, he cautioned, because it betrayed its Jewish foundations by attempting to control the will.[59] These articles supposedly transcended the historical mutations of Judaism and were thus immune to historical contingency. As Hess states, they represent a balance between universal ethical monotheism and particular forms of Jewish identity.[60] Ascher's doctrines included belief in one eternal God of love who revealed himself to Abraham, Isaac, Jacob, and Moses, as well as the doctrines of reward and punishment, of providence ruling the world, and a messiah bringing redemption. He also retained circumcision as symbol of the covenant with God, the Jewish Sabbath and festivals, as well as days of penance and reconciliation.

Despite calling for a Jewish reformation, Ascher took little interest in liturgical reform or the external representations of religion. He kept his distance from the reform movement, although *Leviathan* garnered the limited attention it did among reformers in Berlin after the defeat of Napoleon. Starting in 1814 reform services were held in the Prussian capital in the private homes of Israel Jacobson and Jacob Herz Beer.

They were short-lived. A year after Ascher's death in 1822, King Friedrich Wilhelm III prohibited services outside of existing temples and forbid any changes to traditional ritual, such as prayers and songs, fearing that reform would inhibit 'internal' missions to convert Jews. Ascher's return to pre-Mosaic revelation to justify religious reformation served a purpose similar to ceremonial reform, to retain the loyalty of liberal, enlightened Jews, yet his concern lay more in the philosophy of religion than in its practice.

Salomon Ludwig Steinheim on Primordial Revelation

The persistence of precritical concepts of revelation is most evident in the work of Salomon Ludwig Steinheim, who welcomed ritual reform and sought to ease the burden of religious law. His adherence to revelation without the motive to sanctify the law may reflect concerns about the fragility of Judaism in the early nineteenth century. Conversion rates were high in the 1820s, as Deborah Hertz has shown for Berlin, the result of frustration with the failures of emancipation, as well as of changing German national identities, new socializing patterns, and higher rates of intermarriage. The Prussian government's closure of the Beer temple made conversion, at least in Berlin, the only viable path away from traditional Judaism. State support for missionary societies and activists such as August Tholuck also increased baptism rates, although for young men careerist motives for conversion far outweighed religious convictions.[61] Liberal Jews could not rely on ritual observance to justify loyalty to their religion. But retaining the integrity of the special revelation God entrusted to Jews sanctified both the doctrinal core of Judaism and the historical identity of Jews as the people of revelation.

Steinheim's understanding of revelation in some respects resembles that of Protestant and Catholic orthodoxy. He resisted all mainstream strategies for postcritically rehabilitating revelation, developing instead a positivist defence of the term. Steinheim's "*Offunbarungspositivismus*"[62] insisted upon the unquestioned facticity of revelation, as well as on its capacity for communicating an eternal set of doctrines. Sidestepping Lessing's ditch, Steinheim saw no tension between historical revelation and universal truth. At the same time, Steinheim decoupled the content of the divine truth received by ancient Hebrews from any previous religious sensibilities. Revealed knowledge, in his view, emerged in the period between Noah and Moses. Steinheim steered clear of associating Judaism with natural religion as a way of preserving its unique historical mission and rejected any affinities with paganism. The extent that idealizing primordial revelation jeopardized the historical mission of Jews as the bearers of divine wisdom reverberates in his criticism of Romantic mythologists and idealist philosophers. Revelation occurred, in Steinheim's view, during a particular period in Judaism's history before which true religion did not yet exist, and after which human acceptance of God's word was subject to development.

This idiosyncratic position reflects Steinheim's status as a "lonely prophet"[63] far removed from rabbinic circles and German university life. Born in Bruchhausen, Westphalia, Steinheim attended the gymnasium in Altona before studying medicine in Kiel in 1807. Later as a practicing physician in Altona, he distinguished himself as a public health leader, combatting the typhoid fever that followed Napoleon's troops, as well as later cholera epidemics. For over a decade after the July Revolution in 1830, Steinheim campaigned for the civil and political equality of Jews in Schleswig and Holstein. Hamburg severely restricted the residency of Jews, so many settled in the neighbouring harbour town, then still under Danish rule. Starting in 1833 Steinheim immersed himself in the works of Lessing, Kant, and the German idealists, as well as in Jewish religious thought and philosophy. His goal was to stem the tide of conversion and assimilation by reconciling prevailing philosophy with Judaism. Distressed by ill health and the failures of emancipation, he moved to Rome in 1849 where he completed the final two volumes of *Die Offenbarung nach dem Lehrbegriffe der Synagoge* (1835–65), the only systematic theology of Judaism before the early 1840s.[64]

Steinheim's defence of revelation broke with rationalism, which, in his view, unduly disregarded the historical content of the Jewish Bible and disavowed biblical witness. Convinced by Kant's assault on metaphysical proofs of God, Steinheim declared reason and revelation to be distinct, though interdependent. He likewise rejected the way Lessing historicized revelation to reconcile it with the understanding. Revelation, for Steinheim, had no history. One could only write a history of "emotional adjustment to its teachings and injunctions."[65] The reception of God's word in revealed religion progressed, in his view, from a phase of childhood devotion and unconditional obedience through defiance and temptation before attaining maturity. The knowledge generated by natural religion, by contrast, lacked an identifiable historical inception but progressed from primeval atheism, through myth, to philosophy.

The historical act of revelation was, for Steinheim, epistemologically relevant, an unveiling of otherwise inscrutable truths. Revelation was, he wrote, "a spiritual proclamation of realities, of which we had no knowledge without the direct communication by God or by a divine messenger and of which we had no knowledge prior to this proclamation; nor could we possess or acquire it by means of our natural powers of cognition." [66] Reason could, however, critically evaluate the authenticity of revelation using certain criteria. According to Steinheim, revelation had to disclose something new about God and humankind and be sudden and without precedent. More than a vision or inner awareness, revelation must also derive from an external source and be communicable and comprehensible. It disclosed knowledge about God that reason could not conceive and, importantly, had to be complete in itself, not subject to evolution. The propositional content of revelation was eternal and transcended history despite its presentation at a specific moment in time.

Friedrich Schleiermacher's grounding of religion in subjective feeling wrongly diminished the power of revelation, according to Steinheim, and detracted from the Old Testament's importance as its genuine depository. "The Old Testament was not given in order to reveals laws or statutes," he wrote in contradiction to Mendelssohn, "but in order to reveal a God."[67] According to Steinehim, core truths relating to the unity of a living God, the freedom of the will for God and man, and creation out of nothingness could be extracted from passages throughout the Hebrew Bible. Yet he eschewed the idea of infallible sacred texts. Written and oral law was, for Steinheim, a secondary edifice, a human response to revelation, and not directly of divine origin.

Steinheim also resisted the ontological meaning German idealists attributed to revelation, according to which a self-revealing God came to full realization in the world through the development of human religious consciousness. Revelation, in his view, was a single event in history, not a prolonged educational process, and he neglected on these grounds postbiblical Judaism.[68] The idea of primordial revelation and its reframing as the absolute within idealist histories of religion posed, as Steinheim recognized, a particular threat to the importance of Jews as the recipients of God's word. "Our current generation," Steinheim commented in 1835, "seems to be willfully determined, if not to destroy revelation then at least to distort it by mixing up and confusing it with myths and philosophic theories as to render it unrecognizable."[69] The symbolists and mythologists, by which Steinheim meant Kanne, Creuzer, and Schelling, have caused "devastation in the field of revelation" by presuming "golden days of human omniscience" and a "deep agreement" among the belief systems of the Orient.[70] No continuity could be found in the revealed truths of the Bible and Hinduism or Zoroastrianism, for Steinheim. The notion that Jews had preserved an original faith in its purity, he concluded, was likewise fallacious since only with Abraham did Jews distinguish themselves from other idolatrous peoples.

Reluctance to tarnish the revealed truths of Judaism with the stigma of a pagan inheritance led Steinheim to confront the ways in which Protestant biblical criticism compromised the uniqueness of Hebrew monotheism, such as occurred in Wilhelm Vatke's *Biblische Theologie* (1835). Published in the same year as D.F. Strauss's *Life of Jesus*, Vatke's text had similarly "violent results"[71] for Moses and the Old Testament, Steinheim feared, as Strauss did for the historical Christ. Loyalty to the facticity of revelation distinguished Steinheim from Vatke, who subordinated biblical history to Hegelian philosophy and took a developmental approach to revelation, suggesting, for example, that the Persian cult of light could be a prelude to monotheism. Vatke insinuated that Moses and the patriarchs had been pagans who worshipped Molekh and, as Steinheim interpreted his opponent, might have practiced a cult of human sacrifice, a painful association given the accusations of blood libel that surfaced in the Damascus Affair when the Ottoman Empire accused thirteen Jews of murdering a Christian monk in 1840.[72] In *Die Offenbarung vom Standpuncte der höheren Kritik* (1840) Steinheim rehabilitated the image of Moses. Even if Mosaic law didn't have divine origins, monotheism had matured by his time and Moses himself had delivered the law; it was not the product of a later age.

Steinheim concluded that the historical mission of the Jews was to preserve and proclaim revelation as it had been transmitted in the three covenants to Noah, the patriarchs, and Moses. He drew a delicate balance between the "peculiar nation-building element of revelation"[73] and its universal significance. The ancient Hebrews were particularly receptive to God's word because the absence of higher culture and profound thought shielded them from false doctrines. At the same time the Jewish polity had to fall to strengthen the "world-conquering power of revelation."[74] Judaism was, for Steinheim, the "great institution for the maintenance and preservation of that documented revelation ... with a perpetually rejuvenated people serving as its vessel."[75] It guarded God's doctrines in their pristine form to defeat paganism and philosophy for the future realization of God's kingdom on earth.

The unusual circumference Steinheim drew around revelation positioned him at odds with orthodox, Conservative, and reform Judaism, as they developed in the 1840s. Steinheim, like most reformers, denied the divine origins of the halacha. While regarding the Sabbath as a symbol of revelation, for example, he did not recognize the precise form of its observance as an extension of revelation, and its expression could take various forms.[76] Steinheim wished to detach the essence of Judaism from its ceremonial trappings and envisioned a liturgy that purely reflected his conception of revelation. He viewed the prayer book of the Hamburg Temple, founded in 1818, as not radical enough, since, in his view, it supposedly contained vestiges of ancient pagan traditions, such as animal sacrifice, as well as neo-Platonic, mystical, and Kabbalistic elements that Judaism had absorbed from neighbouring peoples.[77] Subsequent reformers, however, dismantled his propositional concept of revelation, conflated revelation with human religious consciousness, and welcomed the idea of perpetually evolving religious knowledge. Orthodox Jews held closer to Steinheim's propositional concept of revelation but extended its purview to the actual text of the Torah and oral law.

Revelation as Historical Experience: Samson Raphael Hirsch

Tensions between the reform movement and orthodox Judaism were especially pronounced in the free city of Hamburg, where the first enduring reform institution was founded in 1818. The liturgy of the Hamburg Temple departed starkly from precedent. Readings from the Torah were abbreviated to allow more time for the sermon; the prayer book was composed in Hebrew and German; and an organ and choir singing German hymns in the style of church music replaced the traditional melodies of the cantor.[78] Around two-thirds of greater Hamburg's Jewish community, then the largest in the German states, however, still resisted such innovations in the early 1840s, attending a traditional synagogue and refusing marriages with temple families.[79] Leading the resistance against ritual reform in Hamburg was Isaac Bernays, a founder of modern orthodoxy. Commensurate with the demands of Hamburg's vibrant commercial economy, Bernays saw no conflict between traditional religious observance and the adoption of secular education and German culture. Yet he campaigned vigorously against planned expansions of the Temple and, in 1842, against a new edition of the prayer book.

Confessional orthodoxy was ascendant across the German states in the 1830s and 1840s, fuelled by the revivalist movement, the forced union of Prussian churches, ultramontanism, and a reaction against critical-historical scholarship. The resurgence of orthodoxy within Judaism, embodied in Samson Raphael Hirsch, rested upon belief in a supernatural Sinaitic revelation. A positivist philosophy of Jewish historical experience allowed Samson Hirsch to extend the scope of revelation beyond that claimed by Steinheim. He, too, felt no compunction to bridge Lessing's ditch. No rational proof was needed for veracity of revelation. For Hirsch, Jewish national history was the sole repository of God's revelation to humanity; its authenticity lay in continual trans-mission through tradition. Curtailing revelation's purview as the clear communication of divine precepts would have weakened the authority of oral and written law, which Hirsch fought to preserve.

Retreating from Mendelssohn's universalism, Hirsch thus celebrated the historical particularity of his religion, attributing noetic content, including teachings about nature, humanity, and history, to the Torah.[80] All knowledge of God derived from objective revelation to the Jewish people, in his view, not from philosophical speculation. Hirsch denied revelation a human component as a way to transcend the pitfalls of historical contingency and accommodation.[81] There could be no Jewish theology, in his view, which implied a system of human ideas about God, nor was Judaism a confession. Attention to dogma, ethics, and the emotional aspects of faith distracted from the law, for Hirsch. Judaism was, in his view, a theonomy, a society ruled by divine law, requiring strict observance derived from study of the Torah and Talmud.[82]

Born into a family of enlightened traditionalists in Hamburg in 1808, Hirsch experienced from a young age the apprehensions his father, a lace maker turned merchant, had about the reformed Temple. While recognizing that customary belief and practice were no longer com-pelling to many Jews, the circle of community leaders that met in the Hirsch household was concerned about the declining authority of rab-binic tradition. Intended for his father's profession, Hirsch received a secular education at the Hamburg gymnasium, supplemented with religious training at home and with Bernays. In 1828, having decided to become a rabbi, he studied for two years under the distinguished Talmudist Jacob Ettlinger in Mannheim, who later led a withdrawal of traditionalist rabbis from the reformed Braunschweig Rabbinical Con-ference in 1845 and organized the Talmud study circles that sustained a rebirth of orthodoxy.

In 1829 Hirsch enrolled at the university in Bonn to study classical languages, history, and philosophy, emulating the precedent set by Ber-nays of combining secular training with orthodoxy. Abraham Geiger was in his cohort; the two studied the Talmud together and founded a homiletic society for rabbinical candidates. From 1830 to 1841 Hirsch served as chief rabbi for the small Duchy of Oldenburg, supervising Jewish schools and selectively modernizing the local synagogues. He introduced a choir and the German language in services, and even substituted a sermon for the traditional derashah, a Hebrew homily interpreting opaque biblical passages or legal problems. Although an adaptation of Protestant practice, many rabbis by the 1830s culti-vated a specifically Jewish homiletics which, while still edificatory and moralizing, was more heavily exegetical and contained midrashic or haggadic material.[83]

To revive public interest in traditional Judaism Hirsch published the popular *Nineteen Letters about Judaism* (1836), which offered a practical interpretation of the law rather than a systematic religious philosophy. A critical review by Geiger (questioning whether Shavuot indeed commemorated the giving of the law) dissolved their friendship and set the pair up as antagonists in struggles over the future of German Judaism. The author of the first letter, the enlightened Benjamin, confesses a conflicted relationship with traditional Judaism, fearing it inhibited the attainment of happiness, unduly restricted individualism, and isolated Jews from broader society. His correspondent, Naftali, the voice of Hirsch, responds with a defence of written and oral law. Hirsch conceded a substantial role to reason in interpreting the law but cautioned that obedience was paramount as human beings were incapable of judging God's word. "Indisputably," Naftali writes to Benjamin, "man requires revelation of the Divine Will."[84] The letters protocol the continuously unfolding spirit of Judaism, arguing that rabbinic literature actualized revelations found in the Hebrew Bible and was therefore also of divine origin.

A series of preliminary revelations prepared the Israelites for reception of the Torah by teaching the will to submit, according to Hirsch. Unlike Steinheim, he welcomed the idea of a preliminary primordial revelation because it set a precedent for the divine origins of oral law. The dispensations subsequently made to Moses constituted a "historical renewal"[85] of the knowledge needed for a national existence. Naftali assures his enlightened correspondent that Judaism was the "cornerstone on which humanity could be reconstructed."[86] God revealed himself to the patriarchs as the sole creator, the lord of nature and all nations, and as a vindicator of the oppressed. The Torah, by contrast, was a "revelation of how He wants men to live."[87] It did not contain the ideas or religious doctrines that Jews of the time formulated about God but contained the unalterable will of God. Hirsch believed the mitzvoth were designed to shape the world according to God's will by proscribing moral action. They were not intended to spark spiritual contemplation, metaphysical speculation, or a mystical union with God.[88] For this reason "arbitrary curtailment of the Torah and capricious abandonment of the very essence of our life" was, for Naftali, "too high a price" to pay for emancipation.[89]

The *Letters* set the stage for *Horeb: A Philosophy of Jewish Laws and Observances* (1837), which Hirsch designed as a compendium to offset how the catechisms then fashionable for preparing children for confirmation presented Judaism. Jewish catechisms shifted the focus of religious education away from Talmud study and Torah translation, emphasizing enlightened, universal aspects of Judaism and its moral content. Catechistic education likewise cultivated the personal beliefs of girls and boys, rather than train them in ritual observance and the law.[90] Hirsch denied that knowledge of God could be rooted in subjective experience, even if the voice of God did penetrate individual conscience. In his view, Judaism rested on "clear cognitive and intellectual perceptions" and on "the recognition and acceptance of Divine truths that have been objectively documented."[91] Hirsch counteracted the extreme individualism of Kant's self-legislating moral actor and Romantic philosophy by grounding revelation in the collective historical witness of a national community.[92]

Titled after the name given the site of Mosaic revelation in Deuteronomy, *Horeb* refuted claims that Talmudic Judaism had betrayed its biblical origins. The text explored the symbolic and allegorical significance of the mitzvoth to justify loyalty to the minute details of their precepts. Hirsch held Hebrew to be a divine medium of expression, an ideal instrument for succinctly conveying and preserving the profound ideas of revelation. As David Sorkin argues, he rehabilitated the Jewish textual tradition using an outdated Romantic theory of language. Hirsch's theory of Jewish symbolism, by which Hebrew roots contained hidden meanings, drew on the tradition of the Kabbalah as well as on the speculative etymology of the mythologists Kanne and Creuzer.[93] According to Hirsch, God spoke through symbols, and performing the commandments proclaimed the truths of revelation through symbolic action, establishing the Jews as a living example to humanity.

The historical experience of Mosaic revelation established, for Hirsch, the divine origins of both the Torah and the oral law and therefore their eternal truth and authority. At Horeb, the whole of Israel, he wrote, "heard directly the voice of the Lord" and "in that moment became prophetic."[94] Rather than reflect the superstitions of a primitive people, this collective witnessing "guarantees the Torah as unchangeable for all generations … closed for all time." Only a like occurrence before another assembly of two and a half million souls could alter the text. "There is … no stronger evidence for the Divine origin and uniqueness of the Torah," Hirsch later wrote, "than the continuous backsliding, the continuous rebellion against it on the part of the Jewish people … The Torah … has no development and no history; it is rather the people of the Torah which has a history."[95] The historical fate of the Jewish nation was, for Hirsch, to bring truth and knowledge of God to all peoples, translating the particularity of its historical experience into a universal mission.

In 1847 Hirsch accepted a position as chief rabbi of Moravia, for which he was ill-suited as an acculturated German Jew. Local services were still held in Yiddish, and many rabbis distrusted his relative lack of expertise in Talmudic studies.[96] During the Revolutions of 1848–9, he played a minor role in obtaining equality for Hapsburg Jews, presenting an emancipation petition to Franz Joseph I as chairman of the Committee for Civil and Political Rights of the Jews in Moravia. Hirsch and other traditionalists resisted the pressure to sacrifice religious customs for equality under the law. In the context of political upheaval the German states often believed adherence to religious custom signified future loyalty to the state. Reformers gravitated more towards liberalism, and their willingness to overturn the past seemed untrustworthy to secular authorities.[97]

An 1847 Law on the Status of the Jews extended limited political rights to Prussian Jews outside of Posen, while reinforcing occupational restrictions and instituting compulsory membership in a religious community. In recognizing the corporate status of individual religious communities, it also enabled orthodox groups to organize separate synagogues.[98] The Israelitische Religionsgesellschaft, an independent neo-orthodox congregation established in Frankfurt in 1850, enticed Hirsch away from his more prestigious appointment in Nikolsburg to serve a relatively small number of families and to organize a religious school. His vision for members of the neo-orthodox synagogue dedicated in Frankfurt in 1853 was "Torah im derekh eretz" (Torah with the way of the land), taken from the Mishnah and implying strict adherence to traditional Judaism combined with engagement with the secular world.

The relationship between revelation and tradition embraced by Hirsch and neo-orthodoxy differed from Conservative Judaism, which welcomed limited reform on the basis of a positive-historical interpretation of tradition. Significant delimitations between the three main denominations of Judaism occurred along the fault lines of how to historicize the Torah and Talmud.[99] For Hirsch, the entirety of written and oral law originated in divine revelation and was eternal and unchanging despite its historical location. He severely criticized the Breslau Jewish theological seminar opened by Conservative leader Zacharais Frankel in 1854 as a centre for Talmudic studies. Its members, including Hirsch's former student Heinrich Graetz and Bernays's son, accepted the positivity of the revelation at Sinai but conceded that Talmudic Judaism underwent historical development. Frankel and Graetz, recognized change in the halacha; the Talmud, in their view, was the product of religious innovators, not a faithful rendition of the revelation to Moses.[100]

By midcentury, religiously observant Jews, such as Samson Hirsch, were rightfully wary of critical historical scholarship encroaching on religious truths. The *Wissenschaft des Judentums*, founded in 1819, wrested interpretation of the canonical and legal texts of Judaism from the hands of rabbis. The philological techniques Leopold Zunz acquired as a student of F.A. Wolf and August Boeckh allowed him to dismember the providential view of Jewish history as a record of the special relationship between God and his people. Hirsch contended, naively by the new standards of *Wissenschaft*, that religious truth transcended the history that produced it and tolerated no modifications or additions. Imagining an alternative to enlightened universalization, the founders of the *Wissenschaft des Judentums* subjected postbiblical Judaism to critical-philological inquiry with the apologetic goal of forging an alternative collective memory. At midcentury, much to the consternation of Samson Hirsch, two reform-minded rabbis set the revelations imparted to biblical Jews within a broadly idealist philosophy of history aimed, however, at proving their universality.

Jewish Philosophies of Revelation: Salomon Formstecher and Samuel Hirsch

The reform movement was on secure enough grounds in the 1840s for its most radical members to dismantle propositional revelation and accept a progressive acquisition of religious truth that shifted agency towards human subjects. In this period, more radical rabbis began to redefine revelation as an evolving inborn human capacity to recognize the presence of God and make moral judgments. Most retained Judaism's status as a positive religion whose revealed truths were found in the Mosaic books but rejected the doctrine of verbal inspiration. In *Das rationale Judenthum* (1840), for example, the Breslau school inspector Isaac Asher Francolm declared that "in positive revelation we find deciphered the secrets of our own breast."[101] Francolm served as a rabbi and teacher in Königsberg during the early 1820s, where he preached in German and introduced the confirmation of girls. But when traditionalists petitioned the government to prohibit his innovations, he refused to renew his post. Francolm asserted that within each person resided an "original revelation,"[102] a nebulous feeling on which natural religion built. The teachings of the prophets issued from a perfection and intensification of this endowment.

Under the influence of idealist philosophy, other reformers welcomed the idea of progressive revelation as a viable platform for asserting the eternal truth and universality of Judaism. In the 1830s idealist

Protestant philosophies of religion transformed revelation from a term with questionable epistemological merit into an ontological account of how the divine realized itself and came to self-consciousness in the empirical world. The speculative histories of religion penned by Hegel and Schelling, and discussed in Chapter 5, drew the interest but also the critique of two reform rabbis, Solomon Formstecher and Samuel Hirsch (of no relation to the neo-orthodox Samson Hirsch), who objected to how German idealism dismissed the knowledge of God found in Judaism as an antiquated relic and dialectically sublated Judaism within Christianity. Adopting the terminology and certain principles from idealism, the pair subversively refigured Protestant philosophies of revelation to redeem the historical significance of Judaism. In so doing, they divested revelation of its propositional content, reconceiving the term as the historical unfolding of divine being and making God's self-actualization dependent on human agency.

The position Judaism held in Hegel's *Lectures on the Philosophy of Religion* (1832) warranted the rebuttal of scholars arguing for the universality of Judaism's God-consciousness and commitment to ethical freedom. Unlike Kant, Hegel acknowledged that Judaism belonged to the sphere of religious truth but only as a temporary phase through which knowledge of God passed on its way to absolute religion. Even if, for Hegel, Jews were the first to attribute subjectivity to the divine, their limited understanding of God was of a lawgiver specific to the Israelite nation. Jewish law curtailed human autonomy, according to Hegel, instilling fear of a distant master who demanded obedience. As spirit separated from nature, God became unduly remote. Moreover, the refusal of Jews to relinquish an antiquated religion perpetuated a 'negative dialectic' that wilfully refused development.[103]

Michael Meyer rightly cautions that Formstecher was not a Jewish philosophical idealist. Instead he sought to vindicate Judaism against idealism and restore its intellectual respectability in the currency of absolute idealism.[104] This required jettisoning the Christological focus of Hegel and Schelling. Sven-Erik Rose finds Formstecher only "weakly" Hegelian, suggesting that he drew on Hegel merely to reject him.[105] The most faithful Jewish Hegelians were arguably members of the Verein für die Kultur und Wissenschaft der Juden, who applied Hegelian principles to reconceive the meaning of Judaism and its relationship to the state. Hegel had endorsed emancipation in the *Philosophy of Right* (1820) despite his criticism of Judaism on religious grounds.

Redeeming Judaism in idealist terms meant, for Formstecher and Hirsch, asserting its universality. Judaism, in their view, originated as pure idea and its evolving historical manifestations could be interpreted as progressive stages in the actualization of God and his destiny for humanity. Earning recognition for Judaism as an equal, independent, and relevant cultural force could have a "consciously counter-assimilationist purpose,"[106] aiming to strengthen the foundations of the religion through reform, not render Judaism more palatable to a hostile public. Formstecher agreed with other idealists that religion was the means for spirit to become fully self-conscious and attain subjectivity in this world. He retained an epistemological function for revelation in dispensing religious knowledge but also, like Hegel and Schelling, bound the self-actualization of God to the progressive realization of spirit in the human world. Hirsch doubted the necessity of supernatural revelation for the education of the human race but still distinguished Jews as the chosen messengers of God.

Born in 1808 in Offenbach in the Electorate of Hesse, Salomon Formstecher received a traditional Jewish education in Hebrew and Talmudic studies. His father was a successful engraver of printing stock, able to send his son to the University of Giessen to study philology, Protestant theology, and Hegelian philosophy. After obtaining his doctorate in 1831, Formstecher returned to Offenbach to preach. Sabbath services for the liberal Jewish community already included edifying sermons on morality; the synagogue regulations passed in 1832 mandated the use of the German language for sermons, weddings, and prayers for the elector and his family. Formstecher's sermons and essays from this period justify such reforms based on a developmental history of Judaism. He became the chief rabbi of Hesse after ordination in 1842 and was active in the reform rabbinical conferences.[107] The catechism he wrote to prepare adolescents for confirmation based religious education on an appreciation of how knowledge of God's original revelation had progressed through time.[108]

Rather than a philosophy of religion, a genre tainted for Formstecher with paganism, *Die Religion des Geistes* (1841) presented itself as a "scientific theology"[109] of Judaism. Its goal was to restore Judaism's significance for the history of humanity by showing how "in its essential development it elevates itself to the universal religion of civilized humanity."[110] As the religion of spirit, Formstecher argued, Judaism differed fundamentally from the religion of nature, or paganism, but reconciled the principles of both as it actualized absolute spirit in the historical world. The ontology of being upon which this vision built was indebted to Schelling. According to Formstecher, nature and spirit both derived from a single source. "The infinite universe," he wrote, "is the revelation of an organism with the powers of a world soul."[111] Present in the laws of nature and in rational thought, the world-soul found its highest manifestation in human beings as they became self-conscious of their role in the actualization of spirit.

Although Hegel and the later Schelling both eschewed the idea of primordial revelation, Formstecher retained it as an anchor for subsequent religious development. He postulated the existence of a "prehistorical revelation,"[112] reminiscent but diametrically opposed to Schelling's notion of primordial time when God existed as pure potency and had not yet entered the historical world. Spirit stepping out of the world-soul into the empirical world resulted, for Formstecher, in the "objective positing of primal being."[113] This act created the ideals of absolute goodness and beauty, which, in his view, lay dormant in the human soul. Original revelation was perfected, stable, and complete, he concluded, but not conscious of itself. The subsequent relative, historical revelations that constituted all religion, for Formstecher, denoted subjective human knowledge of the absolute. Spirit only attained self-consciousness in humanity through the "becoming conscious of an objectively given revelation."[114] Prophecy constituted the initial mode through which early humans received relative, historical revelation. According to Formstecher, the "primal power (*Urkraft*) of the Absolute" manifested itself most eminently as an ecstatic feeling. Reason and reflective understanding, however, later brought objective revelation to consciousness.

Irreducible to faith or subjective feeling, religion thus progressively acquired objective knowledge of the divine, for Formstecher. He retained the epistemological value of revelation in its absolute form, even as he bestowed existential importance on relative, historical revelation as a vehicle for the self-realization of God as self-conscious spirit. The vessels of revelation were, in his view, historically relative but contained a "substrate" grounded in absolute revelation.[115] Judaism had the distinction of allowing spirit to become universal. Its history, as Formstecher delineated it, advanced dialectically from a period of objectivity to one of subjectivity through several intermediate stages. In the process, revelation progressed from being an unconscious feeling to rationally comprehensible knowledge. Formstecher attributed muted significance to the dispensation on Mt. Sinai in this process. In his view, Jews had acquired divine truth long before Moses, and the Sinaitic revelation offered no new doctrines. But it did renew a covenant already established between God and Israel and allowed Judaism to persevere under hostile conditions. Moses's achievement was to create the first theocracy, a political order in which the divine ideal could be realized. For Formstecher, as for Hegel, spirit required a people and a state to take objective form.

To assert Judaism's universal significance, Formstecher argued that Christianity and Islam were merely missions to the pagan world that cloaked divine truth in transitory forms, then mistook relative for absolute truth; the Trinity, for example, eventually betrayed monotheism. The Reformation confirmed, for Formstecher, that Christianity was on track to eradicate its pagan remnants and resurface as true Judaism, and he attributed a particular role to the German people in Judaism's path to universality. "The Germanic race (*Volksstamm*)," he wrote, "is the first able to comprehend the Protestant principle in its truth, as a protest of the Jewish element against the pagan in Christianity."[116] Yet, rather than purify Christian teachings, speculative philosophy, according to Formstecher, further corrupted them with pantheism and refused to take seriously the "scientific presentation of truth" in Judaism. Among idealists, he noted, Judaism appeared "almost like a ghostly corpse ... as the remains of a Semitic race that, due to its innate Oriental character, remains totally unreceptive for the civilization of the Japhetic, Indo-Germanic race."[117] This remarkable citation indicates the extent to which perceptions of race confirmed belief in the historical obsolescence of Judaism.

Formstecher ended *Die Religion des Geistes* with a messianic prediction that correlated the immanent emancipation of German Jews with Judaism's attaining universal recognition as the fulfilment of absolute prehistorical revelation. Mendelssohn, in his view, marked the moment when Jewish theology attained "the status of a religious science"[118] and revelation became rationally comprehensible. The degree to which German Jews renounced isolation and the external marks of distinction also eased spirit's transition to subjectivity. Full emancipation was necessary, as Hegel argued, for the state to become a purely ethical institution and would occur once every confession was recognized as a necessary revelation of spirit.

The first to respond to Formstecher, Samuel Hirsch found his colleague's speculative history of Judaism overly apologetic and lacking in specific moral or religious recommendations.[119] The two nevertheless shared an intellectual project. The son of a cattle dealer and tradesman, Hirsch was born in Thalfang in 1815 just as Prussia acquired the surrounding territory on the Rhine's left bank. His family educated him at ultraconservative yeshivot in Metz and then Mainz. Hirsch clandestinely read the German works necessary for acceptance at the university in Bonn in 1835, however, where he immersed himself in philosophy, Protestant theology, history, and literature, before training amongst Hegelians at the university in Berlin. Ordained by Samuel Holdheim, he accepted a rabbinate in the Duchy Anhalt-Dessau in 1838, only to be dismissed two years later for lacking piety. Hirsch wrote *Die Religionsphilosophie der Juden* (1842) as an independent scholar in Dessau. Committed to the reform movement, he emerged as a prominent leader at the rabbinical conferences held in Brunswick, Frankfurt, and Breslau between 1844 and 1846. He denounced Bruno Bauer's essay on *Die Judenfrage* (1843), which made Jewish emancipation contingent on relinquishing religious sensibilities, critiquing how Bauer distorted the reformist position when claiming that obedience to the law inhibited freedom.[120]

More radically than Formstecher, Hirsch conceded that philosophy enabled "scientific knowledge of religion."[121] Idealist principles could, in his view, clarify and interpret the truths present in the history of human consciousness. However, Hirsch argued that Hegel misconstrued the role of Judaism in the education of humanity to freedom. *Die Religionsphilosophie der Juden* traces the self-unfolding of spirit. The essential content of religion, for Hirsch, was not the human relationship to God or, as Hegel asserted, the self-actualization of the divine, but the gradual realization of human moral freedom. Human beings were progressively coming to full awareness of their freedom of will and recognizing God as its transcendent source.

Defining religion as an attitude of self-reflection implied that dogma and knowledge of God were necessary only as a means to grasp moral freedom. Revelation transpired in the human consciousness and was "clearly inscribed in every breast, audible to all."[122] The propositional content of revelation was irrelevant to Hirsch, and he explicitly denied the possibility of primordial wisdom. Recent accounts of paganism, in his view, wrongly presumed an *Urvolk* to which God dispensed "a higher wisdom, scientific methods, and a versatile culture."[123] Unlike Hegel, Hirsch drew an absolute distinction between true and false religions, refusing to redeem paganism as a reservoir of partial truths. No dialectical process could elevate the flawed religious sensibilities of other faiths. In paganism, a passive form of religion, humanity renounced freedom and subjugated itself to the sensual world. The pagan consciousness of God admitted no higher spirituality, and its historical dialectic was self-destructive. Sin was a choice, in his view, not an inescapable condition, and Hirsch refused to accept evil as a necessary negative phase in the self-realization of God.[124]

On this basis, Hirsch argued that Judaism did not represent a dialectical outgrowth from paganism but a radical leap towards freedom, a revolt against the deification of nature in which human beings rose to self-chosen liberty. In his view, Abraham recognized the existence of one eternal God and understood that His purpose was the "eternal self-liberation of man and mankind, humanity living in freedom."[125] This destroyed the pagan principle that nature reigned over spirit. Although generally dismissive of the law, Hirsch retained circumcision as the act symbolizing Abraham's commitment to live in absolute freedom and truth. The Hebrew consciousness of God was not a human invention, however, but the result of divine intervention making visible content already latent in humanity. "God did not just reveal his teachings, but himself to Israel,"[126] Hirsch wrote. From the exodus to the building of the second temple, God lived among the ancient Israelites as a father educating his people.

Similarly to Formstecher, Hirsch saw in the extensive religiosity of Christianity as a mechanism for spreading religious truth to pagans and a necessary step towards absolute religion. Jesus, in his view, sought to recover the prophetic voice of Judaism and revitalize an old religion, not found a new faith. He embodied the idea that man exists in the image of God and is destined to realize divine freedom. With the doctrine of eternal sin, however, Pauline Christianity, for Hirsch, broke with the historical Jesus, the acceptance of original sin resurrecting pagan unfreedom. For Hirsch, the Protestant Reformation started liberating Christianity from Pauline influence by instituting greater freedom in state and civil society. Only modern Jews, however, who repudiated slavish adherence to ritual, could fulfill the messianic teaching that man was not condemned to sin and could attain full spiritual freedom.

In 1843 Hirsch found employment as the head rabbi of the liberal Jewish community in the Grand Duchy of Luxembourg, where he remained until 1866, briefly joining the freemasons until his brothers at the Les enfants fortifiés criticized his work as too Jewish. He confirmed his radical critique of revelation in *Die Reform im Judenthume und dessen Gebrauch in der gegenwärtigen Welt* (1844). The "natural revelation"[127] present in every human was a sufficient foundation for morality and salvation, he argued. Submission to a higher authority threatened human autonomy and enslaved spirit. Judaism, he wrote, was "not revelation in the sense of its having been imparted supernatural, transcendent secrets and believing them necessary for salvation." Rather, it should be regarded as the "religion of history."[128] The sacred history of the Jews, as the "history of a people's education,"[129] modelled how humanity could rise to spirituality. Christianity, by contrast, required revealed teachings and dogmas due to its assumption of original sin. Hirsch, in other words, crossed Lessing's ditch by attributing to Judaism the historical role liberal Protestants assigned to Christianity.

For Hirsch, adherence to supernatural revelation threatened Judaism's ability to embody humanity's self-education to freedom. The term 'revelation' was too closely associated with doctrinal propositions and, within German idealism, the self-actualization of God. Hirsch held that religion did not consist in a set of privileged truths about God but in knowledge about humanity. Even without special claim to revelation, the history of the Jews could thus still embody, for Hirsch, a divinely sanctioned model for how other nations could attain moral freedom. His critique of Hegel, nevertheless, fell short of its mark. Hirsch spent his last two decades as a reform rabbi of a German congregation in Philadelphia and reportedly died while reading the *Prolegomena* of Julius Wellhausen.[130] Wellhausen's Hegelian reformulation of the history of ancient Israel similarly dethroned the revelations to Moses but sketched Judaism's degeneration into a rote adherence to the law, the prospect of which might well have broken Hirsch.

By the late 1840s more radical reform congregations were willing to accept the notion that revelation occurred within the soul of each individual. This is particularly apparent in the Berlin Reform Congregation, founded in 1845 on a radically revised liturgy and the first to hold services exclusively on Sundays. The Berlin prayer book, which eliminated almost all Hebrew, echoed the Frankfurt Reform Society in declaring divine truth subject to human judgment and capable of continued development. It defined revelation as "divine illumination of the spirit" and cautioned that it did not "exceed the natural limits of human ability." When the sacred texts of Judaism referred to supernatural events, these had to be interpreted as "a living expression of subjective faith." As a feeling, revelation lacked objective factuality, and prior assertions of its eternal truth were only a response to the living sense of immediacy which ancient Jews felt in the presence of God.[131]

A postcritical appreciation of how the Jewish people embodied revelation could effectively distinguish Judaism from natural religion and the ethical monotheism of liberal Protestants, as seen in the reflections of Samuel Holdheim, who joined the Reform Association in Berlin in 1847. Having had an exclusively Talmudic education in east Prussia, Holdheim only gradually came to locate religious authority in reason and the conscience. Not until the 1840s did he regard Scripture as a human response to divine illumination.[132] But in a criticism of Mendelssohn in 1857 he confirmed that the content of Jewish revelation was not actual historical events, but the "inner ... intuition" with which their "invisible cause" was detected.[133] Revelation as such had two trajectories. The first, like natural religion, entailed recognition of God's self-revelation in nature as a beneficent creator. The second found full expression in the Sinaitic revelation and exceeded the religion of the patriarchs and any wisdom to be derived from nature. Only by appreciating the presence of God in their history could Jews, in his view, understand love, morality, and justice. The subjective illumination of human spirit, which God granted the Jews, distinguished their religion even without the receipt of eternal propositional truths or commandments.

The Genius of Revelation: Abraham Geiger

The most significant Jewish reformer of the nineteenth century, Abraham Geiger, applied critical historical research based in Rabbinic sources to the same moments in Judaism's development that Formstecher and Hirsch subjected to philosophical speculation. He, too, subscribed to the notion of progressive revelation but set chronological limits on its duration, proposing that tradition safeguarded the divine spirit after the building of the Second Temple. Susannah Heschel has convincingly argued that the liberal Geiger salvaged the concept of revelation by reframing Jewish consciousness of God in terms of cultural originality.[134] The possession of an extraordinary "religious genius," Geiger wrote in 1865, uniquely qualified Jews to be the "people of revelation."[135] Their religious awareness did not consist in a set of propositional truths, either derived from the natural world or an external source. Geiger criticized Steinheim for not understanding revelation as "the becoming revealed"[136] of a transcendent personal God. He vested the authority of revelation and the tradition it inspired in the religious consciousness of the people of Israel at various moments in their historical development.

In the 1850s and 1860s there were still no Jewish theological faculties at German universities. Geiger was one of the first Jewish scholars to intensively engage Christian theologians, demonstrating how historical research on the sacred texts of Judaism could transform New Testament scholarship.[137] His approach to Judaism subverted the Romantic cult of genius liberal Protestants, such as Schleiermacher, applied to Jesus in an attempt to detach the origins of Christianity from its Jewish roots. Once belief in a supernatural Christ gave way to the historical Jesus, stressing the autonomous generation of intellectual property helped minimize or eliminate Jewish influence on Christian teachings and, by implication, reinforced perceptions that Jews were foreign to German society. Schleiermacher held that Jesus possessed an exceptional religious consciousness that allowed him to transcend his historical milieu and build a distinct religious community around a radically new revelation. The exceptional character of his cultural production, not miracles or supernatural intervention, served as evidence of divine origin, in this view.[138]

The son of an Orthodox rabbi and teacher, Geiger was raised in a strictly observant Jewish family, receiving early training in Hebrew and traditional Jewish sources. By age eleven, however, exposure to the political uses of myth in classical antiquity had led him to question whether Moses was indeed a prophet and actually encountered the divine on Mt. Sinai.[139] He began university studies in Heidelberg but soon transferred to Bonn to study Arabic under Georg Freytag. Here he pursued Oriental languages, philosophy, history, and theology and briefly collaborated with Samson Hirsch. J.G. Herder's accounts of human spiritual development particularly intrigued Geiger during this period, as did Lessing's theological writings, especially as their work reflected on Judaism. He obtained his first position as a rabbi in Wiesbaden, where he reformed services, eliminating the recitation of medieval poems.

Geiger's chief concern in the 1830s was understanding the historical relationship between Judaism, Christianity, and Islam, for which he turned to the critical analysis of rabbinic literature. His prize essay *Was hat Mohammed aus dem Judenthume aufgenommen?* (1833), which earned Geiger a doctorate from Marburg, argued that the Koran drew heavily from rabbinic sources in its doctrines and retelling of biblical stories. Geiger was not concerned with debating the extent that Islam actually constituted a divine revelation but to prove that its religious imagination, and that of Christianity, was unoriginal and derivative.[140] According to Geiger, Mohammad borrowed his concept of revelation from the Jews and subjected it to modification.[141] Judaism, for Geiger, was the only true religion of revelation and grasped truths that paganism and philosophic speculation compromised.

From 1840 to 1863 Geiger served as a rabbi in Breslau. Despite repeated flare-ups with Rabbi S.A. Titkin, who solicited police assistance to block his first sermon, Geiger quickly emerged as leader of the reform movement. His political engagement on behalf of Jewish equality was equally substantial, enduring through the Revolutions of 1848–9 and German unification, both which he cautiously embraced with a liberal patriotism alert to antisemitism. Geiger was, however, bypassed as too radical for the directorship of the rabbinical seminar Zacharias Frankel assumed in Breslau in 1854. Geiger's *Die Urschrift und Uebersetzungen der Bibel* (1857), which analysed ancient Bible translations from the Second Temple to the Mishnaic period, deviated from the positive-historical approach of Conservative Jews. For Geiger, the Bible and Talmud conveyed revealed doctrines but as human documents did not directly contain the word of God. Enduring conflict led him to the more liberal Jewish community of Frankfurt in 1863. Only at the end of his life could Geiger relinquish his rabbinical duties for scholarship with the founding of the Hochschule für die Wissenschaft des Judentums in Berlin in 1872.

Geiger's analysis of how Christianity related to Judaism was far more controversial and bore higher stakes, especially as it proved knowledge of rabbinic Judaism indispensable to German theological faculties. Protestant biblical scholarship directly concerned Jews, their history, and their religion, but it loomed as an "alien, sometimes antagonistic territory" that precluded Jewish participation.[142] Higher criticism held out the promise of liberating the Old Testament from Christological hermeneutics, but it quickly developed anti-Jewish biases.[143] Many theological journals were closed to Jews, and their overtures met with disinterested, often hostile, colleagues.[144] Massive institutional disparities likewise afflicted the scholarly interactions between Jews and Christians. Jewish scholars engaged the scholarship of Christians, responded to their portrayal of historical and contemporary Judaism, and sought to engage in dialogue. But, Christian scholars regularly ignored the contributions of Jewish theology, dismissing the importance of rabbinical texts in understanding the origins of Christianity.[145]

Geiger had to refute the anti-Judaism of New Testament scholarship, which impeded acceptance of Jewish equality. At the same time, he had to assure his colleagues that reformers did not risk replicating the secession of early Christians. The undefined ethical monotheism that remained after liberal Jews discarded the halacha was often uncomfortably similar to the faith liberal Protestants attributed to Jesus.[146] In *Judaism and its History* (1865), held as lectures in Frankfurt, Geiger argued that Jesus was a Pharisee who sought to liberalize Jewish religious practice, not found a new faith. Under the influence of the Sadducees, a competing religious party, and Greco-Roman paganism, early Christians deviated from the faith of their messiah. Subsequent dogmatic formulations of Christianity further betrayed the pure biblical monotheism of Jesus, who subscribed to the only original, true religion.

A Schleiermacherian conception of religion enabled Geiger in *Judaism and its History* to counter claims that Judaism was an antiquated "ruin."[147] A focus on inner illumination also helped him retain the importance of revelation and tradition, while denying that Judaism entailed blind belief and submission to an external authority. In his view, human beings were distinguished by the possession of spirit, which enabled insight into imperceptible matters. Religion derived from the inborn presentiment that spirit generated of a higher wisdom and freedom, as well as from humanity's consciousness of its own eminence and dependence. A longing or striving for the infinite lay at the heart of individual religious experience, for Geiger, the "aspiration of the spirit after the ideal." As the primordial source of the human spirit, God was the "noblest reality within."[148] The inner presence of the divine was, however, not a mere figment of the imagination, according to Geiger, and historical revelation was not reducible to human spiritual development.

Geiger sketched in his work the progressive self-revelation of God in the history of the Jewish people until its completion with the founding of the Second Temple. A "mere tribe" undistinguished in philosophy, science, and art brought forth, in his view, unprecedented knowledge of God as if prompted by "some inner force." An "aboriginal energy"[149] enabled the Jews to see deeper into the higher life of spirit, feel more vividly the relationship between humanity and the supreme spirit, and attain awareness of morality. This knowledge was "inborn," not garnered from nature or obtained as propositions from a higher source. "It is Revelation," Geiger wrote, "as manifested in the whole nation." Though most concentrated in the prophets, the entire Jewish people from Abraham through the Babylonian exile possessed "the genius of revelation." Unlike Lessing, Geiger did not equate revelation with a developmental process; it entailed "an illumination from a higher mind and spirit, which cannot be explained ... Which all at once appears in existence as a whole, like every new creation proceeding from the Original Spirit."[150] Historical revelation, was, in his view, the point of contact between human reason and the fundamental source of all things and required active rational assent.

By Geiger's account, revelation ceased with the refounding of the Jewish nation after the Babylonian exile. The revealed doctrine was complete, and Israel thoroughly imbued with it. Yet the living spirit behind revelation continued to preserve it. Geiger characterized tradition as the "daughter of Revelation and of equal rank with her," inspired by the same creative spirit but not revelation itself. Judaism was not a relic, finished and closed, but was animated by the vital energy of a continuously advancing tradition. Ceremonial law thus represented, in Geiger's words, "a living stream that ever fertilizes her anew."[151] Jews could not relinquish tradition for a generic ethical monotheism, as it emanated from a higher power. But, as with revelation, the enactment of tradition required human initiative and invited reform. A moral person did not blindly follow the will of an external God; ceremonial law must agree with inner moral conscience and the understanding.[152]

This perspective led Geiger to reconsider the orthodox presumption that Shavuot marked an actual historical revelation to Moses on

Mt. Sinai and to alter the ritual practices associated with the festival. In his 1837 review of Hirsch's *Nineteen Letters*, Geiger had questioned whether biblical sources justified regarding Shavuot as both an early harvest festival and a celebration of God's granting the law. As he later elaborated, according to the Gemara, a rabbinical commentary on the Mishnah, a faction of the Sadducees commemorated Shavuot on the fiftieth day after the Sabbath in the week of Passover, not on the fiftieth day following the second day of Passover. "According to them, it thus cannot also be the festival of revelation," he explained. It is "uncertain based on the Talmud," Geiger concluded, if Shavuot "falls together with the day of receiving the law, in fact, the opposite is probable."[153] Geiger controversially declined the Omer count, the verbal recitation of days between Passover and Shavuot. Orthodox rabbis also criticized his neglect of the mourning observances between festivals on the grounds that the practice started after Talmudic times, as well as his refusal to hold vigil on the night before Shavuot.[154]

Yet, when Martin Maaß in the *Protestantische Kirchenzeitung* dismissed the three Jewish festivals as nothing more than nature cults and "festivals of historical memory"[155] devoid of religious consciousness, Geiger defended the importance of revelation to Jews. Maaß did concede some religious significance to Shavuot given its link with the Ten Commandments, the universal foundation of all morality, in his view. However, educated Jews, he reckoned, must recognize that the subsequent development of religion made the God-consciousness of Moses appear primitive. The revelation at Sinai hardly deserved its own celebration and, by implication, Jews should convert to Christianity.

Geiger himself recognized progressive historical development in Judaism and likewise decoupled Shavuot from an actual historical event. However, the festival of revelation retained its meaning for Jews, he retorted, as "an exalted religious memory,"[156] precisely because they introduced ethical monotheism to humanity. "May our festival of revelation prove its power to you also," Geiger entreated an orthodox critic, "the festival that brings us the most solemn memory ... whether receipt of the law took place a day earlier or later. And may Israel's calling become vividly clear in this festival, and may our calling to proclaim the divine word strengthen and encourage us to carry forth steadfast the light of religion!"[157] Reframing revelation as an inner capacity particular to Jews withstood the dangers historicism posed to religious truth more readily than naive positivism, while asserting both the distinction of Judaism and its universal significance for the development of human religious consciousness. Retaining a positive and propositional concept of revelation had before the 1840s been useful to reformers as a way to offset Christian dismissal of the religion as antiquated and anachronistic, and to the orthodox as justification for the divine origins of written and oral law. Revelation underwent a critical turn in Jewish religious thought later than among liberal Protestants, but under Geiger it had assumed an equally radical form by midcentury.

Chapter Eight

Revelation Imperilled in Protestant Religious Thought, 1820–1850

In the preface to his *Book on Adler*, written in 1846 but withheld from publication to protect the false prophet it denounced, Søren Kierkegaard bemoaned "the confusion the concept of revelation suffers in our confused age."[1] His lament rightly reflects the muddled mélange of meanings that by the 1840s engulfed the term in Protestant religious thought. In this case, Kierkegaard feared that conceiving of revelation as subjective inner experience had encouraged the Danish pastor Adolph P. Adler to proclaim a new doctrine and wrongly attribute it to Christ. Kierkegaard also rejected the rational abstraction typical of speculative Hegelian theology, by which God as absolute idea became manifest in the historical world. Schelling's positive philosophy initially promised to restore, for Kierkegaard, the priority of lived experience in the historical unfolding of the divine, but, severely disappointed by his Berlin lectures, Kierkegaard launched an alternative reconceptualization of religion as an existentialist project in which revelation factored heavily in the transformation of the real, existing self. The main value of revelation, in his view, was neither epistemological nor propositional. For Kierkegaard, revelation was a regulative concept, demanding personal obedience and painful self-examination. A leap of faith was necessary, in his view, to cross Lessing's ditch, and embracing the paradoxes of historical revelation was crucial to self-transformation as a Christian.

A few years earlier, the radical Young Hegelian Ludwig Feuerbach declared that bridging Lessing's ditch, eliding the contradictions of historical revelation, could be achieved only "by self-deception, only by the silliest subterfuges, only by the most miserable, transparent sophisms."[2] In the *Essence of Christianity* (1841) he interpreted the contradictions inherent in revelation as evidence that religion contained merely anthropological truths with the incarnation epitomizing the projection of human nature onto God. Insufficient as a moral authority, revelation's only epistemological value lay for Feuerbach in self-knowledge. "Revelation is simply the self-determination of man,"[3] he declared, like Kierkegaard using the concept to grasp the nature of being. The post-critical attempt to rehabilitate revelation as a subjective and ontological category resulted in two contradictory ends exemplified by Feuerbach and Kierkegaard. Both prospects posed significant difficulties for mainstream Protestant theologians, as they respectively culminated in self-declared atheism and a virulent denunciation of the established church.

This chapter argues that the rebirth of revelation faced renewed obstacles in Protestant religious thought in the decades prior to the Revolutions of 1848–9. The terms on which revelation was rehabilitated, as well as the collapse of Mosaic authorship, magnified the purview of human agency in the acquisition of religious truths. An initial retention of primordial revelation among Protestant theologians offset the implications of historicizing scripture and, for August Tholuck, of grounding religious consciousness in subjective human experience. If God primed the historical world with foundational knowledge of the divine and graced humankind with a higher religious sensibility, then the anthropological aspects of religion could still have a divine provenance. The grounding of an otherwise subjective, radically historical experience of God in an original moment of divine self-disclosure and creation eased the burden of Lessing's ditch, especially among revivalist theologians. By the 1830s, however, Hegelian religious philosophy, the weakening of propositional revelation, and the disrepute in which speculation about Eastern origins had fallen after the Creuzer Affair hastened the erosion of ancient theology. Primordial revelation subsequently factored only in the defence of scriptural literalism and Christian fulfilment theology, safely ensconced within the apologetic schemes of neo-confessionalists seeking to mitigate the effects of recognizing aspects of religion as culturally constructed.

At the same time, the anthropomorphization of religion among liberal Protestants widened the breach between the historical world and the divine realm of transcendence, such that it became unbridgeable without a blind leap of faith. The philosophy of revelation, which extended beyond but engaged with these Protestant theological debates, responded to the bubble bursting around the late Schelling in the 1840s by seeking alternative means to ground revelation in the positive facts of existence. The chapter concludes with analyses of Ludwig Feuerbach and Søren Kierkegaard as related but divergent responses to the subjectivist and ontological turns taken by revelation among German idealists. Both post-idealist critics of speculative reason regarded Schelling's positive philosophy as a failed effort to restore the lived experience of human beings. They agreed that speculative philosophy was cognitively bankrupt, having wrongly detached reason from embodied human beings. But their understanding of how sensuous individuals related to the truths found in religion differed substantially. For Feuerbach, the contradictions surrounding Christian concepts of revelation exposed the anthropological origins of religion in base human functions; he accordingly detached revelation entirely from God. Kierkegaard preferred to catapult over Lessing's ditch, asking individuals to embrace the absolute paradox of faith as justification for obedience to God.

Revelation and Neo-Confessionalism: August Tholuck

Primordial revelation proved difficult for Protestant theologians to relinquish even as critical-historical exegesis undermined its scriptural foundations, suggesting the concept's significance to the politics of confessionalism and its function as a crutch guaranteeing the transcendent quality of historical revelation. Since the Council of Trent, Protestants had derived pre-Mosaic oral tradition from primordial revelation to protect Luther's principle of *sola scriptura* and circumvent the Catholic Church's claim to the authoritative interpretation of tradition. The content of the Mosaic books presumably existed as "unwritten" or "pre-written" scripture directly dispensed by God and inherited through the descendants of Noah's sons.[4] The gradual dismantling of Mosaic authorship at the end of the eighteenth century placed this transmission in question, however, and raised the prospect that the Mosaic books did not contain authentic historical material. Reducing the Pentateuch to a later human creation undermined the principle source base for the existence of primordial revelation.

Yet even among historical-critical readers of the Old Testament, such as the Lutheran theologian Wilhelm Martin Leberecht de Wette (1780–1849), primordial revelation remained an appealing historical paradigm. De Wette's controversial *Beiträge zur Einleitung in das Alte Testamente* (1806–7) interpreted the Pentateuch as a post-exilic composition designed to legitimate the religious views of the Hebrews during the late monarchy. In his view, the Mosaic books reflected the evolving religious consciousness of the Hebrew people and contained little verifiable historical information.[5] Nevertheless, de Wette evoked the inheritance of primordial revelation to champion the spirit of original Mosaism over the later written law of Judaism. "This nation," de Wette wrote of the Hebrews, "preserved the memory of the primordial revelation to humanity, which included the idea of a highest god, more purely than all others."[6] The comparative history of religion de Wette later composed in Basel similarly maintained Judaic primacy. *Ueber die Religion* (1827) argued that the first humans had an immediate, instinctive faith in God, the product of "an emotional intuition or imagination"[7] that generated feelings of dependence, trust, and obligation towards an eternal highest being. Moses made this "transmission from primeval times" into an "object of free cultivation,"[8] ending humanity's subjection to nature.

The Creuzer Affair was likewise not enough to deter Protestant theologians from writing speculative histories of religion that set Christian revelation in relation to venerable pagan precedents. Their evocation of primordial revelation risked the derision of liberal neo-humanists who avoided conjecture about Eastern origins and Christianity's debts to the ancient world.[9] However, the new philosophies of revelation set forth by Schleiermacher and Schelling lent a veneer of credibility to sweeping histories of religion. Having defended Creuzer against his detractors, the Lutheran theologian Ferdinand Christian Baur (1792–1860), for example, rehabilitated his project in the 1820s. Following a Schellingian model of history, Baur's *Symbolik und Mythologie oder die Naturreligion des Alterthums* (1824–5) affirmed the centrality of religious categories in the analysis of myth. Baur saw revelation as the historical process of God's self-manifestation in the world. Early monotheism was visible, in his view, not in individual doctrines or divinities but in the total system of natural religion. The collapse of propositional revelation and its focus on doctrinal content alleviated some of the vulnerabilities that reconstructing speculative lines of transmission entailed and mitigated the problem of assigning derivative status to later faiths. It also shifted the narrative significance of origins from prefiguration to marking the onset of divine self-disclosure and religious consciousness.

The primary function of primordial revelation in the 1820s and 1830s was, however, to offset the subjectification of religion in liberal Protestant theology, a role that increasingly confined the concept to a narrowly conceived orthodoxy. Especially among theologians of the awakening, such as August Tholuck, a repristinization of primordial revelation helped prevent the subjective experience of religious awareness from being entombed in an historical world void of grace. Tholuck is an interesting case because, like Schleiermacher, he viewed inner emotion as a foundation of theological knowledge yet also retained the traditional credibility of objective, external revelation. "Religious self-consciousness knows itself in feeling to be one with truth," he affirmed in 1839.[10] But theologians struggled, Tholuck noted, to explain the "emergence of objective truth from the depths of spirit." According to

Karl Barth, a dilettantish "doctrine of the 'immediate'"[11] allowed Tho-luck to bridge the gulf between subjective revelation and absolute truth. "Knowledge is given through existence,"[12] Tholuck declared in antici-pation of Kierkegaard. In his view, primordial revelation's legacy in the human soul rendered even the misguided faith of pagans more than a profane human projection. Yet he also recognized that without a "posi-tive criterium for revelation," "inferior human creations" would mas-querade as genuine religion.[13] Authentic Christian awakening relied, for Tholuck, both upon a divinely instilled inner capacity for belief and the historical revelations of Christ.

Tholuck's intellectual itinerary runs countercurrent in that philology propelled him to conservative theology at a time when critical-histor-ical methods more often curtailed faith in revelation. Born the son of a poor goldsmith in Breslau, Lower Silesia, Tholuck later described him-self as a suicidal, brooding youth who took refuge in the exotic.[14] By the age of sixteen he had learned nineteen languages under the guidance of Christian Maximillian Habicht, a local Arabist. The young Tholuck kept a polyglot diary in which the only German entries were composed in Greek or Hebrew script.[15] An "ever greater aversion to everything reli-gious"[16] seems to have elicited bouts of depression. Tholuck disdained the local deacon, dismissed the resurrection, and dabbled in natural religion.[17] His final speech at the Magdalenian Gymnasium equated the three prophets, Moses, Jesus, and Mohammad, and argued for the greater significance of Zoroaster, Confucius, and Manu. "I planned to travel to the Orient," Tholuck recalled, to prove "how absurd Christian-ity was compared to the exalted wisdom of the Orientals."[18] Abandon-ing an apprenticeship as a goldsmith, he joined Habicht to study Arabic at the university of Breslau.

Tholuck transferred to Berlin in early 1817, arriving as a "vehe-ment doubter of Christianity."[19] His conversion to biblical Christianity began in the home of the Orientalist Baron Heinrich von Diez, Tho-luck's benefactor and the former Prussian representative to Istanbul, who insisted the deep moral truth Tholuck found in Homer actually came from the Israelites.[20] Following a near death experience, cough-ing blood over Turkish manuscripts, Tholuck decided to embrace God and become a missionary to India. "I put aside almost all my Oriental labors," Tholuck explained.[21] He immersed himself in the revivalist cir-cles of Baron von Kottwitz and began studying theology under August Neander. Tholuck became, in Barth's assessment, "a pure theologian of the Revival."[22] He was a founding member of the Berlin Society for the Advancement of Christianity, taught Hebrew at Johannes Jänicke's missionary school, and tried to convert Prussian Jews.

The choice of Sufi mysticism as a dissertation topic followed from a missionary report that Iranian Sufis were numerous and amenable to conversion.[23] It likewise promised, for Tholuck, to stem the tide of rationalism and deflate the pretentions of speculative philosophy to know God. The mystical sentiment of Eastern religions evoked, for him, the emotion and inner experience crucial to the neopietist revival. While recognizing affinities with other gnostic traditions, his *Ssufismus sive theosophia Persarum pantheistica* (1821) argued that Sufi doctrine originated not in India or Greece but in Muhammad's own mysticism. Tholuck opposed Sylvester de Sacy's argument for its pre-Islamic origins in the remnants of an ancient Persian sect.[24] For Tholuck, Sufism represented a pantheistic, heretical doctrine within Islam, in which "*nihil esse praeter Deum*";[25] creation necessarily emerged from God, and the self awaited reabsorption into the divine. For his *Ssufismus* Tholuck is still recognized as a pioneer in the European study of Islamic mysticism.[26] Schleiermacher, however, found the text inadequately theological and opposed granting Tholuck an appointment in Berlin. Due to de Wette's recent departure and the strength of the Prussian court's sympathies for the awakening, however, Tholuck began his career there with the directive to restore a positive view of the Old Testament.

Tholuck justified Old Testament studies based on the "profound wisdom" of the Israelites and their exceptional custodianship of primordial revelation. God had not entirely neglected other nations, he noted in *Einige apologeitsche Winke für das Studium des Alten Testaments* (1821). Persians, Indians, Greeks, and Romans were, however, "entirely unfit for divine revelation, their knowledge constituting mere tinsel" in contrast with Hebrew monotheism.[27] True knowledge of God appeared only among one nation. The essay mounted an anti-rationalist defence of historical revelation and Mosaic authorship and, accordingly, found a warm reception.[28] Creuzer agreed with his "assumption of an original pure religion" and confessed how "indignant" he was over "the neological urge" to banish supernaturalism from the Bible.[29] Only more extreme conservatives, such as Tholuck's friend and fellow revivalist Rudolf Ewald Stier, argued that he "still conceded and granted to much to pagans," ignoring the absolute distinction of the divinely inspired.[30] Much of Tholuck's work in the following years negotiated the fine line between granting pagan religions the inheritance of primordial revelation, while preserving the distinction of Christianity.

In his *Lehre von der Sünde und vom Versöhner* (1823), an immensely popular text crucial to the awakening, Tholuck acknowledged the full gamut of enlightenment criticisms of revelation. But he also affirmed the concept as key to the first post-Napoleonic generation's struggle to subdue rationalism and natural religion and restore Christian faith. The letters which comprise the text depict the trials of a young theology student, Guido, who nearly succumbs to pantheism after exposure to Spinoza, Schelling, and Schleiermacher at University G. "In the dazzling, magical light of pantheism," Guido confesses to his recently awakened friend, the philology student Julius, "all shades of good and evil ran together, and deadened all color to a dull grey."[31] Guido's rebirth begins with the rehabilitation of his faith in positive revelation, which Julius's second letter defines traditionally as an external dispensation of otherwise inaccessible knowledge, "an historical fact derived from a higher order."[32] Tholuck insisted on the necessity of divine intervention in the development of faith although accepting the compatibility of revelation and reason and the existence of an inborn religious sensibility.[33]

Tholuck's resurrection of traditional revelation justified confidence in the truth of its propositions not with reference to reason, whose prerogatives were limited, but to subjective experience – the "testimony of inner existence," the "unmediated certainty of life."[34] Even the ecstatic inner visions of prophets constituted, in his view, a church-sanctioned form of revelation.[35] This assumption risked, Tholuck realized, reducing revelation to purely human thought or feeling, erasing what he later termed the "difference between God's revelation to man and man's own thought."[36] Tholuck's rather weak solution to the problem was to depict the human spirit as "a living organ of the divine."[37] Primordial revelation ensured that all people inherited "absolute truths, innate to the human spirit."[38] The conviction of faith rested on "subjective grounds" and extended to practitioners of false religions, although God's original presence in the human soul guaranteed each a degree of authenticity. At the same time, Tholuck insisted that inner sensibility be "confirmed, clarified, and expanded through historical revelations."[39] Correspondence between a subjective awakening and objective, external revelation lent credence to the latter, such that the existential conditions of self-constitution established reliable knowledge of God.

A supplement to the letters disproved pagan claims to true revelation despite their shared primordial inheritance.[40] Salvation without Christ was "imperfect,"[41] for Tholuck, because it lacked the sole positive criterium for genuine revelation: the knowledge of sin and forgiveness provided by Christ. Pagan faiths had, moreover, bequeathed a troubling pantheistic legacy to speculative philosophy. Tholuck willingly bestowed an Asian pedigree on European philosophy, at a time when most sought its origin in Greece and subverted its progressive narrative with the idea of repetition and of parity between East and West.[42] Yet the goal of that trajectory was to deflate the current presumption that an "idealistic pantheism was the only true philosophy."[43] Like paganism, speculative philosophy destroyed, in his view, the self-conscious personal God of revelation, as well as any concept of divine individuality, freedom, and morality.

Tholuck's prominent position as an exponent of the revival placed him on the frontlines of the Prussian state's offensive against rationalism. In 1825 he was transferred to Halle, a hotbed of theological rationalism and a major centre for training clergymen. The crown prince, a pietist, and several cabinet ministers attended his inaugural banquet, during which Hegel spoke in favour of Tholuck's mission. Public protests by hostile students and faculty members so unnerved Tholuck after his arrival, however, that he took a year's leave in Rome as the chaplain of the Prussian embassy. The appointment of Ludwig Gerlach to the provincial court in Halle eased Tholuck's return, but civil unrest erupted again in the revolutionary year of 1830 following his denunciation, exposed by leaked student lecture notes, of leading rationalists Julius Wegscheider and Wilhelm Gesenius. Tholuck was forced to seek police protection, but the affair marked a shift in Halle towards pietism and orthodoxy. Along with Hengstenberg, Tholuck emerged as one of the most powerful conservative Protestant theologians in the *Vormärz*.[44] Never strictly dogmatic, his views softened Lutheran orthodoxy with a neopietist emphasis on personal religious experience.

Tholuck's Orientalism persisted through the mid-1820s as a catalyst for unleashing religious sentiment and combatting Hegel, but it placed the authority of biblical revelation in jeopardy. In 1825 Tholuck translated and enlarged his previous Latin renditions of Arabic, Turkish, and Persian manuscripts. His *Blüthensammlung aus der Morgenländischen Mystik* (1825) claimed that, as the antithesis to dry rationalism, Oriental mysticism could help "arouse shallow, sluggish spirits and inspire them to something more exalted than conventional morality and custom."[45] Mystics recognized that conceptual thought failed to adequately grasp every aspect of experience and knowledge. According to Tholuck, mysticism represented the highest form of natural religion; the discovery of God within was, in his words, "the most animated and exalted revelation in the realm of nature."[46] Partly on these grounds Hegel in 1827 deemed the *Blüthensammlung* "itself … consumed by… a thoroughly pantheistic mysticism."[47] Tholuck countered by distinguishing mysticism based on positive biblical revelation.[48] He detected in Schleiermacher's *Speeches* a comparable mystical sensibility, a necessary corrective to his unreligious age; but their extreme emphasis on feeling and intuition suggested to Tholuck that his view of religion was only viable in the East.[49]

Tholuck's selective parcelling of the Oriental inheritance upheld proximity to primordial revelation as a measure of divine truth. His battles with speculative philosophy encouraged increasingly more exclusive genealogies, however, that condemned the slightest deviance from historical revelation. Tholuck's *Speculative Trinitätslehre des späteren Orients* (1826) ostensibly aimed to extract gnostic elements from the positive religion of Islamic sects to understand how Eastern doctrines had infiltrated Jewish and early Christian revelation. The covert goal of Tholuck's text, as Peter Park has elaborated, was to separate philosophical conceptions of God rooted in the speculative Trinity from Christian revelation and in so doing to expose Hegelian philosophy as Oriental, pagan, and pantheistic.[50] In the 1827 edition of his *Encyclopedia* Hegel retorted that Tholuck himself was essentially guilty of anti-trinitarian natural theology and of ignoring other Christian doctrines, such as the resurrection.[51] Tholuck abandoned his Orientalism shortly thereafter, likely having suffered collateral damage in his volleys with Hegel. Tholuck's embrace of Prussian church politics and his popularity as a preacher erased all traces of his youthful radicalism, and by 1845, following the death of Gesenius, the Prussian ministry happily reported that the majority of students in Halle embraced Tholuck's position.[52]

By the 1830s the ancient wisdom narrative was used to justify a narrow neo-confessionalist orthodoxy that maintained the absolute truth of historical revelation against critical-historical exegesis, rationalism, and speculative theology. Among heterodox Protestants, such as Wilhelm Vatke, an infusion of Hegelian philosophy rendered primordial revelation unattractive as a paradigm for the history of religion. Vatke's *Biblische Theologie* (1835) declared invalid "all hypotheses of a primordial revelation and primordial wisdom, however much one endeavors to adorn them with fantasy."[53] Within a Hegelian framework religious consciousness developed gradually from a primitive state. Vatke presumed that spirit slowly came to full self-realization in history and, contradicting de Wette, only gradually attained conscious expression in Judaism. The popular religion of the ancient Hebrews had been an idolatrous nature religion dedicated to the astral god Saturn, whose image, a steer, they transported in a tent through the desert. For this reason Mosaic monotheism, Vatke wrote, "is an absolute act, presumes a prophetic consciousness and can only be correctly understood as revelation."[54] Belief in an original dispensation diminished, in his view, the significance of biblical revelation.

Ultra-conservative Protestant nationalists, such as the little-known comparative mythologist Peter Feddersen Stuhr (1787–1851), who saw no scandal in particularism, likewise denied primordial revelation as an unwarranted granting of religious truth to pagans and a Catholic folly. Born in the Danish province of Schleswig, Stuhr studied philosophy in Heidelberg under Joseph Görres, then *Naturphilosophie* and history under his countryman Heinrich Steffens in Halle. Despite his combative spirit, Stuhr was one of Steffens's favourite students.[55] An early publication on the *Untergang der Naturstaaten* (1811), criticizing the Roman historian B.G. Niebuhr, found commendation in Hegel's philosophy of right.[56] However, Stuhr's understanding of religion as feeling, as well as his more rigorous historicism otherwise unravelled Hegel's logical conceptualism. During the 1840s Stuhr both foreshadowed and stood as an alternative to Schelling's critique of Hegel's philosophy of religion.[57]

Expecting Prussia to unify German speakers, Stuhr distinguished himself in the Wars of Liberation and began his career as secretary of the commission for military studies in Berlin. He continued to teach military and Prussian state history, along with comparative mythology and the philosophy of history and religion after obtaining a professorship at the university.[58] Benedetto Bravo describes Stuhr as hovering "in the margins of 'philology' and 'history,' isolated from all scholarly groups, an ingenious *franc-tireur*." Most of his colleagues, including August Boeckh, found him ill-placed at the university and opposed Stuhr's earning a full chair.[59] As a member of the *Maikäferklub* and *Haller'sche Gesellschaft* in Berlin he frequented the same circles as the Gerlach brothers, whose fusion of religious awakening and Christian Germanicism aligned perfectly with Stuhr's reactionary politics.[60] On the eve of revolution in 1848, Stuhr supported representation by estate as the only protection against an assembly of proletarians and intellectuals.[61]

Stuhr denounced all existing forms of mythological scholarship. Creuzer, in his view, was guilty of "fantastical enthusiasm ... a Jesuitical attempt to glorify the ominous rule of priests."[62] His early essays attacked ancient theology in the Jesuit tradition, condemning as "unbridled insanities"[63] the idea that Indian and Chinese astronomy derived from an *Urwissenschaft* in inner Asia. Stuhr turned against Görres after he was banished from Prussia for publishing *Teutschland und die Revolution* (1819), which challenged state censorship in the aftermath of Kotzebue's murder.[64] Stuhr likewise rejected K.O. Müller's plea to detach Greek mythology from eastern precedents.[65] The historical relationship between paganism and Christianity was a crucial question, for Stuhr. Yet theology and philosophy were distinct disciplines, in his view, and religious truth was the exclusive purview of revelation.[66] Synchronisms did not represent inherited traditions, he concluded, but rose independently from a shared "moral foundation of life in the human soul,"[67] which distinctive historical and geographical contexts shaped accordingly.

Stuhr's *Religions-Systeme der heidnischen Völker des Orients* (1836) derived the diversity of pagan faiths from local environmental conditions. Each *Volk* had a *Heimat*, he noted, whose distinct character determined the "diversity in the dispositions and intuitions of the particular nations."[68] The core of religion was, for Stuhr, not a philosophical concept of the divine, but "living faith," the "soulful power of sentiment" which excessive rationalism disembodied and obscured.[69] He defined religion in Schleiermacherian terms as a "feeling of individual dependency on more universal and higher powers of life."[70] The inner spiritual life of pagans reflected this and was thus, although subject to error and distortion, not reducible to madness and lies. "Not through external doctrines, not through external transmission were the seeds of higher cultivation originally implanted in the human race," Stuhr wrote, "rather they developed everywhere from an independently creative spiritual power where an obliging nature did not restrain the development of spiritual life."[71] When Heinrich Lüken wrote in 1856 that his argument in favour of *Uroffenbarung* was "a solitary one … especially among philologists and mythologists,"[72] he was correct. After the 1830s the paradigm survived largely in the hands of conservative Protestant apologists and Catholic traditionalists.

The Self-Revelation of Humanity: Ludwig Feuerbach

In the 1840s Protestant religious thinkers deepened the ontological significance that Hegel and Schelling attributed to revelation as the purported self-manifestation of God through history. Idealist philosophers had bridged Lessing's ditch by eroding the propositional function of revelation and expanding its relevance for understanding how the self-disclosure of divine being related to the historical world. But a younger generation dissatisfied by both speculative theology and the unfulfilled promises of Schelling's late philosophy steered the debate over revelation towards a more radical philosophy of human existence. In an 1843 letter to Karl Marx, Ludwig Feuerbach wrote dismissively of Schelling, whose Berlin lectures he attended: "his *Philosophia secunda* … could only exist as long as it didn't exist."[73] Schelling's vaunted promise to restore real existing human beings to the history of divine revelation resulted not in compelling answers, but in a project subsequently expanded by two forerunners of existentialist philosophy. Feuerbach rewrote the self-revelation of God through history as the self-revelation of humanity with theology playing a significant yet inhibiting role in the acquisition of self-knowledge. Kierkegaard reenvisioned revelation as demanding absolute, excruciatingly personal obedience to divine authority while at the same time deflating the enlightened human pretension to produce and critique revelation on rationalist grounds. Both trajectories cast postcritical concepts of revelation into doubt, tearing asunder reason and faith, as well as their reconciliation of theology and *Wissenschaft*.

As the son of a prominent Protestant legal reformer in Bavaria, Feuerbach initially imbibed the rational humanism and ethical idealism typical of liberal Protestantism in the Napoleonic era, which his father defended against resurgent Catholicism and the populist pietism of the awakening.[74] The separation of his parents after a mistress bore his father a child, however, propelled Feuerbach into a phase of fervent faith, in which he studied biblical texts as the revealed word of God. For a period, Feuerbach immersed himself in the Christian-German ideology of the post-war patriotic student organizations, idealizing the faith and communalism of medieval Germans. However, a reckoning with Hegelian philosophy dislodged this traditional belief in revelation. As a theology student in Heidelberg, he embraced Karl Daub's efforts to speculatively distil the philosophical truth of Christian dogma.[75]

After moving to Berlin in 1824 Feuerbach found himself reborn as a left-wing Hegelian. He now asserted that speculative philosophy superseded the inadequate form in which historical revelation expressed Christian truth.[76] Feuerbach switched his degree to philosophy, assuming theology was merely an intermediary stage in the development of speculative reason. In 1826, after Feuerbach attended Hegel's lectures for two years, Bavarian King Ludwig I cancelled his stipend, suspecting Feuerbach's father of liberal proclivities. He returned to Bavaria and completed advanced studies in Erlangen. Here, like many of his generation, Feuerbach began the fruitful process of repudiating Hegel, convinced that history did not represent the progressive unfolding and actualization of reason. Hegel's scientific explication of the absolute and its self-revelation through history had, he concluded, wrongly deified reason as a transcendent power that determined the forms of human existence.

The assault Feuerbach waged against the Christian doctrine of personal immortality in the early 1830s combined an activist political agenda with what Warren Breckman terms a "social ontology of the self."[77] Building upon Schelling's examination of the ground of being in the *Freedom* essay, Feuerbach derided belief in the personal God of Christianity as a fantasy of unlimited selfhood, no longer a preliminary stage on the road to truth. Human existence, in his view, had to be understood as historically contingent and necessarily limited, radically distinct from the ideal, transcendent essence Christianity held attainable in a higher life. This critique reinforced a left Hegelian campaign against absolute monarchy, which the Protestant defence of personalism legitimated. In its place, Feuerbach offered a vision of communal integration rooted in the universalizing forces of love and self-transcendence.[78] Conservative pietistic Erlangen had little tolerance for his views, however, and with his dissertation Feuerbach effectively excluded himself from academic employment. Marriage into a family of porcelain manufacturers in 1837 enabled him to write unencumbered in the Bavarian village of Bruckberg.

Feuerbach's dissatisfaction with Schelling's speculative theism, the focus of Erlangen's conservative philosophy department, built from the critique of personalism. Positive philosophy, Feuerbach observed in 1838, derived its legitimacy from an absolute grounding in concrete existence. While this offset the logical abstraction of Hegelian philosophy, it allowed an irrational belief in divine personhood to masquerade as a philosophical corrective. Feuerbach drew upon Jacobi's claim that feeling lay at the heart of religion to unravel the delusions of Schelling's late philosophy, which, in his view, mistakenly projected essential human qualities onto the divine.[79] "Schelling creates his god, he has no god," Feuerbach explained to Marx, "he is the ungodliness of the time, that fancies itself righteous."[80] For the philosophy of religion to be scientific, Feuerbach insisted, it must interpret religion from the perspective of human psychology. The history of revelation's application within theology illuminated nothing, in his view, but the cognitive habits of human beings, which Feuerbach's own humanist, materialist philosophy promised to expose and re-instil with alternative meaning.

Feuerbach styled the masterful *Essence of Christianity* (1841) as a supreme act of revelation, an unveiling of hidden truths about the psychological and epistemological processes behind the formation of religious concepts. The preface promised a "revelation of religion to itself, the awakening of religion to self-consciousness."[81] This, ironically, reclaimed the epistemological privileges of revelation, but as a secular bestowal of new knowledge that liberated human consciousness. Feuerbach modelled the progressive self-revelation of humanity through history on the same dialectical trajectory as the self-revelation of God in speculative theology and idealist philosophy. But he expanded the ontological significance of revelation into a process by which the true nature of species being became manifest. As a step in the acquisition of self-knowledge, religion filled a crucial function in the historical self-revelation of species being, for Feuerbach. A hidden deposit of anthropological wisdom had accumulated, in his view, as religion matured from a naïve, childlike faith to systematized, rational theology. Feuerbach's account of the historical self-revelation of emancipatory self-knowledge declared the original true object of religion to be humanity. The first part of the *Essence of Christianity* details what he saw as the true or anthropological essence of religion, or human consciousness. Under the guise of the divine, he argued, people worshipped their own humanity and celebrated their capabilities as a species, projecting their essential being onto an imagined object. The incarnation, for Feuerbach, offered ultimate proof for the identity of man and God, while reflecting that absolute, pure love for man was the essential condition of the human species. By objectifying the human essence in a false form as God, theology negated the original meaning of religion, however. Part two explores theology's systematization of illusion, the means by which psychological processes of concept formation came to pass for metaphysical or ontological truths. Rendering the esoteric content of theology into unalienated, human terms, Feuerbach presumed, would result in higher, self-conscious knowledge of humanity's own nature.

As the central pillar upholding the truth and objectivity of theology, belief in revelation appeared, for Feuerbach, to be a major culprit in the self-estrangement of humanity, exhibiting "in the clearest manner the characteristic illusion of the religious consciousness."[82] Revelation, he noted in the *Essence of Christianity*, provided the only certain proof for the existence of God, guaranteed the reliability of religious knowledge, and secured the foundations of morality. As the anchor of religious belief, it fettered the understanding and had a debilitating effect on social relations. "The believer," he wrote, can "prove revelation only by incurring contradiction within himself, with truth, with the understanding, only by the most impudent assumptions, only by shameless falsehoods."[83] Theology and speculative philosophy both wrongly presumed the human faculties included the ability to access a transcendent, infinite realm. But the attempt to bridge Lessing's ditch, to reconcile historical revelation and sacred truth, only produced superstition and sophistry. Feuerbach likewise refused to equate revelation with Kantian moral law, arguing that it destroyed "the moral sense ... the divinest feeling in man"[84] by representing just deeds as the commandments of an external lawgiver.

Revelation, in other words, represented the ultimate negation of humanity, for Feuerbach, and reduced human beings to passive objects of an invented God's dictates. "In the belief in revelation," he concluded, "man makes himself a negation, he goes out of and above himself; places revelation in opposition to human knowledge and opinion ...

reason must hold its peace." The contradictions in the concept, however, pointed towards a deeper, anthropological truth. According to Feuerbach, the futility of recent efforts to reconcile revelation and reason had begun to unmask religion as a form of self-alienation. Revelation had to be recognized, in his view, as a human product that provided knowledge about the nature of being. "The contents of the divine revelation are of human origin," he declared, "for they have proceeded not from God as God, but from God as determined by human reason, human wants, that is, directly from human reason and human wants." For this reason, revelation actually disclosed man's latent nature. Specifically, Feuerbach argued that humans had an "inward necessity" to present moral and philosophical doctrines in narrative form and an "equal necessity to represent that impulse as a revelation."[85] The deceptions of the imagination were the source of revelation, and only by curtailing belief could humanity recognize that the structure of its own consciousness had determined God.

In the years following the *Essence of Christianity*, Feuerbach expanded his understanding of the location of revelation, binding it to the sensuous existence of human beings, rather than to consciousness. Responding to criticism from Left Hegelians, a short supplement to the text, *The Essence of Faith according to Luther* (1844), aimed to curb Feuerbach's own tendency towards abstraction by emphasizing sensualism and concrete human existence, rather than seeing God as the objectification of the species idea. It develops the naturalist-existentialist themes he had explored in two short intervening philosophical essays.[86] The work also offered a politically more acceptable forum for critiquing Christianity in the wake of Austria banning his book in 1842 and police searching his premises a year later.[87] God, Feuerbach now proposed, was not the projection of an idealized human essence, but the product of individual desires and wishes. The divine, he wrote, is "the being who expresses, promises, and objectifies human... ...wishes ... nothing but the essence of the human heart – or, rather, emotion – objectified to itself."[88] The assertion that belief in God was a form of self-love or egoism signifies a return to personalism in Feuerbach's work but with a new focus on the particular, individual, contingent body.[89]

The uniqueness of Christian revelation now lay, for Feuerbach, in God's being regarded as a sensual being, not as a being in thought or as the product of reason. "That which is for other peoples (pagans) an *imagined* being, existing only in thought and therefore dubitable," he wrote, "is for Christians a *sensual*, and therefore a certain, being."[90] The concrete, sensuous form of the incarnation guaranteed to Christians that God had an independent existence and was not a figment of the imagination or a human creation. "The essence of Revelation is the essence of sensuality,"[91] Feuerbach concluded. The Christian concept of revelation itself mandated that the sensuous existence of a feeling, willing individual took priority over a detached notion of species being. The sensuous existence of God likewise implied that human beings themselves were not disembodied bearers of abstract reason but conditioned by their spatial and temporal location.

Feuerbach's *Lectures on the Essence of Religion* (1851) more forcefully bound contingent human existence to nature. Delivered in Heidelberg at the request of students who sought, but failed, to secure his academic appointment during the Revolutions of 1848–9, which Feuerbach regarded apathetically, the lectures reflect the empirical realism that characterizes Feuerbach's late or positive philosophy and a deeper concern for the relationship between human subjects and nature.[92] Feuerbach proposed that unconscious nature was the eternal, uncreated being, the first being, and therefore the condition for the origin of human life. A feeling of dependency on nature, fused with self-love and a fear of death, moreover, was the psychological ground of the earliest religions. Pagan faiths indicated that nature was "the ground of human existence … the reality on which man should know himself to be dependent."[93] Theology, Feuerbach now affirmed, was thus both a closet 'anthropology,' probing the drives and unconscious instincts comprising human subjectivity, and physiology, a universal natural science.

Revelation emerges as a quality embodied, sensuous, desiring beings projected onto the natural world in Feuerbach's last work on religion, the *Theogonie* (1857). Here he acknowledged revelation as a crucial power with which nature gods and mythological figures were endowed and, as such, an important feature in the human psychological response to environmental contingencies. The gods did not originate in an act of philosophical speculation, according to Feuerbach; polytheism was not the result of defective or immature reasoning. Rather, the divine was an object of desire, longing, and the wish to escape mortality. Feuerbach insisted, furthermore, on an "inner, indivisible connection between belief in gods and belief in revelation." The will of the gods had to be revealed in order for the faithful to honour their prescriptions. The quality of revelation was essential to the very existence of the gods as living beings even if they were objects of nature, for "the revelation of their existence is therefore simultaneously the revelation of their will." The shining of the sun, for example, was an act of revelation that conveyed to humankind knowledge of its "existence and essence"[94] as a divine being.

Revelation, Feuerbach concluded, was a universal human belief, necessary for people to know what the gods required for felicity and salvation. Its function remained the same within paganism and Christianity, even if the forms assumed by the divine evolved as human desires and wishes responded to changing historical circumstances. The knowledge transmitted through revelation was merely a reflection of what human beings wished to know. If, in the *Essence of Christianity*, deciphering the hidden meaning of revelation promised a liberating knowledge of species being and a reappropriation of the human capacity to reason and act ethically, belief in revelation had by the *Theogonie* become an inescapable component of the human desire to fulfil its wishes and satisfy a subjective need for happiness. In both cases Feuerbach denied revelation the capacity to convey knowledge of a transcendent realm. Its human origins shifted, however, from a necessary cognitive phase in the collective self-objectification and reappropriation of species being to an extension of the instincts and desires of sensuous individuals existing in specific material circumstances.

Karl Barth characterized Feuerbach as the point of intersection where the lines leading from Schleiermacher, Hegel, de Wette, and Tholuck converged, in that each regarded religion, revelation, and the relationship to God as a predicate of man.[95] Whether by exposing religion as an illusion that contained a liberating truth Feuerbach fathered the hermeneutics of suspicion, which Paul Ricoeur associated with Marx, Nietzsche, and Freud, has been debated.[96] Feuerbach's ambition in 1848 to "replace the love of God by the love of man as the only true religion"[97] put a positive and affirmative spin on atheism, but his tracing the belief in revelation to human desire also appeared to later readers as acceptance of religion as a legitimate source of solace and comfort. In either case, Feuerbach's view of revelation carried to the extreme a nearly century-old tendency among theologians to recognize human agency, whether in the form of reason or feeling, in the acquisition of higher truths. Feuerbach erased Lessing's ditch by declaring its irrelevance and welcoming the necessary historical embodiment of cognitive processes. For Feuerbach, the concept of revelation had value solely as an ontological category that unveiled truths about the subjective inner existence of contingent, historical beings and their embodiment in a sensuous, material world.

Søren Kierkegaard: Revelation in Existentialist Thought

Redefining revelation in ontological terms likewise eased the Danish religious philosopher Søren Kierkegaard past the impasses posed by enlightened critique and speculative philosophy. Similarly to Feuerbach, Kierkegaard regarded religion as an existentialist project of self-transformation with revelation serving as a guide to understanding the embodied self. If, for Feuerbach, exposing a defunct God hastened the self-disclosure of humanity to itself, self-knowledge was the path to the divine for Kierkegaard. Although denying the epistemological prerogatives of revelation, he preserved its transcendental origins as an existential communication from God. An infinite qualitative difference separated God and man, according to Kierkegaard, and he resisted all anthropocentric notions of immanence that derived knowledge of the divine from the world of human experience. Revelation, for Kierkegaard, presented absolutely binding, external directives for the individual seeking to live by God's will. Recognition of human insufficiency in the face of revelation's supreme paradoxes demanded, for Kierkegaard, faith, obedience, and the transformation of existence. His insistence on the transcendent origins of revelation became fodder for an early twentieth-century revolt against liberal theology. The existentialist slant Kierkegaard lent to revelation also established the term as a crucial concept in the tradition extending to Martin Heidegger, Paul Tillich, and Jean-Paul Sartre. The theological foundations of Kierkegaard's reappraisal lay, however, in efforts to respond to Lessing's ditch and the perceived failures of speculative theology.

The famously severe upbringing Kierkegaard endured as the child of an overbearing, melancholic father fused the revivalism of the post-Napoleonic period and Lutheran orthodoxy. Having spent his early years as a shepherd on the Jutland moors, Kierkegaard's father remained seeped in the rural pietism of the Herrnhuter congregation while, as a successful entrepreneur in Copenhagen, also affiliating with the Danish state church. Despite the initially close mentorship of the Bishop of Zealand, Jakob Peter Mynster, Kierkegaard quickly found himself disaffected with the urban, elitist Christianity of golden age Denmark. An inheritance from his father was sufficient for Kierkegaard to live as an independent writer, and he set himself the task of pushing the comfortable, prosperous Danish middle class towards the abyss, unmasking the illusion that Denmark was a Christian state. Despite his personal conservatism, aristocratic preferences, and objections to the French Revolution, Kierkegaard welcomed liberalism and rural populism as allies in deflating the religious pretences of the urban cultural elite.[98]

A decade studying theology at the University of Copenhagen in the 1830s, home to a conciliatory moderate supernaturalism, convinced Kierkegaard of the inadequacy of prevailing Protestant responses to the enlightened critique of religion. Schleiermacher visited Copenhagen while Kierkegaard was a student, and although his Danish reception was reserved, Kierkegaard took a tutorial on the *Christian Faith*, pleased with how Schleiermacher captured the sense of inward wonder that religion elicited. Schleiermacher, Kierkegaard later wrote, rightly conceived the feeling of absolute dependence as "a condition of religiousness in the sphere of being"[99] and regarded self-awareness of Christian existence as the foundation of faith. But Kierkegaard feared Schleiermacher reduced religiousness to a static metaphysical condition rather than a struggle in the sphere of becoming.[100] He sympathized with the young Danish Hegelians to the extent they offered an alternative to mediating theology, gaining his first serious exposure to speculative thought in the lectures of the Lutheran theologian Hans Lassen Martensen. But Kierkegaard immediately doubted the compatibility of Hegelian dialectics with the universality of sin and the fallibility of human knowledge.[101] Like Feuerbach, he remained a staunch anti-Hegelian, rejecting basic premises of the master's thought while retaining traces of his edifice.

An encounter with Immanuel Hermann Fichte's "Spekulation und Offenbarung" in December 1837 shaped Kierkegaard's particular response to Hegel and Schleiermacher, confirming his own commitment to the individual, positive aspects of historical revelation and to concrete embodied personhood.[102] In the opening essay of his *Zeitschrift für Philosophie und speculative Theologie*, Fichte distinguished based on their effects on revelation two trajectories in the recent philosophy of religion: the psychological-human approach of Schleiermacher and F.H. Jacobi, and the objective divine tack of Hegel and his followers. The subjective line of religious inquiry, Fichte surmised, captured the inner life of the soul and the particularities of human religious consciousness. But the "divine being in his positive nature and revelation"[103] remained unknowable. Hegel's disciples, by contrast, mistook human self-knowledge for knowledge of the divine with the result that God deceptively became transparent in his revelation, eliminating mystery and the inner substance of the divine.

A synthetic third way, favoured by Fichte, bestowed renewed authority in revelation and corrected, as far as Kierkegaard was concerned, the relationship between philosophy and theology in speculative thought. The religious philosophy Fichte proposed distinguished the divine content of revelation sharply from its subjective human appropriation. He argued for the existence of a "deep and yet common fundamental truth" that extended through all religions and history. This was not, he cautioned, an *Uroffenbarung*, "a closed ... transmitted doctrine, or even a primordial system of knowledge,"[104] but the self-revelation of divine being. Since primeval times," Fichte wrote, "a personal god has disclosed itself to the human race in particular, ever more deeply unveiling revelation."[105] The most pressing project for speculative philosophy, according to Fichte, was to distinguish the divine "thread of revelation" from what was "fantastical-human embellishment."[106] Recognizing the limits of reason did not, in his view, entail capitulating to "authoritarian faith" (*Authoritätsglauben*).[107] Rather, Fichte concluded in anticipation of Kierkegaard, philosophers must embrace the paradoxes of Christianity as "the truth, more deeply satisfying to reason, and thus more suitable to God."[108]

Kierkegaard followed Fichte's admonition that philosophy submit to the authority of positive historical revelation. "The philosophers think that all knowledge, yes, even the existence of the deity, is something man himself produces," he wrote in a journal entry from 20 July 1839, "and that revelation can be referred to only in a figurative sense in somewhat the same sense as one may say the rain falls down from heaven, since the rain is nothing but an earth-produced mist." "But they forget," he continued, severing the transcendent from the human, "that in the beginning God separated the waters of the heaven and of the earth and that there is something higher than the atmosphere."[109] Religion should not aspire to objective rational validation, Kierkegaard concluded, but neither were irrationalism or naïve fideism adequate responses to transcendence. He sought to deconstruct the apparent dichotomy between faith and reason by focusing on the real existential character of religious belief.[110] Already as a student he reflected on the nature of religious existence and reconceived knowledge of the divine as an inward process of self-transformation. "What I really need is to get clear about what I must do, not what I must know," he noted in a famous aphorism from 1835, "What matters is to find a purpose, to see what it really is that God wills that I shall do; the crucial thing is to find a truth which is truth for me, to find the idea for which I am willing to live and die."[111]

After completing his theological exams and abruptly ending an engagement to Regine Olsen, the daughter of a wealthy bourgeois family, Kierkegaard departed for Berlin to hear Schelling's much-anticipated lectures. Enticed by Schelling's claim to prioritize the positivity of experience over pure thought, he found himself "'indescribably'" happy at the start of the lectures on the philosophy of mythology. "Long enough have I sighed and thoughts sighed in me," he wrote, "when [Schelling] mentioned the word 'reality' concerning the relation of philosophy to reality then the fetus of thought leaped with joy in me."[112] Kierkegaard's anticipation quickly ceded to contempt and indifference, however, and he returned to Copenhagen four and a half months later without hearing the lectures on the philosophy of revelation. Like Feuerbach, he sympathized with Schelling's negative critique of Hegel, but forged an alternative solution to how one might conceive of existing reality as an ethical task.

Kierkegaard's two major commentaries on historical revelation in the 1840s are structured as a response to Lessing's ditch and reflect the renewed concern that J.F. Strauss's *Life of Jesus* elicited for the relationship between revelation and history.[113] Although reversing the relative weight Lessing placed on reason and revelation, Kierkegaard found in him a useful ally in the fight against speculative theology, as Lessing also pondered the subjective process of becoming a believer.[114] The *Philosophical Fragments* (1844) address Lessing's temporal gap, or the conditions under which the truth of historical revelation could be acquired. Along with the first section of the longer *Concluding Unscientific Postscript* (1846), they also respond to the metaphysical gap Lessing detected between contingent historical revelation and the universal or necessary truths of reason. The second part of the *Postscript* resolves the crucial existential gap, or how a subjective individual may appropriate the truths of Christianity.[115] Both works are pseudonymous, narrated by Johannes Climacus, who though ignorant of Christianity struggled to become a Christian in an age when, in his view, an excess of knowledge distracted from the task of existence. The texts offered later Protestants a compelling strategy for neutralizing the effects of historical criticism and reconciling faith and history. While maintaining the positivity of revelation, Kierkegaard proposed that genuine faith did not hinge on its facticity.[116]

The so-called "thought project" of the *Fragments* contrasts what Kierkegaard held to be irreconcilable conceptions of how the individual relates to truth: a Socratic model of self-discovery typical of philosophical idealism, in which a teacher elicits already existing knowledge from the learner, and the Christian conception of an external agent bestowing otherwise inaccessible truth on the individual. Unlike Lessing, Kierkegaard held philosophical reason and revelation to be qualitatively different types of truth, such that moving beyond Socrates would never gain humanity access to the transcendent realm. Reason, Kierkegaard wrote, could never advance beyond the "supreme paradox of all thought ... the attempt to discover something that thought cannot think."[117] Only faith, in his view, could embrace the absolute contradiction that in the incarnation the historical and eternal were united.

Revelation, for Kierkegaard, could not become an object of scientific knowledge or intuition because it transcended the categories of the human understanding.[118] Rather, it forced recognition that human error and sin were inevitable and established the insufficiency of reason. Revelation did retain a slight epistemological aspect, for Kierkegaard, as it disclosed otherwise inaccessible truths that the imagination and the understanding could not discover. But its aim was not to enlighten the mind. Unlike Lessing, Kierkegaard did not regard history as the education of the human race. Revelation exposed human standards for grasping reality as inadequate and invited the Christian to set reason aside in an ecstatic moment of passion that embraced the paradox of faith.

Reason's encounter with the absolute paradox of Christianity could, Kierkegaard reckoned, elicit two possible responses: the happy passion of faith, or a taking of offense. Feuerbach, in Kierkegaard's view, represented the offended person who refused the paradox. Reading the *Essence of Christianity* while writing the *Philosophical Fragments*, Kierkegaard agreed that transcendent religion necessarily offended the understanding. He saw Feuerbach's response to the paradox of faith as a legitimate possibility of existence, preferable to conventional theology. Rather than argue against Feuerbach, however, Kierkegaard inverted his projection theory and wielded it against the naturalistic hypothesis. In his view, judging religion by human standards alone resulted in self-alienation of a different kind. Feuerbach became unable to grasp the only real pathway to truth, which led through the faith of subjective existing individuals.[119]

The Christian conception of truth preferred by Climacus closed Lessing's temporal gap by detaching faith from the burden of attaining historical or philosophical certainty. As faith was not a form of knowledge, it was not contingent upon the results of secular, empirical inquiry and required no evidence, testimony, or proof. The problem of revelation's historical reconstruction and transmission was therefore no longer pressing. The temporal gap separating present believers from revelatory events was likewise, for Kierkegaard, inconsequential. Witnesses to the incarnation possessed no special understanding of how God entered time, in his view, and no personal experience of revelation was required. Faith could bring believers across time into contemporaneity with Christ. The simultaneity implied in Kierkegaard's concept of revelation rendered the ancient wisdom narrative meaningless. "Pure humanity is soon done with, likewise world history," Kierkegaard explained in the *Postscript*, "for even such huge helpings as China, Persia, etc., are swallowed up, as though they were nothing, by the hungry monster of the world-historical process."[120] The idea of primordial revelation subordinated particular existing human beings to the transmission of abstract principles and undermined the individual existential task of becoming a Christian.

Lessing's metaphysical gap questioned how historical revelation could be a reliable basis for religious truth and salvation when its very contingency disrupted necessity. Kierkegaard responded by embracing the contingency of history as a vehicle for faith. A particular historical moment, such as the incarnation, could, in his view, be theologically determinative. But this required rejecting Lessing's desire for objective verifiability and philosophical justification. Historical events represented, for Kierkegaard, a "coming into existence,"[121] a free and contingent transition from possibility to actuality that was not subject to the necessities of logic. Historical knowledge could only ever be an approximation, he concluded; it offered no more than probability. Embracing historical revelation had to be a free decision, an expression of the will to faith; the true "organ for the historical,"[122] was, according to Kierkegaard, belief, the only means to negate uncertainty and annul doubt. The ideal of historical objectivity was in fact an obstacle to faith. In the place of Lessing's opposition between the historically contingent and the necessary, Kierkegaard substituted an alternative dialectic between the historical and the eternal. The historical moments constituting subjective existence opened a gateway to the eternal because they directly confronted the paradox of time and eternity through which a believer entered into a relationship with Christ.

The most pressing of Lessing's ditches was, for Kierkegaard, the existential gap or the theological problem of plausibility and appropriation. How did an individual become a Christian in the face of potentially dubious religious truths? Kierkegaard countered with the radical and powerful assertion that truth was subjectivity, existing "only in the becoming, in the process of appropriation."[123] For the religiously existing subject, he wrote in the *Postscript*, "the truth becomes appropriation, inwardness, subjectivity, and the thing is precisely, in existing, to deepen oneself in subjectivity."[124] A genuine appropriation of historical revelation entailed, for Kierkegaard, a personal transformation, a coming into existence of the self. Existence was a task, a continual process of becoming, whose highest ambition was cultivating a relationship with God. The pain and anguish produced by the futile attempt to synthesize the temporal and eternal in one's own life could only be met, Kierkegaard concluded, with a leap of faith, a free, personal decision to cross Lessing's ditch and accept the incarnation as revelation and with it Christ's promise for salvation.

Revelation, in Kierkegaard's analysis, could only be appropriated subjectively and grasped in terms of a paradox. Having no significant external, objective expression, it took form subjectively as a direct, private relationship with God.[125] Revelation therefore factors significantly in the stages of personal transformation that Kierkegaard detailed on the path towards becoming subjective. The self-deceiving aestheticist, who seeks pleasure and ironic social detachment, Kierkegaard noted in *Either/Or* (1843), remained constantly concealed, enigmatical even to himself. By contrast, the prospect of facing judgment after death meant that an ethical existence demanded full self-revelation; judgment would come as a punishment if during life a person did not reveal himself. It is "every man's duty to become revealed," Kierkegaard wrote, "Ethics says that it is the significance of life and of reality that every man become revealed."[126] Self-revelation in the ethical realm took the form of love and required full disclosure of a subject's inner development. On these grounds Kierkegaard found marriage inadvisable if secrets or complications prevented the full self-revelation of the partners to each other.[127]

In this sense, the tragic hero in *Fear and Trembling* commits to the universal by becoming revealed and finds public acclaim in his self-revelation.[128] The knight of faith, by contrast, exemplified for Kierkegaard by the figure of Abraham, is incapable of self-disclosure and cannot communicate his direct experience of revelation. Abraham's compliance with God's command to sacrifice Isaac is incomprehensible within the ethical realm, though he never doubts hearing God's word. In the religious stage, the self admits its inability to fulfil ethical duties. Anxiety, guilt, and suffering accompany the resulting social isolation and in turn encourage repentance and submission to God's will. Secrecy and silence were the only possible expression of a mutual understanding achieved between God and the individual. The absolute relation to the absolute that Abraham achieves cannot be understood and is not outwardly distinguishable from a demonic bond. This made recognizing a genuine revelation difficult.

Kierkegaard's *Book on Adler*, written in 1846 and 1847, grappled with the criteria of a true revelation and the nature of obedience to divine authority, or how to act in the ethical realm in relation to a revelation. Its target, Adolph Peter Adler, was a priest from the island of Bornholm who, after abjuring his former Hegelianism and burning his manuscripts, announced in the preface to an 1843 collection of sermons that he had received a direct revelation from Christ, accompanied by a whistling in his bedroom chimney. Bishop Mynster defrocked Adler for reasons of mental incapacity, and Kierkegaard used the occasion to denounce speculative philosophy and disrespect for God's authority. Revelation, he affirmed, defied human judgment and demanded absolute submission to a transcendent power.

Continued allegiance to Hegel had, for Kierkegaard, rendered Adler emblematic of the confusion that had descended upon his age, in which a "militia of attackers,"[129] including Strauss and Feuerbach, undercut Christian authority in an effort to concoct a new religion. As a rural pastor, Adler discovered the emotional religion of the awakening, leaping from Hegelian philosophy to the sphere of religious inwardness. But he resorted to speculative terms, according to Kierkegaard, when explaining his purported revelation, which, if genuine, would lie beyond human comprehension. This alone exposed the vision as a human creation. "Hegelian philosophy," Kierkegaard wrote, "volatizes the concept of a revelation. It does not deny a revelation but explains it away ... to such an extent that it becomes the expression for the immediacy of the subjectivity, certainly not the individual subjectivity, but the subjectivity that is the human race, humanity."[130] Adler should have curbed his emotion and sought discipline in adherence to Christian concepts.

To preserve revelation's divine origins and radical alterity from the human experience, Kierkegaard denounced Adler's contradictory claims that his doctrine was both divinely inspired and his own intellectual achievement. First Adler announced he was an apostle. Later he claimed authorship of the revelation, declared himself a genius, and expected future refinement of the doctrine. Kierkegaard eliminated the human contribution to revelation by distinguishing sharply between a genius and an apostle. Talented, brilliant, and original, a genius introduced startling ideas, but their provenance was human. The rupture caused by a genius's wisdom was only temporary, as humanity eventually assimilated his ideas into its patrimony. An apostle, by contrast, possessed no extraordinary gifts or profundity. His message had a transcendent origin and was not subject to rational comprehension. A true revelation was, in Kierkegaard's words, "absolutely teleologically positioned paradoxically."[131] It rested on divine authority alone, remained shrouded in mystery, and therefore demanded faith and submission, not comprehension.

Adler showed no indication, Kierkegaard concluded, of submitting to the divine authority that marked a true revelation. His actions in the ethical realm betrayed a lack of conviction, especially his refusal to resign his priesthood and abandon the sphere of the universal represented by the Danish state church. Receipt of a revelation conferred an enormous responsibility, for Kierkegaard, both inwardly and outwardly in relation to the established order. A true apostle would realize his obligation to assert the authority he derived from God. Called to an unceasingly active life as the Lord's messenger, he would go out in the world and proclaim the doctrine, not endlessly evaluate or analyse it. Adler claimed a calling but remained ensconced in literary idleness, behaviour that was blasphemous, according to Kierkegaard, if he indeed had received a revelation. A person called by a revelation may not allow the silence of the grave to become the law of his existence; he must risk the possibility of offence by acting on God's authority.

Following Mynster's death in 1854, Kierkegaard himself launched an aggressive campaign against the Danish state church in newspapers and his own magazine. Denmark had successfully transitioned to liberal constitutionalism in the Revolutions of 1848–9, and he sought to fracture the dominant Christian cultural synthesis by separating church and state and organizing a popular boycott of official Christianity.[132] His concept of revelation veered sharply from the path of orthodoxy and held little relevance for confessional debates or doctrine. The final authority on God's word lay, for Kierkegaard, not in the abstract dictates of Scripture but in the conditions of individual human existence.[133] A Christian proclaimed religious truth by adapting a principle to practice, not by debating a body of philosophical statements. The *Philosophical Fragments* were not translated into German until 1910, reflecting Kierkegaard's virtual irrelevance for liberal Protestant theology and positivist philosophy.[134]

By the mid-nineteenth century propositional revelation was unconvincing as the epistemological anchor of religious truth outside of narrowly orthodox circles. But the implications of the post-Enlightenment revival of revelation as inner subjective experience and as an ontological category describing the nature of being also rendered it unwieldy for more heterodox Protestants. As Feuerbach and Kierkegaard indicate, the main nineteenth-century approaches to revelation veered, on the one hand, into the dangerous territory of extreme anthropomorphism, philosophical reductionism, and a moralism independent of God, and, on the other hand, into existentialist deliberations with no bearing on doctrine. Feuerbach, however, marks an extreme case outside the disciplinary boundaries of theology. His work disassociated revelation from its purportedly transcendent origins by subordinating the concept to reason, inner experience, and religious culture, virtually confining it to the natural sphere of human possibility. Rather than render revelation utterly indefensible for liberal religious thinkers after 1850, as Barth would have it, however, Feuerbach's insights merely drove the wedge deeper between theology and the human sciences, rendering unpalatable the ideas of transcendence that revelation once conveyed within earlier forms of language study or natural history, for example.

After World War I Kierkegaard's work resurfaced and ignited a new generation of dialectical theologians dissatisfied with what many perceived to be an undue erosion of revelation within Protestant theology. Kierkegaard offered Barth an initial ally in his indictment of liberal theology's propensity to ground theological reflection in human experience, providing an "awakening call" that drew him away from Hegel and Schleiermacher.[135] As Barth wrote in the preface to the second edition of his *Epistle to the Romans* (1922), "what Kierkegaard called the 'infinite qualitative distinction' between time and eternity," the cleft between God and man, "is for me ... the essence of philosophy."[136] Dismissing natural theology, Barth eschewed the anthropological optimism of the post-Enlightenment period and denied fallen humanity any inherent faculty to know God.[137] God's existence was, in his view, "distinguished qualitatively from men and from everything human, and must never be identified with anything which we name, or experience, or conceive, or worship, as God."[138] Through a miraculous act of condescension, Barth proposed, God transformed his word into flesh, allowing himself to be known through Christ, Scripture, and the proclamations of the church.

In later years, Barth repudiated Kierkegaard as complicit with what he regarded as the nineteenth century's proclivity to focus on subjective religion at the expense of revelation's objectivity.[139] Lingering traces of Pietism, relentless individualism, and disdain for the church ultimately rendered Kierkegaard unpalatable to Barth. Insisting that the word of God, not human existence, was the proper concern of theology, he ceded Kierkegaard to a rival theological camp that included the Christian existentialist Paul Tillich.[140] Disillusioned by both "empty" moralism and the positivist repristinization of revelation, Tillich found himself "grasped by Kierkegaard" as a theology student in Halle in 1905.[141] Enveloped in ecstasy and miracle, revelation was, for Tillich, the manifestation of the ultimate ground of being that occurred through the mediation of signs and symbols. In his view, there was "no reality, thing, or event which cannot become a bearer of the mystery of being and enter into a revelatory correlation."[142] A phenomenology of human existence, also inspired by Schelling, secured for him the possibility of revelation, a tribute to the long legacy enjoyed by revelation's rebirth in the early nineteenth century.

Conclusion

In his essay "Atheistic Theology" (1914), the Jewish theologian and philosopher Franz Rosenzweig denounced nineteenth-century German religious thinkers for precipitating a "monstrous birth of the divine out of the human."[1] He detected in Judaism and Protestantism the parallel triumph of a "theology hostile to revelation"[2] and an undue erasure of the distinction between God and humanity. The cause, in his view, was twofold: a flight into detailed historical research and an overly rationalistic interpretation of revelation. The nineteenth century, he claimed, tried to render revelation "unobjectionable"[3] but, in truth, so softened and blurred this difficult concept that its higher content sank into an "unworthy vessel."[4] The result, for Rosenzweig, was that the Jewish people were "theologically vaporized,"[5] their special historical mission erased. In his view, an excessive humanization of religion transformed the idea of God's chosen people into that of an ideal but generic human community. In a manner similar to the life of Jesus, the election of the Jewish nation was also subject to such excessive historicization, Rosenzweig believed, that God's interventions appeared mythological. Theology can be "as scientific as it wants," Rosenzweig wrote, "it cannot circumvent the notion of revelation"; divine intervention was necessary, in his view, to bridge the "unfillable cleft" separating God from the recipients of his word.[6]

After World War I, Karl Barth denounced in equally resolute terms the tradition of liberal Protestant theology and "anthropocentric-Christian thought"[7] that had, in his view, eroded the authority of revelation. Led astray by historicism, secular philosophy, and the psychology of religion, nineteenth-century thinkers had wrongly embraced the subjectivity of religion and fallen prey to their own epistemological arrogance. Barth urged those sceptical of revelation to bring themselves "under control" and to adopt "an attitude of attention, of awe, or trust, of obedience to this name." "It is not necessary," he wrote, "first to look for the true revelation on the right hand or on the left: much less ... to ask whether there is such a thing as revelation at all. Revelation need not first be brought in from any quarter, or furnished with proof."[8] Barth advocated a return to the "original, true and strict meaning of the concept" that did not reduce revelation to the manifestation of an idea or to the fulfilment of human yearnings, demands, or speculations.[9] His conception of revelation as an unresolved dialectical presence juxtaposed God's transcendent grace and human sinfulness and stressed the paradox of God's presence and absence in human history.[10] Barth's theology of revelation so artfully bypassed the major criticisms of the nineteenth century that his friend Dietrich Bonhoeffer warned of a new "positivism of revelation" which was "essentially a restoration."[11]

Rosenzweig, too, escaped the radical subjectivity he and Barth attributed to the theology of experience by cultivating a new "phenomenology of revelation."[12] Breaking with critical idealism and distrustful of humanity's cognitive and moral abilities, Rosenzweig embraced a theology of witness and pragmatic verification centred on revelation. In the interpretation of Randi Rashkover, revelation was, for Rosenzweig, performative and commanding, not a propositional dispensation of knowledge. A hidden God, separate from the world, made himself manifest to humanity through the divine act of love. Illumination from a blink of God's eye, Rashkover wrote in the *Star of Redemption* (1921), bestowed "the force to transform the created-being that is touched by this illumination ... into the testimony of a Revelation that has come to pass."[13] The covenant of the Torah called upon Jews to live a life of communal testimony to revelation, even if the intimacy of Sinai was fleeting and the relationship between God and humanity was as tenuous as it was for Barth.

The concerns of WWI-era crisis theologians, such as Barth and Rosenzweig, wrongly occlude the vitality of revelation in the nineteenth century and inadvertently overestimate the degree the Enlightenment secularized European intellectual life. Rosenzweig's and Barth's characterizations of German thought reflect less the actual position revelation held in the nineteenth century than the concerns of their time.[14] World War I destroyed the optimistic narratives of progress, rationality, and ethical humanism that allowed nineteenth-century German religious thinkers to so confidently ground revelation in the world of experience. The relativizing tendencies of historicism seemed exceedingly perilous to crisis theologians, and the restraints imposed by Enlightenment thought represented, in their view, an unjustifiable prohibition on the expression of authoritative truth. In response, Rosenzweig and Barth affirmed the absolute necessity of revelation in overcoming the fallibilities of human nature and the social order, radically separating God and the world. A supposed dilution of revelation in liberal theology became responsible, in their view, for the failure of religion to stem the secularization of European society and its descent into war.

In fact, revelation was a pervasive and vital concept in the nineteenth century. It successfully withstood historical criticism, aligned well with modern philosophy, and proved remarkably amenable to the new standards of *Wissenschaft*. Across the three main German confessions the rebirth of revelation as subjective historical experience and as the progressive realization of divine being through history established its relevance for the modern world. Revelation's compatibility with reason bestowed the privileges of science on theology while opening a fruitful dialog with Kantian philosophy and German idealism. A shift away from propositional revelation alleviated concerns arising from the uncertain contingent historical presentation of transcendent truth while empowering human subjects as crucial partners in the actualization of God's word. Historicization also enabled revelation to be responsive to the rapidly changing political circumstances of postrevolutionary Europe, when secularization, territorial restructuring, considerations of Jewish emancipation, and the challenges of political reform placed new demands on religious thinkers.

The grounding of revelation in historical communities had unforeseen consequences, however. On the one hand, it facilitated the racialization of religion by associating forms of faith with national or ethnic characteristics and by emphasizing historical lines of descent in the receipt, preservation, and corruption of revelation. The claim to authoritative custodianship of revelation was a vector of confessional chauvinism, legitimated the exclusion of Jews from full participation in civic life, and reinforced the political and cultural hegemony of Protestants in many German states. The comparative history of religion likewise enabled European scholars to hierarchically order the world's religions along a continuum of access to revelation that conferred specific historical roles to nations in the unfolding of divine truth and allowed for varying degrees of political and spiritual self-determination. On the other hand, despite creative approaches to documenting God's revelatory presence on earth, the means by which revelation was historicized in the nineteenth century struggled to fully preserve and accommodate divine transcendence, only partially bridging Lessing's ditch.

By the Revolutions of 1848–9, the risks of attributing increased significance to human experience in the unfolding of revelation had become apparent, magnified by the severity of the political instability that threatened the conservative alliance of throne and alter in Europe. The postcritical reinvention of revelation destabilized orthodoxy across the three confessions, proving incompatible with the literal interpretation of Scripture and often compromising religious institutions and practices. By the 1840s it had become apparent that, in its most extreme forms, approaching revelation as subjective inner experience reduced religion to a psychological projection or to a profane expression of cultural particularity. Similarly, understanding revelation as the progressive actualization of divine being through history floundered on God's perceived dependence on the world and on the uncertainty of his transcendence. Recourse to origins, to a moment of primordial revelation, provisionally offered theologians a mechanism for proclaiming God the ultimate source of rationality and religious consciousness, but the decline of the ancient wisdom narrative and the difficulty of guaranteeing the objectivity of subsequent revelations left them vulnerable to their foundation in otherwise subjective experience.

Religious thinkers easily met the danger of revelation being reduced to a human creation without surrendering to the debilitating anthropomorphism Barth and Rosenzweig feared. In limited cases, the theological response to the challenges posed by nineteenth-century concepts of revelation was merely reactionary, evading the concerns raised by the religious Enlightenment. Neo-confessionalist Protestants and orthodox Catholics doubled down on scriptural literalism, God's personal transcendence, and doctrinal conservatism; orthodox Jews similarly maintained the absolute historical facticity of God's revelation on Mt. Sinai, as well as the divine origins of oral law. Among less doctrinaire scholars, however, the new postcritical models of revelation offered a welcome opportunity for religious renewal and for dynamically engaging developments across other fields of inquiry. Rather than excise the term, the Enlightened critique of revelation opened a period of remarkable and productive reflection on a crucial concept in German theology.

Even the most radical advocates of historicism and rationalism in German religious thought still maintained the centrality of revelation in the second half of the nineteenth century. Albrecht Ritschl, for example, whose school dominated Protestant theology after 1875, responded to the crisis of theological historicism, not by retreating to dogma, speculation, or mystical thinking, but by building upon the Christian experience of historical revelation. Unable to ascertain the facticity of the gospels, Ritschl focused theology on the apostolic community's religious and ethical response to God's revelation. In the *Christian Doctrine of Justification and Reconciliation* (1870–4), Ritschl thus deemed theology "incompetent"[15] to enter into proof of Christian revelation. Because divine revelation was "always humanly conditioned," the possibility of "delusion" and "error" could not be eradicated, but Christians, in his view, should accept "the possibility of certainty subject to the conditions under which the human spirit becomes conscious of its relations to God."[16] For Ritchl, Christ was the "perfect revelation of God."[17] Historical study of Jesus and the "bearers of revelation" who "make the revelation of God in Christ efficacious for the community which He founded"[18] created a reliable basis for faith.

The leader of the Marburg school of Neo-Kantian philosophy, Hermann Cohen, by contrast, presented Judaism as a model and source for the religion of reason. Bringing together the traditions of Jewish rationalism and German idealism, Cohen asserted that reason bestowed lawfulness and certainty on religion, providing a necessary counterweight to historical analysis and a viable alternative to approaching religion as feeling. In his analysis the fundamental ideas of religion, including revealed law, were regulative, not constitutive, proscribing ethical imperatives and thought patterns rather than conveying knowledge of a transcendent reality.[19] Tellingly, revelation factored heavily in Cohen's work as a precondition for human rationality. In the posthumous *Religion der Vernunft aus den Quellen des Judentums* (1919), Cohen asserted that revelation was "the foundation of reason for all content of reason."[20] As the "eternal origin,"[21] revelation bestowed rationality on human beings and enabled a relationship to moral law. Cohen gave only secondary importance to the historical fact of revelation at Sinai but still regarded the content of the commandments as crucial to the history of Jews and to the emergence of rational religion.

Increasingly captive to ultramontane postures, German Catholic thinkers, however, reverted to more conventional positions on revelation in the later nineteenth century. The apostolic constitution *Dei Filius*, adopted by the First Vatican Council in 1870, dismissed many of the innovations nineteenth-century Catholic theology had made in the interpretation of revelation. *Dei Filius*'s second chapter granted to reason the ability to arrive at God's existence and know some divine attributes with certainty, breaking with the extreme traditionalist presumption that all knowledge required revelation. However, it likewise deemed revelation in Scripture and unwritten tradition necessary, in contrast to rationalism, because God had ordained humankind to a supernatural end and to blessings that exceeded natural intelligence. While the third chapter held the assent to faith rational, it likewise demanded that reason yield to and obey revelation based on the authority of God. Reason and faith were two mutually reinforcing orders of knowledge, according to the constitution, but separate. The Church derived from God the charge of guarding the deposits of faith, such that sacred doctrines should not be treated as philosophical inventions subject to human perfection.

The persistence of revelation as a concept crucial to German religious thought after 1848 should not, however, obscure that by then the term had lost its association with transcendence for scholars operating outside of theological faculties, for whom Feuerbach's indictments were more compelling. A secularized concept of revelation nevertheless persisted as a category for capturing the constitution of the self and the dynamics of intersubjective engagement, especially among existentialists. When conceived as an historically situated process of self-disclosure or as an elusive encounter between the self and other, revelation raised fundamental questions about identity construction, communication, cultural particularity, and transcendence, as well as about the despair of inhabiting a world left meaningless without an authoritative signifier. It likewise invited reflection on acts of radical creativity, unprecedented innovation, and genius while probing the processes by which knowledge is received, understood, and transmitted. These concerns endured beyond the theological milieu in which the nineteenth century debated revelation, even without the high stakes and presumption of infallible truth that divine origins conveyed.

Notes

Introduction

1 F.W.J. Schelling, *On University Studies*, trans. E.S. Morgan (Athens: Ohio University Press, 1966), 11–12.
2 Schelling, *On University Studies*, 85.
3 Thomas Howard, *Religion and the Rise of Historicism: W.M.L. de Wette, Jacob Burckhardt, and the Theological Origins of Nineteenth-Century Historical Consciousness* (Cambridge: Cambridge University Press, 2000), 15; Grant Kaplan, *Answering the Enlightenment: The Catholic Recovery of Historical Revelation* (New York: Herder & Herder, 2006), 3ff.; Suzanne Marchand, *German Orientalism in the Age of Empire: Religion, Race, and Scholarship* (Cambridge: Cambridge University Press, 2009), xxiv; Samuel Moyn, *Origins of the Other: Emmanuel Levinas between Revelation and Ethics* (Ithaca: Cornell University Press, 2005).
4 Many histories of revelation are internal explorations of confessional disputes. Avery Dulles, *Revelation Theology: A History* (New York: Herder and Herder, 1969); Hans Waldenfels, *Die Offenbarung: Von der Reformation bis zur Gegenwart* (Freiburg: Herder, 1977); Peter Eicher, *Offenbarung: Prinzip neuzeitlicher Theologie* (Munich: Kösel Verlag, 1977); H.D. McDonald, *Theories of Revelation: An Historical Study, 1700–1960* (Grand Rapids: Baker Book House, 1979); Michael Meyer, "'Ob Schrift? Ob Geist' Die Offenbarungsfrage im deutschen Judentum des neunzehnten Jahrhunderts" in *Quaestiones Disputatae*, ed. Karl Rahner and Heinrich Schlier, vol. 92 *Offenbarung* (Basel: Editiones Herder, 1981); Gerhard Heinz, *Untersuchen zur Entstehung des fundamentaltheologischen Offenbarungstraktates der katholischen Schultheologie* (Mainz: Mattias-Grünewald-Verlag, 1984); Gunther Wenz, *Offenbarung: Problemhorizonte moderner evangelischer Theologie* (Göttingen: Vandenhoeck & Ruprecht, 2005); Jan Rohls, *Offenbarung, Vernunft und Religion. Ideengeschichte des Christentums*, vol. 1 (Tübingen: Mohr Siebeck, 2012).

5 See Paul Helm, ed. *Faith & Reason* (Oxford: Oxford University Press, 1999).

6 See Maria Rosa Antognazza, "Revealed Religion: The Continental European Debate" in Knud Haakonssen, *The Cambridge History of Eighteenth-Century Philosophy*, vol. 2 (Cambridge: Cambridge University Press, 2006).

7 Balázs M. Mezei, *Religion and Revelation after Auschwitz* (London: Bloomsburg, 2013), 93.

8 Hans Frei, *The Eclipse of Biblical Narrative: A Study in Eighteenth and Nineteenth Century Hermeneutics* (New Haven: Yale University Press, 1974), 63–5.

9 Gotthold Ephraim Lessing, "On the Proof of the Spirit and of Power" (1777), in *Lessing's Theological Writing*, ed. Henry Chadwick (Stanford: Stanford University Press, 1957), 87.

10 See Gordon E. Michalson, *Lessing's 'Ugly Ditch': A Study of Theology and History* (University Park: Penn State University Press, 1985), 8ff.

11 Avery Dulles, *Models of Revelation* (Maryknoll, NY: Orbis Books, 1992), xix.

12 Howard, *Protestant Theology*, 44–6.

13 See the typology of revelation developed by Avery Dulles in *Models of Revelation*.

14 Martin Jay, *Songs of Experience: Modern American and European Variations on a Universal Theme* (Berkeley: University of California Press, 2005), 82–3.

15 Mark Lilla, *The Stillborn God: Religion, Politics, and the Modern West* (New York: Alfred Knopf, 2007), 249.

16 Marchand, *German Orientalism*, 4–5.

17 See Howard, *Protestant Theology*, 18, and Eduard Hegel, "Die Situation der deutschen Priesterausbildung um die Wende vom 18. zum 19. Jhdt," in *Kirche und Theologie im 19. Jahrhundert*, ed. Georg Schwaiger (Göttingen: Vandenhoeck & Ruprecht, 1975).

18 Hegel, "Die Situation," 25.

19 Hans-Jürgen Brandt, *Eine katholische Universität in Deutschland? Das Ringen der Katholiken in Deutschland um eine Universitätsbildung im 19. Jahrhundert* (Cologne: Böhlau Verlag, 1981), 22–3.

20 Hegel, "Die Situation," 27.

21 Gerald A. McCool, *Nineteenth-Century Scholasticism: The Search for a Unitary Method* (New York: Fordham University Press, 1989), 83.

22 Keith H. Pickus, *Constructing Modern Identities: Jewish University Students in Germany, 1815–1914* (Detroit: Wayne State University Press, 1999), 27.

23 Shmuel Feiner, *The Jewish Enlightenment*, trans. Chaya Naor (Philadelphia: University of Pennsylvania Press, 2004), 369–71.

24 Pickus, *Constructing Modern Identities*, 8.

25 Christian Wiese, *Challenging Colonial Discourse: Jewish Studies and Protestant Theology in Wilhelmine Germany* (Leiden, Brill: 2005), 82.

26 See Olaf Blaschke, "Antisemitismus Nebensache: Verhältnis und Verflechtung von Feindbildkomplexen in der Kulturkampfzeit," in *Antisemitismus und andere Feinseligkeiten: Interaktionen von Ressentiments*, ed. Katharina Rauschenberger and Werner Konitzer (Frankfurt: Campus Verlag, 2015), 75–7.

27 Susannah Heschel, *Abraham Geiger and the Jewish Jesus* (Chicago: University of Chicago Press, 1998), 129, 158–9.

28 See Dulles, *Revelation Theology*, 133. The term is from Paul Althaus in 1941.

1. Historical Revelation in the Protestant Enlightenment

1 Lessing, "On the Proof of the Spirit and of Power" (1777), in *Lessing's Theological Writing*, ed. Henry Chadwick (Stanford: Stanford University Press, 1957), 53.

2 Chadwick, "Introduction," in *Lessing's Theological Writings*, 10.

3 Lessing, "Ein Mehreres aus den Papieren des Ungenannten, die Offenbarung betreffend" (Gegensätze des Herausgebers), in *Gotthold Ephraim Lessings sämmtliche Schriften*, ed. Karl Lachmann, vol. 10 (Berlin: Voss, 1839), 14.

4 Ernst Cassirer, *The Philosophy of the Enlightenment* (Princeton: Princeton University Press, 1951), 175.

5 See Frei, *Eclipse* and Jonathan Sheehan, *The Enlightenment Bible: Translation, Scholarship, Culture* (Princeton: Princeton University Press, 2005).

6 Lessing, "Proof of the Spirit," 87. See Toshimasa Yasukata, *Lessing's Philosophy of Religion and the German Enlightenment: Lessing on Christianity and Reason* (Oxford: Oxford University Press, 2002), 56ff.

7 Frei, *Eclipse*, 52.

8 Frei, *Eclipse*, 63.

9 Karl Aner, *Die Theologie der Lessingzeit* (Hildesheim: Georg Olms, 1964), 4.

10 Jonathan I. Israel, *Radical Enlightenment: Philosophy and the Making of Modernity, 1650–1750* (Oxford: Oxford University Press, 2001), 635.

11 Israel, *Radical Enlightenment*, 13.

12 Steven Nadler, *A Book Forged in Hell: Spinoza's Scandalous Treatise and the Birth of the Secular Age* (Princeton: Princeton University Press, 2011), 20ff.

13 Benedict de Spinoza, *Theological-Political Treatise*, ed. Jonathan Israel, trans. Michael Silverthorne and Jonathan Israel (Cambridge, 2007), 188.

14 Spinoza, *Treatise*, 185.

15 Spinoza, *Treatise*, 194.

16 Spinoza, *Treatise*, 184.

17 Spinoza, *Treatise*, 40.

18 Spinoza, *Treatise*, 27.

19 Israel, *Radical Enlightenment*, 218.

20 Israel, *Radical Enlightenment*, 447ff.
21 Israel, *Radical Enlightenment*, 548ff.
22 Israel, *Radical Enlightenment*, 503–4, 507.
23 Israel, *Radical Enlightenment*, 513–14.
24 Gottfried Wilhelm Leibniz, "Discourse on Metaphysics," in *Discourse on Metaphysics: Correspondence with Arnauld, and Monadology*, intro. Paul Janet, trans. George R. Montgomery (Chicago: Open Court, 1918), 59.
25 Gottfried Wilhelm Leibniz, "Novissima Sinica," in Leibniz, *Writings on China*, trans. Daniel J. Cook and Henry Rosemont (Chicago: Open Court, 1994), 51.
26 Cited in Franklin Perkins, *Leibniz and China: A Commerce of Light* (Cambridge: Cambridge University Press, 2004), 155.
27 Perkins, *Leibniz*, 148.
28 Perkins, *Leibniz*, 146.
29 Jan Rohls, *Offenbarung*, 403.
30 Gottfried Wilhelm Leibniz, *Theodicy: Essays on the Goodness of God, the Freedom of Man, and the Origin of Evil*, ed. and intro. Austin Farrer, trans. E.M. Huggard (La Salle, IL: Open Court, 1985), 91.
31 Leibniz, *Theodicy*, 91.
32 Leibniz, *Theodicy*, 88.
33 Leibniz, *Theodicy*, 103.
34 Avi Lifschitz, *Language and Enlightenment: The Berlin Debates of the Eighteenth Century* (Oxford: Oxford University Press, 2012), 43.
35 Allison P. Coudert, *Leibniz and the Kabbalah* (Dordrecht: Kluwer Academic Publishers, 1995), 45.
36 C.J. Gerhardt, Die philosophischen Schriften Gottfried Wilhelm Leibniz, vol. 3 (Hildesheim: Georg Olms Verlag, 1960), 624–5. See Wouter J. Hanegraaff, *Esotericism and the Academy: Rejected Knowledge in Western Culture* (Cambridge; Cambridge University Press, 2012), 130.
37 Aner, *Die Theologie*, 3f.
38 Israel, *Radical Enlightenment*, 549–50.
39 Christian Wolff, "Discourse on the Practical Philosophy of the Chinese," in *Moral Enlightenment: Leibniz and Wolff on China*, ed. Julia Ching and Willard Gurdon Oxtoby (Sankt Augustin: Institut Monumenta Serica, 1992), 163–4.
40 Suzanne Marchand, *German Orientalism in the Age of Empire: Religion, Race, and Scholarship* (Cambridge: Cambridge University Press, 2009), 33.
41 Peter Hanns Reill, *The German Enlightenment and the Rise of Historicism* (Berkeley: University of California Press, 1975), 33.
42 Christian Wolff, *Natürliche Gottesgelahrheit*, trans. Gottlieb Friedrich Tagen (1742), vol. 1 (Hildesheim: Georg Olms Verlag, 1995), 1.
43 Wolff, *Natürliche Gottesgelahrheit*, vol. 2, 13.
44 Reill, *German Enlightenment*, 95.

45 Wolff, *Natürliche Gottesgelarheit*, vol. 2, 122.
46 Wolff, *Natürliche Gottesgelarheit*, vol. 1, 341.
47 Wolff, *Vernünfftige Gedancken von Gott, der Welt, und der Seele des Menschen* (Halle: Magdeburgischen, 1747), 626.
48 Barth, 142ff.
49 Frei, *Eclipse*, 96.
50 Wolff, *Natürliche Gottesgelarheit*, vol. 2, 117–18.
51 Wolff, *Natürliche Gottesgelarheit*, vol. 2, 121ff, 133ff.
52 Wolff, *Natürliche Gottesgelarheit*, vol. 2, 131f.
53 Wolff, *Natürliche Gottesgelarheit*, 157ff.
54 Frei, *Eclipse*, 96ff.
55 Israel, *Radical Enlightenment*, 544, 552.
56 Aner, *Die Theologie*, 22.
57 Barth, 151.
58 Henry E. Allison, *Lessing and the Enlightenment: His Philosophy of Religion and its Relation to Eighteenth-Century Thought* (Ann Arbor: University of Michigan Press, 1966), 37ff.
59 Aner, *Die Theologie*, 152; Allison, *Lessing and the Enlightenment*, 38.
60 Jonathan Israel, "The Philosophical Context of Hermann Samuel Reimarus' Radical Biblical Criticism," in *Between Philology and Radical Enlightenment: Hermann Samuel Reimarus (1694–1768)*, ed. Martin Mulsow (Leiden: Brill, 2011), 183.
61 Reill, *German Enlightenment*, 162.
62 Reill, *German Enlightenment*, 240.
63 See Ursula Goldenbaum, "The Public Discourse of Hermann Samuel Reimarus and Johann Lorenz Schmidt in the Humburgische Berichte von Gelehrten Sachen in 1736," in *Between Philology and Radical Enlightenment*.
64 Israel, "Reimarus' Radical Bible Criticism," 197.
65 Israel, *Radical Enlightenment*, 472.
66 Hermann Samuel Reimarus, *Vornehmsten Wahrheiten der natürlichen Religion* (Hamburg: Johann Carl Bohn, 1766), unpaginated preface.
67 Israel, "Reimarus' Radical Bible Criticism," 197.
68 Rohls, *Offenbarung*, 429.
69 Anonymous (Reimarus), "Zweytes Fragment: Unmöglichkeit einer Offenbarung, die alle Menschen auf eine gegründete Art glauben könnten," in *Fragmente des Wolfenbüttelschen Ungenannten*, ed. G.E. Lessing (Berlin: Arnold Meyer, 1788), 31.
70 "Zweytes Fragment," 37.
71 "Zweytes Fragment," 41–2.
72 Frei, *Eclipse*, 114.
73 "Zweytes Fragment," 129–30.
74 "Zweytes Fragment," 33.

75 Aner, *Die Theologie*, 4.
76 Barth, 153.
77 Allison, *Lessing and the Enlightenment*, 40.
78 David Sorkin, *The Berlin Haskalah and German Religious Thought: Orphans of Knowledge* (London: Vallentine Mitchell, 2000), 5.
79 Sorkin, *Berlin Haskalah*, 67.
80 Semler, *Versuch einer freiern theologischen Lehrart* (Halle: Hemmerde, 1777), 88–9.
81 Semler, *Lebensbeschreibung von ihm selbst abgefaßt*, vol. 1 (Halle, 1781), 108.
82 Semler, "Historische Einleitung in die Dogmatische Gottesgelersamkeit von ihrem Ursprung und ihrer Beschaffenheit bis auf unsere Zeiten," in *D. Siegmund Jacob Baumgartens Evangelische Glaubenslehre*, ed. Johann Salomon Semler, vol. 1 (Halle: Johann Justinus Gebauer, 1759), 71.
83 Semler, "Historische Einleitung," vol. 1, 52.
84 Semler, "Historische Einleitung," vol. 1, 48.
85 See also Frei, *Eclipse*, 111.
86 Semler, "Historische Einleitung," vol. 1, 52.
87 Semler, *Versuch*, 86.
88 Semler, *Versuch*, 89.
89 Semler, *Versuch*, 84–5.
90 Semler, *Versuch*, 257.
91 Semler, *Versuch*, 97.
92 Reill, *German Enlightenment*, 166, 171–2.
93 Reill, *German Enlightenment*, 169.
94 Reill, *German Enlightenment*, 166.
95 Reill, *German Enlightenment*, 169.
96 Rohls, *Offenbarung*, 467.
97 Allison, *Lessing and the Enlightenment*, 40.
98 Aner, *Die Theologie*, 96.
99 Henry E. Allison, *The Kant-Eberhard Controversy* (Baltimore: Johns Hopkins University Press, 1973), 1973.
100 Gerda Haßler, *Johann August Eberhard (1739–1809): Ein streitbarer Geist an den Grenzen der Aufklärung* (Halle: Hallescher Verlag, 2000), 33–4.
101 Carl Friedrich Bahrdt, *Geschichte seines Lebens, seiner Meinungen und Schicksale*, vol. 4 (Frankfurt/Main: Varrentrapp and Wenner, 1791), 112.
102 Eberhard, *Neue Apologie des Sokrates oder Untersuchung der Lehre von der Seligkeit der Heiden*, 2nd ed., vol. 1 (Berlin: Friedrich Nicolai, 1776), 199.
103 Eberhard, *Sokrates*, vol. 1, 214.
104 Eberhard, *Sokrates*, vol. 1, 210.
105 Allison, *Lessing and the Enlightenment*, 42.
106 Allison, *Lessing and the Enlightenment*, 86ff.
107 Allison, *Lessing and the Enlightenment*, 193–4.

108 Johann David Michaelis, *Dogmatik* (Göttingen: Wittwe Vandenhoek, 1784), 134.
109 William Baird, *History of New Testament Research*, vol. 1 *From Deism to Tübingen* (Minneapolis: Fortress Press, 1992), 129–30.
110 Michaelis, *Dogmatik*, 1ff.
111 Michaelis, *Dogmatik*, 7ff.
112 Michaelis, *Dogmatik*, 137.
113 Michaelis, *Dogmatik*, 27.
114 Israel, *Democratic Enlightenment*, 306.
115 Israel, *Democratic Enlightenment*, 309.
116 Allison, *Lessing and the Enlightenment*, 77–8.
117 Gotthold Ephraim Lessing, "On the Origin of Revealed Religion," in *Philosophical and Theological Writings*, ed. Hugh Barr Nisbet (Cambridge: Cambridge University Press, 2005), 35–6.
118 Allison, *Lessing and the Enlightenment*, 83.
119 Barth, 225.
120 Lessing, "Ein Mehreres aus den Papieren des Ungenannten," 15.
121 Lessing, "Ein Mehreres aus den Papieren des Ungenannten," 13.
122 Israel, *Democratic Enlightenment*, 320–1.
123 Lessing, "Ein Mehreres aus den Papieren des Ungenannten," 19.
124 Lessing, "Ein Mehreres aus den Papieren des Ungenannten," 10.
125 Lessing, "Axiomata," in Gotthold Emphraim Lessing, *Gesammelte Werke*, ed. Paul Rilla, vol. 8 (Berlin: Aufbau-Verlag, 1956), 190.
126 Toshimasa Yasukata, *Lessing's Philosophy of Religion and the German Enlightenment: Lessing on Christianity and Reason* (Oxford: Oxford University Press, 2002), 62–4.
127 Allison, *Lessing and the Enlightenment*, 99.
128 Lessing, "Ein Mehreres aus den Papieren des Ungenannten," 26–7.
129 Lessing, "Proof of the Spirit," in *Philosophical and Theological Writings*, ed. Hugh Barr Nisbet (Cambridge: Cambridge University Press, 2005), 83–5.
130 See discussion in Yasukata, *Lessing's Philosophy*, 58f.
131 Lessing, "Proof of the Spirit," 86–7.
132 Lessing, "Axiomata," 195.
133 Allison, *Lessing and the Enlightenment*, 151.
134 Allison, *Lessing and the Enlightenment*, 134.
135 Gotthold Ephraim Lessing, "The Education of the Human Race," in *Philosophical and Theological Writings*, ed. Hugh Barr Nisbet (Cambridge: Cambridge University Press, 2005), 218.
136 Israel, *Democratic Enlightenment*, 684.
137 Lessing, "Education of the Human Race," 218.
138 Yasukata, *Lessing's Philosophy*, 103.
139 Lessing, "Education of the Human Race," 218–19.

140 Yasukata, *Lessing's Philosophy*, 90.
141 Israel, *Democratic Enlightenment*, 325.
142 Lessing, "Education of the Human Race," 219.
143 Lessing, "Education of the Human Race," 234.
144 Lessing, "Education of the Human Race," 224.
145 Lessing, "Education of the Human Race," 226–7.
146 Lessing, "Education of the Human Race," 230–1.
147 Lessing, "Education of the Human Race," 233–4.
148 Lessing, "Education of the Human Race," 236.
149 Yasukata, *Lessing's Philosophy*, 98.
150 Yasukata, *Lessing's Philosophy*, 114.
151 Lessing, "Education of the Human Race," 236.
152 Yasukata, *Lessing's Philosophy*, 107.
153 Anthony LaVopa, *Fichte: The Self and the Calling of Philosophy, 1762–1799* (Cambridge: Cambridge University Press, 2001), 71.
154 LaVopa, *Fichte*, 76ff.
155 Garrett Green, "Introduction" to J.G. Fichte, *Attempt at a Critique of All Revelation*, trans. Garrett Green (Cambridge University Press, 1978), 19–20.
156 Fichte, *Critique of All Revelation*, 79f.
157 Fichte, *Critique of All Revelation*, 96.
158 Fichte, *Critique of All Revelation*, 104.
159 Fichte, *Critique of All Revelation*, 11.
160 Fichte, *Critique of All Revelation*, 114.
161 Fichte, *Critique of All Revelation*, 121–2.
162 Fichte, "Deduzierter Plan einer zu Berlin zu errichtenden höheren Lehranstalt" (1807), in *Die Idee der deutschen Universität: Die fünf Grundschriften aus der Zeit ihrer Neubegründung durch klassischen Idealismus und romantischen Realismus*, ed. Ernst Anrich (Darmstadt: Hermann Gentner Verlag, 1956), 154–5.
163 Fichte, "Deduzierter Plan," 161.
164 Thomas Howard, *Protestant Theology and the Making of the Modern German University* (New York: Oxford University Press, 2006), 164–5.
165 Immanuel Kant, *Religion within the Limits of Reason Alone*, trans. and introduction, Theodore M. Greene and Hoyt H. Hudson (Chicago: Open Court Publishing, 1934), 11.
166 James J. Dicenso, *Kant's Religion within the Boundaries of Mere Reason: A Commentary* (Cambridge: Cambridge University Press, 2012), 36.
167 Kant, *Religion*, 11.
168 Kant, *Religion*, 94.
169 Kant, *Religion*, 96–7.
170 Kant, *Religion*, 100.
171 Dicenso, *Kant's Religion*, 153.

172 Kant, *Religion*, 97, 106.
173 Kant, *Religion*, 112.
174 Kant, *Religion*, 113.
175 Kant, *Religion*, 143.
176 Kant, *Religion*, 102.
177 Walter Jaeschke, "'Um 1800' – Religionsphilosophische Sattelzeit der Moderne" in *Philosophisch-Theologische Streitsachen*, ed. Georg Essen and Christian Danz (Darmstadt: Wissenschaftliche Buchgesellschaft, 2012), 46.

2. The Comparative History of Religion, 1770–1800

 1 David Hume, *Vier Abhandlungen über die Geschichte der Religion*, trans. Friedrich Gabriel Resewitz (Quedlinburg: Andreas Franz Biesterfeld, 1759).
 2 Peter Jones, *The Reception of David Hume in Europe* (London: Thoemmes Continuum, 2005), 100ff.
 3 See Frank E. Manuel, *The Eighteenth Century Confronts the Gods* (Cambridge: Harvard University Press, 1959).
 4 Manuel, *Eighteenth Century*, 59ff.
 5 J.A.I. Champion, *The Pillars of Priestcraft Shaken; The Church of England and its Enemies, 1660–1730* (Cambridge: Cambridge University Press, 1992), 133ff.
 6 Peter Hanns Reill, "The Hermetic Imagination in the High and Late Enlightenment," in *Auklärung und Esoterik: Rezeption – Integration – Konfrontation*, ed. Monika Neugebauer-Wölk (Tübingen: Niemeyer, 2008), 325.
 7 See Monika Neugebauer-Wölk, "Aufklärung – Esoterik – Wissen. Transformationen des Religiösen im Säkularisierungsprozess. Eine Einführung," in *Aufklärung und Esoterik: Rezeption – Integration – Konfrontation*, 26–8.
 8 Guy G. Stroumsa, *A New Science: The Discovery of Religion in the Age of Reason* (Cambridge: Harvard University Press, 2010), 2–9.
 9 Peter Harrison, *'Religion' and the Religions in the English Enlightenment* (Cambridge: Cambridge University Press, 1990), 28ff.; Eric J. Sharpe, *Comparative Religion: A History* (New York: Charles Scribner's Sons, 1975), 18.
10 Jonathan Z. Smith, *Relating Religion: Essays in the Study of Religion* (Chicago: Chicago University Press, 2004), 186.
11 Harrison, *'Religion'*, 100.
12 Harrison, *'Religion'*,131–2.
13 See Jan Assmann, *Religio Duplex: How the Enlightenment Reinvented Egyptian Religion* (Cambridge: Polity Press, 2014).
14 Harrison, *'Religion'*, 160.

15 Manuel, *Eighteenth Century*, 133.
16 Harrison, '*Religion*', 169, 171.
17 David Hume, "The Natural History of Religion" (1757), in *Principle Writings on Religion*, ed. J.C.A. Gaskin (Oxford: Oxford University Press, 1993), 134.
18 Hume, "Natural History of Religion," 134.
19 Hume, "Natural History of Religion," 176.
20 Hume, "Natural History of Religion," 183.
21 Hume, "Natural History of Religion," 155.
22 Manuel, *Eighteenth Century*, 181.
23 Hume, "Natural History of Religion," 184.
24 Martin Kessler, "Herder's Theology," in *A Companion to the Works of J.G. Herder*, ed. Hans Adler and Wulf Koepke (Rochester: Camden House, 2009), 250.
25 J.G. Herder, *Ideen zur Philosophie der Geschichte der Menschheit*, vol. 1 (Leipzig: Hartknoch, 1841), 212.
26 Justin E.H. Smith, *Nature, Human Nature, and Human Difference: Race in Early Modern Philosophy* (Princeton: Princeton University Press, 2015), 251–2.
27 Herder, *Ideen zur Philosophie*, vol. 1, 212.
28 Johann Gottfried Herder, "Ueber die verschiednen Religionen," in *Herders Sämmtliche Werke*, ed. Bernhard Suphan, vol. 32 (Berlin: Weidmann, 1899), 148.
29 Herder, "Religionen," 146.
30 Herder, "Religionen," 149.
31 Herder, "Religionen," 150–1.
32 Johann Gottfried Herder, "Confirmation Ihro Hochfürstl. Durchlaucht Karoline Luise," in *Sämmtliche Werke*, vol. 31, 606.
33 Herder, "Religionen," 152.
34 Herder, "Confirmation," 611.
35 Christoph Bultmann, *Die biblische Urgeschichte in der Aufklärung: J.G. Herders Interpretation der Genesis als Antwort auf die Religionskritik David Humes* (Tübingen: Mohr Siebeck, 1999), 130, 133.
36 Wulf Koepke, *J.G. Herder* (Boston: Twayne Publishers, 1987), 39.
37 Frederick C. Beiser, *The German Historicist Tradition* (Oxford: Oxford University Press, 2011), 129.
38 Monika Neugebauer-Wölk, "Nicolai-Tiedemann-Herder: Texte und Kontroversen zum hermetischen Denken in der Spätaufklärung," in *Antike Weisheit und kulturelle Praxis: Hermetismus in der Frühen Neuzeit*, ed. Anne-Charlott Trepp and Hartmut Lehmann (Göttingen: Vandenhoeck & Ruprecht, 2001), 429.
39 Neugebauer-Wölk, "Nicolai-Tiedemann-Herder," 431–2.

40 Hans-Georg Kemper, "'Eins in All! Und all in Eins!' 'Christliche Hermetik' als trojanisches Pferd der Aufklärung," in *Aufklärung und Esoterik: Rezeption – Integration – Konfrontation* (2008), 43.

41 Herder to Johann Heinrich Merck, 15 October 1770, in Johann Gottfried Herder, *Briefe*, ed. Wilhelm Dobbek und Gunter Arnold, vol. 1 (Weimar, 1977), 260.

42 Robert T. Clark, *Herder: His Life and Thought* (Berkeley: University of California Press, 1969), 166.

43 Johann Gottfried Herder, *Älteste Urkunde des Menschengeschlechts*, in *Herders sämmtliche Werke*, ed. Bernhard Ludwig Suphan, vol. 6 (Berlin: Weidmann, 1883), 258.

44 Daniel Weidner, "Hieroglyphen und heilige Buchstaben: Herders orientalische Semiotik," in *Herder Yearbook*, vol. 7 (2004), 61.

45 Christoph Bultmann, "Herder's Biblical Studies," in *A Companion to the Works of J.G. Herder*, ed. Hans Adler and Wulf Koepke (Rochester: Camden House, 2009), 153–4, 237.

46 Rudolf Smend, "Herder und die Bibel," in *J.G. Herder: Aspekte seines Lebenswerkes*, ed. Martin Keßler and Volker Leppin (New York: Walter de Gruyter, 2005), 5.

47 Clark, *Herder*, 163.

48 Herder, "Fragmente zu einer 'Archäologie des Morgenlandes'" (1769), in *Werke*, vol. 6, 35.

49 Koepke, *J.G. Herder*, 32.

50 Günter Arnold, Kurt Kloocke, Ernest A. Menze, "Herder's Reception and Influence," in Adler and Koepke, 395.

51 Hamann, "Prolegomena über die neueste Auslegung der ältesten Urkunde," in *Sämtliche Werke*, ed. Josef Nadler, vol. 3 (Vienna: Verlag Herder, 1951), 128.

52 Kant to Hamann, 6 April 1774, in *J.F. Kleuker und Briefe seiner Freunde*, ed. Hennig Ratjen (Göttingen: Diesterische Buchhandlung, 1842), 208.

53 John H. Zammito, *The Genesis of Kant's Critique of Judgment* (Chicago: University of Chicago Press, 1992), 40.

54 Herder, *Urkunde*, 211.

55 Herder, *Urkunde*, 310–1.

56 Herder, *Urkunde*, 276.

57 Herder, "'Archäologie des Morgenlandes,'" 50.

58 Beiser, *German Historicist Tradition*, 130.

59 Clark, *Herder*, 167.

60 Herder, *Urkunde*, 298.

61 Herder, *Urkunde*, 289.

62 Herder, *Urkunde*, 450.

63 Herder, *Urkunde*, 451.

64 Herder, *Urkunde*, 446.
65 Herder, *Urkunde*, 464.
66 Beiser, *German Historicist Tradition*, 144–5.
67 Carl von Prantl, "Meiners, Christoph," in *Allgemeine Deutsche Biographie*, ed. Historische Kommission bei der Bayerischen Akademie der Wissenschaften, vol. 21 (Leipzig: Duncker & Humblot, 1885), S. 224.
68 Friedrich Lotter, "Christoph Meiners und die Lehre von der unterschiedlichen Wertigkeit der Menschen Rassen," in *Geschichtswissenschaft in Göttingen: eine Vorlesungsreihe* (Göttingen: Vandenhoeck & Ruprecht, 1987), 44, 51–2.
69 *Alte Göttinger Landsmannschaften: Urkunden zu ihrer frühesten Geschichte (1737–1813)* (GT: Vandenhoeck & Ruprecht, 1937), 58, 86.
70 Christoph Meiners, *Grundriß der Geschichte der Menschheit*, 2nd ed., (Lemgo: Meer, 1793), 6.
71 See Susanne Zantop, "The Beautiful, the Ugly, and the German: Race, Gernder, and Nationality in Eighteenth-Century Anthropological Discourse," in *Gender and Germanness: Cultural Productions of Nation*, ed. Patricia Herminghouse and Magda Mueller (Berghahn Books, 1997).
72 Lotter, "Christoph Meiners," 52ff.
73 See Paola Rumore, "Im Kampf gegen die Metaphysik: Michael Hißmanns Verständnis der Philosophie," in *Michael Hißmann (1752–1784): Ein materialistischer Philosoph der deutschen Aufklärung*, ed. Heiner F. Klemme, Gideon Stiening, Falk Wunderlich (Berlin: Akademie Verlag, 2013), 60–1.
74 Meiners, *Revision der Philosophie* (Göttingen: Johann Christian Dieterich, 1772), 91–2.
75 Meiners, *Revision*, 104.
76 Meiners, *Revision*, 17.
77 Meiners, *Revision*, 19.
78 John H. Zammito, *Kant, Herder, and the Birth of Anthropology* (Chicago: Chicago University Press, 2002), 278.
79 Manfred Kuehn, "Reception of Hume in Germany," in *The Reception of David Hume in Europe*, Peter Jones (New York: Thoemmes Continuum, 2005), 112.
80 Christoph Meiners, *Versuch über die Religionsgeschichte der ältesten Völker besonders der Egyptier* (Göttingen: J.C. Dieterich, 1775), 327.
81 Meiners, *Versuch*, 256.
82 Meiners, *Versuch*, 11.
83 Meiners, *Versuch*, 63.
84 Christoph Meiners, "Ueber die Mysterien der Alten," in *Vermischte Philosophischen Schriften*, vol. 3 (Leipzig: Weygandsche Buchhandlung, 1776), 208.
85 Meiners, "Mysterien," 205.

86 Markus Meumann, "Zur Rezeption antiker Mysterien im Geheimbund der Illuminaten: Ignaz von Born, Karl Leonard Reinhold und die Wiener Freimaurer-loge 'Zur wahren Eintracht,'" in *Aufklärung und Esoterik*, ed. Monika Neugebauer-Wölk (Tübingen: Meiner, 1999), 292.

87 Florian Ebeling, "Rationale Mysterien," in *Egypt: Temple of the Whole World: Studies in Honor of Jan Assmann* (Boston: Brill, 2003), 67.

88 Monika Neugebauer-Wölk, "Illuminaten" in *Dictionary of Gnosis and Western Esotericism*, ed. Wouter J. Hanegraaff (Boston: Brill, 2006), 593–4.

89 Christoph Meiners, *Historia Doctrinae de Vero Deo Omnium Rerum Actore atque Rectore* (Lemgo: Meyer, 1780). Translated into German by Justus Conrad Mensching as *Geschichte der Lehre vom wahren Gott dem Urheber und Regierer aller Dinge* (Duisburg: Gebrüder Helwig, 1791).

90 Lotter, "Christoph Meiners," 47.

91 Meiners, *Lehre vom wahren Gott*, 17.

92 Peter K.J. Park, *Africa, Asia, and the History of Philosophy: Racism in the Formation of the Philosophical Canon, 1780–1830* (Albany: State University of New York Press, 2013), 78–81.

93 W. Daniel Wilson, "Enlightenment Encounters the Islamic and Arabic Worlds: The German 'Missing Link' in Said's Orientalist Narrative (Meiners and Herder)," in *Encounters with Islam and German Literature and Culture*, ed. James R. Hodkinson and Jeffrey Morrison (Rochester: Camden House, 2009), 78ff.

94 Meiners, *Lehre vom wahren Gott*, 40.

95 Meiners, *Lehre vom wahren Gott*, 57.

96 Meiners, *Lehre vom wahren Gott*, 69.

97 Meiners, *Lehre vom wahren Gott*, 131.

98 Meiners, *Lehre vom wahren Gott*, 141.

99 Meiners, *Grundriß der Geschichte aller Religionen* (Lemgo: Meyersche Buchhandlung, 1785), unpaginated preface.

100 Meiners, *Geschichte aller Religionen*, 11.

101 Christoph Meiners, *Allgemeine kritische Geschichte der Religionen*, vol. 1 (Hannover: Helwingische Hof-Buchhandlung, 1806), 11.

102 Meiners, *Allgemeine kritische Geschichte*, vol. 1, 16.

103 Meiners, *Allgemeine kritische Geschichte*, vol. 1, 2–3.

104 Meiners, *Allgemeine kritische Geschichte*, vol. 1, 117.

105 Meiners, *Allgemeine kritische Geschichte*, vol. 1, 125.

106 Meiners, *Allgemeine kritische Geschichte*, vol. 1, 131.

107 See Michael Vester, *Aufklärung – Esoterik – Reaktion: Johann August Starck (1741–1816): Geistlicher, Gelehrter und Geheinbündler zur Zeit der deutschen Spätaufklärung* (Darmstadt: Verlag der Hessischen Kirchengeschichtlichen Vereinigung, 2012), 41–2; and Erich Donnert,

Anti-Revolutionär-konservative Publizistik in Deutschland am Ausgang des Alten Reiches: J.A. Starck, J.A.C von Grolman, F. Nicolai (Frankfurt: Peter Lang, 2010), 48.

108 See Starck, *Apologie des Ordens der Frey-Mäurer*, 2nd ed. (Berlin: Christian Ludewig Stahlbaum, 1778).

109 See Vester, 152ff.; Henri Veldhuis, *Ein versiegeltes Buch: Der Naturbegriff in der Theologie J.G. Hamanns* (1730–1788) (Berlin: Walter de Gruyter, 1994), 232; John R. Betz, *After Enlightenment: The Post-Secular Vision of J.G. Hamann* (Chichester: Wiley-Blackwell, 2009), 168–9.

110 Johann Georg Hamann, *Mysterienschriften erklärt von Evert Jansen Schoonhoven* (Gütersloh: Gerd Mohn, 1962), 25.

111 Veldhuis, *Ein versiegeltes Buch*, 236.

112 Betz, *After Enlightenment*, 26–7.

113 Betz, *After Enlightenment*, 211.

114 Betz, *After Enlightenment*, 64, 78–80, 112.

115 Betz, *After Enlightenment*, 64.

116 Manuel, *Eighteenth Century*, 169.

117 Timothy J. Beech, *Hamann's Prophetic Mission: A Genetic Study of Three Late Works against the Enlightenment* (Landon: Maney Publisher, 2010), 87–8.

118 Veldhuis, *Ein versiegeltes Buch*, 89.

119 Johann Georg Hamann, *Vetii Epagathi Regiomonticolae Hierophantische Briefe* (Riga: np, 1775), 13.

120 Johann Georg Hamann, "Prolegomena über die neueste Auslegung der ältesten Urkunde" in *Sämtliche Werke*, ed. Nadler, vol. 3, 127.

121 Hamann, *Hierophantische Briefe*, 5.

122 Hamann, *Hierophantische Briefe*, 7.

123 Hamann, *Hierophantische Briefe*, 61.

124 J.A. Starck, *Hephästion* (Königsberg: Gottlieb Lebrecht Hartung, 1775), 72.

125 Starck, *Hephästion*, 1.

126 Starck, *Hephästion*, 17.

127 Vesper, 166.

128 Starck, *Hephästion*, 99.

129 Starck, *Hephästion*, 2nd ed. (1776), unpaginated preface.

130 Veldhuis, *Ein versiegeltes Buch*, 244.

131 Starck, *Hephästion*, 75.

132 Starck, *Hephästion*, 87.

133 Starck, *Hephästion*, 9.

134 Starck, *Hephästion*, 87.

135 "Starck, Johann August, Freiherr von," in *Dictionary of Eighteenth-Century German Philosophers*, ed. Heiner Klemme and Manfred Kuehn, vol. 3 (New York: Continuum, 2010), 1117.

136 Beech, *Hamann's Prophetic Mission*, 165. For detailed discussions of the *Konxompax*, see Beech, *Hamann's Prophetic Mission*, 41ff; Veldhuis, *Ein versiegeltes Buch*, 243ff; Betz, *After Enlightenment*, 198ff; and Hamann, *Mysterienschriften*.

137 Johann Georg Hamann, "Konxompax: Fragmente einer apokrypischen Sibylle über apokalyptische Mysterien," in *Sämtliche Werke*, ed. Nadler, vol. 3, 217.

138 Hamann, "Konxompax," 224.

139 [anonymous], *Freymüthige Betrachtungen über das Christenthum* (Berlin: Christian Friedrich Himburg, 1780), 67.

140 Starck, *Ueber die alten und neuen Mysterien*, 143–4.

141 Ketmia Vere, *Compaß der Weisen*, ed. Adam Michael Birkholz (Berlin: Christian Ulrich Ringmacher, 1779), 28.

142 Vesper, 129ff.

143 See Sigurd Hjelde, "Das Aufkommen der Idee einer Religionswissenschaft: Einige deutsche Ansätze zum Ende des 18. Jahrhunderts," in *Zeitschrift für Religionswissenschaft* 22, no. 2 (2014), 150–75.

144 Richard Popkin, "Some Thoughts about Stäudlin's 'History and Spirit of Skepticism,'" in *The Skeptical Tradition around 1800: Skepticism in Philosophy, Science, and Society*, ed. Johan van der Zande and Richard H. Popkin (Boston: Kluwer Academic Publishers, 1998), 342.

145 Karl Friedrich Stäudlin, *Zur Erinnerung an D. Carl Friedrich Stäudlin: Seine Selbstbiographie*, ed. Johann Tychsen Hemsen (Göttingen: Vandenhoeck und Ruprecht, 1826), 4.

146 Karl Friedrich Stäudlin, *Geschichte und Geist des Skepticismus* (Leipzig: Siegfried Lebrecht Crusius, 1794), iv.

147 Paul Tschackert, "Stäudlin, Karl Friedrich," in *Allgemeine Deutsche Biographie*, ed. Historische Kommission bei der Bayerischen Akademie der Wissenschaften, vol. 35 (Leipzig: Duncker & Humblot, 1893), 516.

148 Karl Friedrich Stäudlin, *Ideen zu einer Kritik des Systems der christlichen Religion* (Göttingen: Vandenhoeck & Ruprecht, 1791), 29.

149 Stäudlin, *Ideen*, 167.

150 Stäudlin, *Skepticismus*, iii.

151 Stäudlin, *Skepticismus*, 123.

152 Stäudlin, *Skepticismus*, v.

153 See Johann Christian Laursen, "Skepticism and the History of Moral Philosophy: The Case of Carl Friedrich Stäudlin," in van der Zande and Popkin, 374ff.

154 John Stroup, "Protestant Church Historians in the German Enlightenment," in *Aufklärung und Geschichte: Studien zur deutschen Geschichtswissenschaft im 18. Jahrhundert*, ed. Hans Erich Bödeker (Göttingen: Vandenhoeck & Ruprecht, 1986), 189–90.

155 See Joachim Ringleben, "Göttinger Aufklärungstheologie – von Königsberg her gesehen," in *Theologie in Göttingen: Eine Vorlesungsreihe,* ed. Bernd Moeller (Göttingen: Vandenhoeck & Ruprecht, 1987).

156 Immanuel Kant, *Critik der Urtheilskraft* (Berlin: Lagarde und Friederich, 1790), 412.

157 Stäudlin, *Ideen,* 10–11.

158 Stäudlin, *Ideen,* 5.

159 Stäudlin, *Ideen,* 17.

160 Stäudlin, *Ideen,* 86.

161 Karl Friedrich Stäudlin, "Vorrede," in *Beiträge zur Philosophie und Geschichte der Religion und Sittenlehre überhaupt und der verschiedenen Glaubensarten und Kirchen insbesondere,* vol. 1 (Lübeck: np, 1797), iii.

162 Stäudlin, "Über den Werth der kritischen Philosophie," in *Beiträge,* vol. 5 (1799), 338.

163 Stäudlin, "Über den Werth der kritischen Philosophie," in *Beiträge,* vol. 4 (1798), 165.

164 Stäudlin, *Selbstbiographie,* 21.

165 Stäudlin, *Selbstbiographie,* 17–18.

166 Laursen, "Skepticism," 373.

167 Immanuel Berger, *Aphorismen zu einer Wissenschaftslehre der Religion* (Leipzig: Joh. Sam. Heinsius, 1796), 4.

168 Berger, *Aphorismen,* 174.

169 Immanuel Berger, "Wie ist die Göttlichkeit des Christenthums für die reine Vernunft-Religion zu erweisen?" in *Beiträge,* vol. 1 (1797), 142.

170 Immanuel Berger, "Ideen zur Philosophie der Religionsgeschichte," in *Beiträge,* vol. 4 (1798), 246.

171 Immanuel Berger, *Geschichte der Religionsphilosophie* (Berlin: Langische Buchhandlung, 1800), 58.

172 Berger, *Geschichte der Religionsphilosophie,* 4.

173 See Immanuel Berger, "Ueber Religionsphilosophie und religiöse Anthropologie," in Schuderoff, ed. *Journal zur Veredelung der Prediger- und Schullehrerstandes,* vol. 2 (Altenburg: Im literarischen Komtoir, 1803).

174 Berger, *Geschichte der Religionsphilosophie,* 34–5.

175 Berger, *Geschichte der Religionsphilosophie,* 47–8.

176 Gunther Stephenson, "Geschichte und Religionswissenschaft im ausgehenden 18. Jahrhundert," in *Numen,* vol. 13 (1966), 54, 56.

177 See R.F. Merkel, "Beiträge zur vergleichenden Religionsgeschichte, I. Ein vergessener deutscher Religionsforscher," in *Archiv für Religionswissenschaft,* vol. 36 (1939), 193–215.

178 Christian Wilhelm Flügge, *Versuch einer historisch-kritischen Darstellung des bisherigen Einflusses der Kantischen Philosophie auf alle Zweige der*

wissenschaftlichen und praktischen Theologie (Hannover: Helwingsche Hofbuchhandlung, 1796), 11.

179 Christian Wilhelm Flügge, "Versuch über das Studium der Religionsgeschichte," in *Beiträge*, vol. 2 (1797), 4.

180 Flügge, "Versuch über das Studium," 4–5.

181 Flügge, "Versuch über das Studium," 16.

182 Christian Wilhelm Flügge, *Geschichte des Glaubens an Unsterblichkeit, Auferstehung, Gericht und Vergeltung*, vol. 1 (Leipzig: Siegfried Lebrecht Crusius, 1794), 78.

183 Christian Wilhelm Flügge, "Fragmente über das Nationale, Locale, und Klimatische in dem Volksglauben verschiedener Völker an Fortdauer nach dem Tode," in *Beyträge zur Geschichte der Religion und Theologie in ihrer Behandlungsart*, ed. Flügge, vol. 1 (Hannover: Helwing, 1797), 97.

184 Christian Wilhelm Flügge, *Der Himmel der Zukunft* (Altona: I.F. Hammerich, 1804), 2.

185 Flügge, "Versuch über das Studium," 40.

186 Flügge, "Versuch über das Studium," 24.

187 Christian Wilhelm Flügge, "Ueber die Mythologie der Hindu's," in *Beyträge*, ed. Flügge, vol. 1, 41.

188 Karl Friedrich Stäudlin, "Anstatt der Vorrede," in *Magazin für Religions- Moral- und Kirchengeschichte* vol. 1(1) (Hannover: Gebrüder Hahn, 1801), 284.

189 Stäudlin, *Selbstbiographie*, 22.

3. God's Word in Comparative Mythology, 1760–1830

1 Gotthilf Heinrich Schubert, *Der Erwerb aus einem Vergangenen und die Erwartungen von einem zukünftigen Leben*, vol. 2 (Erlangen: J.J. Palm und E. Enke, 1856), 2, 291.

2 Johann Arnold Kanne, *Leben und aus dem Leben merkwürdiger und erweckter Christen aus der protestantischen Kirche*, vol. 1 (Bamberg: Carl Friedrich Kunz, 1816), 281.

3 Martin Hirzel, *Lebensgeschichte als Verkündigung: Johann Heinrich Jung-Stilling – Ami Bost – Johann Arnold Kanne* (Göttingen: Vandenhoeck & Ruprecht, 1998), 161.

4 Johann Arnold Kanne, "Das Panglossium Manuskript," cited in Erich Neumann, *Johann Arnold Kanne: Ein vergessener Romantiker: Ein Beitrag zur Geschichte der mystischen Sprachphilosophie* (Friedrich-Alexander-Universität Erlangen, 1827), 83.

5 Gotthilf Heinrich Schubert, *Gotthilf Heinrich Schubert in seinen Briefen: Ein Lebensbild*, ed. Nathanael Bonwetch (Stuttgart, 1918), 155.

6   Paolo Rossi, *The Dark Abyss of Time: The History of the Earth and the History of Nations from Hooke to Vico*, trans. Lydia G. Cochrane (Chicago: University of Chicago Press, 1984), 195ff.

7   Maurice Olender, *The Languages of Paradise: Race, Religion, and Philology in the Nineteenth Century*, trans. Arthur Goldhammer (Cambridge: Harvard University Press, 1992), 19.

8   John Milbank, *The Word Made Strange: Theology, Language, Culture* (Cambridge, MA: Blackwell, 1997), 84ff.

9   Johann David Michaelis, *Ueber den Einfluss der Sprachen auf die Meinungen der Menschen* (London, 1769).

10 See W.M. Alexander, *J.G. Hamann: Philosophy and Faith* (The Hague: Martinus Nijhoff, 1966), 25ff.

11 Johann Georg Hamann, "Über die Auslegung der Heiligen Schrift," in *Sämtliche Werke*, ed. Josef Nadler, vol. 1 (Vienna: Thomas-Morus Presse, 1949), 14.

12 Hamann, "Auslegung," 9.

13 Peter Meinhold, "Hamanns Theologie der Sprache," in *Acta des Internationalen Hamann-Colloqiums in Lüneburg 1976* (Frankfurt/Main: Vittorio Klostermann, 1979), 53–5.

14 James H. Stam, *Inquiries into the Origin of Language: The Fate of a Question* (New York: Harper & Row, 1976), 150.

15 Hamann, "Auslegung," 5.

16 Johann Georg Hamann, "Des Ritters von Rosencreuz letzte Willenserklärung über den göttlichen und menschlichen Ursprung der Sprache," in *Über den Ursprung der Sprache: Zwo Recensionen*, ed. Elfriede Büchsel (Gütersloh: Mohn, 1963), 199.

17 Johann Georg Hamann, "Aesthetica in Nuce" (1762), in *J.G. Hamann: Writings on Philosophy and Language*, ed. Kenneth Haynes (Cambridge: Cambridge University Press, 2007), 65–6.

18 Alexander, *J.G. Hamann*, 27.

19 Johann Georg Hamann, "Brocken," in *Sämtliche Werke*, ed. Josef Nadler, vol. 1, 308.

20 Meinhold, "Hamanns Theologie der Sprache," 56.

21 Hamann, "Aesthetica in Nuce," 66.

22 Stam, *Inquiries into the Origin of Language*, 151.

23 Johann Georg Herder, *Aelteste Urkunde des Menschengeschlechts* (1774, vol. 1), in *Herders Sämmtliche Werke*, ed. Ig Suphan, vol. 6 (Berlin: Weidmannsche Buchhandlung, 1883), 297.

24 Herder, *Aelteste Urkunde*, vol. 1, 275.

25 Herder, *Aelteste Urkunde*, vol. 1, 360.

26 Erich Ruprecht, "Die Frage nach dem Ursprung der Sprache: Eine Untersuchung zu J.G. Hamann's Wirkung auf die deutsche Romantik," in

Acta des Internationalen Hamann-Colloquiums in Lüneburg 1976 (Frankfurt/ Main: Vittorio Klostermann, 1979), 312.

27 Dorit Messlin, *Antike und Moderne: Friedrich Schlegel's Poetik, Philosophie und Lebenskunst* (Berlin: Walter de Gruyter, 2011), 196ff. See also Günter Arnold, Kurt Kloocke, and Ernest A. Menze, "Herder's Reception and Influence," in *A Companion to the Works of J.G. Herder*, ed. Hans Adler and Wulf Koepke (Rochester: Camden House, 2009) and Wolff A. von Schmidt, "Mythologie und Uroffenbarung bei Herder und Friedrich Schlegel," in *Zeitschrift für Religions- und Geistesgeschichte*, ed. E. Benz and H.J. Schoeps (Cologne: Brill, 1973).

28 Friedrich Schlegel to August Wilhelm Schlegel, 27 July 1807 in *Krisenjahre der Frühromantik. Briefe aus dem Schlegelkreis*, ed. Josef Körner, vol. 1 (Bern: Francke Verlag, 1969), 424.

29 Friedrich Schlegel, "Geschichte der alten und neuen Literatur," in *Kritische Friedrich-Schlegel-Ausgabe*, ed. Ernst Behler, J.J. Anstett, and Hans Eichner, vol. 6 (Munich: F. Schöningh, 1979), 385. See also Wolff A. Von Schmidt, "Mythologie und Uroffenbarung bei Herder und Friedrich Schlegel," in *Zeitschrift für Religions- und Geistesgeschichte*, ed. E. Benz and H.J. Schoeps (Cologne: Brill, 1973).

30 Michael Franklin, "Introduction," in Friedrich Schlegel, *On the Language and Wisdom of the Indians*, ed. Michael Franklin (London: Ganesha Publishing, 2001), xi.

31 Robert Cowan, *The Indo-German Identification: Reconciling South Asian Origins and European Destinies, 1765–1885* (Rochester: Camden House, 2010), 90.

32 Friedrich Schlegel, *Philosophische Vorlesungen aus den Jahren 1804 bis 1806*, ed. C.J.H. Windischmann, vol. 2 (Bonn: Eduard Weber, 1837), 226.

33 Adrian Daub, "'All Evil is the Cancellation of Unity': Joseph de Maistre and Late German Romanticism," in *Joseph de Maistre and his European Readers: From Friedrich von Genz to Isaiah Berlin*, ed. Carolina Armenteros and Richard A. Lebrun (Leiden: Brill, 2011), 141.

34 Schlegel, *Philosophische Vorlesungen*, 224.

35 Schlegel, *Philosophische Vorlesungen*, 225.

36 Schlegel, *Philosophische Vorlesungen*, 246.

37 Schlegel, *Vorlesungen über Universalgeschichte*, 14.

38 Schlegel, *Vorlesungen über Universalgeschichte*, 27–8.

39 Claudia Brauers, *Perspektiven des Unendlichen: Friedrich Schlegels ästhetische Vermittlungstheorie* (Berlin: Erich Schmidt, 1996), 201, 207–10.

40 Schlegel, *Philosophische Vorlesungen*, 239.

41 Schlegel, *Philosophische Vorlesungen*, 252–3.

42 Schlegel, *Über die Sprache und Weisheit*, 106–7. Translation in Schlegel, *On the Language and Wisdom of the Indians*, trans. E.J. Millington, 473.

43 Schlegel, *Über die Sprache und Weisheit*, 141.

44 See Messlin, *Antike und Moderne*, 261.
45 Schlegel, *Über die Sprache und Weisheit*, 200.
46 Messlin, *Antike und Moderne*, 281.
47 Schlegel, "Geschichte der alten und neuen Literatur," 114–15.
48 Schlegel, "Philosophische Vorlesungen insbesondere über Philosophie der Sprache und des Wortes" (1828–9), in *Kritische Friedrich-Schlegel-Ausgabe*, ed. Ernst Behler, vol. 10 (Munich: Ferdinand Schöningh, 1969), 373.
49 Schlegel, "Philosophie der Sprache und des Wortes," 361–2.
50 Schlegel, "Philosophie der Sprache und des Wortes," 365.
51 Johann Arnold Kanne, *Leben und aus dem Leben merkwürdiger und erweckter Christen*, vol. 1 (Bamberg: Carl Friedrich Kunz, 1816), xxxiv.
52 Kanne, *Leben*, vol. 1, 273.
53 Kanne, *Leben*, 280.
54 George Williamson, *The Longing for Myth in Germany: Religion and Aesthetic Culture from Romanticism to Nietzsche* (Chicago: University of Chicago Press, 2004), 37.
55 Dieter Schrey, *Mythos und Geschichte bei Johann Arnold Kanne und in der romantischen Mythoogie* (Tübingen: Max Niemeyer Verlag, 1969), 36ff.
56 Schrey, *Mythos und Geschichte bei Johann Arnold Kanne*, 53.
57 Schrey, *Mythos und Geschichte bei Johann Arnold Kanne*, 58.
58 Schrey, *Mythos und Geschichte bei Johann Arnold Kanne*, 43–5.
59 Kanne, *Leben*, 278.
60 F.W.J. Schelling, *Philosophy of Art*, trans. D. W. Stott (Minneapolis: University of Minnesota Press, 1989), 157.
61 Johann Jakob Wagner, *System der Idealphilosophie* (Leipzig: Breitkopf und Härtel, 1804), 111–13.
62 See the discussion in J.J. Wagner, *Organon der menschlichen Erkennitniss* (Ulm: P.L. Adam's Verlags-Buchhandlung, 1851), xxvi.
63 J.J. Wagner, *Ideen zu einer allgemeinen Mythologie der alten Welt* (Frankfurt: Andreäische Buchhandlung, 1808), 65.
64 Kanne, *Erste Urkunden*, 72.
65 Schrey, *Mythos und Geschichte bei Johann Arnold Kanne*, 133.
66 Kanne, *Erste Urkunden*, 47.
67 Stefan Willer, *Poetik der Etymologie: Texturen sprachlichen Wissens in der Romantik* (Berlin: Akademie Verlag, 2003), 204.
68 Kanne, *Erste Urkunden*, 47.
69 Willer, *Poetik der Etymologie*, 134.
70 Kanne, *Erste Urkunden*, 48.
71 Cited in Schrey, *Mythos und Geschichte bei Johann Arnold Kanne*, 212.
72 Patrick M. Erben, *A Harmony of the Spirits: Translation and the Language of Community in Early Pennsylvania* (Durham: University of North Carolina Press, 2012), 21ff.

73 Stam, *Inquiries into the Origin of Language*, 205–6.

74 Kanne's review of *"S'cheik Mahommad Fani's Dabistan, oder von der Religion der ältesten Farsen* ... ins Deutsche übersetzt von F.V. Dalberg," in *Uebersicht der neuesten Literatur* 18 (1809), 72.

75 Cited in Neumann, *Johann Arnold Kanne*, 57.

76 Paola Mayer, *Jena Romanticism and its Appropriation of Jakob Böhme: Theosophy-Hagiography-Literature* (Montreal: McGill-Queen's University Press, 1999), 209.

77 Schrey, *Mythos und Geschichte bei Johann Arnold Kanne*, 215.

78 Johann Arnold Kanne, *Pantheum der Aeltesten Naturphilosophie, die Religion aller Völker* (Tübingen: Cotta, 1811), 11.

79 Kanne's review of *"S'cheik Mahommad Fani's Dabistan,"* 72.

80 Kanne, *Pantheum*, 13.

81 Kanne, *Pantheum*, 2.

82 Kanne, *Leben*, 290.

83 Kanne, "Das Panglossium Manuskript," cited in Neumann, *Johann Arnold Kanne*, 77–9.

84 F.W.J. Schelling, *Historical-critical Introduction to the Philosophy of Mythology*, trans. Mason Richey and Markus Zisselberger (Albany: SUNY Press, 2007), 156.

85 Willer, *Poetik der Etymologie*, 169.

86 Kanne, *Leben* 278.

87 Kanne, *Leben*, 292.

88 Cited in Hartmut Bobzin and Bernhard Forssman, "Orientalistik und Indogermanistik," in *250 Jahre Friedrich-Alexander-Universität-Erlangen-Nürnberg-Festschrift*, ed. Henning Kössler (Erlangen: Universität-Bibliothek, 1993), 478.

89 Jean Paul, "Überchristenthum. Wider-Kanne" (1817–1823), in *Jean Pauls Sämtliche Werke: historisch-kritische Ausgabe*, ed. Eduard Berend and Helmut Pfotenhauer, vol. 4 (Weimar: Hermann Böhlaus Nachfolger, 1934), 47ff.

90 Johann Arnold Kanne, *Christus im alten Testament: Untersuchungen über die Vorbilder und Messianischen Stellen*, vol. 2 (Nuremburg: Riegel und Mießner, 1818), xxvi.

91 Kanne, *Christus*, vol. 2, xxviii–xxxix.

92 Kanne, *Christus*, vol. 1 (1818), vi, 49–50.

93 Friedrich Rückert to Jean Paul Friedrich Richter, 29 June 1811, in Friedrich Rückert, *Briefe*, ed. Rüdiger Rückert, vol. 1, 14–15.

94 Anton von Preußen [J.A. Kanne], *Zwanzig kritische Paragraphen und historische Noten über den Text der Zeit* (Leipzig: Weygand'schen Buchhandlung, 1814), 29–32.

95 Friedrich Rückert, *Gedichte von Rom und andere Texte der Jahre 1817–1818*, ed. Claudia Wiener (Göttingen: Wallstein, 2000), 248.

96 Helmut Prang, *Geist und Form der Sprache* (Wiesbaden: O. Harrassowitz, 1963), 19.

97 Claudia Wiener, *Friedrich Rückerts 'De idea philologiae' als dichtungstheoretische Schrift und Lebensprogramm* (Schweinfurt: Stadtarchiv Schweinfurt, 1994), 46–7.

98 Cited in Amélie Sohr, *Heinrich Rückert in seinem Leben und Wirken* (Weimar: Hermnn Böhlau, 1880), 60.

99 H. Rückert, "Friedrich Rückert als Gelehrter," in *Die Grenzboten: Zeitschrift für Politik, Literatur und Kunst* 25, no. 4 (1866), 135. See also Leopold Magon, *Der Junge Rückert: Sein Leben und Schaffen* (Halle: Max Niemeyer, 1914), 16.

100 H. Rückert, "Friedrich Rückert als Gelehrter," 135.

101 Suzanne Marchand, *German Orientalism in the Age of Empire: Religion, Race, and Scholarship* (Cambridge: Cambridge University Press, 2009), 70.

102 F. Rückert, *Briefe*, vol. 2, 1310.

103 F. Rückert, "Bau der Welt," in *Gesammelte Gedichte von Friedrich Rückert*, vol. 2, (Erlangen: Carl Heyder, 1839), 335–6.

104 Friedrich Rückert, "Dissertatio philologico-philosophica de idea philologiae" (1811), in Claudia Wiener, *Friedrich Rückerts 'De idea philologiae' als dichtungstheoretische Schrift und Lebensprogramm* (Schweinfurt: Stadtarchiv Schweinfurt, 1994), 219.

105 F. Rückert, "Dissertatio," ed. Wiener, 183.

106 H. Rückert, "Friedrich Rückert als Gelehrter," 134 and Prang, *Geist und Form der Sprache*, 25.

107 F. Rückert, "Dissertatio," ed. Wiener, 175.

108 F. Rückert, "Dissertatio," ed. Wiener, 205.

109 See Wiener, 73.

110 F. Rückert, "Dissertatio," ed. Wiener, 207.

111 F. Rückert, "Dissertatio," ed. Wiener, 191.

112 F. Rückert, "Dissertatio," ed. Wiener, 191.

113 Willer, *Poetik der Etymologie*, 172–3.

114 Wiener, 82.

115 F. Rückert, "Dissertatio," ed. Wiener, 181.

116 Willer, *Poetik der Etymologie*, 176.

117 Cited in Schrey, *Mythos und Geschichte bei Johann Arnold Kanne*, 205.

118 Prang, *Geist und Form der Sprache*, 22.

119 Wagner, *Idealphilosophie*, 113, 111.

120 F. Rückert, "Dissertatio," ed. Wiener, 207.

121 F. Rückert, "Dissertatio," ed. Wiener, 213.

122 Friedrich Rückert to Christian Stockmar, 8 March 1813, in *Zeitgedichte und andere Texte der Jahre 1813–1816*, ed. Claudia Wiener and Rudolf Kreutner (Göttingen: Wallstein Verlag, 2009), 669.

123 F. Rückert, "Geharnischte Sonette," in *Friedrich Rückerts gesammelte poetische Werke in zwölf Bänden*, vol. 1 (Frankfurt: J.D. Sauerländer, 1882), 5.

124 E. Groß, "Friedrich Rückerts politisches Glaubensbekenntnis," in *Rückert im Spiegel seiner Zeitgenossen*, 171. See also *Zeitgedichte*, ed. Wiener and Kreutner, 21–2.

125 Prang, *Geist und Form der Sprache*, 129.

126 H. Rückert, "Friedrich Rückert als Gelehrter," 149.

127 *200 Jahre Friedrich Rückert, 1788–1866: Dichter und Gelehrte. Katalog der Ausstellung*, ed. J. Erdmann (Coburg: Druckhaus Neue Presse Coburg, 1988), 22.

128 F. Rückert, "Deutsches Künstlerfest in Rom (1818)," in *Frauentaschenbuch für das Jahr 1823* (Nuremberg: J.L. Schrag), 5.

129 Friedrich Rückert, "Ermuthigung zur Uebersetzung der Hamasa," in *Musenalmanach für das Jahr 1831*, 285.

130 F. Rückert, *Briefe*, vol. 1, 380.

131 See Friedrich Rückert to wife Luise, 24 June 1821, in *Briefe*, vol. 1, 184.

132 Cited in Sohr, *Heinrich Rückert in seinem Leben und Wirken*, 61.

133 Cited in Sohr, *Heinrich Rückert in seinem Leben und Wirken*, 61–2.

134 Cited in Sohr, *Heinrich Rückert in seinem Leben und Wirken*, 53.

135 Prang, *Geist und Form der Sprache*, 167–8.

136 See "Nachrichten von Friedrich Rückerts Leben," in *Gesammelte poetische Werke*, vol. 12, 443.

137 Cited in Sohr, *Heinrich Rückert in seinem Leben und Wirken*, 60.

138 Cited in Prang, *Geist und Form der Sprache*, 216.

139 Friedrich Rückert to Joseph Kopf, 2 February 1842, in *Briefe*, vol. 2, 843.

140 Friedrich Rückert to wife Luise, 21 December 1843, in *Briefe*, vol. 2, 938.

141 Friedrich Rückert to son Heinrich, 28 July 1842, in *Briefe*, vol. 2, 869.

142 F. Rückert, *Liedertagebuch: Werke der Jahre 1850–1851*, ed. R. Kreutner and H. Wollschläger, vol. 1 (Göttingen: Wallstein Verlag, 2003), 298.

143 F. Rückert, *Liedertagebuch*, 298.

144 Paul de Lagarde, "Erinnerungen an Friedrich Rückert," in *Ausgewählte Schriften*, ed. P. Fischer (Munich: J.F. Lehmann, 1934), 49.

145 Williamson, *Longing for Myth in Germany*, 136.

146 See Jan Vanden Heuvel, *A German Life in the Age of Revolution: Joseph Görres, 1776–1848* (Washington: Catholic University of America Press, 2001).

147 Leonardo Lotito, "Die Allegorie des Überschwenglichen: Überlegungen über die Interpretation des Schellingschen Absoluten und des Creuzerschen Symbols im Denken Görres' (1805–1810)," in *Görres Studien: Festschrift zum 150. Todesahr von Joseph von Görres*, ed. Harald Dickerhof (Munich: Schöningh, 1999), 94; Georg Bürke, *Vom Mythos zur Mystik* (Einsiedeln: Johannes Verlag, 1958), 20–4.

148 Joseph Görres, *Glauben und Wissen* (Munich: Scherersche Kunst- und Buchhndlung, 1805), 19.

149 Lotito, "Die Allegorie des Überschwenglichen," 91–3.

150 Görres, *Glauben und Wissen*, 18.
151 Görres, *Glauben und Wissen*, 7.
152 Görres, *Glauben und Wissen*, 11.
153 Görres, *Glauben und Wissen*, 141.
154 See Bürke, *Vom Mythos zur Mystik*.
155 Görres, *Aphorismen über die Kunst* (Koblenz: Lassaulx, 1802), 26.
156 Görres, *Aphorismen über die Kunst*, 47.
157 See Williamson, *Longing for Myth in Germany*, 129.
158 Joseph Görres, "Religion in der Geschichte: Wachstum der Historie," in *Studien*, ed. Daub and Creuzer, vol. 3 (1807), 353–4.
159 Görres, "Wachstum der Historie," 316.
160 Görres, "Wachstum der Historie," 420.
161 See Wolfgang Bopp, *Görres und der Mythos* (Tübingen: Fotodruck Präzis Barvara v. Spangenberg, 1974), 185.
162 Friedrich Creuzer, *Symbolik und Mythologie der alten Völker, besonders der Griechen*, vol. 1 (Leipzig: Karl Wilhlem Leske, 1810), 62–3.
163 Creuzer, *Symbolik und Mythologie*, vol. 1, 61.
164 Creuzer, *Symbolik und Mythologie*, vol. 1, 63.
165 Creuzer, *Symbolik und Mythologie*, vol. 1, 109.
166 Creuzer, *Symbolik und Mythologie*, vol. 1, 42.
167 Görres, *Mythengeschichte*, xxvi.
168 Bopp, *Görres*, 154.
169 Görres, *Mythengeschichte*, 3.
170 Görres, *Mythengeschichte*, 1.
171 Görres, *Mythengeschichte*, 13.
172 Görres, *Mythengeschichte*, 2.
173 Görres, *Mythengeschichte*, 15–16.
174 Peter Michelson, "Der Sog der Myth. Zu Görres' Mythengeschichte," in *Heidelberg im säkularen Umbruch*, ed. Friedrich Strack (Stuttgart, 1987): 444–65.
175 Gershon Greenberg, "Religionswissenschaft and Early Reform Jewish Thought: Samuel Hirsch and David Einhorn," in *Modern Judaism and Historical Consciousness: Identities, Encounters, Perspectives*, ed. Andreas Gotzmann and Christian Wiese (Boston: Brill, 2007), 133.
176 See Bopp, *Görres*, 185ff.

4. Revelation in Nature from Physicotheology to G.H. Schubert

1 Friedrich Wilhelm Joseph Schelling, *Philosophical Investigations into the Essence of Human Freedom*, trans. Jeff Love and Johannes Schmidt (Albany: SUNY Press, 2006), 77.

2   Aleida Assmann, "Schriftspekulationen und Sprachutopien in Antike und
    früher Neuzeit," in *Kabbala und Romantik*, ed. Eveline Goodman-Thau, Gert
    Mattenklott, and Christoph Schulte (Tübingen: Niemeyer, 1994), 32.

3   John H. Zammito, *The Gestation of German Biology: Philosophy and Physiology
    from Stahl to Schelling* (Chicago: Chicago University Press, 2018), 2–3.

4   Martin J.S. Rudwick, "The Shape and Meaning of Earth History," in
    *God and Nature: Historical Essays on the Encounter between Christianity
    and Science*, ed. David C. Lindberg and Ronald L. Numbers (Berkeley:
    Univerity of California Press, 1986), 303–4.

5   See Sibelle Mischer, *Der verschlungene Zug der Seele: Natur, Organismus und
    Entwicklung bei Schelling, Steffens und Oken* (Würzburg: Königshausen &
    Neumann, 1997).

6   Nicolas A. Rupke, "Geology and Paleontology," in *Science and Religion:
    A Historical Introduction*, ed. Gary B. Ferngren (Baltimore: Johns Hopkins
    University Press, 2002), 190–1.

7   See Jonathan Sheehan, *The Enlightenment Bible: Translation, Scholarship,
    Culture* (Princeton: Princeton University Press, 2005).

8   Richard G. Olson, *Science and Religion, 1450–1900: From Copernicus to
    Darwin* (Westport, CT: Greenwood Press, 2004), 137–8, 167.

9   Frederick Gregory, *Nature Lost? Natural Science and the German Theological
    Traditions of the Nineteenth Century* (Cambridge: Harvard University Press,
    1992), 15.

10 Gregory, *Nature Lost*, 114.

11 Marcus Hellyer, *Catholic Physics: Jesuit Natural Philosophy in Early Modern
    Germany* (Notre Dame: University of Notre Dame Press, 2005), 218.

12 See Steven Nadler, "'Whatever is, is in God': Substance and Things in
    Spinoza's Metaphysics," in *Interpreting Spinoza: Critical Essays*, ed. Charlie
    Huenemann (Cambridge: Cambridge University Press, 2008), 65–70.

13 See Hong Han-Ding, *Spinoza und die deutsche Philosophie. Eine Untersuchung
    zur metaphysischen Wirkungsgeschichte des Spinozismus in Deutschland*
    (Aalen, Scientia Verlag, 1989), 35ff.

14 See Han-Ding, *Spinoza und die deutsche Philosophie*, 28ff.

15 Gottfried Wilhelm Leibniz, *Discourse on Metaphysics*, trans. George R.
    Montgomery (Chicago: Open Court Publishing Company, 1902), 4.

16 Lloyd Strickland, ed., *Gottfried Wilhelm Leibniz's Monadology: A New
    Translation and Guide* (Edinburgh: Edinburgh University Press, 2014), 99.

17 Christina Mercer, *Leibniz's Metaphysics: Its Origins and Development*
    (Cambridge: Cambridge University Press, 2001), 453ff.

18 Christian Wolff, *Natürliche Gottesgelahrtheit*, trans. Gottlieb Friedrich
    Hagen, vol. 1 (Halle: Renger, 1742), 1.

19 Christian Wolff, *Vernünfftige Gedancken von den Absichten der natürlichen Dinge*
    (Frankfurt: Rengerische Buchhandlung, 1737), unpaginated 1723 foreword.

20 John O. Reiss, *Not by Design: Retiring Darwin's Watchmaker* (Berkeley: University of California Press, 2009), 75.
21 Christian Wolff, *Preliminary Discourse on Philosophy in General*, trans. Richard J. Blackwell (Indianapolis: Bobbs-Merrill, 1963), 54.
22 Wolff, *Preliminary Discourse*, 51.
23 See Alexander Baumgarten, *Metaphysics. A Critical Translation with Kant's Elucidations, Selected Notes, and Related Materials*, trans. and ed. Courtney D. Fugate and John Hymers (London: Bloomsbury, 2013).
24 Immanuel Kant, *Universal Natural History and Theory of the Heavens*, trans. Stanley L. Jaki (Edinburgh: Scottish Academic Press, 1981), 86.
25 Immanuel Kant, *The One Possible Basis for a Demonstration of the Existence of God*, trans. Gordon Treash (Lincoln: University of Nebraska Press, 1979) 49.
26 See Gordon Treash, "Introduction," in Kant, *The One Possible Basis*, 10ff.
27 Kant, *One Possible Basis*, 233, 235.
28 Kant, *One Possible Basis*, 159.
29 Kant, *One Possible Basis*, 149.
30 Kant, *One Possible Basis*, 119.
31 Kant, *One Possible Basis*, 235.
32 See John H. Zammito, *The Gestation of German Biology: Philosophy and Physiology from Stahl to Schelling* (Chicago: Chicago University Press, 2018), 107–14.
33 Zammito, 132.
34 On the latter, see Hans Peter Reill, "Between Mechanism and Hermeticism: Nature and Science in the Late Enlightenment," in *Frühe Neuzeit, Frühe Moderne? Forschungen zur Vielschichtigkeit von Übergangsprozessen*, ed. Rudolf Vierhaus (Göttingen: Vandenhoeck & Ruprecht, 1992): 393–421.
35 On this, see Mischer, *Der verschlungene Zug der Seele*, 64ff.
36 See Zammito, 29–32.
37 See Julian Jaynes and William Woodward, "In the Shadow of the Enlightenment: Reimarus against the Epicureans," *Journal of the History of the Behavioral Sciences* 10 (1974), 3–15, 144–59, and Zammito, 134ff.
38 Hermann Samuel Reimarus, *Abhandlungen von den vornehmsten Wahrheiten der natürlichen Religion* (Carl Ernst Bohn, 1791), 151.
39 Reimarus, *Abhandlungen*, 163.
40 Reimarus, *Abhandlungen*, 160.
41 Jaynes and Woodward, "In the Shadow of the Enlightenment," 144ff.
42 Immanuel Kant, *Immanuel Kant's Critique of Pure Reason*, trans. Norman Kemp Smith (London: Macmillan, 1950), 500.
43 Kant, *Critique of Pure Reason*, 523–4.
44 Immanuel Kant, *Critique of Judgement*, trans. James Creed Meredith, ed. Nicholas Walker (Oxford: Oxford University Press, 2009), 19.

45 Paul Guyer, *Knowledge, Reason, and Taste: Kant's Response to Hume* (Princeton: Princeton University Press, 2008), 207–9.

46 Kant, *Critique of Judgement*, 228.

47 Kant, *Critique of Judgement*, 203.

48 Kant, *Critique of Judgement*, 228.

49 Kant, *Critique of Judgement*, 266.

50 See Paul Guyer, "From Nature to Morality: Kant's New Argument in the 'Critique of Teleological Judgment,'" in *Kant's System of Nature and Freedom: Selected Essays* (Oxford: Clarendon Press, 2005).

51 Kant, *Critique of Judgement*, 267.

52 Kant, *Critique of Judgement*, 307.

53 See Reed Winegar, "Kant and Hutcheson on Aesthetics and Teleology," in *Kant and the Scottish Enlightenment*, ed. Elizabeth Robinson and Chris W. Surprenant (New York: Taylor and Francis, 2017), 84–5.

54 Friedrich Wilhelm Joseph Schelling, "Introduction to the Outline of a System of the Philosophy of Nature, or On the Concept of Speculative Physics and the Internal Organization of a System of this Science" (1799), in F.W.J. Schelling, *First Outline of a System of the Philosophy of Nature*, trans. Keither R. Peterson (Albany: SUNY Press, 2004), 194.

55 Friedrich Wilhelm Joseph Schelling, *Ideas for a Philosophy of Nature*, trans. Errol E. Harris and Peter Heath (Cambridge: Cambridge University Press, 1988), 34.

56 Schelling, *Ideas*, 33–4.

57 Han-Ding, *Spinoza und die deutsche Philosophie*, 145.

58 Schelling, *First Outline*, 14.

59 Schelling, *First Outline*, 17.

60 Schelling, "Outline of a System," 194.

61 Schelling, "Outline of a System," 228.

62 Schelling, "Outline of a System," 198.

63 Schelling, *Ideas*, 42.

64 Schelling, *Ideas*, 50.

65 Bruce Matthews, *Schelling's Organic Form of Philosophy: Life as the Schema of Freedom* (Albany: SUNY Press, 2011), 43, 66.

66 Friedrich Immanuel Niethammer, *Ueber den Versuch einer Kritik aller Offenbarung* (Jena: C.H. Cuno's Erben, 1792). See Ian Balfour, "Excursus on Revelations, Representation, and Religion in the Age of German Idealism," in Ian Balfour, *The Rhetoric of Romantic Prophecy* (Palo Alto: Stanford University Press, 2002), 233–9.

67 Friedrich Wilhelm Joseph Schelling, "Ueber Offenbarung und Volksunterricht" (1798), in F.W.J. von Schelling, *Sämmtliche Werke* I, vol. 1 (Stuttgart: J.G. Cotta, 1856), 476.

68 Schelling, "Offenbarung und Volksunterricht," 475.

69 Schelling, "Offenbarung und Volksunterricht," 481.
70 Schelling, *Von der Weltseele: Eine Hypothese der höhern Physik zur Erklärung des allgemeinen Organismus* (Hamburg: Friedrich Perthes, 1798), iv.
71 Schelling, *Weltseele*, 195.
72 Schelling, *Weltseele*, 11.
73 Schelling, *Weltseele*, 18.
74 Schelling, *Weltseele*, 174.
75 Schelling, *Weltseele*, 235.
76 Heinrich Heine, *On the History of Religion and Philosophy in Germany*, ed. Terry Pinkard (Cambridge: Cambridge University Press, 2007), 58.
77 Georges Cuvier, "Nature," in *Dictionnaire des Sciences Naturelles*, vol. 34 (Strasbourg: L.G. Levrault, 1825), 267.
78 Toby A. Appel, *Cuvier-Geoffrey Debate: French Biology in the Decades before Darwin* (New York: Oxford University Press, 1987), 107.
79 Bradley Herling, *The German Gita: Hermeneutics and Discipline in the German Reception of Indian Thought, 1778–1831* (New York: Routledge, 2006), 91.
80 Dan Charly Christensen, *Hans Christian Ørsted: Reading Nature's Mind* (Oxford: Oxford University Press, 2013), 274–6.
81 Williamson, *Longing for Myth in Germany*, 46.
82 Christensen, *Hans Christian Ørsted*, 274–6.
83 Schelling, *Von der Weltseele, eine Hypothese der höheren Physik* (Hamburg: Friedrich Perthes, 1806), xxiv.
84 Schelling, *Weltseele* (1806), l–lii.
85 Johann Philipp Gabler, "Einleitung" to Eichhorn, *Urgeschichte*, vol. 1 (Altdorf: Monath und Kußler, 1790), 135.
86 Gabler, "Einleitung," 45.
87 Gabler in *Urgeschichte*, vol. 2 (1792), 587. See also David Julius Pott, *Moses und David keine Geologen: Ein Gegenstück zu Hen. Kirwan's geologischen Versuchen* (Berlin: Friedrich Nicolai, 1799).
88 Charles Dupuis, *Origine de tous les cultes: ou, Religion universelle*, vol. 1 (Paris: Louis Rosier, 1835), xxvi.
89 Dupuis, *Origine*, vol. 1, xxvi.
90 See Jonathan Z. Smith, *Drudgery Divine: On the Comparison of Early Christianities and the Religions of Late Antiquity* (Chicago, 1990), 29–30.
91 Charles Dupuis, *Mémoire explicative du zodique chronologique et mythologique* (Paris: Courcier, 1806), 79.
92 Dupuis, *Mémoire explicative*, 86.
93 Dupuis, *Mémoire explicative*, 65.
94 Dupuis, *Mémoire explicative*, 79.
95 Dupuis, *Mémoire explicative*, 62.
96 Buchwald and Josefowicz, 2.

97 Buchwald and Josefowicz, 57.

98 Charles Dupuis, *Mémoire sur l'origine des constellations, et sur l'explication de la fable par le moyen de l'astronomie* (Paris: Desaint, 1781), 43.

99 Dupuis, *Mémoire sur l'origine des constellations*, 4–5.

100 Buchwald and Josefowicz, 59.

101 See Creuzer's tribute to Dupuis in *Symbolik und Mythologie der alten Völker, besonders der Griechen*, vol. 1, 2nd ed. (Leipzig: Heyer und Leske, 1819), 237–8.

102 Friedrich Creuzer, *Symbolik und Mythologie*, vol. 1 (Leipzig: Karl Wilhelm Leske, 1810), 7.

103 Creuzer, *Symbolik*, vol. 1, 88.

104 Creuzer, *Symbolik*, vol. 1, 62.

105 Creuzer, *Symbolik*, vol. 1, 42–3.

106 Creuzer, *Symbolik*, vol. 1, 92.

107 Creuzer, *Symbolik*, vol. 1, 8.

108 Creuzer, *Symbolik*, vol. 1, 85.

109 Creuzer, *Symbolik*, vol. 1, 75.

110 Creuzer, *Symbolik*, vol. 1, 7.

111 Creuzer, *Symbolik*, vol. 1 (1819), 586ff.

112 Williamson, *Longing for Myth in Germany*, 127.

113 Johann Gottfried Herder, "Gott: Einige Gespräche" (1787), in *Sämmtliche Werke*, vol 16 (Berlin: Weidmannsche Buchhandlung, 1887), 403.

114 "Nekrolog: G.H. Schubert," in *Der Bayerische Landbote* 190 (8 July 1860) (Munich), 759.

115 Gotthilf Heinrich Schubert, *Der Erwerb aus einem Vergangenen und die Erwartungen von einem zukünftigen Leben*, vol. 1 (Erlangen: J.J. Palm and E. Enke, 1854), 208.

116 Schubert, *Erwerb*, vol. 1, 208.

117 Schubert, *Erwerb*, vol. 1, 267–8.

118 Schubert, *Erwerb*, vol. 1, 285.

119 Schubert, *Erwerb*, vol. 1, 267–8.

120 Schubert, *Erwerb*, vol. 1, 266.

121 Miklós Vassányi, *Anima Mundi: The Rise of the World Soul Theory in Modern German Philosophy*, 318.

122 Herder, "Gott: Einige Gespräche," 453, 451.

123 See Chr. J. Kraus, "Ueber den Pantheismus," in *Vermischte Schriften* (Königsberg, 1812) vol. 5, 1–50.

124 Herder, "Ideen zur Philosophie der Geschichte der Menschheit," in *Werke in zehn Bänden*, ed. Martin Bollacher, vol. 6 (Frankfurt: Deutscher Klassiker Verlag, 1989), 17.

125 Herling, *German Gita*, 120.

126 Helmut Zander, *Geschichte der Seelenwanderung in Europa: Alternative religiöse Traditionen von der Antike bis heute* (Darmstadt: Wissenschaftliche Buchgesellschaft, 1999), 356–60.

127 Schubert, *Erwerb*, vol. 1, 271–2.

128 Schubert to Emil Herder, 29 August 1801, in *Gottfried Heinrich Schubert in seinen Briefen: Ein Lebensbild*, ed. G. Nathanael Bonwetsch (Stuttgart: C. Belser, 1918), 54.

129 Aldabert Elschenbroich, *Romantische Sehnsucht und Kosmogonie: Eine Studie zu Gotthilf Heinrich Schuberts 'Geschichte der Seele' und deren Stellung in der deutschen Spätromantik* (Tübingen: Max Niemeyer Verlag, 1971), 53, 21.

130 Margarete Kohlenbach, "Mesmerism," in *Encyclopedia of the Romantic Era*, ed. Christopher John Murray, vol. 2 (New York: Routledge, 2004), 735.

131 Volker Roelcke, "Kabbala und Medizin der Romantik: Gotthilf Heinrich Schubert," in *Kabbala und Romantik*, 131.

132 Schubert, *Erwerb*, vol. 2 (1855), 29.

133 Schubert, *Erwerb*, vol. 2, 112.

134 Martin Buntau, *Die Genesis der Geologie als Wissenschaft* (Berlin: Akademie-Verlag, 1984), 93.

135 Anthony Hallam, *Great Geological Controversies* (Oxford: Oxford University Press, 1983), 23.

136 Schubert, *Erwerb*, vol. 2, 143.

137 Schubert, *Erwerb*, vol. 2 (1854), 229.

138 Adam Heinrich Müller, *Die Elemente der Staatskunst: Oeffentliche Vorlesungen*, vol. 2 (Jena: Gustav Fischer, 1922), 234.

139 Schubert, *Erwerb*, vol. 2, 245. See also Heike Petermann, *Gotthilf Heinrich Schubert: Die Naturgeschichte als bestimmendes Element* (Erlangen: Verlag Palm & Enke, 2008), 195.

140 Frederick Gregory, "Gottfried Heinrich Schubert and the Dark Side of Natural Science," in *Internationale Zeitschrift für Geschichte und Ethik der Naturwissenschaften, Technik, und Medizin* 3 (1995), 255.

141 See Joseph Ennemoser, *Der Magnetismus im Verhältnisse zur Natur und Religion* (Stuttgart: Cotta, 1842).

142 Gotthilf Heinrich Schubert, *Ansichten von der Nachtseite der Naturwissenschaft* (Dresden: Arnoldsche Buchhnadlung, 1808), 2.

143 Schubert, *Erwerb* vol. 2, 240.

144 Schubert, *Erwerb* vol. 2, (1855), 400.

145 Schubert, *Nachtseite*, 3.

146 Schubert, *Nachtseite*, 5.

147 Schubert, *Nachtseite*, 8.

148 Schubert, *Nachtseite*, 63.

149 Schubert, *Nachtseite*, 383.

150 Schubert, *Nachtseite*, 287.

151 Theodore Ziolkowski, *Dresdner Romantik: Politik und Harmonie* (Heidelberg: Universitätsverlag Winter, 2010), 85.

152 Schubert, *Erwerb*, vol. 2, 232.

153 August Tholuck, "Ueber die Wunder der katholischen Kirche und insbesondere über das Verhältniß dieser und der biblischen Wunder zu den Erscheinungen des Magnetismus und Somnambulismus," in *Vermischte Schriften größtentheils apologetischen Inhalts*, vol. 1 (Hamburg: Perthes, 1839), 58.

154 Roelcke, "Kabbala und Medizin der Romantik," 134.

155 A. Assmann, "Schriftspekulationen," 31ff.

156 Gotthilf Heinrich Schubert, *Die Symbolik des Traumes* (Heidelberg: Lambert Schneider, 1968), 55.

157 Schubert, *Symbolik*, 29.

158 Schubert, *Symbolik*, 23.

159 Matt Ffytche, *The Foundation of the Unconscious: Schelling, Freud, and the Birth of the Modern Psyche* (Cambridge: Cambridge University Press, 2012), 146ff.

160 Schubert, *Symbolik*, 2.

161 Schubert, *Symbolik*, 14.

162 Schubert, *Symbolik*, 24.

163 Schubert, *Symbolik*, 156.

164 Schubert, *Symbolik*, 29.

165 Schubert, *Erwerb*, vol. 2, 481.

166 Schubert to Köthe, 8 September 1814, in Bonwetsch, 180.

167 Gotthilf Friedrich Schubert, *Die Symbolik des Traumes mit einem Anhang: Die Sprache des Wachens*, ed. F.H. Ranke, 4th ed. (Leipzig: Brockhaus, 1862), 234.

168 Gerhard Sauder, "Nachwort," in *Symbolik des Traumes* (Heidelberg: Lambert Schneider, 1968), xx.

169 Tholuck, "Ueber die Wunder," 85ff.

170 Friedrich Wilhelm Kantzenbach, *Die Erweckungsbewegung: Studien zur Geschichte ihrer Entstehung und ersten Ausbreitung in Deutschland* (Neuendettelsau: Freimund-Verlag, 1957), 76.

171 Schubert to Gerhard von Kügelgen, 24 February 1812, in Bonwetsch, 265–6.

172 Schubert, *Erwerb*, vol. 3, 1, 166.

173 Schubert, *Erwerb*, vol. 3, 1, 168.

174 Schubert, *Erwerb*, vol. 3, 1, 311.

175 Schubert, *Erwerb*, vol. 3, 1, 316.

176 Schubert to Köthe, 26 February 1819, in Donwetsch, 207.

177 Schubert, *Erwerb*, vol. 3, 1, 555.

178 Warren Breckman, *Marx, the Young Hegelians, and the Origins of Modern Social Theory* (Cambridge: Cambridge University Press, 1999), 111.
179 Schubert, *Erwerb*, vol. 3, 1, 507.
180 Schubert, *Erwerb*, vol. 3, 1, 457.
181 Schubert, *Erwerb*, vol. 3, 1, 358.
182 Schubert, *Erwerb*, vol. 3, 1, 333.
183 Schubert, *Erwerb*, vol. 3, 1, 476.
184 Schubert to Marie von Kügelgen, 5 June 1818, in Bonwetsch, 299.
185 Schubert, *Erwerb*, vol. 1, 18.
186 Richard G. Olson, *Science and Religion, 1450–1900: From Copernicus to Darwin* (Westport, CT: Greenwood Press, 2004), 181–2.
187 Schubert, *Erwerb*, vol. 3, 490.
188 Gotthilf Heinrich Schubert, *Die Urwelt und die Fixsterne: Eine Zugabe zu den Ansichten von der Nachtseite der Naturwissenschaft* (Dresden: Arnoldische Buchhandlung, 1822), 14.
189 Heinrich Friedrich Link, *Die Urwelt und das Alterthum*, vol. 2 (Berlin: Ferdinand Dümmler, 1822), 1.
190 Link, *Urwelt*, vol. 1 (1821), 347.
191 J.G.J. Ballenstedt, *Die Urwelt oder Beweis von dem Daseyn und Untergange von mehr al seiner Vorwelt* (Quendlinburg: Gottfried Basse, 1818), 212.
192 Ballenstedt, *Die Urwelt*, 196, 198.
193 Ballenstedt, *Die Urwelt*, 161.
194 Ballenstedt, *Die Urwelt*, 149.
195 Schubert, *Naturgeschichte*, 454.
196 Gotthilf Heinrich Schubert, "Theologische Wahrheiten und geologische Ketzereien" in *Evangelische Kirchen-Zeitung* 93 (1851), 883–4.
197 Zöckler, *Geschichte der Beziehungen zwischen Theologie und Naturwissenschaft*, 528–9.
198 Martin J.S. Rudwick, "Biblical Flood and Geological Deluge: The Amicable Dissociation of Geology and Genesis," in *Geology and Religion: A History of Harmony and Hostility*, 105–9.
199 Schubert, "Theologische Wahrheiten," 877–9.
200 Schubert, *Naturgeschichte*, 333–4.
201 Schubert, *Urwelt*, 414.
202 Haim Goren, "Zieht hin und erforscht das Land," in *Die deutsche Palästinaforschung im 19. Jahrhundert*, trans. Antje Clara Naujoks (Göttingen: Wallstein Verlag, 2003).
203 Goren, "Zieht hin und erforscht das Land," 122.
204 Schubert, *Erwerb*, vol. 3, 659.
205 Schubert, "Theologische Wahrheiten," 888.
206 Petermann, *Gotthilf Heinrich Schubert*, 82.

5. The Philosophy of Revelation: Schleiermacher, Hegel, and Schelling

1 Karl Barth, *Protestant Theology in the Nineteenth Century: Its Background and History* (Valley Forge: Judson Press, 1973), 395–6.
2 See Johan Walker, "The Autonomy of Theology and the Impact of Idealism: From Hegel to Radical Orthodoxy," in *The Impact of Idealism: The Legacy of Post-Kantian German Thought*, ed. Nicholas Adams, vol. iv (Cambridge: Cambridge University Press, 2013), 169.
3 See Dale Schlitt, "German Idealism's Trinitarian Legacy: The Twentieth Century," in *The Impact of Idealism*, ed. Adams, vol. iv, 72–6; also Wolfhart Pannenberg, "Introduction," in *Revelation as History*, trans. David Granskou and ed. Pannenberg (New York: Macmillan, 1968), 4ff.
4 See Martin Wendte, "The Impact of Idealism on Christology: From Hegel to Tillich," in *The Impact of Idealism*, ed. Adams, vol. iv, 24–47.
5 G.W.F. Hegel, "Faith and Knowledge," in *Hegel: Theologian of the Spirit*, ed. Peter C. Hodgson (Minneapolis: Fortress Press, 1997), 73.
6 See Walter Jaeschke, "Um 1800 – Religionsphilosophische Sattelzeit der Moderne," in *Philosophisch-theologische Streitsachen: Pantheismusstreit – Atheismusstreit – Theismusstreit*, ed. Georg Essen and Christian Danz (Darmstadt: Wissenschaftliche Buchgesellschaft, 2012); and Walter Jaeschke, *Reason in Religion: The Foundations of Hegel's Philosophy of Religion* (Berkeley: University of California Press, 1990), 3ff.
7 Hegel, "Faith and Knowledge," 73.
8 Jaeschke, *Reason in Religion*, 100.
9 Jaeschke, *Reason in Religion*, 5.
10 Douglas Hedley and Chris Ryan, "Nineteenth-Century Philosophy of Religion: An Introduction," in *The History of Western Philosophy of Religion*, ed. Graham Oppy and Nick Trakakis, vol. 4 (Oxford: Oxford University Press, 2009).
11 Jaeschke, *Reason in Religion*, 105ff.
12 See Baláz M. Mezei, *Religion and Revelation after Auschwitz* (London: Bloomsbury, 2013), 94–5.
13 See John Edward Toews, *Hegelianism: The Path toward Dialectical Humanism, 1805–1841* (Cambridge; Cambridge University Press), 57.
14 Karl Barth, *Die Christliche Dogmatik im Entwurf*, ed. Gerhard Sauter, vol. 1 (Zürich: Theologischer Verlag Zürich, 1982).
15 Barth, *Christliche Dogmatik*, vol. 1, 402.
16 Barth, *Christliche Dogmatik*, vol. 1, 405.
17 Hans-Joachim Birkner, "Offenbarung in Schleiermacher's *Glaubenslehre*" (1956), in *Schleiermacher-Studien*, ed. Hermann Fischer (New York: Walter de Gruyter, 1996), 82, 86.

18 Friedrich Schleiermacher, *On Religion: Speeches to its Cultured Despisers*, ed. Richard Crouter (Cambridge: Cambridge University Press, 1988), 72.
19 Schleiermacher, *Speeches*, 24.
20 Schleiermacher, *Speeches*, 26.
21 Jan Rohls, *Protestantische Theologie der Neuzeit*, vol. 1 (Tübingen: Mohr Siebeck, 1997), 328.
22 See Richard B. Brandt, *The Philosophy of Schleiermacher: The Development of his Theory of Scientific and Religious Knowledge* (New York: Harper & Brothers, 1941), 88, and Richard Crouter, "Introduction," in *Friedrich Schleiermacher, On Religion: Speeches to its Cultured Despisers*, ed. Richard Crouter (Cambridge: Cambridge University Press, 1988), xxiv.
23 Crouter, "Introduction," xxxii.
24 Brandt, *Philosophy of Schleiermacher*, 193.
25 Toews, *Hegelianism*, 63.
26 Schleiermacher, *Speeches*, 49.
27 Schleiermacher, *Speeches*, 66.
28 Schleiermacher, *Speeches*, 83.
29 Schleiermacher, *Speeches*, 96.
30 Schleiermacher, *Speeches*, 99–100.
31 Schleiermacher, *Speeches*, 112.
32 Schleiermacher, *Speeches*, 104.
33 Theodore Ziolkowski, *Clio the Romantic Muse: Historicizing the Faculties in Germany* (Ithaca: Cornell University Press, 2004), 88.
34 Hermann Süskind, *Der Einfluss Schellings auf die Entwicklung von Schleiermachers System* (Tübingen: J.C.B. Mohr, 1909), 60–2.
35 Martin Redeker, *Schleiermacher: Life and Thought* (Philadelphia: Fortress Press, 1973), 77.
36 Brandt, *Philosophy of Schleiermacher*, 83.
37 Theodore Vial, "Schleiermacher and the State," in *The Cambridge Companion to Friedrich Schleiermacher*, ed. Jacqueline Mariña (Cambridge: Cambridge University Press, 2005), 273–5.
38 Robert M. Bigler, *The Politics of German Protestantism: The Rise of the Protestant Church Elite in Prussia, 1815–1828* (Berkeley: University of California Press, 1972), 29–31.
39 Vial, "Schleiermacher and the State," 280.
40 See Theodore Ziolkowski, *Clio the Romantic Muse: Historicizing the Faculties in Germany* (Ithaca: Cornell University Press, 2004), 93–6.
41 Johannes Zachhuber, *Theology as Science in Nineteenth-Century Germany: From F.C. Baur to Ernst Troeltsch* (Oxford: Oxford University Press, 2013), 16.
42 Toews, *Hegelianism*, 61.
43 Birkner, "Offenbarung in Schleiermacher's *Glaubenslehre*," 13.

44 Richard Crouter, *Friedrich Schleiermacher: Between Enlightenment and Romanticism* (Cambridge: Cambridge University Press, 2005), 88.

45 Friedrich Schleiermacher, *The Christian Faith*, ed. H.R. Mackintosh and J.S. Stewart (Edinburgh: T&T Clark, 1928), 17–18.

46 Schleiermacher, *Christian Faith*, 26.

47 Schleiermacher, *Christian Faith*, 36.

48 Schleiermacher, *Christian Faith*, 19.

49 Schleiermacher, *Christian Faith*, 51–2.

50 Schleiermacher, *Christian Faith*, 46.

51 Schleiermacher, *Christian Faith*, 72.

52 Schleiermacher, *Christian Faith*, 62.

53 Schleiermacher, *Christian Faith*, 443.

54 Schleiermacher, *Christian Faith*, 593, 597–8.

55 Toews, *Hegelianism*, 32–3.

56 Hegel, "Faith and Knowledge," 74.

57 Cyril O'Regan, *The Heterodox Hegel* (Albany: SUNY Press, 1994), 38.

58 Crouter, *Between Enlightenment and Romanticism*, 75.

59 Crouter, *Between Enlightenment and Romanticism*, 94.

60 G.W.F. Hegel, "Foreword to Hinrichs's Religion" (1822), in *Theologian of the Spirit*, ed. Hodgson, 156.

61 Hegel, "Foreword to Hinrichs's Religion," 161.

62 Hegel, "Foreword to Hinrichs's Religion," 163.

63 Hegel, "Foreword to Hinrichs's Religion," 166–7.

64 See O'Regan, *Heterodox Hegel*, 36–8, and Kipton Jensen, "The Principle of Protestantism: On Hegel's (Mis)Reading of Schleiermacher's Speeches," *Journal of the American Academy of Religion* 71, no. 3 (June 2003): 405–22.

65 Peter C. Hodgson, *Hegel and Christian Theology: A Reading of the Lectures on the Philosophy of Religion* (Oxford: Oxford University Press, 2005), 64–5.

66 O'Regan, *Heterodox Hegel*, 36.

67 Philip M. Merklinger, *Philosophy, Theology, and Hegel's Berlin Philosophy of Religion, 1821–1827* (Albany: SUNY Press, 1993), 4.

68 Toews, *Hegelianism*, 62–6.

69 See Josef Mader's discussion of the two meanings of revelation for Hegel in *Offenbarung als Selbstoffenbarung Gottes: Hegels Religionsphilosophie als Anstoß für ein neues Offenbarungsverständnis in der katholischen Theologie des 19. Jahrhunderts* (Münster: LIT Verlag, 2000), 27ff.

70 O'Regan, *Heterodox Hegel*, 29ff.

71 Hodgson, *Hegel and Christian Theology*, 16–17.

72 Douglas Hedley and Chris Ryan, "Nineteenth-Century Philosophy of Religion: An Introduction," in *Nineteenth-Century Philosophy of Religion*, ed. Graham Oppy and N. N. Trakakis (New York: Routledge, 2013), 11.

73 O'Regan, *Heterodox Hegel*, 48.

74 Hodgson, *Hegel and Christian Theology*, 43.
75 G.W.F. Hegel, *The Phenomenology of Spirit*, trans. A.V. Miller (Oxford: Clarendon Press, 1977), 411.
76 Hegel, *Phenomenology*, 460.
77 Hegel, *Phenomenology*, 459.
78 Hegel, *Phenomenology*, 461.
79 O'Regan, *Heterodox Hegel*, 66.
80 Crouter, *Between Enlightenment and Romanticism*, 95.
81 Mader, *Offenbarung als Selbstoffenbarung Gottes*, 26.
82 Toews, *Hegelianism*, 62–65.
83 Bigler, *Politics of German Protestantism*, 79–80.
84 Toews, *Hegelianism*, 61–2.
85 Crouter, *Between Enlightenment and Romanticism*, 83.
86 The discrepancies and alterations across Hegel's lectures on the philosophy of religion are assiduously detailed in G.W.F. Hegel, *Lectures on the Philosophy of Religion*, ed. Peter C. Hodgson, trans. R.F. Brown, P.C. Hodgson, and J.M. Stewart, 3 vols. (Berkeley: University of California Press, 1984).
87 Toews, *Hegelianism*, 85.
88 Hegel, *Lectures on the Philosophy of Religion*, vol. 1, 126.
89 Hegel, *Lectures on the Philosophy of Religion*, vol. 1, 119.
90 Hegel, *Lectures on the Philosophy of Religion*, vol. 1, 273.
91 See Hodgson, *Hegel and Christian Theology*, 110.
92 Michael H. Hoffheimer, "Race and Law in Hegel's Philosophy of Religion," in *Race and Racism in Modern Philosophy*, ed. Andrew Walls (Ithaca: Cornell University Press, 2005), 201.
93 Jaeschke, *Reason in Religion*, 269–71.
94 Hodgson, *Hegel and Christian Theology*, 240.
95 Jaeschke, *Reason in Religion*, 272; Hodgson, *Hegel and Christian Theology*, 212.
96 Hodgson, *Hegel and Christian Theology*, 206.
97 Hegel, *Lectures on the Philosophy of Religion*, vol. 2, 237–8.
98 Hegel, *Lectures on the Philosophy of Religion*, vol. 2, 272.
99 Hoffheimer, "Race and Law," 202.
100 Hegel, *Lectures on the Philosophy of Religion*, vol. 2, 240.
101 Hoffheimer, "Race and Law," 206–7.
102 Timo Slootweb, "Hegel's Philosophy of Judaism," in *Hegel's Philosophy of the Historical Religions*, ed. Bart Labuschagne and Timo Slootweg (Leiden: Brill, 2012), 128.
103 Hegel, *Lectures on the Philosophy of Religion*, vol. 3, 170–1.
104 Toews, *Hegelianism*, 141–2.
105 Hodgson, *Hegel and Christian Theology*, 93.

106 Hegel, *Lectures on the Philosophy of Religion*, vol. 3, 254–5.
107 See Mader, *Offenbarung als Selbstoffenbarung Gottes*, 27–9.
108 See Jaeschke, *Reason in Religion*, 352.
109 Toews, *Hegelianism*, 142ff.
110 Toews, *Hegelianism*, 155ff.
111 Jaeschke, *Reason in Religion*, 387.
112 Peter Steinacker, "Die Bedeutung der Philosophie Schellings für die Theologie Paul Tillichs," in *Studien zu einer Theologie der Moderne*, ed. Hermann Fischer (Frankfurt/Main: Athenäum, 1989), 42.
113 George S. Williamson, *The Longing for Myth in Germany: Religion and Aesthetic Culture from Romanticism to Nietzsche* (Chicago: Chicago University Press, 2004), 42.
114 Friedrich Wilhelm Joseph Schelling, "Ueber Offenbarung und Volksunterricht" (1798), in F.W.J. von Schelling, *Sämmtliche Werke* I, vol. 1 (Stuttgart: J.G. Cotta, 1856), 480–1.
115 Friedrich Wilhelm Joseph Schelling, *System of Transcendental Idealism* (1800), trans. Peter Heath, intro. Michael Vater (Charlottesville: University Press of Virginia, 1978), 211.
116 Andrew Bowie, *Schelling and Modern Philosophy: An Introduction* (London: Routledge, 1993), 45.
117 Emil L. Fackenheim, *The God Within: Kant, Schelling, and Historicity*, ed. John Burbidge (Toronto: University of Toronto Press, 1996), 67–8.
118 Schelling, *System of Transcendental Idealism*, 211–2.
119 Schelling, *System of Transcendental Idealism*, 223.
120 Schelling altered the medicine the physician prescribed for her. Thomas O'Meara, "Revelation in Schellings Lectures on Academic Studies," in *Los Comienzos filosoficos de Schelling*, ed. Ignacio Falgueras (Málaga: Servicio de Publicaciones de la Universidad de Mélaga, 1988), 122.
121 Vincent A. McCarthy, *Quest for a Philosophical Jesus: Christianity and Philosophy in Rousseau, Kant, Hegel, and Schelling* (Macon, GA: Mercer University Press, 1986), 179–80.
122 Friedrich Wilhelm Joseph Schelling, "Vorlesungen über die Methode des akademischen Studiums," in F.W.J. von Schelling, *Sämmtliche Werke* I, vol. 5 (Stuttgart: J.G. Cotta, 1859), 305.
123 Schelling, "Vorlesungen über die Methode," 299.
124 McCarthy, *Quest for a Philosophical Jesus*, 178–80.
125 Friedrich Wilhelm Joseph Schelling, *Philosophy and Religion* (1804), trans. Klaus Ottmann (Putnam CT: Spring Publications, 2010), 44.
126 Günter Zöller, "Church and State: Schelling's Political Philosophy of Religion," in *Interpreting Schelling: Critical Essays*, ed. Lra Ostaric (Cambridge: Cambridge University Press, 2013): 200–15.
127 See Essen and Danz, eds. *Philosophisch-theologische Streitsachen*.

128 Friedrich Wilhelm Joseph Schelling, *Ueber das Verhältniß der bildenden Künste zu der Natur* (Munich: Philipp Krüll, 1807), 5.
129 Schelling, *Ueber das Verhältniß*, 37.
130 F.H. Jacobi, "Von den göttlichen Dingen und ihrer Offenbarung" (1811), in *Religionsphilosophie und spekulative Theologie. Quellenband*, ed. Walter Jaeschke (Hamburg: Felix Meiner Verlag, 1994), 193.
131 McCarthy, *Quest for a Philosophical Jesus*, 181.
132 Friedrich Wilhelm Joseph Schelling, *Philosophical Investigations into the Essence of Human Freedom*, trans. Jeff Love and Johannes Schmidt (Albany: SUNY Press, 2006), 58.
133 Schelling, *Freedom*, 18.
134 Schelling, *Freedom*, 59.
135 Schelling, *Freedom*, 29.
136 F.W.J. Schelling, *The Ages of the World*, trans. Jason M. Wirth (Albany: SUNY Press, 2000), 16.
137 Xavier Tilliette, *Schelling: Biographie*, trans. Susanne Schaper (Stuttgart: Klett-Cotta, 2004), 330.
138 Edward Allen Beach, *The Potencies of God(s): Schelling's Philosophy of Mythology* (Albany: SUNY Press, 1994), 257.
139 Jan Vanden Heuvel, *A German Life in the Age of Revolution: Joseph Görres, 1776–1848* (Washington: Catholic University of America Press, 2001), 293ff.
140 Peter Koslowski, *Philosophien der Offenbarung: Antiker Gnostizismus, Franz von Baader, Schelling* (Paderborn: Ferdinand Schöningh, 2001).
141 Beach, *Potencies*, 79.
142 Bruce Matthews, "Introduction," in F.W.J. Schelling, *The Grounding of Positive Philosophy: The Berlin Lectures*, trans. Bruce Matthews (Albany: SUNY Press, 2007), 11.
143 Tilliette, *Schelling*, 390.
144 F.W.J. Schelling, *Urfassung der Philosophie der Offenbarung*, ed. Walter E. Ehrhardt, vol. 2 (Hamburg: Felix Meiner Verlag, 1992), 431.
145 Kaplan, *Answering the Enlightenment*, 83–4.
146 John Edward Toews, *Becoming Historical: Cultural Reformation and Public Memory in early Nineteenth-Century Berlin* (Cambridge: Cambridge University Press, 2004), 13–14.
147 Schelling, *The Grounding of Positive Philosophy*, 187.
148 Schelling, *The Grounding of Positive Philosophy*, 183.
149 Beach, *Potencies*, 102.
150 Schelling, *Urfassung*, vol. 1, 29.
151 Beach, *Potencies*, 103, 106–7.
152 Schelling, *Urfassung*, vol. 1, 10.
153 Friedrich Wilhelm Joseph Schelling, *Historical-critical Introduction to the Philosophy of Mythology*, trans. Mason Richey and Markus Zisselberger (Albany: SUNY Press, 2007), 98.

154 Schelling, *Historical-Critical Introduction*, 99.
155 Schelling, *Urfassung*, vol. 1, 9.
156 Schelling, *Urfassung*, vol. 1, 266.
157 Schelling, *Urfassung*, vol. 1, 351.
158 Schelling, *Urfassung*, vol. 2, 420.
159 Beach, *Potencies*, 242.
160 Schelling, *Urfassung*, vol. 2, 608.
161 Schelling, *Urfassung*, vol. 2, 699.
162 Toews, *Becoming Historical*, 11.
163 Cited in Tilliette, *Schelling*, 392.
164 Toews, *Becoming Historical*, 14.
165 Tilliette, *Schelling*, 426.
166 Friedrich Engels, *Schelling und die Offenbarung: Kritik des neuesten Reaktionsversuchs gegen die freie Philosophie* (Leipzig: Robert Binder, 1842), 13.

6. The Epistemology of Grace: Revelation in Catholic Theology, 1770–1850

 1 Franz Anton Staudenmaier, *Encyklopädie der theologischen Wissenschaften als System der gesammten Theologie*, vol. 1 (Mainz, 1840), 146.
 2 Staudenmaier, *Encyklopädie*, 143–4.
 3 Staudenmaier, *Encyklopädie*, 317
 4 Staudenmaier, *Encyklopädie*, 147.
 5 See Franz Anton Staudenmaier, *Geist der göttlichen Offenbarung* (Gießen: B.G. Ferber, 1837), 143–4.
 6 Gerhard Heinz, *Divinam christianae religionis originem probare. Untersuchung zur Entstehung des fundamentaltheologischen Offenbarungstraktates der katholischen Schultheologie* (Mainz: Mattias-Grünewald-Verlag, 1984), 285.
 7 Franz-Josef Niemann, *Jesus als Glaubensgrund in der Fundamentaltheologie der Neuzeit. Zur Genealogie eines Traktats* (Innsbruck: Tyrolia-Verlag, 1983), 14.
 8 Heinz, *Divinam christianae religionis originem probare*, 143.
 9 Heinz, *Divinam christianae religionis originem probare*, 162.
10 Horst Möller, *Vernunft und Kritik: Deutsche Aufklärung im 17. und 18. Jahrhundert* (Frankfurt: Suhrkamp, 1986), 86. See also Heribert Raab, "Die 'katholische Ideenrevolution' des 18. Jhts," in *Katholische Aufklärung – Aufklärung im katholischen Deutschland*, ed. Harm Klueting (Hamburg: Felix Meiner Verlag, 1993), 106.
11 Mader, *Offenbarung als Selbstoffenbarung Gottes*, 7.
12 Avery Dulles, *A History of Apologetics* (San Francisco: Ignatius Press, 1999), 237.
13 See McCool, *Nineteenth-Century Scholasticism*, 18–21.

14 McCool, *Nineteenth-Century Scholasticism*, 18–21.
15 Norbert Hötzel, *Die Uroffenbarung im französischen Traditionalismus* (Munich: Max Hueber Verlag, 1962), 69.
16 Gabriel Motzkin, *Time and Transcendence: Secular History, the Catholic Reaction, and the Rediscovery of the Future* (Dordrecht: Kluwer Academic Publishers, 1992), 178.
17 Karl Eschweiler, *Die katholische Theologie im Zeitalter des deutschen Idealismus*, ed. Thomas Marschler (Münster: Monsenstein und Vannerdat, 2010), lvi-lviii, 138.
18 Motzkin, *Time and Transcendence*, 163–5.
19 Heinz, *Divinam christianae religionis originem probare*, 283.
20 Philip Caldwell, *Liturgy as Revelation: Re-Sourcing a Theme in Catholic Theology* (Minneapolis: Fortress Press, 2014), 10.
21 Michael Printy, *Enlightenment and the Creation of German Catholicism* (Cambridge: Cambridge University Press, 2009), 21.
22 Möller, *Vernunft und Kritik*, 89.
23 Philipp Schäfer, *Kirche und Vernunft: Die Kirchen in der katholischen Theologie der Aufklärungszeit* (Munich: Max Hueber Verlag, 1974), 5, 83ff., 101–2.
24 Möller, *Vernunft und Kritik*, 87.
25 Schäfer, *Kirche und Vernunft*, 271, 278.
26 Ulrich L. Lehner, *Enlightened Monks: The German Benedictines, 1740–1803* (Oxford: Oxford University Press, 2011), 20–6.
27 Raab, "Die 'katholische Ideenrevolution,'"106–10.
28 See Möller, *Vernunft und Kritik*, 87.
29 Motzkin, *Time and Transcendence*, 168.
30 Gerald P. Fogarty, "The Catholic Church and Historical Criticism of the Old Testament," in *Hebrew Bible/Old Testament: The History of its Interpretation*, ed. Magne Sæebø, vol. 3, part 1 *The Nineteenth Century – A Century of Modernism and Historicism* (GT: Vandenhoeck & Ruprecht, 2013), 246–7.
31 Donald J. Dietrich, *The Goethezeit and the Metamorphosis of Catholic Theology in the Age of Idealism* (Frankfurt: Peter Lang, 1979), 43.
32 See Bruno Bianco, "Wolffianismus und katholische Aufklärung. Storchenaus' Lehre vom Menschen," in *Katholische Aufklärung*, ed. Harm Kleuting, 70–1.
33 Lehner, *Enlightened Monks*, 203.
34 Johann Michael Sailer, "Benekict Stattlers kurzgefaste Biographie" (1798), in *Sämmtliche Werke: Biographische Schriften*, vol. 1 (Sulzbach: Seidel, 1841), 118.
35 Benedikt Stattler, *Allgemeine katholisch-christliche theoretische Religionslehre aus hinreichenden Gründen der göttlichen Offenbarung und der Philosophie* (Munich: Schulfondsbücherverlag, 1791), 207.
36 Stattler, *Religionslehre*, 171.
37 Stattler, *Religionslehre*, 191.

38 Stattler, *Religionslehre*, 170.

39 Stattler, *Religionslehre*, 175.

40 Neumann, *Johann Arnold Kanne*, 268–9.

41 Schäfer, *Kirche und Vernunft*, 150.

42 Ulrich L. Lehner, "Benedict Stattler (1728–1897): The Reinvention of Catholic Theology with the Help of Wolffian Metaphysics," in *Enlightenment and Catholicism in Europe: A Transnational History*, ed. Jeffrey D. Burson and Ulrich L. Lehner (University of Notre Dame Press, 2014), 187.

43 Lehner, "Stattler," 180–4.

44 Lehner, "Stattler," 186.

45 Niemann, *Jesus als Glaubensgrund*, 268–70.

46 Michael Printy, "Catholic Enlightenment and Reform Catholicism in the Holy Roman Empire," in *A Companion to the Catholic Enlightenment in Europe*, ed. Michael O'Neill Printy and Ulrich Lehner (Leiden: Brill, 2010), 205.

47 Niemann, *Jesus als Glaubensgrund*, 280–1; Lehner, "Beda Mayr (1742–1794): Ecumenism and Dialogue with Modern Thought," in *Enlightenment and Catholicism in Europe: A Transnational History*, ed. Jeffrey D. Burson and Ulrich L. Lehner (Notre Dame: University of Notre Dame Press, 2014), 196.

48 Beda Mayr, *Vertheidigung der natürlichen, christlichen und katholischen Religion nach den Bedürfnissen unsrer Zeiten*, vol. 2, part 1 (Augsburg: Matthäus Riegers, 1789), 12, 25.

49 Mayr, *Vertheidigung*, vol. 1 (Augsburg: Matthäus Riegers, 1787), 455.

50 Mayr, *Vertheidigung*, vol. 1, 492.

51 Mayr, *Vertheidigung*, vol. 1, 501.

52 Mayr, *Vertheidigung*, vol. 1, 501.

53 Lehner, *Enlightened Monks*, 218–19.

54 Christoph Böttigheimer, "Einführung zur Geschichte des Verhältnisses des Katholismus zu Kant," in *Kant und der Katholismus. Stationen einer wechselhaften Geschichte*, ed. Norbert Fischer (Freiburg: Herder, 2005), 85.

55 Norbert Hinski, "Kant im Auf und Ab der katholischen Kantrezeption," in *Kant und der Katholismus*, ed. Fischer, 203–4.

56 Aloysius Winter, "Einführung zur katholischen Kantdeutung nach der Indizierung der *Kritik der reinen Vernunft*" in *Kant und der Katholismus*, ed. Fischer, 319.

57 Thomas Fliethman, *Vernünftig Glauben: Die Theorie der Theologie bei Georg Hermes* (Würzburg: Echter Verlag, 1997), 220, 279.

58 Dietrich, *Goethezeit and Metamorphosis*, 50.

59 Georg Hermes, *Einleitung in die christkatholische Theologie, vol. 1 Philosophische Einleitung* (Münster: Coppenrathsche Buch- und Kunsthandlung, 1819), xv.

60 Hermes *Philosophische Einleitung*, viii.

61 Hermes *Philosophische Einleitung*, 261.

62 Hermes *Philosophische Einleitung*, x.
63 Hermes *Philosophische Einleitung*, 605.
64 Hermes *Philosophische Einleitung*, 511.
65 Hermes *Philosophische Einleitung*, 513.
66 Hermes *Philosophische Einleitung*, 217.
67 Hermes *Philosophische Einleitung*, 221.
68 Hermes *Philosophische Einleitung*, 558ff.
69 Hermes *Philosophische Einleitung*, 221–2.
70 Georg Hermes, *Christkatholische Dogmatik*, ed. J.H. Achterfeldt, vol. 3 (Münster: Coppenrath, 1834), 183.
71 Bernhard Reardon, *Religion in the Age of Romanticism: Studies in Early Nineteenth-Century Thought* (Cambridge: Cambridge University Press, 1985), 123.
72 Reardon, *Religion in the Age of Romanticism*, 125.
73 McCool, *Nineteenth-Century Scholasticism*, 66.
74 See Herman. H. Schwedt, "Georg Hermes (1775–1831), seine Schule und seine wichtigsten Gegner," in *Christliche Philosophie im katholischen Denken des 19. und 20. Jahrhunderts*, ed. Emerich Coreth, Walter M. Neidl, and Georg Pfligersdorfer, vol. 1 (Graz: Verlag Styria, 1987), 223ff.
75 On Catholic histories of religion, see Anton Anwander, *Die allgemeine Religionsgeschichte im katholischen Deutschland während der Aufklärung und Romantik* (Salzburg: Anton Pustet, 1932).
76 Joseph Ringmüller, *Allgemeine Religions- und Staatsgeschichte von der Weltschöpfung an bis auf gegenwärtige Zeiten* (Wurzburg: Stahel, 1772), 360.
77 Ringmüller, *Allgemeine Religions- und Staatsgeschichte*, 340.
78 Ringmüller, *Allgemeine Religions- und Staatsgeschichte*, 581.
79 Conrad Aloys Prechtl, "Religionsgeschichte der ganzen Welt und aller Zeiten," in *Anhang zu dem dreyzehnten bis vier und zwanzigsten Bande der allgemeinen deutschen Bibliothek* (Berlin: Friedrich Nicolai, 1777), 250.
80 Prechtl, "Religionsgeschichte," 201.
81 Prechtl, "Religionsgeschichte," 207.
82 Hartmut Böhme, *Fetishism and Culture: A Different Theory of Modernity* (Boston: De Gruyter, 2014), 144.
83 Christoph Meiners, *Historische Vergleichung der Sitten, und Verfassungen, der Gesetze, und Gewerbe, des Handels, und der Religion, der Wissenschaften und Lehranstalten des Mittelalters mit denen unsers Jahrhunderts in Rücksicht auf die Vortheile, und Nachtheile der Aufklärung*, vol. 3 (Hannover: Helwig, 1794), 487.
84 Christoph Nebgen, *Konfessionelle Differenzerfahrungen: Reiseberichte vom Rhein (1648–1815)* (Munich: De Gruyter, 2014), 25.
85 Meiners, *Vergleichung*, vol. 3 (1794), 483ff.

86 Johann Gottlieb Lindemann, *Geschichte der Meinungen älterer und neuerer Völker, im Stande der Rohheit und Cultur, von Gott, Religion, und Priesterthum*, vol. 1 (Stendal: Franzen und Grosse, 1784), 46.

87 Lindemann, *Geschichte der Meinungen*, vol. 6 (1792), 77.

88 Lindemann, *Geschichte der Meinungen*, vol. 1, 63.

89 Lindemann, *Geschichte der Meinungen*, vol. 6, 3.

90 Lindemann, *Geschichte der Meinungen*, vol. 6, 235.

91 See Böhme, *Fetishism and Culture*, 156–8; and Peter Melville Logan, *Victorian Fetishism: Intellectuals and Primitives* (Albany: SUNY Press, 2009), 28.

92 Franz Michael Vierthaler, "Von dem Unterrichte in der Religion," in *Ausgewählte pädagogische Schriften*, ed. Leopold Glöckl, vol. 6 (Freiburg im Breisgau: Herder, 1893), 153.

93 Franz Michael Vierthaler, *Philosophische Geschichte der Menschen und Völker*, vol. 1 (Salzburg: Waisenbuchhandlung, 1787), 273.

94 Anwander, *Allgemeine Religionsgeschichte*, 115.

95 Vierthaler, *Philosophische Geschichte*, vol. 1, 377.

96 Vierthaler, *Philosophische Geschichte*, vol. 1, 525.

97 Vierthaler, *Philosophische Geschichte*, vol. 1, 380.

98 Vierthaler, *Philosophische Geschichte*, vol. 1, 588.

99 Manfred Weitlauff, "Friedrich Leopold Graf zu Stolbergs *Geschichte der Religion Jesu Christi* (1806–1818)," in *Friedrich Leopold Graf zu Stolberg (1750–1819): Beiträge zum Eutiner Symposium im September 1997*, ed. Frank Baudach, Jürgen Behrens, and Ute Pott (Eutin: Struve, 2002), 250–1.

100 See Norberg Oellers, "Stolberg, das Christentum und die Antike. Der Streit mit Schiller" in *Friedrich Leopold Graf zu Stolberg*, ed. Baudach, Behrens, and Pott.

101 Leo Scheffczyk, *Friedrich Leopold zu Stolbergs 'Geschichte der Religion Jesu Christi': Die Abwendung der katholischen Kirchengeschichtsschreibung von der Aufklärung und ihre Neuorientierung im Zeitalter der Romantik* (Munich: Karl Zink Verlag, 1952), 46.

102 Cited in Scheffczyk, *Friedrich Leopold zu Stolbergs 'Geschichte der Religion Jesu Christi,'* 46.

103 Eleoma Joshua, *Friedrich Leopold Graf zu Stolberg and the German Romantics* (New York: Peter Lang, 2005), 142.

104 See Scheffczyk, *Friedrich Leopold zu Stolbergs 'Geschichte der Religion Jesu Christi,'* 76–7.

105 Friedrich Leopold Stolberg, *Geschichte der Religion Jesu Christi*, vol. 1 (Hamburg, 1809), 475.

106 Heike Vierling-Ihrig, *Schule der Vernunft: Leben und Werk des Aufklärungspädagogen Cajetan von Weiller (1762–1826)* (Munich: Stadtarchiv München, 2001), 68ff.

107 O'Meara, *Romantic Idealism*, 208.

108 Kajetan Weiller, "Vorlesung des Director v. Weiller," in *Friedrich Heinrich Jacobi nach seinem Leben, Lehren und Wirken* (Munich: Fleichmann, 1819), 43.

109 Weiller, "Vorlesung," 50.

110 Albert Mues, "Editionspraxis in dürftiger Zeit am Beispiel der F.H. Jacobi-Werkausgabe Band 3," in *Grundlegung und Kritik: Briefwechsel zwischen Schelling und Fichte, 1794–1802*, ed. Jörg Jantzen, Thomas Kisser, and Hartmut Traub (New York: Rodopi, 2005), 169.

111 Weiller, *Ideen zur Geschichte der Entwickelung des religiösen Glaubens*, vol. 1 (Munich: Fleischmann, 1808), 132.

112 Weiller, *Ideen*, vol. 3, 30.

113 See Helmut Wiesner, *Religion und Vernunft im Frühwerk Friedrich Brenners (1810–1818)*, vol. 1 *Allgemeine Offenbarungslehre und Theorie der jüdischen Religion* (Würzburg: Echter Verlag, 1984), 171.

114 Friedrich Brenner, *Katholische Dogmatik, oder, System der katholischen speculativen Theologie*, vol. 1 (Rottenburg: Bäuerle, 1831), 27–8.

115 Gerhard Förch, *Theologie als Darstellung der Geschichte in der Idee: Zum Theologiebegriff Friedrich Brenners, 1784–1848* (Würzburg: Echter Verlag, 1980), 6.

116 Wiesner, *Religion und Vernunft*, 258.

117 Friedrich Brenner, *Versuch einer historisch-philosophischen Darstellung der Offenbarung als Einleitung in die Theologie* (Bamberg: Joseph Anton Goebhardt, 1810), 4.

118 Friedrich Brenner, *Freye Darstellung der Theologie in der Idee des Himmelreichs*, vol. 1 (Bamburg: Goebhardt, 1815), 40.

119 Adolf Dyroff, *Carl Joseph Windischmann (1775–1839) und sein Kreis* (Cologne: J.P. Bachem, 1916), 80–1.

120 Windischmann to Franz Bopp, 2 February 1815, in Salomon Lefmann, *Franz Bopp: Sein Leben und seine Wissenschaft* (Berlin: Reimer, 1891), vol. 1, 17.

121 Karl Joseph Hieronymus Windischmann, *Kritische Betrachtungen über die Schicksale der Philosophie in der neueren Zeit* (Frankfurt: Andreäische Buchhandlung, 1825), 123.

122 Windischmann, *Kritische Betrachtungen*, 122.

123 Karl Joseph Hieronymus Windischmann, *Philosophie im Fortgang der Weltgeschichte*, part 1, *Die Grundlagen der Philosophie im Morgenland*, vol. 4 (Bonn: Adolph Marcus, 1834), vol. 4, 1530.

124 Windischmann, *Philosophie*, vol. 1 (1827), 26.

125 Dyroff, *Carl Joseph Windischmann*, 75.

126 Windischmann, *Philosophie*, vol. 2 (1829), 522–36.

127 Windischmann, *Philosophie*, vol. 1, xlv.

128 Mader, *Offenbarung als Selbstoffenbarung Gottes*, 4–6, 342–3.

129 See O'Meara, *Romantic Idealism*, 4–10.

130 Peter Jonkers, "Hegel on Catholic Religion," in *Hegel's Philosophy of the Historical Religions*, ed. Bart Labuschagne and Timo Slootweg (Leiden: Brill, 2012), 203.

131 Jonkers, "Hegel on Catholic Religion," 180–4.

132 Jakob Sengler, *Ueber das Wesen und die Bedeutung der speculativen Philosophie und Theologie: Allgemeine Einleitung* (Mainz: F. Kupferberg, 1834), 72ff.

133 Sengler, *Ueber das Wesen*, 58.

134 Peter Hünermann, "Nicht: Theologie oder Religionswissenscahft – sondern: Theologie der Religionen," in *Adolf von Haarlack: Christentum, Wissenschaft und Gesellschaft*, ed. Kurt Nowak, Otto Gerhard Oexle, Trutz Rendtorff, and Kurt-Victor Segle (Göttingen: Vandenhoeck & Ruprecht, 2003), 276–8.

135 Wayne L. Fehr, *The Birth of the Catholic Tübingen School: The Dogmatics of Johann Sebastian Drey* (Chico, CA: Scholars Press, 1981), 8–9.

136 Anonymous [J.S. Drey], "Aphorismen über den Ursprung unserer Erkenntnisse von Gott – ein Beitrag zur Entscheidung der neuesten Streitigkeiten über den Begriff der Offenbarung," in *Tübinger theologische Quartalschrift* (1826), 266.

137 "Aphorismen," 249.

138 "Aphorismen," 169.

139 Fehr, *The Birth of the Catholic Tübingen School*, 9.

140 O'Meara, *Romantic Idealism*, 100.

141 Johann Sebastian Drey, *Kurze Einleitung in das Studium der Theologie mit Rücksicht auf den wissenschaftlichen Standpunct und das katholische System* (Tübingen: Heinrich Laupp, 1819), 3–4, 10–11.

142 O'Meara, *Romantic Idealism*, 108.

143 Fehr, *The Birth of the Catholic Tübingen School*, 49.

144 Johann Sebastian Drey, *Die Apologetik als wissenschaftliche Nachweisung der Göttlichkeit des Christenthums in seiner Erscheinung*, vol. 1 (Mainz: F. Kupferberg, 1838), 132.

145 Drey, *Apologetik*, vol. 1, 118.

146 Drey, *Apologetik*, vol. 1, 158.

147 Drey, *Apologetik*, vol. 1, 162.

148 Drey, *Apologetik*, vol. 1, 164.

149 Drey, *Apologetik*, vol. 1, 10.

150 Staudenmaier, *Encyklopädie*, 271.

151 Staudenmaier, *Encyklopädie*, 247.

152 Staudenmaier, *Encyklopädie*, 318.

153 In Peter Knoodt, *Anton Günther: Eine Biographie*, vol. 1 (Vienna: Wilhelm Braumüller, 1881), 84–5.

154 In Knoodt, *Anton Günther*, 104–5.

155 Anton Günther, *Vorschule zur speculativen Theologie des positiven Christenthums*, vol. 2 [1827], in *Anton Günther's gesammelte Schriften*, vol. 2 (Frankfurt: Minerva, 1968), vii.

156 Anton Günther and J.H. Pabst, *Janusköpfe. Zur Philosophie und Theologie* [1833], in *Anton Günther's gesammelte Schriften*, vol. 5 (Frankfurt: Minerva, 1968), 19.

157 Günther and Pabst, *Janusköpfe*, 18.

158 Günther and Pabst, *Janusköpfe*, 21.

159 Günther and Pabst, *Janusköpfe*, 22–3.

160 Anton Günther, "Protestantismus und Philosophie," in *Lydia, Philosophisches Taschenbuch* I (Vienna, 1849), 61.

161 Anton Günther, *Vorschule zur speculativen Theologie des positiven Christenthums*, vol. 1 [1827], in *Anton Günther's gesammelte Schriften*, vol. 1 (Frankfurt: Minerva, 1968), 97.

162 Günther and Pabst, *Janusköpfe*, 1.

163 Günther, *Vorschule*, vol. 2, 74.

164 Günther and Pabst, *Janusköpfe*, 110.

165 Günther, *Vorschule*, vol. 1, 29.

166 Günther, *Vorschule*, vol. 1, 22.

167 Günther, *Vorschule*, vol. 1, 108.

168 Günther, *Vorschule*, vol. 1, 17.

169 Günther and Pabst, *Janusköpfe*, 257.

170 Adam Bunnell, *Before Infallibility: Liberal Catholicism in Biedermeier Vienna* (Rutherford: Fairleigh Dickinson University Press, 1990), 83.

171 Günther, *Vorschule*, vol. 1, 35.

172 Günther, *Vorschule*, vol. 1, 111.

173 Günther, *Vorschule*, vol. 1, 34.

174 Günther, *Vorschule*, vol. 1, 57.

175 Günther, *Vorschule*, vol. 1, 229.

176 Günther and Pabst, *Janusköpfe*, 110.

177 Günther, *Vorschule*, vol. 2, xxi.

178 On Günther's approach to revelation, see Karl Beck, *Offenbarung und Glaube bei Anton Günther* (Vienna: Herder, 1967) and Joseph Pritz, *Glauben und Wissen bei Anton Günther: Eine Einführung in sein Leben und Werk mit einer Auswahl aus seinen Schriften* (Vienna: Herder, 1963).

179 Paul Wenzel, *Das wissenschaftliche Anliegen des Güntherianismus. Ein Beitrag zur Theologiegeschichte des 19. Jahrhunderts* (Essen: Ludgerus-Verlag, 1961), 47ff.

180 Pritz, *Glauben und Wissen bei Anton Günther*, 58.

181 McCool, *Nineteenth-Century Scholasticism*, 135.

182 McCool, *Nineteenth-Century Scholasticism*, 133–4.

183 Joseph Kleutgen to P. Haßlacher, 1 August 1855, in Konrad Deufel, *Kirche und Tradition: Ein Beitrag zur Geschichte der theologischen Wende im 19. Jahrhundert am Beispiel des kirchlich-theologischen Kampfprogramms P. Joseph Kleutgens S.J.* (Munich: Ferdinand Schöningh, 1978), 51.

184 See Hubert Wolf, *The Nuns of Sant'Ambrogio: The True Story of a Convent Scandal*, trans. Ruth Martin (Oxford: Oxford University Press, 2015).

185 See Theo Schäfer, *Die erkenntnistheoretische Kontroverse Kleutgen-Günther* (Paderborn: Ferdinand Schöningh, 1961).

186 Joseph Kleutgen, *Die Theologie der Vorzeit vertheidigt*, vol. 1 (Münster: Theissing, 1867), 4.

187 See McCool, *Nineteenth-Century Scholasticism*, 209–13.

188 Kleutgen, *Theologie der Vorzeit*, vol. 1, 8.

189 Kleutgen, *Theologie der Vorzeit*, vol. 5 (1874), 22.

190 Kleutgen, *Theologie der Vorzeit*, vol. 5, 337.

7. Revelation in Jewish Religious Thought from Mendelssohn to Geiger

1 A.Z. Idelsohn, *Jewish Liturgy and its Development* (New York: Dover Publication, 1995), 198–9, 331ff.

2 Bernhard Beer, "Das Wochenfest in der neuen Synagoge zu Dresden," *Allgemeine Zeitung des Judenthums* 4, no. 26 (1840), 376–7. See the detailed account of this service in Michael A. Meyer, *Response to Modernity: A History of the Reform Movement in Judaism* (Oxford: Oxford University Press, 1988), 106.

3 Samson Raphael Hirsch, "Reflections on the Jewish Calendar Year," in *Judaism Eternal: Selected Essays from the Writings of Rabbi Samson Raphael Hirsch*, trans. I. Grunfeld, vol. 1 (London: Soncino Press, 1956), 106.

4 Andrea Bieler, *Die Sehnsucht nach sem verlorenen Himmel: Jüdische und christliche Refleionen zu Gottesdienstreform und Predigtkultur im 19. Jahrhundert* (Stuttgart: Kohlhammer, 2003), 173.

5 Leopold Zunz, "Die Einheit Gottes," in *Predigten, gehalten in der neuen Israelitischen Synagoge zu Berlin* (Berlin: Schlesinger, 1823), 55.

6 Samuel Hirsch, *Die Messiaslehre der Juden in Kanzelvorträgen* (Leipzig: Heinrich Hunber, 1843), 234ff.

7 Michael A. Meyer, *Judaism within Modernity: Essays on Jewish History and Religion* (Detroit: Wayne State University Press, 2001), 112.

8 Nathan Rotenstreich, *Tradition and Reality: The Impact of History on Modern Jewish Thought* (New York: Random House, 1972), 11.

9 David N. Myers, *Resisting History: Historicism and its Discontents in German-Jewish Thought* (Princeton: Princeton University Press, 2003), 14.

10 Rotenstreich, *Tradition and Reality*, 15.
11 George Y. Kohler, *Reading Maimonides' Philosophy in 19th Century Germany: The Guide to Religious Reform* (New York: Springer, 2012), 2, 38.
12 Eliezer Schweid, "Halevi and Maimonides as Representatives of Romantic Versus Rationalistic Conceptions of Judaism," in *Kabbala und Romantik*, ed. Eveline Goodman-Thau, Gert Mattenklott, and Christoph Schulte (Tübingen: Nieymeyer, 1994), 184–5.
13 Kohler, *Reading Maimonides' Philosophy*, 345.
14 Susannah Heschel, *Abraham Geiger and the Jewish Jesus* (Chicago: University of Chicago Press, 1998), 67.
15 David Sorkin, *The Berlin Haskalah and German Religious Thought: Orphans of Knowledge* (London: Vallentine Mitchell, 2000), 6.
16 Ran HaCohen, *Reclaiming the Hebrew Bible: German-Jewish Reception of Biblical Criticism*, trans. Michelle Engel (New York: De Gruyter, 2010), 7.
17 Heschel, *Abraham Geiger and the Jewish Jesus*, 2–3.
18 See Myers, *Resisting History*.
19 Emil L. Frackenheim, *Quest for Past and Future: Essays in Jewish Theology* (Bloomington: Indiana University Press, 1968), 210.
20 Sorkin, *Berlin Haskalah*, 4.
21 Eliezer Schweid, *A History of Modern Jewish Religious Philosophy*, vol. 1 *The Period of the Enlightenment*, trans. Leonard Levin (Leiden: Brill, 2011), 34, 37.
22 David Sorkin, *The Transformation of German Jewry, 1780–1840* (New York: Oxford University Press, 1987), 21ff.
23 Mosche Pelli, *The Age of Haskalah: Studies of Hebrew Literature of the Enlightenment in Germany* (Leiden: Brill, 1979), 18.
24 HaCohen, *Reclaiming the Hebrew Bible*, 33.
25 Sorkin, *Transformation*, 22.
26 Jonathan M. Hess, *Germans, Jews, and the Claims of Modernity* (New Haven: Yale University Press, 2002), 7ff.
27 Sorkin, *Transformation*, 54–7.
28 Schweid, *History*, 235.
29 Allan Arkush, *Moses Mendelssohn and the Enlightenment* (Albany: SUNY Press, 1994), 196.
30 Cited in David Sorkin, *Moses Mendelssohn and the Religious Enlightenment* (Berkeley: University of California Press, 1996), 84.
31 Sorkin, *Mendelssohn*, 78–81.
32 Moses Mendelssohn, *Jerusalem, or on Religious Power and Judaism*, trans. Allan Arkush (Hannover: Brandeis University Press, 1983), 90.
33 Micahel Meyer, "'Ob Schrift? Ob Geist' Die Offenbarung im deutschen Judentum des neunzehnten Jahrhunderts," in *Quaestiones Disputatae*, ed.

Karl Rahner and Heinrich Schlier, vol. 92 *Offenbarung* (Basel: Editiones Herder, 1981), 166.

34 Mendelssohn, *Jerusalem*, 97.

35 Michah Gottlieb, *Faith and Freedom: Moses Mendelssohn's Theological-Political Thought* (New York: Oxford University Press, 2011), 46.

36 Arkush, *Moses Mendelssohn*, 184–6.

37 Mendelssohn, *Jerusalem*, 127.

38 Sorkin, *Transformation*, 67.

39 Hess, *Germans, Jews, and the Claims of Modernity*, 96–7.

40 Karl Erich Grözinger, *Jüdisches Denken: Theologie – Philosophie – Mystik*, vol. 3 (Frankfurt: Campus Verlag, 2009), 491–3.

41 Meyer, *Response*, 15.

42 Hess, *Germans, Jews, and the Claims of Modernity*, 149–53.

43 See Nathan Rotenstreich, *Jews and German Philosophy: The Polemics of Emancipation* (New York: Schocken Books, 1984), 3–4, and Schweid, *History of Modern Jewish Religious Philosophy*, 132ff.

44 Meyer, *Response*, 64f.

45 Noah H. Rosenbloom, *Tradition in an Age of Reform: The Religious Philosophy of Samson Raphael Hirsch* (Philadelphia: The Jewish Publication Society of America, 1976), 15–17.

46 Hess, *Germans, Jews, and the Claims of Modernity*, 149.

47 Hess, *Germans, Jews, and the Claims of Modernity*, 157.

48 Michael Mack, *German Idealism and the Jew: The Inner Anti-Semitism of Philosophy and German Jewish Responses* (Chicago: University of Chicago Press, 2003), 9f, 32ff.

49 Hess, *Germans, Jews, and the Claims of Modernity*, 139.

50 Samuel Ascher, *Leviathan oder ueber Religion in Rücksicht des Judenthums* (Berlin: Franke, 1792), 158.

51 Ascher, *Leviathan oder ueber Religion*, 75.

52 Ascher, *Leviathan oder ueber Religion*, 107.

53 Ascher, *Leviathan oder ueber Religion*, 123.

54 Ascher, *Leviathan oder ueber Religion*, 63.

55 Ascher, *Leviathan oder ueber Religion*, 237.

56 Christoph Schulte, *Die jüdische Aufklärung: Philosophie, Religion, Geschichte* (Munich: C.H. Beck, 2002), 184ff.

57 Ascher, *Leviathan oder ueber Religion*, 165.

58 Ascher, *Leviathan oder ueber Religion*, 229.

59 Ascher, *Leviathan oder ueber Religion*, 108.

60 Hess, *Germans, Jews, and the Claims of Modernity*, 160.

61 Deborah Hertz, *How Jews Became Germans: The History of Conversion and Assimilation in Berlin* (New Haven: Yale University Press, 2007), 189ff.

62 Micha Brumlik, "Der Begriff der Offenbarung bei Steinheim und Schelling," in *'Philo des 19. Jahrhunderts': Studien zu Salomon Ludwig Steinheim*, ed. Julius H. Schoeps, Anja Bagel-Bohlan, Margret Heitmann, and Dieter Lohmeier (Hildesheim: Georg Olms Verlag, 1993), 72.

63 Michael A. Meyer, "Solomon Ludwig Steinheim and the Reform Movement," in *'Philo des 19. Jahrhunderts,'* ed. Schoeps, Bagel-Bohlan, Heitmann, and Lohmeier, 157.

64 Meyer, "Steinheim," 154.

65 Solomon Steinheim, *The Revelation according to the Doctrine of Judaism: A Criterion*, trans. Joshua O. Haberman, in *Philosopher of Revelation: The Life and Thought of S.L. Steinheim*, ed. Joshua O. Haberman (Philadelphia: Jewish Publication Society, 1990), 65.

66 Steinheim, *Revelation*, 96–7.

67 Steinheim, *Revelation*, 287.

68 Meyer, "Steinheim," 157.

69 Steinheim, *Revelation*, 135.

70 Steinheim, *Revelation*, 129.

71 Solomon Steinheim, *Die Offenbarung vom Standpuncte der höheren Kritik: Eine Prüfung der Darstellung des Herrn Prof. W. Vatke* (Kiel: Universitäts-Buchhandlung, 1840), v.

72 HaCohen, *Reclaiming the Hebrew Bible*, 86–113.

73 Steinheim, *Revelation*, 77.

74 Steinheim, *Revelation*, 80.

75 Steinheim, *Revelation*, 86.

76 Haberman, *Philosopher of Revelation*, 20.

77 Meyer, "Steinheim," 144–5.

78 Meyers, *Response*, 56–7.

79 Meyers, *Response*, 114.

80 Grözinger, *Jüdisches Denken*, vol. 3, 498.

81 Meyer, *Judaism within Modernity*, 118.

82 I. Grunfeld, "Introduction," in *Judaism Eternal*, xxxvii, xliv.

83 Alexander Altmann, "The New Study of Preaching in Nineteenth-Century German Jewry," in *Studies in Nineteenth-Century Jewish Intellectual History*, ed. Alexander Altmann (Cambridge: Harvard University Press, 1964), 79.

84 Ben Uziel (Samson Raphael Hirsch), *The Nineteen Letters about Judaism*, trans. Karin Paritzky, ed. Joseph Elias (New York: Feldheim Publishers, 1996), 76.

85 Samson Raphael Hirsch, *Neunzehn Briefe über Judenthum* (Altona: Hammerich, 1836), 35. German original: "geschichtlich zum zweitenmale."

86 Samson Hirsch, *Nineteen Letters*, 106.

87 Samson Hirsch, *Nineteen Letters*, 115.

88 Joseph Elias, "Editor's Notes," in Samson Hirsch, *Nineteen Letters*, 151.

89 Samson Hirsch, *Nineteen Letters*, 226–7.
90 See Jacob J. Petuchowski, "Manuals and Catechisms of the Jewish Religion in the Early Period of Emancipation," in *Studies in Nineteenth-Century Jewish Intellectual History*, ed. Alexander Altmann (Cambridge: Harvard University Press, 1964), 51ff.
91 Samson Raphael Hirsch, "Belief and Knowledge," in Samson Hirsch, *Collected Writings*, vol. 2 (New York: Philipp Feldheim, 1984), 141.
92 Grunfeld, "Introduction," lxxvi-ii.
93 Sorkin, *Transformation*, 166ff.
94 Samson Raphael Hirsch, *Horeb: A Philosophy of Jewish Laws and Observations*, trans. I. Grunfeld (London: Soncino Press, 1962), 20.
95 Samson Raphael Hirsch, "Reflections on the Jewish Calendar Year," 90.
96 Rosenbloom, *Tradition in an Age of Reform*, 90.
97 Robert Liberles, *Religious Conflict in Social Context: The Resurgence of Orthodox Judaism in Frankfurt am Main, 1838–1877* (Westport, CT: Greenwood Press, 1985), 80–2.
98 Liberles, *Religious Conflict in Social Context*, 85.
99 Myers, *Resisting History*, 28.
100 Meyer, *Judaism within Modernity*, 117.
101 Isaac Ascher Francolm, *Das rationale Judenthum* (Breslau: M. Friedländer, 1840), 155–6.
102 Francolm, *Judenthum*, 14.
103 See Schweid, *History*, 146ff.
104 Meyer, *Response to Modernity*, 70.
105 Sven-Erik Rose, *Jewish Philosophical Politics in Germany, 1789–1848* (Waltham: Brandeis University Press, 2014), 46.
106 Wiese, *Challenging Colonial Discourse*, 25.
107 See Bettina Kratz-Ritter, *Salomon Formstecher: Ein deutscher Reformrabbiner* (Hildesheim: Georg Olms, 1991).
108 Salomon Formstecher, *Mosaische Religionslehre für die israelitische Religionsschule* (Gießen: Ernst Heinemann, 1860).
109 Salomon Formstecher, *Die Religion des Geistes, eine wissenschaftliche Darstellung des Judenthums nach seinem Charakter, Entwicklungsgange und Berufe in der Menschheit* (Frankfurt: Johann Christian Hermann, 1841), 5.
110 Formstecher, *Religion des Geistes*, 4.
111 Formstecher, *Religion des Geistes*, 19.
112 Formstecher, *Religion des Geistes*, 53.
113 Formstecher, *Religion des Geistes*, 33.
114 Formstecher, *Religion des Geistes*, 53.
115 Formstecher, *Religion des Geistes*, 57.
116 Formstecher, *Religion des Geistes*, 394.
117 Formstecher, *Religion des Geistes*, 8.

118 Formstecher, *Religion des Geistes*, 424.
119 Eliezer Schweid, *A History of Modern Jewish Religious Philosophy*, vol. II (Leiden: Brill, 2011), 70.
120 See Rotenstreich, *Jews and German Philosophy*, 85ff.
121 Samuel Hirsch, *Die Religionsphilosophie der Juden oder das Princip der jüdischen Religionsanschauung und sein Verhältniß zum Heidenthum, Christenthum und zur absoluten Philosophie* (Leipzig: Heinrich Hunger, 1842), 8.
122 Samuel Hirsch, *Religionsphilosophie*, 457–8.
123 Samuel Hirsch, *Religionsphilosophie*, 107.
124 Emil L. Fackenheim, "Samuel Hirsch and Hegel," in Alexander Altmann, *Studies in Nineteenth-Century Jewish Intellectual History* (Cambridge, MA: Harvard University Press, 1964), 189.
125 Samuel Hirsch, *Religionsphilosophie*, 521.
126 Samuel Hirsch, *Religionsphilosophie*, 618.
127 Samuel Hirsch, *Die Reform im Judenthum und dessen Gebrauch in der gegenwärtigen Welt* (Leipzig: H. Hunger, 1844), 33.
128 Samuel Hirsch, *Die Reform im Judenthume*, 35–6.
129 Samuel Hirsch, *Die Reform im Judenthume*, 37.
130 See Elmar P. Ittenbach, *Samuel Hirsch: Rabbiner – Religionsphilosoph – Reformer* (Berlin: Hentrich & Hentrich Verlg, 2014).
131 *Gebetbuch der Genossenschaft für Reform im Judenthum*, vol. 1 (Berlin: Selbst-Verlage der Genossenschaft, 1848), vi-vii. Translation taken from Plaut, *Rise of Reform Judaism: A Sourcebook*, 58.
132 Meyer, *Response*, 81.
133 Samuel Holdheim, *Moses Mendelssohn und die Denk- und Glaubensfreiheit im Judenthume* (Berlin: Huber, 1859), 28.
134 Heschel, *Abraham Geiger and the Jewish Jesus*, 158ff.
135 Abraham Geiger, *Judaism and its History in Two Parts*, trans. Charles Newburgh (Lanham, MD: University Press of America, 1985), 46.
136 Abraham Geiger, "Steinheim," in *Jüdische Zeitschrift für Wissenschaft und Leben*, ed. Abraham Geiger, vol. 10 (Breslau: Schletter, 1872), 290.
137 Heschel, *Abraham Geiger and the Jewish Jesus*, 7–8.
138 Heschel, *Abraham Geiger and the Jewish Jesus*, 158–9.
139 Heschel, *Abraham Geiger and the Jewish Jesus*, 25.
140 Heschel, *Abraham Geiger and the Jewish Jesus*, 61.
141 Abraham Geiger, *Was hat Mohammed aus dem Judenthume aufgenommen?* (Bonn: F. Baaden, 1833), 80.
142 HaCohen, *Reclaiming the Hebrew Bible*, 2.
143 HaCohen, *Reclaiming the Hebrew Bible*, 26.
144 Nils H. Roemer, *Jewish Scholarship and Culture in Nineteenth-Century Germany: Between History and Faith* (Madison: University of Wisconsin Press, 2005), 5, 26.

145 Wiese, *Challenging Colonial Discourse*.

146 Heschel, *Abraham Geiger and the Jewish Jesus*, 3–4, 17.

147 Geiger, *Judaism*, 15.

148 Geiger, *Judaism*, 21–2.

149 Geiger, *Judaism*, 38–9.

150 Geiger, *Judaism*, 46–7.

151 Geiger, *Judaism*, 86–7.

152 Meyer, *Judaism within Modernity*, 121

153 Abraham Geiger, "Die letzten zwei Jahre. Sendschreiben an einen befreundeten Rabbiner" (1840), in *Abraham Geiger's Nachgelassene Schriften*, ed. Ludwig Geiger, vol. 1 (Berlin: Luis Gerschel, 1875), 42–3.

154 See Geiger, "Die letzten zwei Jahre."

155 Cited in Abraham Geiger, "Die protestantische Kirchenzeitung und der Fortschritt im Judenthume," in *Jüdische Zeitschrift für Wissenschaft und Leben*, ed. Abraham Geiger, vol. 1 (Breslau: Schletter, 1862), 80.

156 Geiger, "Die protestantische Kirchenzeitung," 81.

157 Geiger, "Die protestantische Kirchenzeitung," 45–6.

8. Revelation Imperilled in Protestant Religious Thought, 1820–1850

1 Søren Kierkegaard, *The Book on Adler: The Religion Confusion of the Present Age Illustrated by Magister Adler as a Phenomenon*, trans. Howard V. Hong and Edna H. Hong (Princeton: Princeton University Press, 1998), 3.

2 Ludwig Feuerbach, *The Essence of Christianity*, trans. George Eliot (New York: Harper & Brothers, 1957), 211.

3 Feuerbach, *Essence of Christianity*, 206.

4 See John H. Sailhammer, *The Meaning of the Pentateuch: Revelation, Composition and Interpretation* (Danvers Grove, IL: IVP Academic, 2009), 182–93.

5 Thomas Howard, *Religion and the Rise of Historicism: W.M.L. de Wette, Jacob Burckhardt, and the Theological Origins of Nineteenth-Century Historical Consciousness* (Cambridge: Cambridge University Press), 38–41.

6 Wilhelm Martin Leberecht de Wette, *Christliche Sittenlehre*, Part II: *Allgemeine Geschichte der christlichen Sittenlehre* (Berlin: G. Reimer, 1819), 21.

7 Wilhelm Martin Leberecht de Wette, *Ueber die Religion, ihre Erscheinungsformen und ihren Einfluß auf das Leben* (Berlin: G. Reimer, 1827), 188–89.

8 de Wette, *Ueber die Religion*, 418.

9 Suzanne Marchand, *German Orientalism in the Age of Empire: Religion, Race, and Scholarship* (Cambridge: Cambridge University Press, 2009), 72–4.

10 August Tholuck, "Einleitende Bermerkungen in das Studium der paulinischen Briefe," in *Vermischte Schriften größtentheils apologetischen Inhalts*, vol. 2 (Hamburg: Perthes, 1839), 300.

11 Karl Barth, *Protestant Theology in the Nineteenth Century: Its Background and History* (Valley Forge: Judson Press, 1972), 499.

12 August Tholuck, *Die Lehre von der Sünde und vom Versöhner, oder Die wahre Weihe des Zweiflers*, 2nd ed. (Hamburg: Friedrich Perthes, 1825), 84.

13 Tholuck, *Lehre von der Sünde*, 285.

14 August Tholuck, "Mein Leben," in Sung-Bong Kim, *"Die Lehre von der Sünde und vom Versöhner"; Tholucks theologische Entwicklung in seiner Berliner Zeit* (Frankfurt/Main: Peter Lang, 1992), 183.

15 Leopold Witte, *Das Leben Friedrich August Gottreu Tholuck's*, vol. 1 (Bielefeld: Belhagen & Klasing, 1884), 26.

16 Tholuck, "Mein Leben," 184.

17 Witte, *Friedrich August Gottreu Tholuck's*, 45, 50.

18 Tholuck, "Mein Leben," 190.

19 Witte, *Friedrich August Gottreu Tholuck's*, 63.

20 Witte, *Friedrich August Gottreu Tholuck's*, 61.

21 Tholuck, "Mein Leben," 195.

22 Barth, *Protestant Theology*, 495.

23 Witte, *Friedrich August Gottreu Tholuck's*, 247.

24 See August Tholuck, *Blüthensammlung aus der Morgenländischen Mystik nebst einer Einleitung über Mystik überhaupt und Morgenländische insbesondere* (Berlin: Ferdinand Dümmler, 1825), 34.

25 August Tholuck, *Ssufismus sive theosophia Persarum pantheistica* (Berlin: Ferdinand Duemmler, 1821), 222.

26 Annemarie Schimmel, *Mystical Dimensions of Islam* (Chapel Hill: University of North Carolina Press, 2011), 9.

27 August Tholuck, *Einige apologeitsche Winke für das Studium des Alten Testaments* (Berlin: Maurer, 1821), 15.

28 Witte, *Friedrich August Gottreu Tholuck's*, 266ff.

29 Creuzer to Tholuck, 5 August 1821, cited in Witte, *Friedrich August Gottreu Tholuck's*, 267.

30 Rudolf Ewad Stier to Tholuck, 14 June 1821, cited in Witte, *Friedrich August Gottreu Tholuck's*, 268.

31 Tholuck, *Lehre von der Sünde*, 10.

32 Tholuck, *Lehre von der Sünde*, 77.

33 See Kim, *"Die Lehre von der Sünde und vom Versöhner,"* 107ff.

34 Tholuck, *Lehre von der Sünde*, 284–5.

35 August Tholuck, *Die Propheten und ihre Weissagungen* (Gotha: Perthes, 1861), 67.

36 Tholuck, "Einleitende Bermerkungen," 300.

37 Tholuck, *Lehre von der Sünde*, 286.
38 Tholuck, *Lehre von der Sünde*, 88.
39 Tholuck, *Lehre von der Sünde*, 84.
40 Tholuck, *Lehre von der Sünde*, 211.
41 Tholuck, *Lehre von der Sünde*, 80.
42 Peter K.J. Park, *Africa, Asia, and the History of Philosophy: Racism in the Formation of the Philosophical Canon, 1780–1830* (Albany: SUNY Press, 2013), 144.
43 Tholuck, *Lehre von der Sünde*, 224.
44 See Bigler, *Politics of German Protestantism*, 100–108.
45 Tholuck, *Blüthensammlung*, ii–iii.
46 Tholuck, *Blüthensammlung*, 27.
47 Georg Wilhelm Friedrich Hegel, *Encyklopädie der philosophischen Wissenschaften im Grundrisse* (Berlin: Duncker and Humblot, 1845), 522.
48 Tholuck, *Blüthensammlung*, 10.
49 Tholuck, *Blüthensammlung*, 45.
50 Park, *Africa, Asia, and the History of Philosophy*, 136.
51 Park, *Africa, Asia, and the History of Philosophy*, 145.
52 Bigler, *Politics of German Protestantism*, 120.
53 Wilhelm Vatke, *Die biblische Theologie wissenschaftlich dargestellt*, vol. 1 (Berlin: G. Bethge, 1835), 660.
54 Vatke, *Biblische Theologie*, 707.
55 Henrich Steffens, *Was ich erlebte: Aus Erinnerung niedergeschrieben*, vol. 6 (Breslau: Josef Max, 1842), 188.
56 See Dr. E. M-n, "P.F. Stuhr, Die Religions-Systeme der heidnischen Völker des Orients," in *Literarische Zeitung* 48 (23 November 1836), 898.
57 Karl Riedel, *Schellings religionsgeschichtliche Ansicht nach Briefen aus München mit einer vergleichenden Zugabe: Peter Feddersen Stuhr über Urgeschichte und Mythologie* (Berlin: Rücker und Püchler, 1841).
58 See "Die Berliner Historiker," in *Hallische Jahrbücher für deutsche Wissenschaft und Kunst* 109 (7 May 1841), 436.
59 Benedetto Bravo, *Philologie, Histoire, Philosophie de l'Histoire, Étude sur J.G. Droysen, Historien de l'Antiquité* (New York: Georg Olms, 1968), 166.
60 See Ronald Roggen, *'Restauration' – Kampfruf und Schimpfwort: Eine Kommunikationsanalyse zum Hauptwerk des Staatstheoretikers Karl Ludwig von Haller (1768–1854)* (Freiburg: Universitätsverlag, 1999), 154, and Uta Motschmann, *Handbuch der Berliner Vereine und Gesellschaften, 1786–1815* (Berlin: de Gruyter, 1815), 459.
61 Robert M. Berdahl, *The Politics of the Prussian Nobility: The Development of a Conservative Ideology, 1770–1848* (Princeton: Princeton University Press, 1988), 337.
62 Peter Feddersen Stuhr, *Das Verhältniss der christlichen Theologie zur Philosophie und Mythologie* (Berlin: E.H. Schroeder, 1842), 14. See also

Stuhr's "Allgemeiner Ueberblick über die Geschichte der Behandlung und Deutung der Mythen seit dem Mittelalter," in *Zeitschrift für spekulative Theologie*, ed. Bruno Bauer, vol. 3 (1–2) (Berlin: Ferdinand Dümmler, 1837) and his *Untersuchungen über die Ursprünglichkeit und Alterthümlichkeit der Sternkunde unter den Chinesen und Indiern* (Berlin: Fr. Laue, 1831).

63 Stuhr, *Untersuchungen*, 2.

64 Peter Feddersen Stuhr, *Deutschland und der Gottesfriede: Sendschreiben an Görres* (Berlin: Maurersche Buchhandlung, 1820), 26.

65 Peter Feddersen Stuhr, "Karl Otfried Müller als Mythologe," in *Hallische Jahrbücher für deutsche Wissenschaft und Kunst* 292–9 (1838), 2355.

66 See Peter Feddersen Stuhr, *Das Verhältniss der christlichen Theologie zur Philosophie und Mythologie* (Berlin: E.H. Schroeder, 1842), 19.

67 Stuhr, "Müller als Mythologe," 2373.

68 Peter Feddersen Stuhr, *Die Religions-Systeme der heidnischen Völker des Orients* (Berlin: Veit, 1836), xix.

69 Stuhr, *Religions-Systeme*, iv.

70 Stuhr, *Religions-Systeme*, vii.

71 Stuhr, *Religions-Systeme*, xlvii.

72 Heinrich Lüken, *Die Traditionen des Menschengeschlechts oder die Uroffenbarung Gottes unter den Heiden* (Münster: Aschendorff'sche Buchhandlung, 1856), v.

73 Ludwig Feuerbach, "Herr von Schelling (1843)," in Ludwig Feuerbach, *Sämtliche Werke*, ed. Wilhelm Bolin and Friedrich Jodl, vol. 4 (Stuttgart: Frommann, 1959), 436.

74 John E. Toews, *Hegelianism: The Path toward Dialectical Humanism, 1805–1841* (Cambridge: Cambridge University Press, 1980), 176–7.

75 Toews, *Hegelianism*, 179–80.

76 Toews, *Hegelianism*, 183.

77 Warren Breckman, *Marx, the Young Hegelians, and the Origins of Radical Social Theory: Dethroning the Self* (Cambridge: Cambridge University Press, 1999), 104.

78 Breckman, *Young Hegelians*, 99–102, 107.

79 Breckman, *Young Hegelians*, 113–22.

80 Feuerbach, "Herr von Schelling (1843)," 439.

81 Feuerbach, *Essence of Christianity*, xli.

82 Feuerbach, *Essence of Christianity*, 206.

83 Feuerbach, *Essence of Christianity*, 212.

84 Feuerbach, *Essence of Christianity*, 209.

85 Feuerbach, *Essence of Christianity*, 206–8.

86 Van A. Harvey, *Feuerbach and the Interpretation of Religion* (Cambridge: Cambridge University Press, 1995), 11–12, 147–51.

87 Harvey, *Feuerbach and the Interpretation of Religion*, 149.
88 Ludwig Feuerbach, *The Essence of Faith According to Luther*, trans. Melvin Cherno (New York: Harper & Row, 1967), 112.
89 Breckman, *Young Hegelians*, 129.
90 Feuerbach, *Essence of Faith*, 65.
91 Feuerbach, *Essence of Faith*, 68.
92 Mark W. Wartofsky, *Feuerbach* (Cambridge: Cambridge University Press, 1977), 367.
93 Ludwig Feuerbach, *Lectures on the Essence of Religion*, trans. Ralph Manheim (New York: Harper & Row, 1967), 37.
94 Feuerbach, *Theogonie nach den Quellen des classischen, hebräischen und christlichen Alterthums* in *Sämtliche Werke*, ed. Wilhelm Bolin and Friedrich Jodl, vol. 9 (Stuttgart: Frommann, 1960), 235.
95 Barth, *Protestant Theology*, 523.
96 Compare Harvey, *Feuerbach and the Interpretation of Religion*, 6ff., with Garrett Green, "Feuerbach and the Hermeneutics of Imagination," in *Biblical Interpretation: History, Context, and Reality*, ed. Christine Helmer (Leiden: Brill, 2005), 160.
97 Feuerbach, *Lectures*, 285.
98 Bruce H. Kirmmse, *Kierkegaard in Golden-Age Denmark* (Bloomington: University of Indiana Press, 1990), 3–5.
99 Cited in Richard E. Crouter, "Schleiermacher: Revisiting Kierkegaard's Relationship to Him," in Jon Stewart, ed. *Kierkegaard and his German Contemporaries*, vol. II *Theology* (Burlington, VT: Ashgate, 2007), 219.
100 See Crouter, "Schleiermacher."
101 Niels Thulstrup, *Kierkegaard's Relation to Hegel* (Princeton: Princeton University Press, 1980), 76.
102 See Thulstrup, *Kierkegaard's Relation to Hegel*, 127–32.
103 I.H. Fichte, "Spekulation und Offenbarung," in *Zeitschrift für Philosophie und speculative Theologie* vol. 1 (Bonn: Eduard Weber, 1837), 10.
104 Fichte, "Spekulation und Offenbarung," 21.
105 Fichte, "Spekulation und Offenbarung," 24.
106 Fichte, "Spekulation und Offenbarung," 22.
107 Fichte, "Spekulation und Offenbarung," 25.
108 Fichte, "Spekulation und Offenbarung," 27.
109 Kierkegaard, *Journals and Papers*, vol. 2 (1970), 526.
110 Jerry H. Gill, "Faith Not without Reason: Kant, Kierkegaard and Religious Belief," in *Kant and Kierkegaard on Religion*, ed. D.Z. Phillips and Timothy Tessin (New York: St. Martin's Press, 2000), 63.
111 Søren Kierkegaard's Journals & Papers IA Gilleleie, 1 August 1835.
112 Cited in Thulstrup, *Kierkegaard's Relation to Hegel*, 267.

113 See Jon Stewart, "Daub: Kierkegaard's Paradoxical Appropriation of a Hegelian Sentry," in *Kierkegaard and his German Contemporaries*, vol. II *Theology*.

114 See Claus v. Bormann, "Lessing," in *Kierkegaard's Teachers*, ed. Albert Anderson, Niels Thulstrup, and Marie Mikulová (Copenhagen: C.A. Reitzels Forlag, 1982).

115 See Matthew A. Benton, "The Modal Gap: The Objective Problem of Lessing's Ditch(es) and Kierkegaard's Subjective Reply," *Religious Studies* 42 (2006), 32.

116 Gordon Michalson, *Lessing's 'Ugly Ditch': A Study of Theology and History* (University Park: Penn State University Press, 1985), 2, 13.

117 Johannes Climacus, *Philosophical Fragments or A Fragment of Philosophy*, trans. Howard V. Hong, ed. Søren Kierkegaard (Princeton: 1962), 46.

118 Steven M. Emmanuel, *Kierkegaard and the Concept of Revelation* (Albany: SUNY University Press, 1996), 37.

119 See Jonathan Malesic, "Illusion and Offense in Philosophical Fragments: Kierkegaard's Inversion of Feuerbach's Critique of Christianity," *International Journal of the Philosophy of Religion* 62 (2007): 43–55, and István Szakó "Feuerbach: A Malicious Demon in the Service of Christianity," in *Kierkegaard and His German Contemporaries: Tome I Philosophy*, ed. Jon Stewart (Burlington, VT: Ashgate, 2007).

120 Søren Kierkegaard, *Concluding Unscientific Postscript to the Philosophical Crumbs*, ed. and trans. Alastair Hannay (Cambridge: Cambridge University Press, 2009), 295.

121 Kierkegaard, *Fragments*, 73.

122 Kierkegaard, *Fragments*, 81.

123 Kierkegaard, *Postscript*, 66.

124 Kierkegaard, *Postscript*, 161.

125 Avi Sagi, *Kierkegaard, Religion, and Existence: The Voyage of the Self*, trans. Batya Stein (Atlanta: Rodopi, 2000), 126–7.

126 Søren Kierkegaard, *Either/Or*, trans. Walter Lowrie (Princeton: Princeton University Press, 1949), 269.

127 Kierkegaard, *Either/Or*, 92, 98.

128 Søren Kierkegaard, *Fear and Trembling, and The Sickness Unto Death*, trans Walter Lowrie (Princeton: Princeton University Press, 1949), 203.

129 Kierkegaard, *Adler*, 5.

130 Kierkegaard, *Adler*, 120.

131 Kierkegaard, *Adler*, 175.

132 Kirmmse, *Kierkegaard in Golden-Age Denmark*, 451ff.

133 Sagi, *Kierkegaard, Religion, and Existence*, 132–3.

134 Niels Thulstrup, "Introduction," in Johannes Climacus, *Philosophical Fragments*, xcvi.

135 Karl Barth, "Mein Verhältnis zu Søren Kierkegaard," *Orbis Litterarum* 18, nos. 3–4 (1963): 98.
136 Karl Barth, *The Epistle to the Romans*, trans. Edwyn C. Hoskyns (Oxford: Oxford University Press, 1977), 10.
137 Trever Hard, "Revelation," in *The Cambridge Companion to Karl Barth*, ed. John Webster (Cambridge, 2000), 54.
138 Barth, *Epistle*, 330–1.
139 Barth, "Mein Verhältnis zu Søren Kierkegaard," 100.
140 Kimlyn J. Bender, "Søren Kierkegaard and Karl Barth: Reflections on a Relation and a Proposal for Future Investigation," *International Journal of Systematic Theology* 17, no. 3 (2015), 305.
141 Paul Tillich, *A History of Christian Thought: From its Judaic and Hellenistic Origins to Existentialism*, ed. Carl E. Braaten (New York: Simon & Schuster, 1967), 458–9.
142 Paul Tillich, *Systematic Theology*, vol. 1 (Chicago: University of Chicago Press, 1973), 118.

Conclusion

1 Franz Rosenzweig, "Atheistic Theology" (1914), in *Philosophical and Theological Writings*, trans. Paul W. Franks and Michael L. Morgan (Indianapolis: Hackett, 2000), 23.
2 Rosenzweig, "Atheistic Theology," 18.
3 Rosenzweig, "Atheistic Theology," 15.
4 Rosenzweig, "Atheistic Theology," 19.
5 Rosenzweig, "Atheistic Theology," 16.
6 Rosenzweig, "Atheistic Theology," 24.
7 Barth, "Mein Verhältnis zu Søren Kierkegaard," 100.
8 Karl Barth, "The Christian Apprehension of Revelation," trans. J.O. Cobham and R.J.C Gutteridge, in *Revelation*, ed. John Baille and Hugh Martin (London: Faber and Faber, 1937), 43–4.
9 Barth, "Christian Apprehension of Revelation," 48.
10 See Avery Dulles, *Models of Revelation* (New York: Orbis Books, 1992), 84–5. Barth's concept of transcendence, as Samuel Moyn has shown, set a precedent for an influential notion of human 'alterity' developed by Emmanuel Levinas. Once secularized, God's radical distinction fed into the idea of the ethical human 'other,' which in post-Holocaust philosophy demanded recognition within the experience of the self. See Samuel Moyn, *Origins of the Other: Emmanuel Levinas between Revelation and Ethics* (Ithaca: Cornell University Press, 2005).
11 Dietrich Bonhoeffer, "An Eberhard Bethge 30.4.44," in *Widerstand und Ergebung: Briefe und Aufzeichnungen aus der Haft*, ed. Christian Gremmels,

Eberhard Bethge, Renate Bethge, and Ilse Tödt (Gütersloh: Christian Kaiser, 1998), 404.

12 Randi Rashkover, *Revelation and Theopolitics: Barth, Rosenzweig and the Politics of Praise* (New York: T&T Clark, 2005), 4.

13 Franz Rosenzweig, *The Star of Redemption*, trans. Barbara E. Galli (Madison: University of Wisconsin Press, 2005), 174.

14 On Barth, see Rudy Koshar, "Where is Karl Barth on Modern European History?" *Modern Intellectual History* 5, no. 2 (2008): 333–62.

15 Albrecht Ritschl, *The Christian Doctrine of Justification and Reconciliation*, ed. H.R. Mackintosh and A.B. Macaulay (Edinburgh: T&T Clark, 1900), 24.

16 Ritschl, *Christian Doctrine*, 154.

17 Ritschl, *Christian Doctrine*, 452.

18 Ritschl, *Christian Doctrine*, 109.

19 See Frederick Beiser, *Hermann Cohen: An Intellectual Biography* (Oxford: Oxford University Press, 2018).

20 Hermann Cohen, *Die Religion der Vernunft aus den Quellen des Judentums* (Leipzig: Gustav Fock, 1919), 97.

21 Cohen, *Religion der Vernunft*, 98.

Bibliography

Adams, Nicholas, ed. *The Impact of Idealism: The Legacy of Post-Kantian German Thought*. 4 vols. Cambridge: Cambridge University Press, 2013.

Adler, Hans, and Wulf Koepke, eds. *A Companion to the Works of J.G. Herder*. Rochester, NY: Camden House, 2009.

Alexander, W.M. *J.G. Hamann: Philosophy and Faith*. The Hague: Martinus Nijhoff, 1966.

Allison, Henry E. *Lessing and the Enlightenment: His Philosophy of Religion and its Relation to Eighteenth-Century Thought*. Ann Arbor: University of Michigan Press, 1966.

–. *The Kant-Eberhard Controversy*. Baltimore: Johns Hopkins University Press, 1973.

–, ed. *Essays on Kant*. Oxford: Oxford University Press, 2012.

Alte Göttinger Landsmannschaften: Urkunden zu ihrer frühesten Geschichte. 1737–1813. Göttingen: Vandenhoeck & Ruprecht, 1937.

Altman, Alexander, ed. *Studies in Nineteenth-Century Jewish Intellectual History*, ed. Cambridge, MA: Harvard University Press, 1964.

Aner, Karl. *Die Theologie der Lessingzeit*. Hildesheim, Germany: Georg Olms, 1964.

[Anonymous]. *Freymüthige Betrachtungen über das Christenthum*. Berlin: Christian Friedrich Himburg, 1780.

Anrich, Ernst, ed. *Die Idee der deutschen Universität: Die fünf Grundschriften aus der Zeit ihrer Neubegründung durch klassischen Idealismus und romantischen Realismus*. Darmstadt, Germany: Hermann Gentner Verlag, 1956.

Antognazza, Maria Rosa. "Revealed Religion: The Continental European Debate." In *The Cambridge History of Eighteenth-Century Philosophy*, Vol. 2, edited by Knud Haakonssen, 666–82. Cambridge: Cambridge University Press, 2006.

Anwander, Anton. *Die allgemeine Religionsgeschichte im katholischen Deutschland während der Aufklärung und Romantik.* Salzburg: Anton Pustet, 1932.

Appel, Toby A. *Cuvier-Geoffrey Debate: French Biology in the Decades before Darwin.* New York: Oxford University Press, 1987.

Arkush, Allan. *Moses Mendelssohn and the Enlightenment.* Albany: SUNY Press, 1994.

Armenteros, Carolina, and Richard A. Lebrun, eds. *Joseph de Maistre and his European Readers: From Friedrich von Genz to Isaiah Berlin.* Leiden, The Netherlands: Brill, 2011.

Ascher, Samuel. *Leviathan oder ueber Religion in Rücksicht des Judenthums.* Berlin: Franke, 1792.

Assmann, Jan. *Religio Duplex: How the Enlightenment Reinvented Egyptian Religion.* Cambridge: Polity Press, 2014.

Bagel-Bohlan, Anja, Margret Heitmann, and Dieter Lohmeier, eds. *'Philo des 19. Jahrhunderts': Studien zu Salomon Ludwig Steinheim.* Hildesheim, Germany: Georg Olms Verlag, 1993.

Bahrdt, Carl Friedrich. *Geschichte seines Lebens, seiner Meinungen und Schicksale.* 4 vols. Frankfurt: Varrentrapp and Wenner, 1791.

Baird, William. *From Deism to Tübingen.* Vol. 1 of the *History of New Testament Research.* Minneapolis: Fortress Press, 1992.

Balfour, Ian. "Excursus on Revelations, Representation, and Religion in the Age of German Idealism." In *The Rhetoric of Romantic Prophecy*, edited by Ian Balfour. Stanford: Stanford University Press, 2002.

Ballenstedt, J.G.J. *Die Urwelt oder Beweis von dem Daseyn und Untergange von mehr als einer Vorwelt.* Quendlinburg, Germany: Gottfried Basse, 1818.

Barth, Karl. "The Christian Apprehension of Revelation." In *Revelation*, translated by J.O. Cobham and R.J.C. Gutteridge and edited by John Baille and Hugh Martin. London: Faber and Faber, 1937.

–. "Mein Verhältnis zu Søren Kierkegaard." *Orbis Litterarum* 18, nos. 3–4 (1963): 97–100.

–. *Protestant Theology in the Nineteenth Century: Its Background and History.* Valley Forge, PA: Judson Press, 1973.

–. *The Epistle to the Romans.* Translated by Edwyn C. Hoskyns. Oxford: Oxford University Press, 1977.

–. *Die Christliche Dogmatik im Entwurf,* Vol. 1. Edited by Gerhard Sauter. Zürich: Theologischer Verlag Zürich, 1982.

Baudach, Frank, Jürgen Behrens, and Ute Pott, eds. *Friedrich Leopold Graf zu Stolberg (1750–1819).* Eutin, Germany: Struve, 2002.

Baumgarten, Alexander. *Metaphysics. A Critical Translation with Kant's Elucidations, Selected Notes, and Related Materials.* Translated and edited by Courtney D. Fugate and John Hymers. London: Bloomsbury, 2013.

Beach, Edward Allen. *The Potencies of God(s): Schelling's Philosophy of Mythology.* Albany: SUNY Press, 1994.

Beck, Karl. *Offenbarung und Glaube bei Anton Günther.* Vienna: Herder, 1967.

Beech, Timothy J. *Hamann's Prophetic Mission: A Genetic Study of Three Late Works against the Enlightenment.* London: Maney Publisher, 2010.

Beer, Bernhard. "Das Wochenfest in der neuen Synagoge zu Dresden." *Allgemeine Zeitung des Judenthums* 4, no. 26 (1840): 376–7.

Behler, Ernst, J.J. Anstett, and Hans Eichner, eds. *Kritische Friedrich-Schlegel-Ausgabe.* 36 vols. Munich: F. Schöningh, 1979.

Beiser, Frederick C. *The German Historicist Tradition.* Oxford: Oxford University Press, 2011.

Bender, Kimlyn J. "Søren Kierkegaard and Karl Barth: Reflections on a Relation and a Proposal for Future Investigation." *International Journal of Systematic Theology* 17, no. 3 (2015): 296–318.

Benton, Matthew A. "The Modal Gap: The Objective Problem of Lessing's Ditch(es) and Kierkegaard's Subjective Reply." *Religious Studies* 42 (2006): 27–44.

Berdahl, Robert M. *The Politics of the Prussian Nobility: The Development of a Conservative Ideology, 1770–1848.* Princeton: Princeton University Press, 1988.

Berger, Immanuel. *Aphorismen zu einer Wissenschaftslehre der Religion.* Leipzig: Joh. Sam. Heinsius, 1796.

–. "Wie ist die Göttlichkeit des Christenthums für die reine Vernunft-Religion zu erweisen?" *Beiträge zur Philosophie und Geschichte der Religion und Sittenlehre* 1 (1797): 140–6.

–. "Ideen zur Philosophie der Religionsgeschichte." *Beiträge zur Philosophie und Geschichte der Religion und Sittenlehre* 4 (1798): 222–89.

–. *Geschichte der Religionsphilosophie.* Berlin: Langische Buchhandlung, 1800.

–. "Ueber Religionsphilosophie und religiöse Anthropologie." *Journal zur Veredelung der Prediger- und Schullehrerstandes* 2 (1803): 90–112.

"Die Berliner Historiker." *Hallische Jahrbücher für deutsche Wissenschaft und Kunst* 109 (1841): 433–6.

Betz, John R. *After Enlightenment: The Post-Secular Vision of J.G. Hamann.* Chichester: Wiley-Blackwell, 2009.

Bieler, Andrea. *Die Sehnsucht nach dem verlorenen Himmel: Jüdische und christliche Reflekionen zu Gottesdienstreform und Predigtkultur im 19. Jahrhundert.* Stuttgart: Kohlhammer, 2003.

Bigler, Robert M. *The Politics of German Protestantism: The Rise of the Protestant Church Elite in Prussia, 1815–1828.* Berkeley: University of California Press, 1972.

Birkholz, Adam Michael, ed. *Compaß der Weisen.* Berlin: Christian Ulrich Ringmacher, 1779.

Birkner, Hans-Joachim. "Offenbarung in Schleiermacher's *Glaubenslehre.*" In *Schleiermacher-Studien,* edited by Hermann Fischer. New York: Walter de Gruyter, 1996.

Bobzin, Hartmut, and Bernhard Forssman, "Orientalistik und Indogermanistik." In *250 Jahre Friedrich-Alexander-Universität-Erlangen-Nürnberg-Festschrift,* edited by Henning Kössler. Erlangen: Universität-Bibliothek, 1993.

Bödeker, Hans Erich, ed. *Aufklärung und Geschichte: Studien zur deutschen Geschichtswissenschaft im 18. Jahrhundert*. Göttingen: Vandenhoeck & Ruprecht, 1986.

Böhme, Hartmut. *Fetishism and Culture: A Different Theory of Modernity*. Boston: De Gruyter, 2014.

Bonhoeffer, Dietrich. *Widerstand und Ergebung: Briefe und Aufzeichnungen aus der Haft*. Edited by Christian Gremmels, Eberhard Bethge, Renate Bethge, and Ilse Tödt. Gütersloh, Germany: Christian Kaiser, 1998.

Bonwetsch, G. Nathanael, ed. *Gottfried Heinrich Schubert in seinen Briefen: Ein Lebensbild*. Stuttgart: C. Belser, 1918.

Bopp, Wolfgang. *Görres und der Mythos*. Tübingen: Fotodruck Präzis Barvara v. Spangenberg, 1974.

Bormann, Claus v. "Lessing." In *Kierkegaard's Teachers*, edited by Albert Anderson, Niels Thulstrup, and Marie Mikulová. Copenhagen: C.A. Reitzels Forlag, 1982.

Bowie, Andrew. *Schelling and Modern Philosophy: An Introduction*. London: Routledge, 1993.

Brandt, Hans-Jürgen. *Eine katholische Universität in Deutschland? Das Ringen der Katholiken in Deutschland um eine Universitätsbildung im 19. Jahrhundert*. Cologne: Böhlau Verlag, 1981.

Brandt, Richard B. *The Philosophy of Schleiermacher: The Development of his Theory of Scientific and Religious Knowledge*. New York: Harper & Brothers, 1941.

Brauers, Claudia. *Perspektiven des Unendlichen: Friedrich Schlegels ästhetische Vermittlungstheorie*. Berlin: Erich Schmidt, 1996.

Bravo, Benedetto. *Philologie, Histoire, Philosophie de l'Histoire, Étude sur J.G. Droysen, Historien de l'Antiquité*. New York: Georg Olms, 1968.

Breckman, Warren. *Marx, the Young Hegelians, and the Origins of Radical Social Theory: Dethroning the Self*. Cambridge: Cambridge University Press, 1999.

Brenner, Friedrich. *Versuch einer historisch-philosophischen Darstellung der Offenbarung als Einleitung in die Theologie*. Bamberg, Germany: Joseph Anton Goebhardt, 1810.

–. *Freye Darstellung der Theologie in der Idee des Himmelreichs*. Bamberg, Germany: Goebhardt, 1815.

–. *Katholische Dogmatik, oder, System der katholischen speculativen Theologie*. Rottenburg, Germany: Bäuerle, 1831.

Bultmann, Christoph. *Die biblische Urgeschichte in der Aufklärung: J.G. Herders Interpretation der Genesis als Antwort auf die Religionskritik David Humes*. Tübingen: Mohr Siebeck, 1999.

Bunnell, Adam. *Before Infallibility: Liberal Catholicism in Biedermeier Vienna*. Rutherford, NJ: Fairleigh Dickinson University Press, 1990.

Buntau, Martin. *Die Genesis der Geologie als Wissenschaft*. Berlin: Akademie-Verlag, 1984.

Bürke, Georg. *Vom Mythos zur Mystik.* Einsiedeln, Switzerland: Johannes Verlag, 1958.

Burson, Jeffrey D., and Ulrich L. Lehner, eds. *Enlightenment and Catholicism in Europe: A Transnational History.* Notre Dame, IN: University of Notre Dame Press, 2014.

Caldwell, Philip. *Liturgy as Revelation: Re-Sourcing a Theme in Catholic Theology.* Minneapolis: Fortress Press, 2014.

Cassirer, Ernst. *The Philosophy of the Enlightenment.* Princeton: Princeton University Press, 1951.

Chadwick, Henry ed. *Lessing's Theological Writing.* Stanford: Stanford University Press, 1957.

Champion, J.A.I. *The Pillars of Priestcraft Shaken; The Church of England and its Enemies, 1660–1730.* Cambridge: Cambridge University Press, 1992.

Ching, Julia, and Willard Gurdon Oxtoby, eds. *Moral Enlightenment: Leibniz and Wolff on China.* Saint Augustin, Germany: Institut Monumenta Serica, 1992.

Christensen, Dan Charly. *Hans Christian Ørsted: Reading Nature's Mind.* Oxford: Oxford University Press, 2013.

Clark, Robert T. *Herder: His Life and Thought.* Berkeley: University of California Press, 1969.

Coreth, Emerich, Walter M. Neidl, and Georg Pfligersdorfer, eds. *Christliche Philosophie im katholischen Denken des 19. und 20. Jahrhunderts.* Graz, Austria: Verlag Styria, 1987.

Coudert, Allison P. *Leibniz and the Kabbalah.* Dordrecht: Kluwer Academic Publishers, 1995.

Cowan, Robert. *The Indo-German Identification: Reconciling South Asian Origins and European Destinies, 1765–1885.* Rochester, NY: Camden House, 2010.

Creuzer, Friedrich. *Symbolik und Mythologie der alten Völker, besonders der Griechen.* Vol. 1. Leipzig: Karl Wilhelm Leske, 1810.

–. *Symbolik und Mythologie der alten Völker, besonders der Griechen,* vol. 1, second edition. Leipzig: Heyer und Leske, 1819.

Crouter, Richard. *Friedrich Schleiermacher: Between Enlightenment and Romanticism.* Cambridge: Cambridge University Press, 2005.

Cuvier, Georges. "Nature" in *Dictionnaire des Sciences Naturelles.* Vol. 34. Strasbourg, France: L.G. Levrault, 1825.

Deufel, Konrad. *Kirche und Tradition: Ein Beitrag zur Geschichte der theologischen Wende im 19. Jahrhundert am Beispiel des kirchlich-theologischen Kampfprogramms P. Joseph Kleutgens S.J.* Munich: Ferdinand Schöningh, 1978.

Dicenso, James J. *Kant's Religion within the Boundaries of Mere Reason: A Commentary.* Cambridge: Cambridge University Press, 2012.

Dickerhof, Harald, ed. *Görres Studien: Festschrift zum 150. Todesjahr von Joseph von Görres.* Paderborn: Schöningh, 1999.

Dietrich, Donald J. *The Goethezeit and the Metamorphosis of Catholic Theology in the Age of Idealism.* Frankfurt: Peter Lang, 1979.

Donnert, Erich. *Anti-Revolutionär-konservative Publizistik in Deutschland am Ausgang des Alten Reiches: J.A. Starck, J.A.C von Grolman, F. Nicolai.* Frankfurt: Peter Lang, 2010.

Drey, Johann Sebastian. *Kurze Einleitung in das Studium der Theologie mit Rücksicht auf den wissenschaftlichen Standpunct und das katholische System.* Tübingen: Heinrich Laupp, 1819.

–. [Anonymous]. "Aphorismen über den Ursprung unserer Erkenntnisse von Gott – ein Beitrag zur Entscheidung der neuesten Streitigkeiten über den Begriff der Offenbarung." *Tübinger theologische Quartalschrift* 8 (1826): 237–84.

–. *Die Apologetik als wissenschaftliche Nachweisung der Göttlichkeit des Christenthums in seiner Erscheinung.* Vol. 1. Mainz, Germany: F. Kupferberg, 1838.

Dulles, Avery. *Revelation Theology: A History.* New York: Herder and Herder, 1969.

–. *Models of Revelation.* New York: Orbis Books, 1992.

–. *A History of Apologetics.* San Francisco: Ignatius Press, 1999.

Dupuis, Charles. *Mémoire sur l'origine des constellations, et sur l'explication de la fable par le moyen de l'astronomie.* Paris: Desaint, 1781.

–. *Mémoire explicative du zodique chronologique et mythologique.* Paris: Courcier, 1806.

–. *Origine de tous les cultes: ou, Religion universelle.* Vol. 1. Paris: Louis Rosier, 1835.

Dyroff, Adolf. *Carl Joseph Windischmann (1775–1839) und sein Kreis.* Cologne: J.P. Bachem, 1916.

Ebeling, Florian. "Rationale Mysterien." In *Egypt: Temple of the Whole World: Studies in Honor of Jan Assmann,* edited by Sibylle Meyer. Boston: Brill, 2003.

–. *The Secret History of Hermes Trismegistus: Hermeticism from Antiquity to Modern Times.* Ithaca, NY: Cornell University Press, 2007.

Eberhard, Johann August. *Neue Apologie des Sokrates oder Untersuchung der Lehre von der Seligkeit der Heiden.* 2nd ed. Vol. 1. Berlin: Friedrich Nicolai, 1776.

–. *Vorbereitung zur natürlichen Theologie.* Halle, Germany: Waisenhaus, 1781.

Eberhard, Johann August, and Immanuel Kant. *Preparation for Natural Theology: With Kant's Notes and the Danzig Rational Theology Transcript.* Translated and edited Courtney D. Fugate and John Hymers. New York: Bloomsbury Academic, 2016.

Eicher, Peter. *Offenbarung: Prinzip neuzeitlicher Theologie.* Munich: Kösel Verlag, 1977.

Elschenbroich, Aldabert. *Romantische Sehnsucht und Kosmogonie: Eine Studie zu Gotthilf Heinrich Schuberts 'Geschichte der Seele' und deren Stellung in der deutschen Spätromantik.* Tübingen: Max Niemeyer Verlag, 1971.

Emmanuel, Steven M. *Kierkegaard and the Concept of Revelation.* Albany: SUNY University Press, 1996.

Engels, Friedrich. *Schelling und die Offenbarung: Kritik des neuesten Reaktionsversuchs gegen die freie Philosophie.* Leipzig: Robert Binder, 1842.

Ennemoser, Joseph. *Der Magnetismus im Verhältnisse zur Natur und Religion.* Stuttgart: Cotta, 1842.

Erben, Patrick M. *A Harmony of the Spirits: Translation and the Language of Community in Early Pennsylvania.* Durham: University of North Carolina Press, 2012.

Erdmann, J., ed. *200 Jahre Friedrich Rückert, 1788–1866: Dichter und Gelehrte. Katalog der Ausstellung.* Coburg, Germany: Druckhaus Neue Presse Coburg, 1988.

Eschweiler, Karl. *Die katholische Theologie im Zeitalter des deutschen Idealismus.* Edited by Thomas Marschler. Münster, Germany: Monsenstein und Vannerdat, 2010.

Essen, Georg, and Christian Danz, eds. *Philosophisch-theologische Streitsachen: Pantheismusstreit – Atheismusstreit – Theismusstreit.* Darmstadt, Germany: Wissenschaftliche Buchgesellschaft, 2012.

Fackenheim, Emil L. *The God Within: Kant, Schelling, and Historicity.* Edited by John Burbidge. Toronto: University of Toronto Press, 1996.

Fehr, Wayne L. *The Birth of the Catholic Tübingen School: The Dogmatics of Johann Sebastian Drey.* Chico, CA: Scholars Press, 1981.

Feiner, Shmuel. *The Jewish Enlightenment.* Translated by Chaya Naor. Philadelphia: University of Pennsylvania Press, 2004.

Ferngren, Gary B., ed. *Science and Religion: A Historical Introduction.* Baltimore: Johns Hopkins University Press, 2002.

Feuerbach, Ludwig. *The Essence of Christianity.* Translate by George Eliot. New York: Harper & Brothers, 1957.

–. *Sämtliche Werke.* Edited by Wilhelm Bolin and Friedrich Jodl. 13 vols. Stuttgart: Frommann, 1959.

–. *The Essence of Faith According to Luther.* Translated by Melvin Cherno. New York: Harper & Row, 1967.

–. *Lectures on the Essence of Religion.* Translated by Ralph Manheim. New York: Harper & Row, 1967.

Ffytche, Matt. *The Foundation of the Unconscious: Schelling, Freud, and the Birth of the Modern Psyche.* Cambridge: Cambridge University Press, 2012.

Fichte, I.H. "Spekulation und Offenbarung." *Zeitschrift für Philosophie und speculative Theologie* 1 (1837): 1–31.

Fichte, Johann Gottlieb. *Attempt at a Critique of All Revelation.* Translated by Garrett Green. Cambridge: Cambridge University Press, 1978.

Fischer, Norbert, ed. *Kant und der Katholismus. Stationen einer wechselhaften Geschichte.* Freiburg: Herder, 2005.

Fischer, Wolfdietrich, ed. *Rückert im Spiegel seiner Zeitgenossen und der Nachwelt.* Wiesbaden: Harrassowitz, 1988.

Fliethman, Thomas. *Vernünftig Glauben: Die Theorie der Theologie bei Georg Hermes*. Würzburg: Echter Verlag, 1997.

Flügge, Christian Wilhelm. *Geschichte des Glaubens an Unsterblichkeit, Auferstehung, Gericht und Vergeltung*. 3 vols. Leipzig: Siegfried Lebrecht Crusius, 1794–9.

–. *Versuch einer historisch-kritischen Darstellung des bisherigen Einflusses der Kantischen Philosophie auf alle Zweige der wissenschaftlichen und praktischen Theologie*. Hannover: Helwingsche Hofbuchhandlung, 1796.

–, ed. *Beyträge zur Geschichte der Religion und Theologie in ihrer Behandlungsart*. 2 vols. Hannover: Helwing, 1797–8.

–. *Der Himmel der Zukunft*. Altona, Germany: I.F. Hammerich, 1804.

Förch, Gerhard. *Theologie als Darstellung der Geschichte in der Idee: Zum Theologiebegriff Friedrich Brenners, 1784–1848*. Würzburg, Germany: Echter Verlag, 1980.

Formstecher, Salomon. *Die Religion des Geistes, eine wissenschaftliche Darstellung des Judenthums nach seinem Charakter, Entwicklungsgange und Berufe in der Menschheit*. Frankfurt: Johann Christian Hermann, 1841.

–. *Mosaische Religionslehre für die israelitische Religionsschule*. Gießen, Germany: Ernst Heinemann, 1860.

Frackenheim, Emil L. *Quest for Past and Future: Essays in Jewish Theology*. Bloomington: Indiana University Press, 1968.

Francolm, Isaac Ascher. *Das rationale Judenthum*. Breslau, Poland: M. Friedländer, 1840.

Franklin, Michael. "Introduction." In *On the Language and Wisdom of the Indians*, edited by Michael Franklin. London: Ganesha Publishing, 2001.

Frei, Hans W. *The Eclipse of Biblical Narrative: A Study in Eighteenth and Nineteenth Century Hermeneutics*. New Haven, CT: Yale University Press, 1974.

Gabler, Johann Philipp. "'Einleitung' to Eichhorn." In *Urgeschichte*. Vol. 1. Altdorf, Switzerland: Monath und Kußler, 1790.

Gebetbuch der Genossenschaft für Reform im Judenthum. Vol. 1. Berlin: Selbst-Verlage der Genossenschaft, 1848.

Geiger, Abraham. *Was hat Mohammed aus dem Judenthume aufgenommen?* Bonn: F. Baaden, 1833.

–, ed. *Jüdische Zeitschrift für Wissenschaft und Leben*. 11 vols. Breslau, Poland: Schletter, 1862–75.

–. "Die letzten zwei Jahre. Sendschreiben an einen befreundeten Rabbiner." In *Abraham Geiger's Nachgelassene Schriften*, edited by Ludwig Geiger. Vol. 1. Berlin: Luis Gerschel, 1875.

–. *Judaism and its History in Two Parts*. Translated by Charles Newburgh. Lanham, MD: University Press of America, 1985.

Gerhardt, C.J. *Die philosophischen Schriften Gottfried Wilhelm Leibniz*. Hildesheim, Germany: Georg Olms Verlag, 1960.

Goodman-Thau, Eveline, Gert Mattenklott, and Christoph Schulte, eds. *Kabbala und Romantik*. Tübingen: Nieymeyer, 1994.

Goren, Haim. *"Zieht hin und erforscht das Land": Die deutsche Palästinaforschung im 19. Jahrhundert*. Translated by Antje Clara Naujoks. Göttingen: Wallstein Verlag, 2003.

Görres, Joseph. *Glauben und Wissen*. Munich: Scherersche Kunst- und Buchhndlung, 1805.

–. "Religion in der Geschichte: Wachstum der Historie." In *Studien*, edited by Carl Daub and Friedrich Creuzer. Vol. 3 (1807): 313–480.

Gottlieb, Michah. *Faith and Freedom: Moses Mendelssohn's Theological-Political Thought*. New York: Oxford University Press, 2011.

Gotzmann, Andreas, and Christian Wiese, eds. *Modern Judaism and Historical Consciousness: Identities, Encounters, Perspectives*. Boston: Brill, 2007.

Gregory, Frederick. *Nature Lost? Natural Science and the German Theological Traditions of the Nineteenth Century*. Cambridge, MA: Harvard University Press, 1992.

–. "Gottfried Heinrich Schubert and the Dark Side of Natural Science." *Internationale Zeitschrift für Geschichte und Ethik der Naturwissenschaften, Technik, und Medizin* 3 (1995): 255–69.

Grözinger, Karl Erich. *Jüdisches Denken: Theologie – Philosophie – Mystik*. Frankfurt: Campus Verlag, 2009.

Günther, Anton. "Protestantismus und Philosophie." *Lydia, Philosophisches Taschenbuch I*. Vienna (1849): 1–176.

–. *Gesammelte Schriften*. 9 vols. Frankfurt: Minerva, 1968.

Guyer, Paul. *Kant's System of Nature and Freedom: Selected Essays*. Oxford: Clarendon Press, 2005.

–. *Knowledge, Reason, and Taste: Kant's Response to Hume*. Princeton: Princeton University Press, 2008.

Haberman, Joshua O., ed. *Philosopher of Revelation: The Life and Thought of S.L. Steinheim*. Philadelphia: Jewish Publication Society, 1990.

HaCohen, Ran. *Reclaiming the Hebrew Bible: German-Jewish Reception of Biblical Criticism*. New York: De Gruyter, 2010.

Hallam, Anthony. *Great Geological Controversies*. Oxford: Oxford University Press, 1983.

Hamann, Johann Georg. *Vetii Epagathi Regiomonticolae hierophantische Briefe*. Riga, Latvia, 1775.

–. *Johann Georg Hamanns, des Magus in Norden, Leben und Schriften*. Edited by Karl Hermann Gildemeister. 6 vols. Gotha, Germany: F. A. Perthes, 1857–73.

–. *Sämtliche Werke*. Edited by Josef Nadler. 6 vols. Vienna: Verlag Herder, 1949–51.

–. *Mysterienschriften erklärt von Evert Jansen Schoonhoven*. Gütersloh, Germany: Gerd Mohn, 1962.

–. *Über den Ursprung der Sprache: Zwo Recensionen* Edited by Elfriede Büchsel. Gütersloh, Germany: Mohn, 1963.

–. *J.G. Hamann: Writings on Philosophy and Language.* Edited by Kenneth Haynes. Cambridge: Cambridge University Press, 2007.

Han-Ding, Hong. *Spinoza und die deutsche Philosophie. Eine Untersuchung zur metaphysischen Wirkungsgeschichte des Spinozismus in Deutschland.* Aalen, Germany: Scientia Verlag, 1989.

Hanegraaff, Wouter J., ed. *Dictionary of Gnosis and Western Esotericism.* Boston: Brill, 2006.

–. *Esotericism and the Academy: Rejected Knowledge in Western Culture.* Cambridge: Cambridge University Press, 2012.

Harrison, Peter. *'Religion' and the Religions in the English Enlightenment.* Cambridge: Cambridge University Press, 1990.

Harvey, Van A. *Feuerbach and the Interpretation of Religion.* Cambridge: Cambridge University Press, 1995.

Haßler, Gerda. *Johann August Eberhard. 1739–1809. Ein streitbarer Geist an den Grenzen der Aufklärung.* Halle, Germany: Hallescher Verlag, 2000.

Hegel, Georg Wilhelm Friedrich. *Encyklopädie der philosophischen Wissenschaften im Grundrisse.* Berlin: Duncker and Humblot, 1845.

–. *The Phenomenology of Spirit.* Translated by A.V. Miller. Oxford: Clarendon Press, 1977.

–. *Lectures on the Philosophy of Religion.* Edited by Peter C. Hodgson, translated by R.F. Brown, P.C. Hodgson, and J.M. Stewart. 3 vols. Berkeley: University of California Press, 1984.

Heine, Heinrich. *On the History of Religion and Philosophy in Germany.* Edited by Terry Pinkard. Cambridge: Cambridge University Press, 2007.

Heinz, Gerhard. *Divinam christianae religionis originem probare. Untersuchung zur Entstehung des fundamentaltheologischen Offenbarungstraktates der katholischen Schultheologie.* Mainz, Germany: Mattias-Grünewald-Verlag, 1984.

Hellyer, Marcus. *Catholic Physics: Jesuit Natural Philosophy in Early Modern Germany.* Notre Dame, IN: University of Notre Dame Press, 2005.

Helm, Paul, ed. *Faith & Reason.* Oxford: Oxford University Press, 1999.

Helmer, Christine, ed. *Biblical Interpretation: History, Context, and Reality.* Leiden, The Netherlands: Brill, 2005.

Herder, Johann Gottfried. *Herders Sämmtliche Werke.* Edited by Bernhard Ludwig Suphan. 33 vols. Berlin: Weidmannsche Buchhandlung, 1877–1913.

–. *Briefe.* Edited by Wilhelm Dobbek und Gunter Arnold. Vol. 1. Weimar, 1977.

–. *Werke in zehn Bänden.* Edited by Martin Bollacher. 10 vols. Frankfurt: Deutscher Klassiker Verlag, 1985–2000.

Herling, Bradley. *The German Gita: Hermeneutics and Discipline in the German Reception of Indian Thought, 1778–1831.* New York: Routledge, 2006.

Hermes, Georg. *Christkatholische Dogmatik*. Edited by J.H. Achterfeldt. 3 vols. Münster: Coppenrath, 1834.

–. *Einleitung in die christkatholische Theologie*. Vol. 1 *Philosophische Einleitung*. Münster, Germany: Coppenrathsche Buch- und Kunsthandlung, 1819.

Hertz, Deborah. *How Jews Became Germans: The History of Conversion and Assimilation in Berlin*. New Haven, CT: Yale University Press, 2007.

Heschel, Susannah. *Abraham Geiger and the Jewish Jesus*. Chicago: University of Chicago Press, 1998.

Hess, Jonathan M. *Germans, Jews, and the Claims of Modernity*. New Haven, CT: Yale University Press, 2002.

Heuvel, Jan Vanden. *A German Life in the Age of Revolution: Joseph Görres, 1776–1848*. Washington, DC: Catholic University of America Press, 2001.

Hirsch, Samson Raphael. *Neunzehn Briefe über Judenthum*. Altona, Germany: Hammerich, 1836.

–. *Judaism Eternal: Selected Essays from the Writings of Rabbi Samson Raphael Hirsch*. Translated by I. Grunfeld. 2 vols. London: Soncino Press, 1956.

–. *Horeb: A Philosophy of Jewish Laws and Observations*. Translated by I. Grunfeld. London: Soncino Press, 1962.

–. *Collected Writings*. 9 vols. New York: Philipp Feldheim, 1984.

–. [Ben Uziel]. *The Nineteen Letters about Judaism*. Translated by Karin Paritzky, edited by Joseph Elias. New York: Feldheim Publishers, 1996.

Hirsch, Samuel. *Die Religionsphilosophie der Juden oder das Princip der jüdischen Religionsanschauung und sein Verhältniß zum Heidenthum, Christenthum und zur absoluten Philosophie*. Leipzig: Heinrich Hunger, 1842.

–. *Die Messiaslehre der Juden in Kanzelvorträgen*. Leipzig: Heinrich Hunber, 1843.

–. *Die Reform im Judenthum und dessen Gebrauch in der gegenwärtigen Welt*. Leipzig: H. Hunger, 1844.

Hirzel, Martin. *Lebensgeschichte als Verkündigung: Johann Heinrich Jung-Stilling – Ami Bost – Johann Arnold Kanne*. Göttingen: Vandenhoeck & Ruprecht, 1998.

Hjelde, Sigurd. "Das Aufkommen der Idee einer Religionswissenschaft: Einige deutsche Ansätze zum Ende des 18. Jahrhunderts." *Zeitschrift für Religionswissenschaft* 22, no. 2 (2014): 150–75.

Hodgson, Peter C., ed. *Hegel: Theologian of the Spirit*. Minneapolis: Fortress Press, 1997.

–. *Hegel and Christian Theology: A Reading of the Lectures on the Philosophy of Religion*. Oxford: Oxford University Press, 2005.

Hoffheimer, Michael H. "Race and Law in Hegel's Philosophy of Religion." In *Race and Racism in Modern Philosophy*, edited by Andrew Walls. Ithaca, NY: Cornell University Press, 2005.

Holdheim, Samuel. *Moses Mendelssohn und die Denk- und Glaubensfreiheit im Judenthume*. Berlin: Huber, 1859.

Hötzel, Norbert. *Die Uroffenbarung im französischen Traditionalismus.* Munich: Max Hueber Verlag, 1962.

Howard, Thomas. *Protestant Theology and the Making of the Modern German University.* New York: Oxford University Press, 2006.

–. *Religion and the Rise of Historicism: W.M.L. de Wette, Jacob Burckhardt, and the Theological Origins of Nineteenth-Century Historical Consciousness.* Cambridge: Cambridge University Press, 2000.

Huenemann, Charlie, ed. *Interpreting Spinoza: Critical Essays.* Cambridge: Cambridge University Press, 2008.

Hume, David. *Vier Abhandlungen über die Geschichte der Religion.* Translated by Friedrich Gabriel Resewitz. Quedlinburg, Germany: Andreas Franz Biesterfeld, 1759.

–. "The Natural History of Religion." In *Principle Writings on Religion*, edited by J.C.A. Gaskin. Oxford: Oxford University Press, 1993.

Hünermann, Peter. "Nicht: Theologie oder Religionswissenschaft – sondern: Theologie der Religionen." In *Adolf von Haarlack: Christentum, Wissenschaft und Gesellschaft*, edited by Kurt Nowak, Otto Gerhard Oexle, Trutz Rendtorff, and Kurt-Victor Segle. Göttingen: Vandenhoeck & Ruprecht, 2003.

Idelsohn, A.Z. *Jewish Liturgy and its Development.* New York: Dover Publication, 1995.

Israel, Jonathan I. *Radical Enlightenment: Philosophy and the Making of Modernity, 1650–1750.* Oxford: Oxford University Press, 2001.

Ittenbach, Elmar P. *Samuel Hirsch: Rabbiner – Religionsphilosoph – Reformer.* Berlin: Hentrich & Hentrich Verlg, 2014.

Jacobi, F.H. "Von den göttlichen Dingen und ihrer Offenbarung." In *Religionsphilosophie und spekulative Theologie. Quellenband*, edited by Walter Jaeschke. Hamburg: Felix Meiner Verlag, 1994.

Jaeschke, Walter. *Reason in Religion: The Foundations of Hegel's Philosophy of Religion.* Berkeley: University of California Press, 1990.

Jantzen, Jörg, Thomas Kisser, and Hartmut Traub, eds. *Grundlegung und Kritik: Briefwechsel zwischen Schelling und Fichte, 1794–1802.* New York: Rodopi, 2005.

Jay, Martin. *Songs of Experience: Modern American and European Variations on a Universal Theme.* Berkeley: University of California Press, 2005.

Jaynes, Julian, and William Woodward. "In the Shadow of the Enlightenment: Reimarus against the Epicureans." *Journal of the History of the Behavioral Sciences* 10 (1974): 3–15, 144–59.

Jensen, Kipton. "The Principle of Protestantism: On Hegel's (Mis)Reading of Schleiermacher's Speeches." *Journal of the American Academy of Religion* 71, no. 3 (2003): 405–22.

Jones, Peter, ed. *The Reception of David Hume in Europe.* London: Thoemmes Continuum, 2005.

Joshua, Eleoma. *Friedrich Leopold Graf zu Stolberg and the German Romantics.* New York: Peter Lang, 2005.

Kanne, Johann Arnold. "*S'cheik Mahommad Fani's Dabistan, oder von der Religion der ältesten Farsen...* ins Deutsche übersetzt von F.V. Dalberg." *Uebersicht der neuesten Literatur* 18 (1809).

—. *Pantheum der Aeltesten Naturphilosophie, die Religion aller Völker.* Tübingen: Cotta, 1811.

—. [Anton von Preußen]. *Zwanzig kritische Paragraphen und historische Noten über den Text der Zeit.* Leipzig: Weygand'schen Buchhandlung, 1814.

—. *Leben und aus dem Leben merkwürdiger und erweckter Christen.* Bamberg, Germany: Carl Friedrich Kunz, 1816.

—. *Christus im alten Testament: Untersuchungen über die Vorbilder und Messianischen Stellen.* Vol. 2. Nuremburg: Riegel und Mießner, 1818.

Kant, Immanuel. *Critik der Urtheilskraft.* Berlin: Lagarde und Friederich, 1790.

—. *Religion within the Limits of Reason Alone.* Translation and introduction by Theodore M. Greene and Hoyt H. Hudson. Chicago: Open Court Publishing, 1934.

—. *Immanuel Kant's Critique of Pure Reason.* Translated by Norman Kemp Smith. London: Macmillan, 1950.

—. *The One Possible Basis for a Demonstration of the Existence of God.* Translated by Gordon Treash. Lincoln: University of Nebraska Press, 1979.

—. *Universal Natural History and Theory of the Heavens.* Translated by Stanley L. Jaki. Edinburgh: Scottish Academic Press, 1981.

—. *Critique of Judgement.* Translated by James Creed Meredith. Oxford: Oxford University Press, 2007.

Kantzenbach, Friedrich Wilhelm. *Die Erweckungsbewegung: Studien zur Geschichte ihrer Entstehung und ersten Ausbreitung in Deutschland.* Neuendettelsau, Germany: Freimund-Verlag, 1957.

Kaplan, Grant. *Answering the Enlightenment: The Catholic Recovery of Historical Revelation.* New York: Herder & Herder, 2006.

Keßler, Martin, and Volker Leppin, eds. *J.G. Herder: Aspekte seines Lebenswerkes.* New York: Walter de Gruyter, 2005.

Kierkegaard, Søren. *Either/Or.* Translated by Walter Lowrie. Princeton, NJ: Princeton University Press, 1949.

—. *Fear and Trembling, and The Sickness unto Death.* Translated by Walter Lowrie. Princeton, NJ: Princeton University Press, 1949.

—. [Climacus, Johannes]. *Philosophical Fragments, or A Fragment of Philosophy.* Edited by Søren Kierkegaard, translated by Howard V. Hong. Princeton, NJ: Princeton University Press, 1962.

—. *Søren Kierkegaard's Journals and Papers.* Edited by Howard Hong, Edna Hong, and Gregor Malantschuk. 7 vols. 1967–78.

–. *The Book on Adler: The Religion Confusion of the Present Age Illustrated by Magister Adler as a Phenomenon*. Translated by Howard V. Hong and Edna H. Hong. Princeton, NJ: Princeton University Press, 1998.

–. *Concluding Unscientific Postscript to the Philosophical Crumbs*. Edited and translated by Alastair Hannay. Cambridge: Cambridge University Press, 2009.

Kilcher, Andreas B. *Die Sprachtheorie der Kabbala als ästhetisches Paradigma: Die Konstruktion einer ästhetischen Kabbala seit der Frühen Neuzeit*. Stuttgart: J.B. Metzler, 1998.

Kim, Sung-Bong. *"Die Lehre von der Sünde und vom Versöhner"; Tholucks theologische Entwicklung in seiner Berliner Zeit*. Frankfurt/Main: Peter Lang, 1992.

Kirmmse, Bruce H. *Kierkegaard in Golden-Age Denmark*. Bloomington: University of Indiana Press, 1990.

Klemme, Heiner F., Gideon Stiening, and Falk Wunderlich, eds. *Michael Hißmann (1752–1784) Ein materialistischer Philosoph der deutschen Aufklärung*. Berlin: Akademie Verlag, 2013.

Kleutgen, Joseph. *Die Theologie der Vorzeit vertheidigt*. Vol. 1. Münster, Germany: Theissing, 1867.

Klueting, Harm, ed. *Katholische Aufklärung – Aufklärung im katholischen Deutschland*. Hamburg: Felix Meiner Verlag, 1993.

Knoodt, Peter. *Anton Günther: Eine Biographie*. Vol. 1. Vienna: Wilhelm Braumüller, 1881.

Koepke, Wulf. *J.G. Herder*. Boston: Twayne Publishers, 1987.

Kohlenbach, Margarete. "Mesmerism." In *Encyclopedia of the Romantic Era*, edited by Christopher John Murray. Vol. 2. New York: Routledge, 2004.

Kohler, George Y. *Reading Maimonides' Philosophy in 19th Century Germany: The Guide to Religious Reform*. New York: Springer, 2012.

Kölbi-Ebert, Martina, ed. *Geology and Religion: A History of Harmony and Hostility*. London: Geological Society, 2009.

Körner, Josef, ed. *Krisenjahre der Frühromantik. Briefe aus dem Schlegelkreis*. Vol. 1. Bern: Francke Verlag, 1969.

Koslowski, Peter. *Philosophien der Offenbarung: Antiker Gnostizismus, Franz von Baader, Schelling*. Paderborn, Germany: Ferdinand Schöningh, 2001.

Kratz-Ritter, Bettina. *Salomon Formstecher: Ein deutscher Reformrabbiner*. Hildesheim, Germany: Georg Olms, 1991.

Kraus, Chr. J. *Vermischte Schriften über staatswirthschaftliche, philosophische und andere wissenschaftliche Gegenstände*. Vol. 5. Königsberg, Prussia: Friedrich Nicolovius, 1812.

Labuschagne, Bart, and Timo Slootweg, eds. *Hegel's Philosophy of the Historical Religions*. Leiden, The Netherlands: Brill, 2012.

Lagarde, Paul de. "Erinnerungen an Friedrich Rückert." In *Ausgewählte Schriften*, edited by P. Fischer. Munich: J.F. Lehmann, 1934.

Laughland, John. *Schelling versus Hegel: From German Idealism to Christian Metaphysics*. Aldershot, UK: Ashgate, 2007.

LaVopa, Anthony. *Fichte: The Self and the Calling of Philosophy, 1762–1799*. Cambridge: Cambridge University Press, 2001.

Lefmann, Salomon. *Franz Bopp: Sein Leben und seine Wissenschaft*. Berlin: Reimer, 1891.

Lehner, Ulrich L. *Enlightened Monks: The German Benedictines, 1740–1803*. Oxford: Oxford University Press, 2011.

Leibniz, Gottfried Wilhelm. *Theodicy: Essays on the Goodness of God, the Freedom of Man, and the Origin of Evil*. Edited and introduced by Austin Farrer, translated by E.M. Huggard. La Salle, IL: Open Court, 1985.

Lessing, Gotthold Emphraim, ed. *Fragmente des Wolfenbüttelschen Ungenannten*. Berlin: Arnold Meyer, 1788.

–. *Gotthold Ephraim Lessings sämmtliche Schriften*. Edited by Karl Lachmann. Vol. 10. Berlin: Voss, 1839.

–. *Discourse on Metaphysics*. Translated by George R. Montgomery. Chicago: Open Court Publishing Company, 1902.

–. *Discourse on Metaphysics: Correspondence with Arnauld, and Monadology*. Translated by George R. Montgomery. Chicago: Open Court, 1918.

–. *Gesammelte Werke*. Edited by Paul Rilla. 10 vols. Berlin: Aufbau-Verlag, 1954–8.

–. *Writings on China*. Translated by Daniel J. Cook and Henry Rosemont. Chicago: Open Court, 1994.

–. *Philosophical and Theological Writings*. Edited by Hugh Barr Nisbet. Cambridge: Cambridge University Press, 2005.

Liberles, Robert. *Religious Conflict in Social Context: The Resurgence of Orthodox Judaism in Frankfurt am Main, 1838–1877*. Westport, CT: Greenwood Press, 1985.

Lifschitz, Avi. *Language and Enlightenment: The Berlin Debates of the Eighteenth Century*. Oxford: Oxford University Press, 2012.

Lilla, Mark. *The Stillborn God: Religion, Politics, and the Modern West*. New York: Alfred Knopf, 2007.

Lindberg, David C., and Ronald L. Numbers, eds. *God and Nature: Historical Essays on the Encounter between Christianity and Science*. Berkeley: University of California Press, 1986.

Lindemann, Johann Gottlieb. *Geschichte der Meinungen älterer und neuerer Völker, im Stande der Roheit und Cultur, von Gott, Religion, und Priesterthum*. Vol. 1. Stendal, Germany: Franzen und Grosse, 1784.

Link, Heinrich Friedrich. *Die Urwelt und das Alterthum*. Vol. 2. Berlin: Ferdinand Dümmler, 1822.

Logan, Peter Melville. *Victorian Fetishism: Intellectuals and Primitives*. Albany: SUNY Press, 2009.

Lotter, Friedrich. "Christoph Meiners und die Lehre von der unterschiedlichen Wertigkeit der Menschen Rassen." In *Geschichtswissenschaft in Göttingen: eine Vorlesungsreihe*. Göttingen: Vandenhoeck & Ruprecht, 1987.

Lüken, Heinrich. *Die Traditionen des Menschengeschlechts oder die Uroffenbarung Gottes unter den Heiden*. Münster: Aschendorff'sche Buchhandlung, 1856.

M-n, E. "P.F. Stuhr, Die Religions-Systeme der heidnischen Völker des Orients." *Literarische Zeitung* 48 (23 November 1836).

Mack, Michael. *German Idealism and the Jew: The Inner Anti-Semitism of Philosophy and German Jewish Responses*. Chicago: University of Chicago Press, 2003.

Mader, Josef. *Offenbarung als Selbstoffenbarung Gottes: Hegels Religionsphilosophie als Anstoß für ein neues Offenbarungsverständnis in der katholischen Theologie des 19. Jahrhunderts*. Münster, Germany: LIT Verlag, 2000.

Magon, Leopold. *Der junge Rückert: Sein Leben und Schaffen*. Halle, Germany: Max Niemeyer, 1914.

Malesic, Jonathan. "Illusion and Offense in Philosophical Fragments: Kierkegaard's Inversion of Feuerbach's Critique of Christianity." *International Journal of the Philosophy of Religion* 62 (2007): 43–55.

Manuel, Frank E. *The Eighteenth Century Confronts the Gods*. Cambridge, MA: Harvard University Press, 1959.

Marchand, Suzanne. *German Orientalism in the Age of Empire: Religion, Race, and Scholarship*. Cambridge: Cambridge University Press, 2009.

Mariña, Jacqueline, ed. *The Cambridge Companion to Friedrich Schleiermacher*. Cambridge: Cambridge University Press, 2005.

Matthews, Bruce. *Schelling's Organic Form of Philosophy: Life as the Schema of Freedom*. Albany: SUNY Press, 2011.

Mayer, Paola. *Jena Romanticism and its Appropriation of Jakob Böhme: Theosophy-Hagiography-Literature*. Montreal: McGill-Queen's University Press, 1999.

Mayr, Beda. *Vertheidigung der natürlichen, christlichen und katholischen Religion nach den Bedürfnissen unsrer Zeiten*. Augsburg, Germany: Matthäus Riegers, 1789.

McCarthy, Vincent A. *Quest for a Philosophical Jesus: Christianity and Philosophy in Rousseau, Kant, Hegel, and Schelling*. Macon, GA: Mercer University Press, 1986.

McCool, Gerald A. *Nineteenth-Century Scholasticism: The Search for a Unitary Method*. New York: Fordham University Press, 1989.

McDonald, H.D. *Theories of Revelation: An Historical Study, 1700–1960*. Grand Rapids, MI: Baker Book House, 1979.

Meiners, Christoph. *Revision der Philosophie*. Göttingen: Johann Christian Dieterich, 1772.

–. *Versuch über die Religionsgeschichte der ältesten Völker besonders der Egyptier.* Göttingen: J.C. Dieterich, 1775.

–. *Vermischte Philosophischen Schriften.* 3 vols. Leipzig: Weygandsche Buchhandlung, 1775–6.

–. *Grundriß der Geschichte aller Religionen.* Lemgo, Germany: Meyersche Buchhandlung, 1785.

–. *Geschichte der Lehre vom wahren Gott dem Urheber und Regierer aller Dinge.* Translated by Justus Conrad Mensching. Duisburg, Germany: Gebrüder Helwig, 1791.

–. *Grundriß der Geschichte der Menschheit,* 2nd ed. Lemgo, Germany: Meer, 1793.

–. *Historische Vergleichung der Sitten, und Verfassungen, der Gesetze, und Gewerbe, des Handels, und der Religion, der Wissenschaften und Lehranstalten des Mittelalters mit denen unsers Jahrhunderts.* 3 vols. Hannover: Helwig, 1793–4.

–. *Allgemeine kritische Geschichte der Religionen.* Vol. 1. Hannover: Helwingische Hof-Buchhandlung, 1806.

Meinhold, Peter. "Hamanns Theologie der Sprache." In *Acta des Internationalen Hamann-Colloqiums in Lüneburg 1976.* Frankfurt/Main: Vittorio Klostermann, 1979.

Mendelssohn, Moses. *Jerusalem, or on Religious Power and Judaism.* Translated by Allan Arkush. Hannover: Brandeis University Press, 1983.

Mercer, Christina. *Leibniz's Metaphysics: Its Origins and Development.* Cambridge: Cambridge University Press, 2001.

Merkel, R.F. "Beiträge zur vergleichenden Religionsgeschichte." *Archiv für Religionswissenschaft* 36 (1939): 193–215.

Merklinger, Philip M. *Philosophy, Theology, and Hegel's Berlin Philosophy of Religion, 1821–1827.* Albany: SUNY Press, 1993.

Messlin, Dorit. *Antike und Moderne: Friedrich Schlegel's Poetik, Philosophie und Lebenskunst.* Berlin: Walter de Gruyter, 2011.

Meyer, Michael A. "'Ob Schrift? Ob Geist' Die Offenbarungsfrage im deutschen Judentum des neunzehnten Jahrhunderts." In *Quaestiones Disputatae,* edited by Karl Rahner and Heinrich Schlier. Vol. 92. Basel: Editiones Herder, 1981.

–. *Response to Modernity: A History of the Reform Movement in Judaism.* Oxford: Oxford University Press, 1988.

–. *Judaism within Modernity: Essays on Jewish History and Religion.* Detroit: Wayne State University Press, 2001.

Mezei, Balázs M. *Religion and Revelation after Auschwitz.* London: Bloomsburg, 2013.

Michaelis, Johann David. *Ueber den Einfluss der Sprachen auf die Meinungen der Menschen.* London, 1769.

–. *Dogmatik.* Göttingen: Wittwe Vandenhoek, 1784.

Michalson, Gordon E. *Lessing's 'Ugly Ditch': A Study of Theology and History.* University Park: Penn State University Press, 1985.

Michelson, Peter. "Der Sog der Mythe. Zu Görres' Mythengeschichte." In *Heidelberg im säkularen Umbruch*, edited by Friedrich Strack. Stuttgart: Klett-Cotta, 1987.

Milbank, John. *The Word Made Strange: Theology, Language, Culture.* Cambridge, MA: Blackwell, 1997.

Mischer, Sibelle. *Der verschlungene Zug der Seele: Natur, Organismus und Entwicklung bei Schelling, Steffens und Oken.* Würzburg: Königshausen & Neumann, 1997.

Möller, Horst. *Vernunft und Kritik: Deutsche Aufklärung im 17. und 18. Jahrhundert.* Frankfurt: Suhrkamp, 1986.

Motschmann, Uta. *Handbuch der Berliner Vereine und Gesellschaften, 1786–1815.* Berlin: de Gruyter, 2015.

Motzkin, Gabriel. *Time and Transcendence: Secular History, the Catholic Reaction, and the Rediscovery of the Future.* Dordrecht: Kluwer Academic Publishers, 1992.

Moyn, Samuel. *Origins of the Other: Emmanuel Levinas between Revelation and Ethics.* Ithaca, NY: Cornell University Press, 2005.

Müller, Adam Heinrich. *Die Elemente der Staatskunst: Oeffentliche Vorlesungen.* Vol. 2. Jena, Germany: Gustav Fischer, 1922.

Mulsow, Martin, ed. *Between Philology and Radical Enlightenment: Hermann Samuel Reimarus. 1694–1768.* Leiden, The Netherlands: Brill, 2011.

Myers, David N. *Resisting History: Historicism and its Discontents in German-Jewish Thought.* Princeton, NJ: Princeton University Press, 2003.

Nadler, Steven. *A Book Forged in Hell: Spinoza's Scandalous Treatise and the Birth of the Secular Age.* Princeton, NJ: Princeton University Press, 2011.

Nebgen, Christoph. *Konfessionelle Differenzerfahrungen: Reiseberichte vom Rhein. 1648–1815.* Munich: De Gruyter, 2014.

"Nekrolog: G.H. Schubert." *Der Bayerische Landbote* 190 (8 July 1860).

Neugebauer-Wölk, Monika, ed. *Aufklärung und Esoterik.* Hamburg: Meiner, 1999.

–, ed. *Aufklärung und Esoterik: Rezeption-Integration-Konfrontation.* Tübingen: Niemeyer, 2008.

Neumann, Erich. *Johann Arnold Kanne: Ein vergessener Romantiker. Ein Beitrag zur Geschichte der mystischen Sprachphilosophie.* Eisleben, Germany: A. Klöppel, 1927.

Niemann, Franz-Josef. *Jesus als Glaubensgrund in der Fundamentaltheologie der Neuzeit. Zur Genealogie eines Traktats.* Innsbruck: Tyrolia-Verlag, 1983.

Niethammer, Friedrich Immanuel. *Ueber den Versuch einer Kritik aller Offenbarung.* Jena: C.H. Cuno's Erben, 1792.

Olender, Maurice. *The Languages of Paradise: Race, Religion, and Philology in the Nineteenth Century.* Translated by Arthur Goldhammer. Cambridge, MA: Harvard University Press, 1992.

Olson, Richard G. *Science and Religion, 1450–1900: From Copernicus to Darwin*. Westport, CT: Greenwood Press, 2004.

O'Meara, Thomas. "Revelation in Schelling's Lectures on Academic Studies." In *Los Comienzos filosóficos de Schelling*, edited by Ignacio Falgueras. Málaga: Servicio de Publicaciones de la Universidad de Mélaga, 1988.

Oppy, Graham, and N.N. Trakakis, eds. *Nineteenth-Century Philosophy of Religion*. New York: Routledge, 2013.

O'Regan, Cyril. *The Heterodox Hegel*. Albany: SUNY Press, 1994.

Ostaric, Lara, ed. *Interpreting Schelling: Critical Essays*. Cambridge: Cambridge University Press, 2013.

Pannenberg, Wolfhart, ed. *Revelation as History*. Translated by David Granskou. New York: Macmillan, 1968.

Park, Peter K.J. *Africa, Asia, and the History of Philosophy: Racism in the Formation of the Philosophical Canon, 1780–1830*. Albany: SUNY Press, 2013.

Paul, Jean. *Jean Pauls Sämtliche Werke: Historisch-kritische Ausgabe*. Edited by Eduard Berend and Helmut Pfotenhauer. 47 vols. Weimar: Hermann Böhlaus Nachfolger, 1934.

Pelli, Mosche. *The Age of Haskalah: Studies of Hebrew Literature of the Enlightenment in Germany*. Leiden, The Netherlands: Brill, 1979.

Perkins, Franklin. *Leibniz and China: A Commerce of Light*. Cambridge: Cambridge University Press, 2004.

Petermann, Heike. *Gotthilf Heinrich Schubert: Die Naturgeschichte als bestimmendes Element*. Erlangen: Verlag Palm & Enke, 2008.

Phillips, D.Z., and Timothy Tessin, eds. *Kant and Kierkegaard on Religion*. New York: St. Martin's Press, 2000.

Pickus, Keith H. *Constructing Modern Identities: Jewish University Students in Germany, 1815–1914*. Detroit: Wayne State University Press, 1999.

Pott, David Julius. *Moses und David keine Geologen: Ein Gegenstück zu Hen. Kirwan's geologischen Versuchen*. Berlin: Friedrich Nicolai, 1799.

Prang, Helmut. *Geist und Form der Sprache*. Wiesbaden: O. Harrassowitz, 1963.

Prantl, Carl von. "Meiners, Christoph." In *Allgemeine Deutsche Biographie*, edited by Historische Kommission bei der Bayerischen Akademie der Wissenschaften. Vol. 21. Leipzig: Duncker & Humblot, 1885.

Prechtl, Conrad Aloys. "Religionsgeschichte der ganzen Welt und aller Zeiten." In *Anhang zu dem dreyzehnten bis vier und zwanzigsten Bande der allgemeinen deutschen Bibliothek*. Berlin: Friedrich Nicolai, 1777.

Printy, Michael. *Enlightenment and the Creation of German Catholicism*. Cambridge: Cambridge University Press, 2009.

Printy, Michael, and Ulrich Lehner, eds. *A Companion to the Catholic Enlightenment in Europe*. Leiden, The Netherlands: Brill, 2010.

Pritz, Joseph. *Glauben und Wissen bei Anton Günther: Eine Einführung in sein Leben und Werk mit einer Auswahl aus seinen Schriften*. Vienna: Herder, 1963.

Ratjen, Hennig, ed. *J.F. Kleuker und Briefe seiner Freunde*. Göttingen: Diesterische Buchhandlung, 1842.

Reardon, Bernhard. *Religion in the Age of Romanticism: Studies in Early Nineteenth-Century Thought*. Cambridge: Cambridge University Press, 1985.

Redeker, Martin. *Schleiermacher: Life and Thought*. Philadelphia: Fortress Press, 1973.

Reill, Peter Hanns. "Between Mechanism and Hermeticism: Nature and Science in the Late Enlightenment." In *Frühe Neuzeit, Frühe Moderne? Forschungen zur Vielschichtigkeit von Übergangsprozessen*, edited by Rudolf Vierhaus. Göttingen: Vandenhoeck & Ruprecht, 1992.

–. *The German Enlightenment and the Rise of Historicism*. Berkeley: University of California Press, 1975.

Reimarus, Hermann Samuel. *Vornehmsten Wahrheiten der natürlichen Religion*. Hamburg: Johann Carl Bohn, 1766.

–. *Abhandlungen von den vornehmsten Wahrheiten der natürlichen Religion*. Hamburg: Carl Ernst Bohn, 1791.

Reiss, John O. *Not by Design: Retiring Darwin's Watchmaker*. Berkeley: University of California Press, 2009.

Riedel, Karl. *Schellings religionsgeschichtliche Ansicht nach Briefen aus München mit einer vergleichenden Zugabe: Peter Feddersen Stuhr über Urgeschichte und Mythologie*. Berlin: Rücker und Püchler, 1841.

Ringleben, Joachim. "Göttingener Aufklärungstheologie – von Königsberg her gesehen." In *Theologie in Göttingen: Eine Vorlesungsreihe*, edited by Bernd Moeller. Göttingen: Vandenhoeck & Ruprecht, 1987.

Ringmüller, Joseph. *Allgemeine Religions- und Staatsgeschichte von der Weltschöpfung an bis auf gegenwärtige Zeiten*. Wurzburg: Stahel, 1772.

Robinson, Elizabeth, and Chris W. Surprenant, eds. *Kant and the Scottish Enlightenment*. New York: Taylor and Francis, 2017.

Roemer, Nils H. *Jewish Scholarship and Culture in Nineteenth-Century Germany: Between History and Faith*. Madison: University of Wisconsin Press, 2005.

Roggen, Ronald. *'Restauration' – Kampfruf und Schimpfwort: Eine Kommunikationsanalyse zum Hauptwerk des Staatstheoretikers Karl Ludwig von Haller. 1768–1854*. Freiburg: Universitätsverlag, 1999.

Rohls, Jan. *Protestantische Theologie der Neuzeit*. Vol. 1. Tübingen: Mohr Siebeck, 1997.

–. *Offenbarung, Vernunft und Religion: Ideengeschichte des Christentums*. Vol. 1. Tübingen: Mohr Siebeck, 2012.

Rose, Sven-Erik. *Jewish Philosophical Politics in Germany, 1789–1848*. Waltham, MA: Brandeis University Press, 2014.

Rosenbloom, Noah H. *Tradition in an Age of Reform: The Religious Philosophy of Samson Raphael Hirsch*. Philadelphia: The Jewish Publication Society of America, 1976.

Rossi, Paolo. *The Dark Abyss of Time: The History of the Earth and the History of Nations from Hooke to Vico*. Translated by Lydia G. Cochrane. Chicago: University of Chicago Press, 1984.

Rotenstreich, Nathan. *Tradition and Reality: The Impact of History on Modern Jewish Thought*. New York: Random House, 1972.

–. *Jews and German Philosophy: The Polemics of Emancipation*. New York: Schocken Books, 1984.

Rückert, Friedrich. "Deutsches Künstlerfest in Rom." In *Frauentaschenbuch für das Jahr 1823*. Nürnberg: J.L. Schrag, 1820.

–. "Ermuthigung zur Uebersetzung der Hamasa." In *Musenalmanach für das Jahr 1831*. Leipzig: Weidmann, 1831.

–. *Gesammelte Gedichte von Friedrich Rückert*. 6 vols. Erlangen: Carl Heyder, 1838.

–. *Friedrich Rückerts gesammelte poetische Werke in zwölf Bänden*. Frankfurt: J.D. Sauerländer, 1882.

–. *Briefe*. Edited by Rüdiger Rückert. 2 vols. Schweinfurt: Rückert-Gesellschaft, 1977.

–. *Gedichte von Rom und andere Texte der Jahre 1817–1818*. Edited by Claudia Wiener. Göttingen: Wallstein, 2000.

–. *Liedertagebuch: Werke der Jahre 1850–1851*. Edited by R. Kreutner and H. Wollschläger. Vol. 1. Göttingen: Wallstein Verlag, 2003.

Ruprecht, Erich. "Die Frage nach dem Ursprung der Sprache: Eine Untersuchung zu J.G. Hamann's Wirkung auf die deutsche Romantik." In *Acta des Internationalen Hamann-Colloquiums in Lüneburg 1976*. Frankfurt/Main: Vittorio Klostermann, 1979.

Sæbø, Magne, ed. *Hebrew Bible/Old Testament: The History of its Interpretation*. Vol. 3, part 1 *The Nineteenth Century – A Century of Modernism and Historicism*. Göttingen: Vandenhoeck & Ruprecht, 2013.

Sagi, Avi. *Kierkegaard, Religion, and Existence: The Voyage of the Self*. Translated by Batya Stein. Atlanta: Rodopi, 2000.

Sailer, Johann Michael. *Sämmtliche Werke: Biographische Schriften*. Vol. 1. Sulzbach: Seidel, 1841.

Sailhammer, John H. *The Meaning of the Pentateuch: Revelation, Composition and Interpretation*. Danvers Grove, IL: IVP Academic, 2009.

Schäfer, Philipp. *Kirche und Vernunft: Die Kirche in der katholischen Theologie der Aufklärungszeit*. Munich: Max Hueber Verlag, 1974.

Schäfer, Theo. *Die erkenntnistheoretische Kontroverse Kleutgen-Günther*. Paderborn: Ferdinand Schöningh, 1961.

Scheffczyk, Leo. *Friedrich Leopold zu Stolbergs 'Geschichte der Religion Jesu Christi': Die Abwendung der katholischen Kirchengeschichtsschreibung von der Aufklärung und ihre Neuorientierung im Zeitalter der Romantik*. Munich: Karl Zink Verlag, 1952.

Schelling, F.W.J. *Von der Weltseele: Eine Hypothese der höheren Physik.* Hamburg: Friedrich Perthes, 1798.

–. *Von der Weltseele, eine Hypothese der höheren Physik.* Hamburg: Friedrich Perthes, 1806.

–. *Ueber das Verhältniß der bildenden Künste zu der Natur.* Munich: Philipp Krüll, 1807.

–. *Sämmtliche Werke.* 14 vols. Stuttgart: J.G. Cotta, 1856.

–. *On University Studies.* Translated by E.S. Morgan. Athens: Ohio University Press, 1966.

–. *System of Transcendental Idealism.* Translated by Peter Heath. Charlottesville: University Press of Virginia, 1978.

–. *Ideas for a Philosophy of Nature.* Translated by Errol E. Harris and Peter Heath. Cambridge: Cambridge University Press, 1988.

–. *Philosophy of Art.* Translated by D.W. Stott. Minneapolis: University of Minnesota Press, 1989.

–. *Urfassung der Philosophie der Offenbarung.* Edited by Walter E. Ehrhardt. Hamburg: Felix Meiner Verlag, 1992.

–. *The Ages of the World.* Translated by Jason M. Wirth. Albany: SUNY Press, 2000.

–. *First Outline of a System of the Philosophy of Nature.* Translated by Keither R. Peterson. Albany: SUNY Press, 2004.

–. *Philosophical Investigations into the Essence of Human Freedom.* Translated by Jeff Love and Johannes Schmidt. Albany: SUNY Press, 2006.

–. *The Grounding of Positive Philosophy: The Berlin Lectures.* Translated by Bruce Matthews. Albany: SUNY Press, 2007.

–. *Historical-critical Introduction to the Philosophy of Mythology.* Translated by Mason Richey and Markus Zisselberger. Albany: SUNY Press, 2007.

–. *Philosophy and Religion.* Translated by Klaus Ottmann. Putnam, CT: Spring Publications, 2010.

Schimmel, Annemarie. *Mystical Dimensions of Islam.* Chapel Hill: University of North Carolina Press, 2011.

Schlegel, Friedrich. *On the Language and Wisdom of the Indians.* Translated by E.J. Millington.

–. *Über die Sprache und Weisheit der Indier: Ein Beitrag zur Begründung der Altertumskunde.* Heidelberg, 1808.

–. *Philosophische Vorlesungen aus den Jahren 1804 bis 1806.* Edited by C.J.H. Windischmann. Vol. 2. Bonn: Eduard Weber, 1837.

Schleiermacher, Friedrich. *The Christian Faith.* Edited by H.R. Mackintosh and J.S. Stewart. Edinburgh: T&T Clark, 1928.

–. *On Religion: Speeches to its Cultured Despisers.* Edited by Richard Crouter. Cambridge: Cambridge University Press, 1988.

Schmidt, Wolff A. von. "Mythologie und Uroffenbarung bei Herder und Friedrich Schlegel." In *Zeitschrift für Religions- und Geistesgeschichte*, edited by E. Benz and H.J. Schoeps. Cologne: Brill, 1973.

Schrey, Dieter. *Mythos und Geschichte bei Johann Arnold Kanne und in der romantischen Mythologie*. Tübingen: Max Niemeyer Verlag, 1969.

Schubert, Gotthilf Heinrich. *Ansichten von der Nachtseite der Naturwissenschaft*. Dresden: Arnoldsche Buchhnadlung, 1808.

–. *Die Urwelt und die Fixsterne: Eine Zugabe zu den Ansichten von der Nachtseite der Naturwissenschaft*. Dresden: Arnoldische Buchhandlung, 1822.

–. "Theologische Wahrheiten und geologische Ketzereien." *Evangelische Kirchen-Zeitung* 93, no. 94 (1851): 875–88.

–. *Der Erwerb aus einem Vergangenen und die Erwartungen von einem zukünftigen Leben*. 3 vols. Erlangen: J.J. Palm und E. Enke, 1854–6.

–. *Die Symbolik des Traumes*. Edited by F.H. Ranke. 4th ed. Leipzig: Brockhaus, 1862.

–. *Gotthilf Heinrich Schubert in seinen Briefen: Ein Lebensbild*. Edited by Nathanael Bonwetch. Stuttgart, 1918.

–. *Die Symbolik des Traumes*. Heidelberg: Lambert Schneider, 1968.

Schulte, Christoph. *Die jüdische Aufklärung: Philosophie, Religion, Geschichte*. Munich: C.H. Beck, 2002.

Schwaiger, Georg, ed. *Kirche und Theologie im 19. Jahrhundert: Referate und Berichte des Arbeitskreises Katholische Theologie*. Göttingen: Vandenhoeck & Ruprecht, 1975.

Schweid, Eliezer. *A History of Modern Jewish Religious Philosophy*. Translated by Leonard Levin. 2 vols. Leiden: Brill, 2011.

Semler, Johann Salomon. "Historische Einleitung in die Dogmatische Gottesgelersamkeit." In *D. Siegmund Jacob Gaumbartens Evangelische Glaubenslehre*, edited by Johann Salomon Semler. Vol. 1. Halle: Johann Justinus Gebauer, 1759.

–. *Versuch einer freiern theologischen Lehrart*. Halle, Germany: Hemmerde, 1777.

–. *Lebensbeschreibung von ihm selbst abgefaßt*. 2 vols. Halle, Germany, 1781–2.

Sengler, Jakob. *Ueber das Wesen und die Bedeutung der speculativen Philosophie und Theologie: Allgemeine Einleitung*. Mainz: F. Kupferberg, 1834.

Sharpe, Eric J. *Comparative Religion: A History*. New York: Charles Scribner's Sons, 1975.

Sheehan, Jonathan. *The Enlightenment Bible: Translation, Scholarship, Culture*. Princeton, NJ: Princeton University Press, 2005.

Smith, Jonathan Z. *Drudgery Divine: On the Comparison of Early Christianities and the Religions of Late Antiquity*. Chicago, 1990.

–. *Relating Religion: Essays in the Study of Religion*. Chicago: Chicago University Press, 2004.

Sohr, Amélie. *Heinrich Rückert in seinem Leben und Wirken.* Weimar: Hermann Böhlau, 1880.

Sorkin, David. *The Transformation of German Jewry, 1780–1840.* New York: Oxford University Press, 1987.

–. *Moses Mendelssohn and the Religious Enlightenment.* Berkeley: University of California Press, 1996.

–. *The Berlin Haskalah and German Religious Thought: Orphans of Knowledge.* London: Vallentine Mitchell, 2000.

Spinoza, Benedict de. *Theological-Political Treatise.* Edited by Jonathan Israel, translated by Michael Silverthorne and Jonathan Israel. Cambridge: Cambridge University Press, 2007.

Stam, James H. *Inquiries into the Origin of Language: The Fate of a Question.* New York: Harper & Row, 1976.

Starck, Johann August. *Hephästion.* Königsberg: Gottlieb Lebrecht Hartung, 1775.

–. *Apologie des Ordens der Frey-Mäurer.* 2nd edition. Berlin: Christian Ludewig Stahlbaum, 1778.

"Starck, Johann August, Freiherr von." In *Dictionary of Eighteenth-Century German Philosophers,* edited by Heiner Klemme and Manfred Kuehn. Vol. 3. New York: Continuum, 2010.

Stattler, Benedikt. *Allgemeine katholisch-christliche theoretische Religionslehre aus hinreichenden Gründen der göttlichen Offenbarung und der Philosophie.* Munich: Schulfondsbücherverlag, 1791.

Staudenmaier, Franz Anton. *Geist der göttlichen Offenbarung.* Gießen: B.G. Ferber, 1837.

–. *Encyklopädie der theologischen Wissenschaften als System der gesammten Theologie.* Vol. 1. Mainz, 1840.

Stäudlin, Karl Friedrich. *Ideen zu einer Kritik des Systems der christlichen Religion.* Göttingen: Vandenhoeck & Ruprecht, 1791.

–. *Geschichte und Geist des Skepticismus.* Leipzig: Siegfried Lebrecht Crusius, 1794.

–. "Vorrede." In *Beiträge zur Philosophie und Geschichte der Religion und Sittenlehre überhaupt und der verschiedenen Glaubensarten und Kirchen insbesondere.* Vol. 1. Lübeck, 1797.

–. "Über den Wert der kritischen Philosophie, vornehmlich in moralischer und religiöser Hinsicht." *Beiträge zur Philosophie und Geschichte der Religion und Sittenlehre* 4 (1798): 83–189.

–. "Anstatt der Vorrede." In *Magazin für Religions- Moral- und Kirchengeschichte.* Vol. 1.1. Hannover: Gebrüder Hahn, 1801.

–. *Zur Erinnerung an D. Carl Friedrich Stäudlin: Seine Selbstbiographie.* Edited by Johann Tychsen Hemsen. Göttingen: Vandenhoeck und Ruprecht, 1826.

Steffens, Henrich. *Was ich erlebte: Aus Erinnerung niedergeschrieben.* 6 vols. Breslau: Josef Max, 1842.

Steinacker, Peter. "Die Bedeutung der Philosophie Schellings für die Theologie Paul Tillichs." In *Studien zu einer Theologie der Moderne,* edited by Hermann Fischer. Frankfurt/Main: Athenäum, 1989.

Steinheim. *Die Offenbarung vom Standpuncte der höheren Kritik: Eine Prüfung der Darstellung des Herrn Prof. W. Vatke.* Kiel: Universitäts-Buchhandlung, 1840.

Stephenson, Gunther. "Geschichte und Religionswissenschaft im ausgehenden 18. Jahrhundert." *Numen* 13 (1966): 43–79.

Stewart, Jon, ed. *Kierkegaard and his German Contemporaries.* Vol. 2 *Theology.* Burlington, VT: Ashgate, 2007.

–, ed. *A Companion to Kierkegaard.* Chichester: Blackwell, 2015.

Stolberg, Friedrich Leopold. *Geschichte der Religion Jesu Christi.* 16 vols. Hamburg, 1809.

Strickland, Lloyd, ed. *Gottfried Wilhelm Leibniz's Monadology: A New Translation and Guide.* Edinburgh: Edinburgh University Press, 2014.

Stroumsa, Guy G. *A New Science: The Discovery of Religion in the Age of Reason.* Cambridge, MA: Harvard University Press, 2010.

Stuhr, Peter Feddersen. *Deutschland und der Gottesfriede: Sendschreiben an Görres.* Berlin: Maurersche Buchhandlung, 1820.

–. *Untersuchungen über die Ursprünglichkeit und Alterthümlichkeit der Sternkunde unter den Chinesen und Indiern.* Berlin: Fr. Laue, 1831.

–. *Die Religions-Systeme der heidnischen Völker des Orients.* Berlin: Veit, 1836.

–. "Allgemeiner Ueberblick über die Geschichte der Behandlung und Deutung der Mythen seit dem Mittelalter." In *Zeitschrift für spekulative Theologie,* edited by Bruno Bauer. Vol. 3.1–2. Berlin: Ferdinand Dümmler, 1837.

–. "Karl Otfried Müller als Mythologe." *Hallische Jahrbücher für deutsche Wissenschaft und Kunst* 294–9 (1838): 2345–50, 2353–7, 2361–4, 2369–73, 2377–81, 2391–2.

–. *Das Verhältniss der christlichen Theologie zur Philosophie und Mythologie.* Berlin: E.H. Schroeder, 1842.

Süskind, Hermann. *Der Einfluss Schellings auf die Entwicklung von Schleiermachers System.* Tübingen: J.C.B. Mohr, 1909.

Tholuck, August. *Einige apologetsche Winke für das Studium des Alten Testaments.* Berlin: Maurer, 1821.

–. *Ssufismus sive theosophia Persarum pantheistica.* Berlin: Ferdinand Duemmler, 1821.

–. *Blüthensammlung aus der Morgenländischen Mystik nebst einer Einleitung über Mystik überhaupt und Morgenländische insbesondere.* Berlin: Ferdinand Dümmler, 1825.

–. *Die Lehre von der Sünde und vom Versöhner, oder Die wahre Weihe des Zweiflers.* 2nd ed. Hamburg: Friedrich Perthes, 1825.

–. *Vermischte Schriften größtentheils apologetischen Inhalts.* 2 vols. Hamburg: Perthes, 1839.

–. *Die Propheten und ihre Weissagungen.* Gotha: Perthes, 1861.

Thulstrup, Niels. *Kierkegaard's Relation to Hegel.* Princeton, NJ: Princeton University Press, 1980.

Tillich, Paul. *A History of Christian Thought: From its Judaic and Hellenistic Origins to Existentialism.* Edited by Carl E. Braaten. New York: Simon & Schuster, 1967.

—. *Systematic Theology.* Vol. 1. Chicago: University of Chicago Press, 1973.

Tilliette, Xavier. *Schelling: Biographie.* Translated by Susanne Schaper. Stuttgart: Klett-Cotta, 2004.

Toews, John E. *Hegelianism: The Path toward Dialectical Humanism, 1805–1841.* Cambridge: Cambridge University Press, 1980.

—. *Becoming Historical: Cultural Reformation and Public Memory in Early Nineteenth-Century Berlin.* Cambridge: Cambridge University Press, 2004.

Trepp, Anne-Charlott, and Hartmut Lehmann, eds. *Antike Weisheit und kulturelle Praxis: Hermetismus in der Frühen Neuzeit.* Göttingen: Vandenhoeck & Ruprecht, 2001.

Tschackert, Paul. "Stäudlin, Karl Friedrich." In *Allgemeine Deutsche Biographie*, edited by Historische Kommission bei der Bayerischen Akademie der Wissenschaften. Vol. 35. Leipzig: Duncker & Humblot, 1893.

Vanden Heuvel, Jan. *A German Life in the Age of Revolution: Joseph Görres, 1776–1848.* Washington, DC: Catholic University of America Press, 2001.

Vassányi, Miklós. *Anima Mundi: The Rise of the World Soul Theory in Modern German Philosophy.* New York: Springer, 2011.

Vatke, Wilhelm. *Die biblische Theologie wissenschaftlich dargestellt.* Vol. 1. Berlin: G. Bethge, 1835.

Veldhuis, Henri. *Ein versiegeltes Buch: Der Naturbegriff in der Theologie J.G. Hamanns. 1730–1788.* Berlin: Walter de Gruyter, 1994.

Vester, Michael. *Aufklärung – Esoterik – Reaktion: Johann August Starck. 1741–1816. Geistlicher, Gelehrter und Geheimbündler zur Zeit der deutschen Spätaufklärung.* Darmstadt: Verlag der Hessischen Kirchengeschichtlichen Vereinigung, 2012.

Vierling-Ihrig, Heike. *Schule der Vernunft: Leben und Werk des Aufklärungspädagogen Cajetan von Weiller (1762–1826).* Munich: Stadtarchiv München, 2001.

Vierthaler, Franz Michael. *Philosophische Geschichte der Menschen und Völker.* Vol. 1. Salzburg: Waisenbuchhandlung, 1787.

—. "Von dem Unterrichte in der Religion." In *Ausgewählte pädagogische Schriften*, edited by Leopold Glöckl. Vol. 6. Freiburg im Breisgau: Herder, 1893.

Wagner, Johann Jakob. *System der Idealphilosophie.* Leipzig: Breitkopf und Härtel, 1804.

—. *Ideen zu einer allgemeinen Mythologie der alten Welt.* Frankfurt: Andreäische Buchhandlung, 1808.

—. *Organon der menschlichen Erkenntniss.* Ulm: P.L. Adam's Verlags-Buchhandlung, 1851.

Waldenfels, Hans. *Die Offenbarung: Von der Reformation bis zur Gegenwart.* Freiburg: Herder, 1977.

Wartofsky, Mark W. *Feuerbach*. Cambridge: Cambridge University Press, 1977.

Webster, John, ed. *The Cambridge Companion to Karl Barth*. Cambridge: Cambridge University Press, 2000.

Weidner, Daniel. "Hieroglyphen und heilige Buchstaben: Herders orientalische Semiotik." *Herder Yearbook 7* (2004): 45–68.

Weiller, Kajetan. *Ideen zur Geschichte der Entwickelung des religiösen Glaubens.* Vol. 1. Munich: Fleischmann, 1808.

–. "Vorlesung des Director v. Weiller." In *Friedrich Heinrich Jacobi nach seinem Leben, Lehren und Wirken*. Munich: Fleichmann, 1819.

Wenz, Gunther. *Offenbarung: Problemhorizonte moderner evangelischer Theologie.* Göttingen: Vandenhoeck & Ruprecht, 2005.

Wenzel, Paul. *Das wissenschaftliche Anliegen des Güntherianismus. Ein Beitrag zur Theologiegeschichte des 19. Jahrhunderts*. Essen: Ludgerus-Verlag, 1961.

Wette, W.M.L. de. *Christliche Sittenlehre*. Part 2: *Allgemeine Geschichte der christlichen Sittenlehre*. Berlin: G. Reimer, 1819–21.

–. *Ueber die Religion, ihre Erscheinungsformen und ihren Einfluß auf das Leben.* Berlin: G. Reimer, 1827.

Wiener, Claudia, ed. *Friedrich Rückerts 'De idea philologiae' als dichtungstheoretische Schrift und Lebensprogramm*. Schweinfurt: Stadtarchiv Schweinfurt, 1994.

Wiener, Claudia, and Rudolf Kreutner, eds. *Zeitgedichte und andere Texte der Jahre 1813–1816*. Göttingen: Wallstein Verlag, 2009.

Wiese, Christian. *Challenging Colonial Discourse: Jewish Studies and Protestant Theology in Wilhelmine Germany*. Leiden, The Netherlands: Brill, 2005.

Wiesner, Helmut. *Religion und Vernunft im Frühwerk Friedrich Brenners. 1810–1818*. Vol. 1 *Allgemeine Offenbarungslehre und Theorie der jüdischen Religion*. Würzburg: Echter Verlag, 1984.

Willer, Stefan. *Poetik der Etymologie: Texturen sprachlichen Wissens in der Romantik*. Berlin: Akademie Verlag, 2003.

Williamson, George S. *The Longing for Myth in Germany: Religion and Aesthetic Culture from Romanticism to Nietzsche*. Chicago: Chicago University Press, 2004.

Wilson, W. Daniel. "Enlightenment Encounters the Islamic and Arabic Worlds: The German 'Missing Link' in Said's Orientalist Narrative (Meiners and Herder)." In *Encounters with Islam and German Literature and Culture*, edited by James R. Hodkinson and Jeffrey Morrison. Rochester, NY: Camden House, 2009.

Windischmann, Karl Joseph Hieronymus. *Kritische Betrachtungen über die Schicksale der Philosophie in der neueren Zeit*. Frankfurt: Andreäische Buchhandlung, 1825.

–. *Philosophie im Fortgang der Weltgeschichte*. Part 1: *Die Grundlagen der Philosophie im Morgenland*. Vol. 4. Bonn: Adolph Marcus, 1834.

Witte, Leopold. *Das Leben Friedrich August Gottreu Tholuck's.* Vol. 1. Bielefeld: Belhagen & Klasing, 1884.

Wolf, Hubert. *The Nuns of Sant'Ambrogio: The True Story of a Convent Scandal.* Translated by Ruth Martin. Oxford: Oxford University Press, 2015.

Wolff, Christian. *Vernünfftige Gedancken von den Absichten der natürlichen Dinge.* Frankfurt: Rengerische Buchhandlung, 1737.

–. *Natürliche Gottesgelahrtheit.* Translated by Gottlieb Friedrich Hagen. Vol. 1. Halle: Renger, 1742.

–. *Vernünfftige Gedancken von Gott, der Welt, und der Seele des Menschen.* Halle: Magdeburgischen, 1747.

–. *Preliminary Discourse on Philosophy in General.* Translated by Richard J. Blackwell. Indianapolis: Bobbs-Merrill, 1963.

Yasukata, Toshimasa. *Lessing's Philosophy of Religion and the German Enlightenment: Lessing on Christianity and Reason.* Oxford: Oxford University Press, 2002.

Zachhuber, Johannes. *Theology as Science in Nineteenth-Century Germany: From F.C. Baur to Ernst Troeltsch.* Oxford: Oxford University Press, 2013.

Zammito, John H. *The Genesis of Kant's Critique of Judgment.* Chicago: University of Chicago Press, 1992.

–. *The Gestation of German Biology: Philosophy and Physiology from Stahl to Schelling.* Chicago: Chicago University Press, 2018.

Zande, Johan van der, and Richard H. Popkin, eds. *The Skeptical Tradition around 1800: Skepticism in Philosophy, Science, and Society.* Boston: Kluwer Academic Publishers, 1998.

Zander, Helmut. *Geschichte der Seelenwanderung in Europa.* Darmstadt: Wissenschaftliche Buchgesellschaft, 1999.

Zantop, Susanne. "The Beautiful, the Ugly, and the German: Race, Gernder, and Nationality in Eighteenth-Century Anthropological Discourse." In *Gender and Germanness: Cultural Productions of Nation,* edited by Patricia Herminghouse and Magda Mueller. New York: Berghahn Books, 1997.

Ziolkowski, Theodore. *Clio the Romantic Muse: Historicizing the Faculties in Germany.* Ithaca NY: Cornell University Press, 2004.

–. *Dresdner Romantik: Politik und Harmonie.* Heidelberg: Universitätsverlag Winter, 2010.

Zöckler, Otto. *Geschichte der Beziehungen zwischen Theologie und Naturwissenschaft.* 2 vols. Gütersloh: Bertelsmann, 1877–79.

Zunz, Leopold. "Die Einheit Gottes." In *Predigten, gehalten in der neuen Israelitischen Synagogue zu Berlin.* Berlin: Schlesinger, 1823.

Index

GERMAN AND EUROPEAN STUDIES

General Editor: Jennifer L. Jenkins